DATE DUE

MAR 2 4			
5/25/79			
1-19-90			
GAYLORD			PRINTED IN U.S.A.

THE STORY OF THE WORLD'S
LITERATURE

SHAKESPEARE.

SHAKESPEARE

RUOTOLO 32

THE STORY OF THE WORLD'S LITERATURE

·

BY

JOHN MACY

ILLUSTRATED
BY
ONORIO
RUOTOLO

·

LIVERIGHT. N.Y.

7936

THE STORY OF THE WORLD'S LITERATURE

REVISED EDITION

FOR
MY DAUGHTER
MARGARET

CONTENTS

PART I

THE ANCIENT WORLD

Contents

PART II

THE MIDDLE AGES

PART III

MODERN LITERATURE BEFORE THE NINETEENTH CENTURY

Contents

Contents

Contents

Contents

ILLUSTRATIONS

Illustrations

PREFACE

The purpose of this book is to give an account of the books
of the world that are of greatest importance to living people.
What is important is a question, or a multitude of questions,
which the individual must, if he can, answer for himself, and
it is at the same time a matter which has been determined by
the general consensus of opinion. But not absolutely determined; for importance is a relative term, and general opinions
are vague abstractions difficult to define. A mere list of the
names of authors and books, each one significant to a considerable number of readers, would constitute a catalogue of
much greater bulk than this volume. Therefore in our review
many books of real value are omitted and many others are
only mentioned. Every reader will miss some of his favorites
and will find their places occupied by authors whom he does
not so highly esteem. This is as it should be and will, I hope,
stimulate those differences of opinion which contribute to the
consensus of opinion and which give to the discussion of literature and the other arts much of its interest and pleasure.

In this book the selection, the proportion, the final judgment
as to what to include and what to leave out are mine; and the
result is necessarily limited and shaded in emphasis by personal enthusiasms and deficiencies of knowledge and appre-
ciation. I can give only a one-man view of a vast subject.
My most learned critic says with some justice: "What you
have actually written is not *The Story of Literature,* but *Casual Observations on a Few Writers I Happen to Have Read.*"
I confidently reply that I have been guided not only by other
books, the master critics and the routine historians, but by the

wise counsels of learned friends. I have to thank especially Dr. Ludwig Lewisohn, Dr. Antonio Calitri, Professor A. H. Rice, Mr. Ernest Boyd, Dr. A. J. Barnouw, Dr. Hendrik Van Loon, Mr. Pitts Sanborn, Mr. Howard Irving Young, Mr. Thomas R. Smith, Mr. Manuel Komroff, Mr. Hugo Knudsen, who have set me right at many points and have helped me to solve, so far as I have solved it, the main problem of what our survey should include. Dr. Lewisohn is almost wholly responsible for the two chapters, XL and XLI, on German literature.

Since this book is addressed to readers of English, relatively more space is devoted to English and American literature than would be warranted from the point of view of an Olympian or a visitor from Mars who should comprehend dispassionately the total thought of our planet. By the same token we have ignored entire national literatures of unquestionable richness. A Roumanian, a Pole, an Hungarian, a Finn, for example, may justly dismiss this book forthwith by saying: "You have not even a short chapter on the literature of my country which contains this, and this, and this man of genius, and yet you pretend to be telling some sort of story about the literature of the world!" The answer is that some national literatures seem not to have become a part of the corporate literature of Europe but have remained shut off within national and linguistic boundaries. Such isolation can persistently confine a writer of genius who ought to be universally known, our ignorance of whom is our loss. I have talked with Poles whose enthusiasm for their national literature, ancient and modern, makes one believe in its greatness, but apparently the translators have opened the door for us only a crack, and so far as I can discover the only Polish novelist of broad European reputation is Henri Sienkiewicz. An American scholar born in Hungary tells me that the only countryman of his who is clearly visible in our prospect is Jókai. Here is Riedl's *History of Hungarian Literature*, a fairly fat book sketching the thought of a nation, and not one of the hundred names is known to me, or, I dare say, to many of my American or English readers.

I cite these examples not as a judgment of Polish and Hungarian literature—that would be absurd!—but as illustrations of the interesting fact that in crowded Europe people who have fraternized and fought with each other for centuries may still remain intellectual strangers. Or the acquaintance may be one-sided. An educated Hungarian knows French literature as a matter of course; an educated Frenchman need not know a word of Hungarian or a single book written by an Hungarian. It is not necessary for admirers of the Danish critic, George Brandes, to know Danish; it is necessary for him to know English, French, German, Italian. The dominant languages have imposed their literatures on our Babel world. And it may be the very richness of those dominant literatures which has shouldered into obscurity work of supreme merit in other literatures. Yet as a rule the supreme thing will in time burst the limits of nationality and language and become the common property of mankind. This is not to say, however, that there are not many fine works which should be better known than they are both at home and abroad.

If our survey cannot pretend to completeness but omits whole nations, whole periods and important individuals in the nations and periods discussed, it does aim at, and I hope arrives at, a kind of organic unity and continuity. The contours of the sketch, which are imperfectly filled in, are coherent and give an impression of the total landscape. Our vision is rapid and fleeting, as from an airplane. We see the salient features, the outstanding peaks. But we do not stop to measure them or to dwell on their ample slopes. We linger for fifteen minutes over Shakespeare, who cannot be comprehended in less than fifteen years—or fifty.

It may be that Shakespeare did not devote every waking hour of fifteen or fifty years to the works of Shakespeare and other works in which he may have been interested. Certainly the ordinary reader has other things to read than Shakespeare and other things to do than read. The most omnivorous student devouring books for many years will become intimate with only a few thousand and will acquire a skimming acquaintance with a few thousand more.

Scores of people are required to keep up the catalogues of the great treasuries of books like the British Museum and the New York Public Library which contain two million volumes. But these printed multitudes need not disturb our peace of mind. Books overlap and duplicate and plagiarize honestly or dishonestly. So that a very few thousand volumes do contain the essential wisdom of the world. And that admirable and enviable person, the well-read man, the man who has "read everything," is a humanly possible person. In order to be "well read" it is not necessary to have labored through all the acknowledged classics. It is enough to have dug into a few of them and blandly to ignore the rest. One of the most sensitive and highly literate men I know does not happen to have read Dante, and he has no intention of trying to read him. Why should he, if he does not feel like it, or if the accidents of reading happen not to have turned his eyes and fingers to the works of the greatest poet? He knows other poets, and they are enough. The solemn notion cherished by Matthew Arnold, Schopenhauer, and other immensely learned men, who were endowed with humor and good sense, that there is some kind of moral obligation to spend one's days and nights with only the good and the great seems to me practical nonsense and a violation of the finer values of literature. Let us read broadly or narrowly according to the needs of our individual natures and let literary authority go hang itself on the lamp post in front of the Public Library. That way of putting it may be too strong, but it expresses a conviction which has been strengthened by many months of study in preparing this book, and by years of reading before I thought of writing such a book. It is not intelligent to read too much. Let us not become what Alexander Pope neatly characterized:

> The bookful blockhead ignorantly read,
> With loads of learned lumber in his head.

And there is this to consider: if you spend all your reading time frowning over the great classics, what becomes of those books which are not among the tremendous immortals but are your intimate companions, less than great but dearer perhaps than the great? Sometimes the volume that we carry in our coat pocket is not the work of an overwhelming major poet, but a little book by a minor poet—I have been bothered all my life to determine which are major and which are minor poets. And what shall we do with the odd books for which we care so much? To save *Alice in Wonderland* and *The Bab Ballads,* I would gladly throw overboard a good deal of very important literature. The little craft are lovelier than the great liners; or at least they have a loveliness in a small style which the liner cannot run down.

With little books or big books it is possible to be at home if you paddle your own canoe, look out for the great swells which may swamp you, and if you cultivate a kind of impudent curiosity about literature. Not to take it too hard, yet not to take it with silly irresponsibility. Literature from

Preface

Mother Goose to *Hamlet* is the story of human life. It may be a tale told by an idiot full of sound and fury signifying nothing. But it is the only story we know, the only story the human being can be interested in; and some of its lesser chapters are the most wise and amusing. So there are small books which are great friends and great books which remain remote strangers or intolerable bores. Since we are trying to lay out a more or less rational course through literature and must make our survey conform to the natural outlines, we shall not be heretical or eccentric too far beyond reason. Yet I venture to suggest two or three radical but not at all original suspicions about literature. One is that the real treasure often lies in a small casket. Another: that if you do not happen to like this or that great man you can let him pass and be better off for not having your intellectual bones broken. Still another is that because there are too many books for any sane person to bother his head about there are enough for any sane person to read with laughing delight or with the sad interest of intellectual curiosity. The art of reading is one of the fine arts. It is not so great, so creative as one of the seven arts. To write a good page is of course harder than to read it. And yet there exists the receptive creator without whom all art is dead. He is the person who sees the picture, who hears the symphony, who reads the book. It is to the reader of books that this book is addressed.

Hastings-on-Hudson

NOTE

To keep this book up-to-date, an appendix on contemporary world literature, writers, and data on historical changes has been added.

THE
STORY OF THE WORLD'S LITERATURE

PART I

THE ANCIENT WORLD

CHAPTER I

THE MAKING OF BOOKS

Of making many books there is no end.
—*Ecclesiastes.*

THE printed page at which we happen to be looking is, like thousands of other pages which we have read or disregarded, part of a wonderful romance that began many centuries ago. The page itself, any printed page, a thing consisting of black marks on white paper, belongs to a great story. It is so vast that none of us can have read it all. We do not know just how or when it started. It is continued every day, and we shall never see the end of it.

The plot, so far as it has developed, includes all other plots; for it is the story of stories. No two readers will see the outlines of this all-embracing plot in just the same proportions or be equally interested in all parts of it. But those outlines, however drawn, make a fascinating story. It was not invented by one man. The author is the Human Race.

We today are a living part of the story. So let us start from where we are at the present hour, and run swiftly back to the beginning. That will give us our bearings and afford a preliminary survey of the course we hope to follow until we arrive again at our own times.

Our eyes are upon a printed page. We have had the same experience so often that we do not stop to think about it. A newspaper or a magazine is delivered at our door for a few cents. We can buy a book, one of the world's masterpieces, for a dollar or two, or we can get it for nothing from a public library. We take all that for granted, and have ceased to marvel at it. Yet what a wonderful thing it is!

Consider first some of the mechanical processes that intervene between an author's mind and a reader's mind. The chief miracle-worker is the Printing Press, which has probably had more influence on modern civilization than any other invention. Before the press begins to turn, metal type has been set either by hand or, more often, by linotype or monotype machines, which are so ingenious that they almost think, though they require skillful men to operate them. Meanwhile paper factories have converted trees or rags into thin white sheets like this. The sheets flow through the press over the inked types. The binders fold and stitch the sheets and clothe them in covers of cardboard or buckram or leather. And in a few days the finished book is placed in the hands of a reader in almost any part of the world.

Now take a comparatively short step back to the time when there were no power presses, when printing, like all other manufacturing processes, was done by hand. In those days they made beautiful books, not more beautiful than we can make today, but more satisfactory than most that we do make in one respect: the paper was usually better, being of linen fiber, whereas most of the paper that we use is made from woodpulp with very strong acids and soon turns yellow and crumbles. As a wise historian has said, we are printing today "not upon sand but upon dust heaps." The preservation of recent literature, and of much of the older literature, depends on continuous reprinting. And on the whole what modern men allow to go "out of print" is not worth keeping, though possibly some very valuable things may be lost.

It is well to remember that every improvement is accompanied by some disadvantages. Our immediate ancestors with their hand presses and handmade paper produced books that are physically more durable than many of the books that we make today. But there was much bad printing done in the age before steam. For the sake of economy the type was often painfully small, and not as a rule so clear and sharp as the small type made by modern methods. Before the power press, books were fewer and relatively more expensive than they are now. Not many people could afford to own books, and, for that matter, not many people knew how to read them.

AN EARLY PRINTING PRESS

Our next stage backward in time is a longer one, though it is short in relation to the whole of human history. We come to the age before the printing press. And we linger with admiration in the little shop of Johann Gutenberg in the city of Mainz, Germany. We are in the presence of the father of printing. The year is about 1450 A. D. Gutenberg's contribution to the art seems to have been the discovery of a method of casting movable types, which could be set up in rows to form lines and pages. We do not know what kind of press he used to make the impact between the types and the paper. And we do not know just what books he printed, for there is none in the museums which bears his name. Latin Bibles, of which copies exist, are ascribed to him, and he may have had a hand in them, even if they were completed by his partners and successors. All the printers and readers in the world may salute Father Gutenberg and may disregard the many controversies that relate to his obscure biography. Like some other inventors to whom the whole world is in debt, he fell heavily in debt himself; his creditor took his tools and types, and Gutenberg died poor. There is no doubt, however, that the creditor made good use of Gutenberg's material. Within half a century the art of printing had spread over Europe from Italy to Holland.

GUTENBERG

We think of literature as something printed, because most of the books, ancient and modern, that we have seen are printed. But the story of literature before Gutenberg is at least ten times as long as the part of the story since the first printing press.

If we continue our journey into the past we come to a time when there was little or no paper in Europe. Paper was invented by the Chinese. The Arabs learned the art of making paper from the Chinese, and taught it to their Christian brothers in the western nations. Thus we owe this indispensable substance, which is the vehicle of almost all modern written and printed communication, to two branches of the human race whose culture and language are not European but Asiatic. By the fourteenth century paper was in common use throughout Europe. But it was not plentiful, because the process of manufacture was slow and laborious. People did not waste it or litter the streets with it as we do. And gentlemen and scholars practised a very fine style of penmanship (with goose-quill pens—"pen" means "feather") not only for the sake of elegance but for the sake of economy, to write many words clearly in small space.

Before paper came into general use, books and private letters and documents were written on parchment or vellum, that is, leather, specially prepared. Leather is relatively durable stuff, and there are still preserved in the museums skinrolls at least three thousand years old. The Jews wrote their sacred books, including the Old Testament, on leather, and even today in the synagogues we find the rolls, or scrolls, of skin. We still use parchment for certain writings which we wish to keep for a long time; a familiar example is the college diploma, which is often called a "sheepskin." Lambs, kids and calves have fed our bodies with their flesh and have given their hides for our shoes and garments; but the chief service of these animals is that they bear our most precious burden, the literature of thousands of years. We order "veal" at the butcher's and forget, perhaps, that "vellum," on which old books were inscribed, is from the same French word for calf. The story of literature is essentially the story of words; so that if we stop to explain the meaning of a word we are not really stopping but are going on with our tale. For a long time I thought that "parchment" had something to do with "parch," because the skin was dried, tanned, in the hot sun. That is the kind of guessing that we all indulge in until we look up the facts; then we find that the facts are more entertaining than our ignorant surmises. "Parchment" comes from Pergamum, a city in Asia Minor, where, about two hundred years before the Christian era, there was manufactured a fine quality of skin for writing material. The king of Pergamum, so the story goes, built up a large library, which was one of the wonders of the world. He and his scribes discovered a process of treating leather so that both surfaces could be written upon, and this made possible the book or volume, as we know it, with right and left hand pages.

The parchment books preserved for us almost all that remains of Greek and Latin literature, and most of the writings of the Christian world for fourteen centuries. Scribes copied upon the tough parchment old masterpieces which they found written on more fragile papyrus; we shall say a word or two about papyrus in a moment. These scribes were usually monks and priests who lived and worked in monasteries, which for many centuries were the safest places for men of learning. Most of the scribes were interested, of course, in the sacred scriptures, the Bible and other writings which they regarded as holy. Some of the monkish scribes had a sneaking fondness for pagan, that is, non-Christian literature. Many of them took great delight in a book as a work of art and spent years in decorating or illuminating a text. In our museums of art and libraries are gorgeous specimens of their work, the great initial letters of inlaid gold and the colors as brilliant as if they had been painted yesterday.

Sometimes the monks, who were poor fellows, ran short of parchment, of new material. But there were stored in the monastery or to be bought in the market old parchments already written on. The old writing could be cleaned off to leave a fairly fresh surface for new writing. The monks often erased pagan literature and used the second-hand parchment for books of Christian devotion. Such a manuscript is called a palimpsest, which means something that has been "scraped again." Sometimes the erasure was not thorough, and scholars have been able, by treating the parchment with chemicals, to decipher the original writing. In this way they have recovered many passages of ancient literature which but for the palimpsest would have been lost. The survival or the disappearance of many of the books of antiquity is largely a matter of accident, though some, the Bible, for instance, were carefully cherished and constantly recopied. The fate of books in a world of decay, fire, and warfare is an exciting story. Imagine the joy of a scholar who, rummaging among old manuscripts, comes upon a lost work by a classic writer. Such discoveries are made from time to time, and to some readers they are as thrilling as the discovery of the North Pole.

The use of parchment, or of leather, as a writing material goes back to a very remote past. But if you had lived in Rome or Athens before the fourth century of the Christian era and had tried to buy a copy of a poem by Virgil or Homer, you would have been offered not a volume written on leather but a roll of dried vegetable fiber called papyrus. As everybody knows, our word "paper" is derived from it. Papyrus is a tough water plant which grew in Egypt. It may have been the "bulrush" in which Moses was found. The stalk was split, pressed, and dried, and then pasted into strips and rolled. The Egyptians exported it to Greece and Rome and other neighboring countries. Almost all the best Greek and Latin literature was written on it until the stouter parchment came into general use. The Greek name for the fiber of the papyrus was *biblos,* which therefore meant the book that was written on it; and that is why our book of books is called the Bible.

When we say that the ancient Egyptians were wonderful people, the first things we think of are the pyramids, the sphinx, mummies, the rediscovered tombs of kings. But the pyramids, which seem built for eternity, are not such an important contribution to civilization as the fragile rolls of papyrus on which not only the Egyptians but all the peoples living on the Mediterranean Sea wrote their thoughts. Not only did the Egyptians furnish the material for writing; they seem to have been the first people with direct influence on Europe who devised a system of writing which represented spoken sounds. The key to that system was lost for many centuries, and it was only within the last hundred years that scholars learned to decipher the Egyptian picture writings or hieroglyphics. (That word means "sacred carvings"). The story of how the secret of old Egypt was unriddled is one of the most romantic chapters in the archeological annals of literature. In 1799 Boussard, a French engineer attached to Napoleon's army in Egypt, found the famous Rosetta stone, which contains a long decree of Egyptian priests in honor of one of the kings. It is inscribed in three versions, in hieroglyphic, in the popular or common language of Egypt, and in Greek. Since Greek was a known language it became possible, after much effort, to make out the parallel Egyptian characters. The decipherment was made by a French scholar, J. F. Champollion. Today the Egyptologist can read the picture writings on a mummy case or an obelisk, and has made the silent Sphinx yield something of her inscrutable reticence.

EGYPTIAN WRITER

Even if scholars had never learned to read the Egyptians in their own language, the wisdom of Egypt would not have been altogether lost. For it was absorbed by other nations, the Greeks and the Romans, and so came down to us, though in diluted and imperceptible form. But we may be sure that when Alexander the Great founded in Egypt the city named after him, which became the center of Greek culture, and when the susceptible Antony and the cooler Cæsars defeated Cleopatra, or were won by her, the conquerors learned something from the conquered.

WRITING ON STONE

Not far from Egypt, up the eastern coast of the Mediterranean were the Phœnicians. They were near neighbors of the Hebrews, who had many contests with them. The prophet Ezekiel pronounces a curse upon the chief Phœnician city, Tyre, whose splendid wealth he describes. They were a busy trading folk, not, it seems, much given to the cultivation of literature; we have only a few fragments of their writings preserved by the Greeks. And yet these Phœnicians, whose cities have vanished, were in a very important sense the fathers of every book we have ever read. For they invented the alphabet, the letter instead of the Egyptian picture-sign. Almost every letter on this page, after centuries of modification and development, owes its shape to the Phœnicians. Just when they invented the alphabet we can only guess. It must have been at least a thousand years before Christ. By this time the use of papyrus was well established; its smooth surface made possible an easy running style of handwriting. The Phœnicians, who were enterprising

MENEPTAH (A SUPPOSED PHARAOH)
(From a mural painting at Tebe)

merchants, bought papyrus from the Egyptians and sold it to the Greeks and other people. With the papyrus they sold the alphabet.

If we go one more step in our backward journey we come to the time when writing material was almost immovable, the stone age of literature. The early Egyptians and other peoples carved their records on walls and pillars. We have never quite outgrown the stone age, for our churches, public buildings, and tombs bear chiseled inscriptions, the purpose of which is to make lasting memorials of important events, prominent persons, civic and religious ideas. If all our books were destroyed, an historian five thousand years from now could reconstruct from our stone buildings a rough sketch of the kind of people we are and of the language we use.

In a similar way we reconstruct the life of people who engraved the stones of the remote past. But even stones disintegrate, and without continuously renewed books whole languages are buried. And even when the stones are intact, and the people that carved them are still living, a public library all of stone, inside and out, walls and books too, has certain disadvantages. You cannot take a book home and read it by your own fireside.

The Babylonians of the great empire in western Asia wrote on clay bricks and cylinders. These were an improvement on stone in that they were portable. But it must have been inconvenient to order a copy of the latest popular book and have it delivered in the form of a ton of brick. Of course nothing like that ever happened, for there was no such thing as popular reading. Only a few priests and scribes knew how to read and write; and most of the writings dealt with religious subjects and the exploits of monarchs.

Literature depends on the use of some light, smooth, flexible substance which makes possible easy transcription, multiplication and exchange of written thought. There is one substance, strong, light and easy to handle, which deserves a place in our story: that is, wood. The old Saxons, from whom the back-bone, the structure, of our English language is descended, wrote on boards made from the beech tree, and that is why these printed sheets bound together are called a "book." If you were lying under a beech tree reading a book, perhaps it would not occur to you that there was much resemblance between the name of the living thing overhead, which gives shade, and the name of the living thing in your hand, which gives light. But a modern German would hear the similarity of the two words; he calls the beech tree *buche*, and the book, *buch*. It was a red-letter day, or perhaps a black letter day, when our ancestors learned to saw wood. They used the boards to build houses and to write messages and records. Remember that when we say ancestors we mean intellectual ancestors, the people in northern Europe, who cut messages on trees, and the Egyptian school children whose "slate" was a slab of wood.

The early Romans wrote not only on boards but on the bark of trees. Their word for book, *liber*, originally meant inner bark. Some form of that word is the name for book in all the modern languages that are descended from Latin. The French say *livre;* the Italians and the Spanish say *libro*. And the English word "library" is from the same stem or root.

That a bark should be a root is not a bad joke but a sober fact. The tree of language and literature, which is the tree of knowledge, the tree of life, grows in strange and wonderful ways. The past lives in us in new forms. This sheet of paper is made from wood fiber, and so it is related physically to the wood on which many centuries ago our forefathers made their primitive inscriptions. The piece of furniture on which you lay this book is a "table," and the block of paper on which you make notes is a "tablet," because the Latin word for "board" is *tabula*. On the same table is a book, probably full of old photographs, called an "album." Why is it called that? Album means "white." In old Rome a high official, the Pontifex Maximus, who was a sort of Secretary of State, wrote the events of the year on a white tablet. That is why our precious family records, faded photographs and pressed flowers, are in a book called an "album."

Our tree of life, our tree of knowledge, is a miraculous tree, so bewildering that one hardly knows how to picture it. It is of wood, it grows from stone; it is a nest for birds that give us pens; it shelters animals that give us leather. And under it, a companion of all living things, is a Man reading a book and thinking thoughts.

CHAPTER II

THE BEGINNINGS OF LITERATURE

In the beginning was the Word.
—*St. John.*

IMAGINE a pile of books as high as the tallest building in the world, and let the pile represent the many centuries that man as a thinking and speaking creature has lived upon this earth. Only the top volume, an inch or two thick, will represent the printed book as we know it since the invention of the printing press. The three or four volumes below the top volume will represent all the hand-written books on parchment and leather. Below them the next half dozen volumes will be of stone and clay and wood. Downward for a few feet will be books with crude signs and marks and pictures that no living man could read. And all the rest of the column, clear to the ground, is blank! Either because those "books" were never written on, or because the writings have long since been obliterated.

So the greater part of our imagined column (a true tower of Babel!) does not consist of books, after all; if there was ever any literature there, we do not know it, we can only

guess that it might have been. But during the ages represented by the blank part of the pile men were communicating
by word of mouth. It is a reasonable conjecture that men
talked before they wrote. We can allow ourselves a contradiction, and say that there was a kind of literature before
literature.

Some of the materials of literature, the thoughts, must have
been created long before they were written down. We can
fancy—and without fancy there would not be much literature
worth reading—that our distant fathers who lived in caves sat
round the fire and told stories about wild animals they had
met, about their exploits in combats with neighboring tribes,
and mysterious tales, "myths," as we call them, about the
gods of forest and stream. Who can doubt that they sang
songs, that they imparted to their children such wisdom as
they had, and so made traditions of law, tribal customs, religion?

We surmise all this from evidence which may seem shaky
but which is as solid as much of the ground on which we build
our beliefs. In the first place, the earliest stories and myths
that we find written are not "childish" but are highly developed and full of wisdom. They could not have been made in
a day. They must have grown up through many generations.
In the second place, there are still living in odd corners of the
world people whom we assume to be like our ancient ancestors.
We call them "savages," which means people who live in the
woods, and we call ourselves "civilized," which means that
we live in cities. We regard ourselves as immensely superior
to savages, and we have no doubt advanced a little beyond
them. But when our wisest students go and live among savages they find stories and laws which have been handed down
for countless generations. Even if the savages can write in

some primitive way, their spoken wisdom is richer than their
written wisdom. We guess that our ancestors were savages of
about the same kind, and that they thought and spoke the
fundamental ideas of literature before they developed the art
of writing.

And though some of the myths of living primitive people

OUR MOTHERS TAUGHT US SONGS

and of our remote ancestors are not childish but are elaborate
and "grown-up," yet there is a certain resemblance between
young or uncultivated races and the children of civilized parents. We were all brought up on oral literature. Our mothers
taught us songs, nursery rhymes, fairy tales, and rules for good

behavior before we learned to spell any word longer than
c-a-t, before we could make sense out of a printed page. Our
first knowledge of language is somewhat like the imperfect
knowledge of music to which many of us are limited all our
lives; we enjoy orchestras and operas, and we sing and play
a little, but never learn to read music as a musician reads it.

The oral language is the basis of the written language.
What makes us superior to the other animals is the possession
of speech by which men taught each other and their children
for ages before they scratched signs on trees and on the walls
of caves. Without writing knowledge did not accumulate
rapidly; and things had to be learned over and over again by
each new generation. We can realize this if we remember
how quickly ideas and languages change even when men have
learned to write. Without special study we cannot read the
English of the twelfth century, and if one of the people of
that time should come to life, we could not understand his
speech. He would be a foreigner from a strange land, though
his blood might be in our veins.

Yet however shifting and perishable spoken language may
be, it does carry on from one person to another, from father
to son, from mother to baby, the elementary ideas by which
we live. And it may preserve and pass down much that is
beautiful. The illiterate mountain folk of Kentucky and
Tennessee repeat long poems which have descended to them
from old ballads that their forefathers brought over from
England. Modern scholars have taken down some of these
oral versions and compared them with the old printed or written versions; and many of the poems, though a good deal
changed, have not been spoiled by their long journey through
the memories and the speech of many generations. This experience, which we have been able to study in our own time,

teaches us what may have happened in the past, how something like literature can flourish even among the illiterate.

It seems to us a terrible handicap not to be able to read and write. But not many centuries ago, in the dark ages of Europe, there were comparatively few literate people, and some of the most active men in government, war, and business could not sign their names. But they were not necessarily ignorant. They spoke and listened, and so they had access to the ideas of their fellow-men.

It is impossible to set too high a value on reading and writing. But to show how much more important is speech, let us consider for a moment the case of a child who is born deaf or loses his hearing in early infancy. He is cut off from the living language and grows up a "dummy" with less knowledge than the illiterate man who can hear. The deaf child misses much of the unconscious education that most of us get before we begin to study in a methodical way. There are special schools for the deaf which do splendid work; they teach these defective children not only to read and write but to speak—one of the finest achievements of modern education. But we are not writing a treatise on education. We bring the deaf child into our story of literature only for the sake of illustrating how the spoken language comes first.

After man has learned to write he continues to speak, and written ideas and spoken ideas act on each other, so that it is almost impossible to tell which form of idea among educated people contributes most to the other. And how and why ideas "turn up" in the world, get from one brain to another, is a never ending problem.

In the broader sense of "literature," we are all writing and speaking it every day, though perhaps without much skill. This idea is humorously twisted by the great French dramatist, Molière, in a play called *Le Bourgeois Gentilhomme*. The middle-class gentleman, Monsieur Jourdain, a good. honest citizen, is trying to educate himself and his family. One of his teachers tells him the difference between prose and poetry. Monsieur Jourdain is surprised to learn that he has been talking prose all his life and never knew it before.

It may surprise us to learn that we have been talking both prose and poetry all our lives. That is true if we think of ourselves as the human race and not merely as this or that individual person. The human race probably composed, recited, memorized and wrote poetry before it wrote literary prose. Poetry is the language of feeling, and prose is the language of reason. Men feel strongly before they think reasonably. The first writers, or composers, were priests. They gave shape to war-songs, stories of heroes and religious beliefs. They wanted the people to remember. And we have all found that it is easier to memorize verse than prose. Verses stick in the head, whereas prose seems to go in one ear and out the other. Here again we can see a relation between the childhood of the individual and the childhood of literature. Most children are poetic in their response to sound and rhyme and in their phrases.

We can say, then, that literature begins as poetry, in the history of the race, and in the heart of the individual. The wisest poet keeps something of the vision of a child. Though he may think a thousand things that a child could not understand, he is always a beginner, close to the original meanings of life. That is why some poems written many centuries ago are as beautiful as any written by the greatest poets of modern times. The older poets recited their verses, addressed them to the ear of a listener rather than to the eye of a reader. Modern poetry, too, if it is to be fully enjoyed, must be heard. The plays of Shakespeare, for example, were made to be spoken in a theater rather than studied in a book. Literary prose also began in oratory and declamation. People heard before they read, and they spoke before they wrote. The written language is merely an extension of speech. "In the beginning was the Word." This sentence, the first in the Gospel according to St. John, is meant to apply to all creation. We may apply it to Man the Thinker, the Speaker, the Writer.

CHAPTER III

THE MYSTERIOUS EAST

Let the East and the West without a breath
Mix their dim lights like life and death
To broaden into boundless day.

—*Tennyson.*

MORE than three-fifths, almost two-thirds, of the human race live in Asia, and it is probable that in earlier times the relative number, as compared with Europe, was even greater than it is now. In Asia were the oldest dead civilizations of which we have any record, and certainly in the greatest of the grand divisions are the oldest civilizations which have a continuous life to the present day. A Chinese can read the wisdom of his ancestors back to a time when, as the American philosopher, Mr. Dooley, dramatically puts it, our ancestors were in the woods throwing stone hatchets at each other.

No doubt these venerable nations have much to teach us. But of the ancient peoples of Asia only those who lived in the western part of the continent have had much effect on our thought. The Jews who gave us the Old Testament were so

close to Europe that they were themselves almost Europeans
So far as we are intellectually concerned, the people in the
eastern and southern parts of Asia were, until recent times,
as far away as if they dwelt on another planet. Before the
eighteenth century travelers and traders brought back to Europe strange tales of China, or Cathay, and of India, but they
were more interested in fabrics and spices than they were in
literary ideas. And as late as the middle of the nineteenth
century Japan was a closed book to western eyes.

The aged book of the Far East is not yet open to us, for the
simple reason that we cannot read it and the work of translation has only begun. We show more enterprise in sending
soldiers to steal cities than in sending scholars to borrow
thoughts. However, we shall not be too severe on ourselves.
Sympathetic missionaries have proved that they could learn
as well as teach. And men armed with commissions to govern
the heathen and licenses to bear the "white man's burden"
have also equipped themselves with note-books and diction-
aries. The eastern Asiatics have sent us their own learned
emissaries, political, religious, and literary, who have mastered our tongues and interpreted their people to us. There
are professors of Oriental languages in almost every European and American university. Quite recently it has become
the fashion for our poets and men of letters to go to Asia for
inspiration and to enrich our literature with translations and
adaptations.

And yet in this book we must be guilty of an absurd disproportion and devote only one short chapter to the literatures of four or five nations which are older than ours and
perhaps wiser. The disproportion is to some extent excused
by sheer ignorance, and to some extent justified by the magnitude of the literatures which are blood of our blood and bone

of our bone. The West has been thinking so fast that we have
not time for the timeless East. It is but a flying visit that we
shall make to central, southern, and eastern Asia, and we shall
make it in a spirit of frank ignorance and respectful curiosity.
So we shall not be disobedient to the teaching of an old Chinese proverb: "When you know, to know that you know, and
when you do not know, to know that you do not know—that
is true knowledge."

The proverb is one of the many wise sayings of Confucius,
the sage of China, who lived about five hundred years before
Christ. Confucius was like Jesus in several respects. He was
a teacher who went among the people and talked. He
preached the Golden Rule in a negative form: "What you
do not wish others should do unto you, do not do unto them."
In his love of moderation and his faith in the power of calm
self-examination he is like Socrates and other Greek philosophers. He was a modest man, practicing the humility which
he taught and claiming little merit for himself. Later his
disciples and followers exalted him and all but deified him,
and it is they who are the authors of many of the books of
wisdom associated with his name, though of course his thought
is the foundation of them.

The chief work of Confucius, besides the influence of his
wise and gentle personality, was the collection and preservation of ancient Chinese literature. This consists of legendary
history, poetry, and moral teachings. The ethical precepts of
Confucius are very practical and are a common-sense comple-
ment to the mysticism of Lao Tzŭ who taught the "Way" of
getting in tune with infinite nature. These two sages and their
disciples, Mencius, the follower of Confucius, and Chuang
Tzŭ, the exponent of Lao Tzŭ, together dominated Chinese
learning for centuries and still inform the common thought of

millions of people. Except stray maxims of Confucius very little of the enormous mass of Chinese literature has passed into western languages. But recently there has been increased enthusiasm for Chinese lyric poets. The greatest of these was Li Po, who lived in the eighth century of our era. To suggest him in western terms, he seems to have been a combination of François Villon, Omar Khayyám, and Heine, a delightful and dissolute pagan. The following bit is from the translation of Li Po's works by Shigeyoshi Obata:

> A lovely woman rolls up
> The delicate bamboo blind.
> She sits deep within,
> Twitching her moth eyebrows.
> Who may it be
> That grieves her heart?
> On her face one sees
> Only the wet traces of tears.

This fragment gives only a hint of Li Po's humanity and grace. The interested reader will turn to Mr. Obata's volume of translations, and an exquisite small volume of translations with explanatory notes by Arthur Waley, called *The Temple*. Chinese graphic art and sculpture are known at least slightly to everyone who has visited a museum or even looked into the window of a dealer in Oriental wares; there is no barrier of language, though there may be other barriers, between a western eye and the beauty of a Chinese vase. The experts tell us that the Chinese poets are very close in spirit, so far as one art can resemble another, to those lovely carved ivories and porcelains and embroidered silks. Literature is only one of the vehicles through which widely separated peoples communicate their visions.

The spirit of Japan, which has become in recent times much

closer to the western world than China, is known to us, if we can pretend to know it, almost wholly through the fine arts, as distinct from literature. The wonderful prints and pottery and screens have been imported into Europe and America almost too abundantly for the integrity of the Japanese artist to withstand the temptation to commercialism. But the verse of Japan is unspoiled; there is no western market for it and most of it was written long ago. The Japanese borrowed their classical literature from China in somewhat the same way that

THUNDER GOD
(From Korin)

modern Europe derived its fundamental ideas from Greece and Rome. But Japanese lyric poetry is original and spontaneous. The golden age of Japanese poetry was the eighth century, and the two chief poets were Hitómaro and Akáhito. The Japanese lyric is short and suggestive, but the charm which it has for the Japanese and for the European student of Japanese literature is a fact that we must accept on faith,

for few English translations that I have seen are better than
trivial commonplace. This must be the fault of the translators. On this point, which is important not only for our
knowledge of Japanese poetry but for the whole problem of
literary communication between Oriental and Occidental
people, we may well quote Lafcadio Hearn, who was the most
eloquent and sympathetic interpreter in English of Japanese
life. "The Japanese poem," he says, "seems to me exactly
the Japanese coloured print in words—nothing much more.
Still, how the sensation of that which has been is flashed into
heart and memory by the delicious print or the simple little
verse." Later he writes to a Japanese pupil these question-
raising sentences: "A great poem by Heine, by Shakespeare,
by Calderon, by Petrarch, by Hafiz, by Saadi, remains a great
poem *even when it is translated into the prose of another
language.* It touches the emotion or the imagination in every
language. But poetry which cannot be translated is of no
value in world literature; and it is not even true poetry."
For us the most illuminating glimpses of Japan are through
Lafcadio Hearn's books, notably *Kotto, A Japanese Miscellany,* and *Japanese Fairy Tales,* which are written with exquisite art. And there are fine things in the collection of
translations by Hearn of *Japanese Lyrics.*

Japan has become a modern nation half Europeanized on
the surface and seems less remote from us than India which
inertly resists the pressure of European ideas though subdued
by European guns and machinery. Yet the Hindus are our
first cousins, being a branch of the great division of the human
race known as Aryan or Indo-European. They attained a
high degree of civilization thirty or more centuries ago, and
their religious philosophy is much older than Greek and contributed much to Greek speculation. Long before the gentle

voice was heard upon the shores of Galilee the Hindu preachers taught the brotherhood of man and the fatherhood of God.

It is one of the ironies of history that the people of India have not found their western brothers very fraternal and that they were divided among themselves by a rigidly un-

JAPANESE MASKS

democratic system of hereditary classes or castes. But the failure of the Hindus to convert the world to universal brotherhood or to realize in their own lives the highest ideals of their sages is only the failure that defeats all noble dreams, that has defeated every religion, including Christianity, down to the present hour. But the thought, the idea, remains, even if it does not practically prevail. That is what literature is, the record of an idea, no matter how life ignores it or people refuse to accept it. The Hindus were from earliest times exceedingly capable and fertile in the expression of their ideas, and their writings have been carefully preserved, suffering less change and loss than the literature of any other race whose records extend over such a long period of time. The thought of the Hindus comes to us in two ways, one ancient, the other modern. The ancient influence was through the Greek and passed into our system vaguely and indirectly. The early Greek philosophers, notably Pythagoras, learned from the Indian philosophers that wisdom is the contemplation of the spirit, that behind material things is the essence, the idea; and this is the basis of Plato's philosophy, which runs through all modern philosophy, and is in our souls, whether or not we have any consciousness of origins. There is a Hindu saying: "The spirit dwells in all men, but not all men are aware of this."

The other way in which Hindu thought has come into the literature of the western world is through modern scholarship. While European armies were conquering India, students and lovers of art were translating the literature of India, and their work has been supplemented by that of Hindu scholars educated in English universities, who were zealous to interpret their country to Europe. So that India is now an almost open book to western eyes. But it is a vast book, which has been thousands of years in the making, and not many of us can read far in it. An attractive glimpse is afforded by a small volume of selections edited by Brian Brown, called the *Wisdom of the Hindus.* It contains aphorisms and hymns from the *Rig-Veda* (verse wisdom), the most ancient of Indian religious thought, by which millions of Hindus govern their lives, and which to unbelieving westerners has much beauty and good sense. Even more interesting are the passages in verse from the two great Indian epics, the *Mahābhārata,* and the *Rāmāyana,* which are full of romantic color and spirited adventure. The increasing interest in Sanskrit literature (Sanskrit is the name that the Hindus give to their ancient written language) is indicated by the publication in the popular Everyman's Library of a translation of *Sakuntala,* the masterpiece of India's chief dramatic poet, Kālidāsa. The translation by Arthur Ryder is delicate and poetic, and we can understand Goethe's enthusiasm for this play.

The most influential of all Indian thinkers is the Buddha

Gotama, the founder of Buddhism. He lived about five hundred years before Christ, and his followers, at first in India (where Buddhism afterward declined), and in eastern and central Asia have outnumbered those of any other religious teacher. He was a preacher, not a writer, and he belongs in

BUDDHA

our record only because his doctrines permeated Asiatic thought and he and the ideas associated with him are the subject of an enormous literature. The English reader will find the life and beliefs of Buddha treated with some charm in Edwin Arnold's once very popular poem, the *Light of Asia.*

And the spirit of Buddhism as felt by a western student is beautifully interpreted in Lafcadio Hearn's *Gleanings in Buddha Fields.*

Translations of original Buddhist literature are accessible in the collection of English versions called the *Sacred Books of the East.* Among western nations interest in Buddhism has been confined to philosophers and scholars like Schopenhauer; it never made much impression on popular thought, because Christianity had triumphed in the West, and because the Oriental elements in Christianity are as much as the western mind can assimilate. Buddhism is too Oriental for us, perhaps to our loss. It teaches that the cause of all pain is desire, and therefore, the way to avoid pain is to get rid of all desire, that the end of life is *Nirvana,* oblivion. It is essentially a retreat from life, out of key with the more active European intelligence, and not acceptable to our way of thinking unless, as may well be, our civilization goes down in desperate defeat. This does not mean that it is a timid philosophy; it appealed to courageous men, men as unlike as Schopenhauer, the pessimist, and Emerson, the serene optimist. But even their literary power failed to carry the message of Buddhism far into European thought.

The Christian world has been similarly impervious to another great Asiatic religion, known as "Islam." Indeed the nations of Europe and the followers of the prophet were, for reasons not wholly religious, continuously at war, and the conflict has not yet ceased. Beginning in the seventh century of our era the Arabs under Mohammed and his successors made sweeping conquests in Asia and Africa, capturing converts by the sword as well as by the tongue. Today there are more than two hundred million members of the faith. The sacred and holy book of "Islam" is the *Koran* or *Quran,* a compilation of the teachings of Mohammed (Muhammad—Peace be upon him) which were revealed to him piecemeal. Since all of his followers are required to study the *Koran,* it is the most extensively read book in the world. There is an English translation of it by J. M. Rodwell which is probably better than the earlier version which Carlyle found so bewildering. Carlyle's eloquent essay on Mohammed in *Heroes and Hero-Worship,* is a just, or more than just, account of the greatness of Mohammed, and is of more than incidental interest to readers of English literature as illustrating Carlyle's wide sympathies and freedom from provincial prejudice. Nothing but a sense of duty could carry any European through the *Koran.* But it is tingling with life and honesty. "Sincerity, in all senses," says Carlyle, "seems to me the merit of the *Koran."* It is unlikely that we who do not read our own Bible any too assiduously, will spend much time reading the *Koran.* Nevertheless a book which has guided the lives of millions of people for twelve centuries is an important document in the story of the books of the world.

Mohammed was *never* venerated as a deity. Witness the sacred prayer:

"La ilaha illa Allah! Mohammed Rasul Allah!"
Translation: "There is no God but one God! Mohammed is a *Messenger* of God!"

The religion is called "Islam"—a word meaning: submission to God's will. The members of this religion are designated "Muslims" or "Moslems" (the English spelling varies) —a Moslem being one who surrenders to the will of God, thus—fatalism! Terms such as "Mohammedanism" or "Mohammedans" are utterly rejected by those who are informed and are erroneous and European in origin.

Probably the average American would cheerfully give up the whole *Koran* for any half dozen of that glorious collection

FROM A PERSIAN BAS-RELIEF ON THE TOMB
OF CIRO IN MURGAB

of stories, the *Thousand and One Nights* or the *Arabian
Nights' Entertainments*. They first became known to Europe
in a French translation early in the eighteenth century and were
immediately popular, spreading from one country to another.
The stories of Aladdin and his lamp, of Sinbad the

EXCHANGE OF OLD LAMPS FOR NEW
(*Arabian Nights*)

Sailor, of Ali Baba and the Forty Thieves are as well known to children of all ages in Europe as any tale of Hans Christian Andersen. And the good Caliph of Bagdad, Haroun Al Raschid, whatever he was in history, is one of the great monarchs in fiction. Undoubtedly the stories full of myth and magic have the most universal charm. But there is also a great variety of tales of another character, not all of them quite acceptable to modern taste but all told with an artfully artless gusto. These old storytellers are interested in the yarn, the adventure, for its own sake, rather than in character, but in El Samet, the garrulous barber, they created a humorous figure who can hold his own with any of the comic types of fiction. The *Arabian Nights* seems to western readers (and students of Arabic literature say that it is so) to be a compendium of the secular life of the Orient, of Persia, Egypt, and India, from which many of the stories were drawn.

The poetry of the Orient which has made the most broad and forceful impression in the west is that of Persia, and this is as it should be, for the supremacy of Persian poetry was acknowledged by the other peoples of eastern Asia, the Arabians and the Turks, and its beauty has appealed to European translators who were artists as well as scholars. To English readers the best known of Persian poems, probably of all Oriental poems, is the *Rubáiyát* of Omar Khayyám. Edward FitzGerald's translation is an English classic, and we shall reserve our word about it until we come to the English poets of the nineteenth century. The great epic poet of Persia is Firdusī who lived in the tenth century A. D. He wrote the *Shāhnāma*, or *Book of Kings*, which is the history of Persia from earliest times. It is a stupendous work of great length and is said to have episodes and passages of great beauty (there seems to be no easily readable English version). One distinction it has among the heroic poems of the world. It is the only poem, with the possible exception of the *Lusiads* of the Portuguese poet, Camoens, which became the accepted national epic during the life-time of the author. One episode from the *Book of Kings*, not a translation but an original version, is the subject of Matthew Arnold's *Sohrab and Rustum,* a poem of intellectual rather than emotional interest. The value of an epic is that it expresses the tradition of a race or a nation; it need not be narrowly nationalistic, indeed it must have universal qualities to be great in its own country and to be imported across boundaries of space and time. The bird that flies is poetry less heavily organized than an epic, something more quotable. Beside the thoroughly Englished and transformed Omar, there are two Persian lyric poets who are to us more than names, Saadi and Hāfiz. Saadi's most famous books, the *Būstān* (*Fruit-Garden*) and *Gūlistān* (*Rose-Garden*), both accessible in English, are philosophic and moral discussions and maxims, not so profound as to be dull, and sharp enough to shine through translations. Edwin Arnold's version of part of the *Gūlistān* did much, on account of Arnold's literary vogue, to make Saadi known to English readers.

Hāfiz was less moralistic than his father-in-law, Saadi, and had more of the spirit of Omar, loving wine, women, song, and nature. And even more than Omar, whose fatalism is somewhat melancholy and pessimistic, Hāfiz feels, at least sometimes, the joy of life.

At the close of this chapter let me say again that it is an absurd violation of the spirit of the ages to glance for only three minutes at a literature like that of China which has been a highly civilized institution for at least thirty centuries. Professor Herbert Giles in his *History of Chinese*

Literature takes us back, conjecturally, a good many centuries before Confucius, who was born about five hundred and fifty years before Christ. Yet the writings of that ancient people, however wise and beautiful, have made almost no impression on the thought of Europe; indeed they remained unknown in Europe until modern scholars began to investigate and translate. There is no doubt much in the Chinese mind which is sympathetic with us, and probably we are making a profound mistake not to get better acquainted with it. A citizen of Pekin can afford to smile tolerantly at our ignorance and perhaps repeat the proverb with which Professor Giles concludes his book: "Without error there could be no such thing as truth."

CHAPTER IV

JEWISH LITERATURE

To understand that the language of the Bible is fluid, passing, and literary, not rigid, fixed, and scientific, is the first step toward a right understanding of the Bible.

—*Matthew Arnold.*

ET us at the outset agree to consider the Bible as literature, to read and enjoy as we should read and enjoy any other book or collection of books, for its beauty, poetry, wisdom, narrative interest, historical value—all that may in the broadest sense be called literary. Whether the Bible is the Word of God, whether it is inspired from cover to cover in a sense of the word "inspiration" that does not apply to any other book in the world, whether it is our moral duty to read it and accept it as the whole truth and nothing but the truth; these are questions which we can leave to theologians and to members of the various Jewish and Christian churches. Our interest here is literature, not religion.

There is, however, one purely religious consideration, a matter of fact which nobody can deny, which no intelligent person would wish to deny. It is the religious value of the

Bible above all its other possible values, it is the special love
for it in the hearts of religious people and the devout study
of it by religious teachers which caused it to be read or listened
to by countless millions of people for many centuries. The
religious motive, the missionary spirit, rather than pure literary interest, accounts for the wide distribution of the Bible
in many languages and for much of the scholarship that has
been devoted to it. If it had not been for the pious zeal of
our forefathers, many of whom had no literary sense whatever, the Bible would have been a book known only to the
learned, as remote from us as the sacred books of India. It
is owing primarily to religion, to faith, which we may or
may not accept, that the phrases of the Bible are part of our
daily speech, and that its principal stories, metaphors, and
parables are almost universally understood. Very few mod-
erately intelligent people have to consult an encyclopedia to
find out what a politician means when he refers to Armaged-
don, and the most ignorant unbeliever may in ordinary conversation quote or misquote Proverbs without the slightest
notion of where the words come from.

Our thought and our language are shot through and through
with the Bible. And the reason for that is, as a matter of
history, religious, not literary. The religious interest in the
Bible still prevails. And though it may be true that in the
old days the Bible was read more faithfully than it is today,
the records of the American Bible Society show that hundreds of thousands of copies are printed every year; and we
in America know from casual observation that there is a copy
in almost every private house.

So that we must recognize that the moving power of the
Bible is religious. Without that power most of it would not
have been written and most of us would never have heard

RUTH
"She stood in tears amid the alien corn"

of it. Nevertheless it is proper for us to disregard all theological argument and to emphasize the importance of the
Bible in the intellectual tradition of all people who speak
European languages, to find in it the manifold glories which
are unvexed by controversies, and, as Pope said of the cross
on the lady's breast:

Which Jews might kiss, and infidels adore.

It may be that we do not know the Bible by heart as did
some of our ancestors who read a chapter every day. But it
is a matter of course among scholars and amateurs of literature
to regard the Bible as part of the necessary culture of every
educated person, to study its historical portions as one would
study Herodotus or Gibbon, to enjoy its poetic books as one
would enjoy Shakespeare or Goethe. This attitude is a gain
for literature and history, and it can hardly be a loss for religion in the broadest sense. Indeed it seems a misfortune
for all the higher interests of life that mere sectarian conflicts could take the Bible into the courts of a great state
like California and have it ruled out of the public schools.
Whoever does not know the Bible in a general way and does
not know its simplest details well enough to recognize them
when he meets them in speech or in literature must be to
some extent a stranger to the mental life of his race and will
be lost in many of the finest pages in the literature of his own
people.

The Old Testament is the basis of Hebrew literature and
of the Jewish religion. It is also the foundation of the Christian religion and therefore the central book, or collection
of books, in the literature of Christian nations. There is no
other book like this in the whole history of human thought.

It has often happened that nations and races have adopted the religions, and so the literatures, of their neighbors. For example, Buddhism, which arose in India, has flourished in China and other nations to the east of India rather than in the land of its origin. All the old religions of Greece, Rome, and northern Europe yielded to Christianity. But the Old Testament has the unique distinction of being root and trunk of two religions which later branch away from each other. At the last word of the Old Testament Jew and Christian part company and become antagonistic while holding a common reverence for the common source! Surely the history of human thought is an amazing and amusing thing to contemplate.

At this point let us make a brief note, inadequate of course, on Jewish literature, after the Christian with his New Testament went one way and the Jew went another. As the second part and fulfillment of the Christian Bible is the New Testament, so the second part and fulfillment of the Jewish Bible is the *Tal-*

THE BOOK OF THE LAW

mud. This is a collection of laws and comments on them by generations of rabbis. They are based on oral tradition which is supposed to go back to Moses, and they have been held sacred by orthodox Jews down to the present time. The fact that the Jew of Europe was engaged in a perpetual struggle with the Gentile to preserve his religious and racial integrity made him cling to his traditional laws and apply to the study of them a vast amount of scholarship. Since it has controlled the lives of countless members of a prolific race and embodies the wisdom of their finest thinkers, the *Talmud* is one of the great books of the world. But on account of the intellectual isolation of the Jew it has had little effect on surrounding literatures, and probably few non·Jewish readers have ever looked into it. In the English translation it occupies twenty volumes, and the books relating to it are an immense library. Some of its proverbs have strayed into Gentile literature, and one often meets quotations from it in fiction which portrays Jewish characters.

The Old Testament includes thirty-nine books, or if we disregard the division of Samuel, Kings, and Chronicles, thirty-six. Just why these books, which are called the "canon" of the Old Testament, were accepted and certain other books were relegated to the Apocrypha as not authoritative, is a question for theologians and historians. From our literary point of view the story of Judith and the shrewd wisdom of Ecclesiasticus are just as entertaining, whether or not they are incorporated in the official Bible.

The accepted books of the Old Testament fall into three groups: the books of the law; the books of the prophets; and the miscellaneous group of scriptures which includes books as unlike as Ruth and Job. This classification is according to subject-matter and except that the books of law, the Pentateuch, are the first five, it does not exactly correspond to the order in which the books appear. For example, Ruth follows Judges and the Song of Solomon precedes Isaiah. Nor does the order in which the books are printed correspond to the probable order in which they were written—a complicated question on which scholars do not agree. Perhaps this question of order and grouping is not of first importance to the ordinary reader who may properly regard each book separately as he would the plays of Shakespeare or the novels of Dickens, and with more justice in the case of the Bible since it is an artificial unit, the work of many writers.

A more practical problem is the physical form of the Bible. It is usually printed in a single volume so large that it is uncomfortable to hold or so small that the type is difficult to read. This problem has been all but perfectly solved by some of the beautiful editions on India paper published by the Oxford University Press. An edition by Eyre and Spottiswoode in four volumes is a delight to the hand and the eye. Professor Richard Moulton divided his *Modern Reader's Bible* into twenty-one volumes. It is also issued in a one-volume edition complete. He grouped the sentences into more or less logical paragraphs, eliminating the divisions into numbered verses which often give a jerky and broken effect to the stately biblical prose. His arrangement is no doubt strange and distasteful to old-fashioned readers, but it certainly makes for fluent consecutive reading.

Whatever the historical reason may be for the order of the books of the Bible, there is no reason why we should read them in that order. Not all the books are equally interesting, and it is well not to let the duller passages, such as the tiresome genealogies and rather dry priestly laws, deter us from plunging ahead into the magnificent stories and poems. Though every page is precious to the devout, many readers will find that inspiration, whatever its source, reaches a supreme height in certain episodes, dramas, biographies, lyrical and prophetic poems; and that on the other hand matters of great importance in the history of man and his religious account of himself are obscure, dull, and difficult.

Often the obscurity is due to brevity. Much is compressed into these books, and it has not yet been explained why the many scribes who worked over them resisted the temptation to expand and elaborate much more than they did. Perhaps they knew the value of a suggestive outline without detail, and perhaps they were mutually jealous to keep out each other's interpolations.

An astonishing example of much said and more implied in a short space is the first four chapters of Genesis. Adam, by inference, is dead in the fourth verse of the fifth chapter, and in a few pages before that we have the whole story of creation, of the Garden of Eden, Adam and Eve, Cain and Abel. And the rest of Genesis, which is shorter than a short modern novel, contains the lives of Noah, Abraham and Isaac, Jacob, Joseph and his brethren, and much else besides. Tolstoy, who spoke not only as a religious zealot but as past master of the art of fiction, said that the story of Joseph is a perfect narrative. It may be that one reason for this is that Joseph is a living character, a flesh-and-blood man of adventure, whereas his ancestors back to Adam grow more and more mythical and shadowy. It is doubtful if any later imagination could add much of interest to the story of Joseph, and that in itself is a test of literary perfection. Later poets, Milton, for example, have been able to enrich the vague story of the creation and the fall of man, not because it is imperfect for its purposes but because it suggests and invites an infinite variety of poetic interpretation.

Exodus, the second book of the Old Testament, is the first part of the biography, or, according to old tradition, the

CAIN

autobiography, of Moses. This biography which embodies the history of Israel continues through Leviticus, Numbers, and Deuteronomy, to the conclusion of the Pentateuch. It is an heroic epic story of the migration and reëstablishment of a people under a great leader. Moses was made, or made himself, the vehicle of many Jewish laws, some of which have only a sort of tribal and parochial interest, and only a few of which, like the Ten Commandments, are wrought into the beliefs and habits of modern people. But even the minor and obsolete laws are not difficult to read and understand. And throughout there are those marvelous flashes of poetic phrasing which light even the darkest pages of the Old Testament. Of the poetry of the Bible we shall say a word presently.

The limitations of this volume do not permit us to consider even superficially each book of the Bible in turn, and our purpose lies far away from scholarly explanation and from what is called Higher Criticism. But we may in a sort of informal commentary remind ourselves of some of the outstanding books and passages of the Bible.

Joshua, the successor of Moses, is distinguished for three miraculous performances. He led the people of Israel dryshod through the river Jordan. He took the city of Jericho by means of trumpetings and shoutings. And he caused the sun and the moon to stand still. The book of Joshua is an epic in itself, the exploits of a hero and the history of a people interwoven with myth and religion. And it contains at least one minor romance which is material for the novelist and the playwright. This is the story of Rahab, who betrayed her city to Joshua and was spared when her fellow-townsmen were put to the sword. For Joshua was a ruthless general, the forerunner of Cromwell and many other pious murderers. The conquests of Joshua were not so extensive as those

MOSES

MOSES

of Alexander, but they bore somewhat the same relation to the history of the Jews as those of Alexander to the history of the Greeks. One difference is that the facts about Alexander are fairly well established, whereas some of the triumphs of Israel ascribed to Joshua seem to have taken place after he slept with his fathers. But that is a question for historians, and the answer to it does not affect one way or another the literary value of the vigorous narrative. And whoever, assuming a scientific attitude, is inclined to argue about the astronomical disturbances is taking a really unscientific attitude toward literature.

The next book is Judges. Near the beginning of it we meet one of the heroines of the Bible, Deborah, in her way as fine a figure as Joan of Arc, though we know less about her. She inspired Barak to lead their people to victory. And after the victory she and Barak sing a duet of exultation and praise which is said to be one of the oldest Hebrew poems. It contains that wonderful phrase which many victors and many hopeful of victory have used: "The stars in their courses fought against"—whoever the enemy was.

Judges also contains the dramatic story of Samson. He belongs to the breed of legendary superhuman heroes like Hercules. His revengeful self-sacrifice is a supreme tragic climax. The finest poetic development of the story is Milton's *Samson Agonistes,* and the theme is effectively treated by the French composer Saint-Saëns in an opera which is extraordinary among modern operas in having a dignified and coherent plot. If we seem to be stressing those parts of the Bible which are narrative units, there is strong justification for this emphasis. As Robert Louis Stevenson pointed out, narrative is the "typical mood" of literature. Everybody is ready to listen to a story on almost every occasion, whereas we often find it difficult to fix our attention on an argument or an explanation of fact. The Hebrew writers, like the writers of all other races, conveyed much of their wisdom, the part that is on the whole best remembered, in some form of story. The Bible is rich in narratives, which are of two principal kinds, those which purport to chronicle events and those which teach moral lessons by allegory and parable. This is true both of the Old Testament and of the New Testament. For the central theme of the New Testament is the biography of Jesus, and Jesus often spoke in parable; indeed it is his favorite method of instruction.

SAMSON

After Judges is the great little Book of Ruth, in four short chapters, less than a hundred verses all told. This brief story is said to be very important for the much that it implies about the status of women and the laws of inheritance among the early Jewish tribes. However that may be, the much that is implied for most readers is a profound and tender pathos; the hearts of two women are revealed with an emotional power which is quite beyond analysis. The toughest cynic must rejoice in the happy ending, by which the lives of two women are fulfilled—a rare thing in human experience and unique in Old Testament literature, where, as a rule, the world bears heavily on men and women alike. The motive that makes this story universal is homesickness, which almost everybody has felt. Keats in his *Ode to a Nightingale* condenses this beautiful pain into three lines which, like the original Bible story, make us all believe in one kind of miracle—the miracle of expression:

> Perhaps the self-same song that found a path
> Through the sad heart of Ruth, when, sick for home,
> She stood in tears amid the alien corn.

The four books of Kings, which in our Bible are divided into two books of Samuel and two of Kings, are the story of the most splendid days of the Jewish monarchy, when Israel triumphed under great men and, according to the indignant prophets, abused its triumph, forgot God, and went the bitter way of punishment, defeat, and captivity. These four books are a superb epic, solid and noble in construction, like a great arch. There must have been at least one master poet at work on these books, and perhaps there were many, for epics grow and are probably not the creation of single minds.

See how the story builds up. Samuel, a devout and valiant man, struggles against external and internal enemies. But he grows old, and his sons are feeble and corrupt. Saul is called in, a tragic character, not equal to the task, finally humiliated and rejected. His son, Jonathan, a brave fighter and a fine soul, later the bosom friend of his chief, is not strong enough or old enough to take command of Israel. All this is a mounting preparation for the coming of David, the supreme figure in the Old Testament, captain and poet, a marvel of physical prowess, for he slew Goliath, and a man of intellect, for he "behaved himself wisely."

It is easy to understand why the biblical writers made David the forefather of Jesus. Whatever the genealogical facts may be, the literary and spiritual descent is clear. The new king, the new hero must be derived from the stock of the bravest of the old kings. David is founder of a new royal house; Jesus is founder of a new kingdom of heaven, or rediscoverer of an old kingdom. That David wore purple and gold and Jesus went barefoot, that David fought in bloody wars and Jesus was a pacific non-resistant, that David was guilty of adultery and Jesus led an immaculate life—these incongruities may puzzle the religious side of our minds. But as human stories they are perfectly explicable and not inconsistent at all. David, even more than Joseph, and much more than the somewhat shadowy Saul, is a real flesh-and-blood character. Like all epic heroes he is veiled in myth and endowed with superhuman qualities. But we seem to know him, his passions, sorrows, angers, his tolerance and affection, his extraordinary strength of will and his quite ordinary weaknesses. He is as definitely drawn as Achilles in the *Iliad*. Some of the Bible narratives are confused or indistinct. The story of David is a masterpiece.

And almost equally clear and strong is the story of David's son, Solomon, the wise, the magnificent. Solomon in all his glory is not a mere man; he is Israel in all its glory at its greatest period of wealth and expansion. The writers are eloquent in their descriptions of the splendor of the king and his possessions. And there is a strain of pathos in this; for the accounts were written after Israel had fallen on evil days, and the chroniclers look back with evident regret to the time when the Jews were prosperous. There is, moreover, a contradiction in the character of the traditional Solomon, which may well have been a contradiction in the character of the actual man. He is a paragon of wisdom, even without nine-tenths of the worldly proverbs and saintly utterances that were later attributed to him. At the same time he is foolish, at least in his old age; for he is led into idolatry by women (biblical writers, both Jewish and Christian, put an undue heap of responsibility on women for the troubles of this world), and he does not leave his kingdom in sound condition. His immediate successors are not quite worthy of father Solomon and grandfather David.

With the decline of the temporal kings comes the fiercest of the prophets, Elijah, and after him his disciple, Elisha. They are miracle-workers, who in some of their deeds, like the dividing of the Jordan, look back to Moses, and in other deeds, like the raising of the dead and the increase of the widow's food, look forward to the Messiah. But they are not very lovable characters. Their unsuccessful attempts to keep the people in the true faith seem to have made them hard and vengeful. The punishment evoked upon errant kings is understandable. But the penalty of bloody death visited upon forty little children who mocked Elisha is incredibly ruthless, if the story is to be taken literally. The Hebrew historians evidently did not try to soften or explain away the misdeeds even of their heroes and prophets. And that is why their prose is often so brutally powerful. Indeed the things which they had to record were bitterly tragic, for in spite of two or three good kings, such as Hezekiah and Josiah, things went from bad to worse; with the fall of Jerusalem at the hands of Nebuchadnezzar, king of Babylon, and the captivity and exile of the Jews, the great days of Israel were at an end.

The two books of Chronicles contain parallel or supplementary accounts of much that has appeared in the preceding books. The next two books, Ezra and Nehemiah, re-
count the return of the Jews from Babylon and the rebuilding
of Jerusalem. These books should be read with the two
books of Esdras (another form of Ezra), which for reasons
too complicated to explain here were separated from the
books with which they logically belong, and were put in the
Apocrypha. It is rather cheering to come to these books
after the disaster and gloom of Kings. Nehemiah and Ezra
are builders, with what we should call a constructive pro-
gram. Nehemiah restored Jerusalem in a physical sense, and
Ezra, according to the declaration imputed to him, restored
it in a spiritual sense by rewriting the laws and records which
had been lost. How he and five scribes wrote two hundred
and four books in forty days is one of the finest tales in the
story of books, no matter whether it happened or not.

And let us say again that the question of what happened
and the question of the religious significance of any recorded
event are the business of the theological historian. Our interest is in what we broadly call literary quality, though, to
be sure, we cannot keep the various kinds of interest completely separated. It is a matter of emphasis. We are certainly justified in emphasizing strongly the literary value of
the Book of Esther, which may be regarded, without irreverence, as an early example of historical romance. To the
Jews (and therefore to the Christians who took over the
Hebrew Old Testament almost as a whole) Esther was a
sacred book. The reason is that it exalts the wit and beauty
of the Jewish queen of a Persian king. She and her foster
father, Mordecai, turn the tables on Haman and save the

DAVID

Jews from destruction; in memory of this the Jews still celebrate the feast of Purim. Whether this story be sacred or "profane" (in the true sense of the word), it is a hair-raising story. Murderous plotting and counter-plotting, with a beautiful intelligent woman at the center of it all—this is surely the richest kind of romantic material. The narrative is direct and condensed, so condensed, indeed, either by ac-cident or by literary art, that, as the familiar phrase runs, "much is left to the imagination."

A sister heroine to Esther is Judith, who in the Greek and the Latin versions of the Bible immediately precedes Esther. In our English Protestant Bible Judith has been relegated to the Apocrypha. We who are merely literary can follow the fortunes of a lady, especially when our adventure is so simple a thing as moving from one book to another. The adven-tures of Judith are not simple but are exciting and creepy. How she charms Holofernes and cuts off his head when he is drunk makes a stirring tale. The literary form which we call the novel is a modern invention, but prose narrative in-volving plot and character is very ancient.

The most powerful example of dramatic narrative in the Bible is the Book of Job, in which there is contest of char-acter with circumstance, of man with the forces of evil and adversity, finally saved by unflinching patience and trust. It is a tremendous drama with Man, Satan, and God as the chief persons. And quite possibly an even sterner and greater drama underlies and historically precedes the version that we have. The idea of this earlier drama was discovered or developed by the late Morris Jastrow. The elaborate learn-ing of Bible scholars is far beyond our scope. But Jastrow's idea adds immensely to the dramatic interest of the Book of

Job. He thinks that originally Job was a terrific rebel against Heaven, like Satan, or Lucifer, or Prometheus, that he refused to give in, no matter how much he suffered. His rebellion was so blasphemous and defiant that later scribes softened and weakened the story, made him merely long-suffering, and rewarded his fidelity with a happy old age.

Whatever the historical basis of this interpretation, its poetic and human value is evident; it enriches the story if it does not explain it. The drama as we have it peters out on a conventional happy ending; Job receives riches and more sons and daughters to compensate for the children who were taken away from him at the beginning of his trials. That compensation is, humanly and dramatically, an impotent conclusion. Children, even seven sons and three "fair" daughters, are not as sheep and camels and oxen and asses to be dealt out in quantity; a parent longs for the first children who were taken away from him. One feels that the curtain falls on this drama, as it now stands, with a too simply satisfactory finality. But if the drama breaks down, the poetry, verse by verse, is sustained up to the last chapter. Dip into it almost anywhere, and you shall find a golden phrase.

And here, as we pass from Job to the Book of Psalms, is our place for a word about the poetry of the Bible. Those who read Hebrew tell us that the beauty of the original text cannot be rendered in another language; and they are probably right, for anybody who has tried to translate from one tongue to another knows that poetry is a strange fluid that somehow spills when it is passed between vessels of different shapes and metals. But we have reason to believe—and many scholars to whom Hebrew is foster-mother if not mother tongue support the belief—that we who inherit the English Bible are wonderfully fortunate, that if we have lost something by not being able to read Hebrew, we have gained much by being, in our language, English.

The reason for the gain is evident if we consider how the Bible came to us. The Old Testament was in Hebrew and in another Semitic language, Aramaic. It was translated into Greek some time before the Christian era; the Greek version is called the Septuagint from the Latin word for seventy, because according to tradition the translation was made by seventy scholars. There were also Latin versions; the text prepared by Jerome at the end of the fourth century A. D., called the Vulgate (that is "published" or "commonly circulated"), is still with some revisions, the official version of the Roman Catholic Church. Before the seventeenth century there were several English versions of the Bible, partial or complete, of which the most important is that of William Tyndale in the sixteenth century. Tyndale was a remarkable scholar, familiar with Hebrew, Greek, and Latin, and master of an English style which was both dignified and popular. His personality still lives in the pages of the English Bible as we know it, so that he has been truly called the father of English prose, for of course the Bible has influenced all modern English writing, even writing that seems far away from it in tone and substance.

When at the beginning of the seventeenth century the Authorized Version was made at the bidding, or with the sanction, of King James, all circumstances conspired to produce the rich poetic prose of the Bible. It is no wonder that many pious Englishmen have believed that the Lord looked with special favor upon this work. The best scholars of the universities and of the English church collaborated in harmonious devotion to the task. Between them they knew all that was knowable about earlier versions of the Scriptures in all languages. They therefore had all the resources of ancient languages to draw upon and they were sensitive to the vocabulary and rhythms of Hebrew, Greek, and Latin. Thus they enlarged the English language without violating its native structure and character.

The time was ripe. The English language was at exactly the right stage of development for the rendering of books full of poetry and sonorous prophecy. For it was the great age of poetry, the age of Shakespeare; and the prose of the period was at once flexible and stately, free and solid; it had not yet been subjected to the rationalizing process which came with the eighteenth century. Almost every master of prose in the spacious days of Elizabeth and James wrote biblical English, or, to put it the other way round, the translators of the Bible wrote Elizabethan English.

If, therefore, there are beauties and shades of meaning in the Hebrew, and perhaps in the Greek and the Latin, which do not appear in the English, yet we may be fairly sure that the authorized English Bible has merits peculiarly its own. Indeed several competent critics, acquainted with ancient and modern versions, have boldly declared that our Bible is of all versions the literary masterpiece.

Let us insist again on "literary," for we are not concerned with the problems of accuracy which have no doubt been satisfactorily solved by the later group of scholars, English and American, who in the nineteenth century gave us the Revised Version. Many of us who are not at all old-fashioned prefer some of the "authorized" phrases to the "revised." "Faith, hope, and charity" is a lovely sequence of words which cannot be displaced by the jolting monosyllables, "faith, hope, and love." The revisers tell us that the psalmist does not say, "unto thee will I sing with the harp," but "unto thee will I play with the harp." Well, maybe so; but it takes a poet to sing with the harp, and that word, "sing," will go on singing above the authority of all scholarship past or to come.

It is in no nationalistic spirit, since I am an American, nor, I trust, in provincially ignorant limitation to the only language I know well, that I suggest a comparison between any of the great phrases of the English Bible with the corresponding phrases in French or even in the stalwart German of Luther. I merely make the suggestion without argument.

However much the informing genius of the Hebrew may have been modified or overlaid by the genius of English, the English translators did not seriously weaken or falsify the spirit of the original; and, as the Bible tells us more than once, it is the spirit and not the letter that counts. The translators rose to their task, and nowhere more splendidly than in the poetic books which lie in the heart of the Old Testament: Job, Psalms, Proverbs, Ecclesiastes, The Song of Songs. These books are as full of metaphor as the honeycomb of honey. And the melody of the tongue, be it just or not, is as choice silver.

The Song of Songs ends in a beautiful cadence: "Make haste, my beloved, and be thou like to a roe or to a young hart upon the mountains of spices." We turn the page to Isaiah, the first of the long list of solemn prophets whose note is often lyric but seldom lovely. Isaiah, of course, is not the first, for prophecy is as old as Moses, and all the later prophets go back at least as far as Elijah. His mantle seems to have fallen not only on Elisha but on all succeeding soothsayers of Israel. And it is a dark mantle curiously woven of gloom and faith. The prophets are most eloquent when they are deploring the sins of the people, threatening them with the punishment of God (which in large measure they have already received), and at the same time exhorting them to trust in God. Whether they are melancholy and pessimistic or filled with zeal and adoration, they are almost always poetic; the gift of prophecy implied the gift of expression, and there seems to have been a traditional prophetic style, a kind of literary school in which the prophet studied his masters. The form sometimes is apparently as deliberate and self-conscious as that of any modern sophisticated poet. Take, for example, some of the haunting phrases that begin the chapters of Isaiah: "Woe to the land shadowing with wings," "The burden of the desert of the sea," "The burden of the valley of vision." Such melodious lines, whatever the original lines may be, are not accidental but are the work of highly artistic poets.

Such generalizations, and many more, apply to all the prophets. But we must remember, even in a brief survey, that behind the various prophetic books are more or less distinct individuals, whose separate characteristics remain in spite of the later priestly editing to which they have been subjected. And the differences are not obliterated in our English Bible where the prophets are all transmuted into what is, in spite of its variety, a uniform style. Isaiah, the noblest of the prophets, is at once judge and consoler; he denounces the wicked, but he proclaims the power of the everlasting Jehovah to redeem Jerusalem and comes at last to a vision of the Messiah. His combination of severity and high hope results in almost dramatic contrasts of emotion, and the book closes in a beautiful crescendo as if it were designed like a symphony. Some scholars believe that the contrasts in Isaiah are inconsistent with the idea of single authorship, and they support their belief with arguments that are no doubt valid. Let them dispute as they will. From a human and artistic point of view there is no reason why a poet of sufficient genius should not have felt and expressed these many moods. If Jewish editors and scribes long ago put Isaiah together out of originally disparate material, they did the work with great skill and made one of the finest and strongest units in the Old Testament.

Jeremiah, the second of the four major prophets, is not so majestic as Isaiah, but he is equally passionate and in his way quite as eloquent. He speaks from the darkest days of Jewish history just before the captivity, and after the fall of Jerusalem he suffered imprisonment and exile. It is no wonder that he is pessimistic. But the pessimism of Jeremiah is found not so much in the Book of Jeremiah as in Lamentations which is ascribed to him; it is from that book that we derive the idea which informs our word "jeremiad." The prophet is not a mere calamity-howler. He is a rebel against the state, which is rotten, and against the religion of the state, which in the hands of the scribes has become formalistic and empty. From that rebellion rises a wonderful idea which is new in literature and which leads directly to the New Testament. If the state has failed and if the relations between the state and Jehovah as a national and tribal deity have failed, there remains the greater thing, the relation between God and the individual. "I will take you (saith the Lord) one of a city, and two of a family." The new covenant is between God and whoever believes in him. Thus the gloomy Jeremiah becomes the prophet if not the originator of an idea which is still fundamental in the faith of millions of people. This vigorous violent man who hurls metaphors like spears proves to be the greatest dreamer of them all. And the somberly beautiful dirge, the Lamentations, which is appended to his book, is not properly his last word. His real last word reappears in Paul's Epistle to the Romans.

Ezekiel, too, is a dreamer, fond of visions and allegories, which are elaborate literary parables full of splendid images. The parable has always been a favorite vehicle for conveying religious ideas. Ezekiel is a great master of the parabolic art, and he is the forerunner of much apocalyptic literature (apocalyptic means revealing the hidden), of which the finest example is the Revelation, the concluding book of the New Testament. The apocalyptic allegory is very effective in the hands of a true poet. When Ezekiel represents the fallen king of Egypt as a ruined cedar with broken branches, the effect is more tragic than if the Pharaoh had been portrayed throughout as a man. Such is the nature of poetry, of the imaginative faculty, that a thing is more impressive if it is disguised (and yet not disguised) as something else. Ezekiel does not conceal all his thoughts in mysterious wheels and clouds of fire. He can step out of his wrapping of figures and deliver flagellating rebukes and moral precepts in plain prose like Jeremiah. But he is on the whole the most intricate and fantastic of the prophets.

Daniel, the fourth of the major prophets, is the most adventurous and most popular. Probably the Christian and Jewish boys who have been named Daniel outnumber all the Jeremiahs, Ezekiels, and Hoseas put together and at least equal the Davids, Josephs, and Samuels. Much happens in this short book of Daniel. We need not inquire too curiously whether these things happened to a man who lived in Babylon during the captivity of the Jews or in the imagination of a writer who lived centuries after King Nebuchadnezzar was dust. The purpose of the book is to console and inspire the Jews and this purpose is realized by very simple means.

Daniel is a seer who can interpret dreams which the heathen
magicians fail to read, and by virtue of this gift he becomes
mighty in the court of a foreign king. He is immune from
physical harm when he is cast into the den of lions, and so
are his three friends who are cast into the fiery furnace. Thus
the superiority of the Jewish intellect and the power of God
to save the Jews from their enemies are both demonstrated
in dramatic fashion. The visions of Ezekiel are complicated
and puzzling. The visions of Daniel are clear as a tale in
a story-book for children; indeed, he explains his own dreams,
as well as the dreams of the king, with naïve plainness, and
everybody understands the handwriting on the wall—except
the king and his professional soothsayers, who seem to have
been remarkably stupid even for heathen. Daniel is a sort
of second Joseph, for both men by their wits and the favor of
God win high places in alien governments.

The twelve brief books of the minor prophets which conclude the Old Testament decline in interest because most
of the ideas in them have been expressed more fully and
powerfully in the preceding books. But these lesser prophets
are important if only because some of the greater prophets
owe much to them. For it should be remembered that the
order of the books in the Old Testament is not a consistently
chronological order. Amos and Hosea were both among
the most ancient prophets; they were trail-breakers, lamps
to the feet of later writers. Amos is perhaps the earliest
prophet whose words were written down more or less under
his direction, the first to think of prophecy as a written document as well as oral teaching.

And Hosea, although what remains of his words is not so
rich and abundant as the words of Isaiah or Jeremiah, is as
fine a spirit as either; his emotional conflict, like that of

Jeremiah, between desperation and hope, between indignation and trust, is the very heart of the Old Testament. If he was relegated to the appendix of minor prophets, the reason is not that he was in any sense a minor person. Most of the other minor prophets do seem minor in every sense. We cannot leave them, however, without reminding ourselves of one remarkable short book, which tells in four chapters the pregnant story of Jonah. How Jonah was cast into the sea, was swallowed up by a great fish (the Bible does *not* say "whale"), and was vomited out upon dry land—such is the familiar miraculous story. In this case, as in some of the exploits of Daniel, the prophecy is expressed in terms of a symbolic adventure. Jonah represents Israel swallowed up and by the grace of God delivered or reborn. So the story of Jonah has immense significance. It is one of many expressions of the idea that not only Israel but all mankind is to be reborn. The final development of that idea, so far as it is found in the Bible, is the story of the Christ, the New Testament.

There are many avenues of approach to the New Testament, all of which are broad enough for an innumerable multitude of pilgrims. Let us approach it over the generously wide highway of biography. The New Testament, whatever else it may be, is the biography of the most important individual that ever lived or was ever imagined. In the so-called Christian nations no other story has been so widely read or recited or discussed; no other chronicle in religious or secular history has affected so many millions of people. Even people who are indifferent or hostile to any form of Christian faith know at least the outlines of the story, for it has permeated the life and the literature of all European countries.

The story of Jesus, indeed, is only an outline as it is recorded in the four Gospels of Matthew, Mark, Luke, and John, and the supplementary account in the Acts of the Apostles. The gospel narratives taken together constitute a very short book, which becomes still shorter if we consider the passages in which one gospel repeats another. There is an element of irony in the contrast between the brevity of this biography of the Prince of Peace and the imposing size of the memoirs of some latter-day politicians and major-generals. The apostles and their immediate successors were not primarily writers; they were, like their Master, preachers and teachers who went about inspiring and converting the people by word of mouth. And even the epistles of Paul, the most learned expounder of the teachings of Jesus, seem like sermons committed to writing from necessity because he could not at the time visit the congregation or the person whom he addressed.

Many years after the crucifixion there grew up an enormous literature, which of course is not in the Bible, and which has been voluminously added to from the time of the Church Fathers down through the nineteenth century. From the material in the New Testament and from non-biblical sources many later writers have tried to reconstruct a coherent Life of Christ, to fill in the historical and social background, and reconcile or explain the differences between the several gospels. One such attempt, the *Life of Jesus* by the French philosopher, Ernest Renan, has become an accepted literary masterpiece; I mention it as an example but do not presume to assess its historical value, especially as its sceptical attitude offended many Christians and removed it from the region of

pure letters into the vexed realm of controversy, where I
have neither the wisdom nor the will to follow it.

Most of us cannot hope to get more than a glimpse into
the great mass of modern literature concerning the Bible.
There is undoubtedly much information in this literature

JESUS

for whoever has sufficient learning and patience to find it.
But I cannot help being reminded, without undue frivolity,
of the remark of the old preacher about a laborious volume
of commentaries: "It is a great book, and the Bible throws
much light on it." Though the biblical record is incomplete,
its very incompleteness gives every reader the imaginative

right to fill it in with his own dreams and conjectures; the New Testament narratives as they stand are extraordinarily rich and clear for all their condensation. Certainly they are the basis of all we know or need to know, and until the ordinary reader is fairly familiar with them, verse by verse, he will not have occasion to go very far into the literature that has grown up about them. That there is much more which might have been told is indicated by the concluding words of the Gospel according to John: "And there are also many other things which Jesus did, the which if they should be written every one, I suppose that even the world itself could not contain the books that should be written." What those things were we shall never be told. But what stands written is enough.

The New Testament is more than the biography of Jesus. It is the extension of his life through the disciples and apostles, especially Paul, who is second in importance only to Jesus and without whose genius the Galilean might never have conquered the western world. Between the four Gospels and Revelation he is the principal character and the leading thinker. Thanks to his letters we know not only his theology, his interpretation of the message of Jesus, but his own character. And it is a very engaging character, courageous, persuasive, aggressive and conciliatory. It is possible to disagree with his religious and philosophical discourses, but it is not possible to withhold admiration for his skill in expressing himself or for his bravery and energy which are attested by other witnesses. The miracles ascribed to him may be an attempt of his followers to magnify him; he himself laid claim to no power except the faith that was in him. The episodes in his life which are on a simple human plane are as credible as they are noble, for example his defense before

Agrippa which in its adroitness and boldness is quite in keeping with his letters. There surely was a great man, resourceful in difficult situations and charming, even humorous, in the fine little epistle to Philemon. We can easily agree with Agrippa: "Almost thou persuadest me." For Paul overcame the "almost" in many who heard him and in many more who came after him. That is a matter of history, which there is no gainsaying.

The New Testament closes with the Apocalypse, The Revelation of St. John the Divine. It is a mystical poem, full of ecstatic visions and allegorical figures which appear in swirling confusion; and to the attempt to resolve that confusion there has been devoted as much poetic and scholarly interpretation as has been applied to any part of the Bible. No explanation of this strange book can be quite satisfactory to anybody but the man who makes the explanation. One of the most interesting is that of Emanuel Swedenborg, the Swedish philosopher and theologian of the eighteenth century, who based his vision of the New Jerusalem primarily on Revelation. The details of the Apocalypse must always remain blind and blurred. The main idea, in its simplest terms, is the promise of a holy city which shall succeed or supplant this sinful world. The city, like all good things in the Bible, is for the faithful; the pit still yawns for the unbelieving. The contrast between the lake of fire and the city of clear gold lightened by the glory of God is poetically and artistically splendid as the climax of this collection of terrific and consoling books.

CHAPTER V

GREEK HISTORY AND HISTORIANS

It is my duty to report all that is said; but I am not obliged to believe it all alike.

—Herodotus.

WE shall begin our short account of Greek literature by glancing at the historians. History, be it understood, is not an early form of literature; it develops late, after a nation has had centuries of experience and has expressed itself in poetry, drama, and other artistic types. This is true of Jewish literature as we find it in the Bible, though there the historical elements are so confused by ethical and religious motives that the sharpest modern scholarship is baffled in its effort to separate the purely historical writing from the rest and to determine the approximate date of composition. In the case of Greek literature we know with almost perfect definiteness when the writing of history began and where the line is to be drawn between the fact and legend; for the Greek told his own story with critical precision, with a highly civilized detachment and coolness of judgment unknown to the Hebrew. The writing of history, as we understand the word, began in Greece with

Herodotus. To be sure, in the long process of life and literature, no form or method is suddenly invented by any single
individual. That is the first lesson of history: ideas grow
and pass from mind to mind. The goddess Pallas Athene
sprang full-armed from the forehead of Zeus, but nobody
knew better than did Herodotus himself that such things happen to goddesses in poetry, not to the thoughts of human
beings. For he was a critic, an investigator, a sceptic. That
he has been called the father of history and that later historians down to our present "scientific" age have been willing
to concede him the title tells us much about him and even
more about the civilization in which he lived.

And what a civilization it was! In the small city of Athens
in the fifth century before Christ there lived more men of
genius than ever happened to live in any other place at any
other time. There is nothing comparable to the Athens of
Pericles until almost twenty centuries later we come to another
small city, Florence. No historian, not the wisest disciple of
Herodotus, can explain just why so many men of brains were
assembled on this particular spot of the world at this particular moment. All we know is that it is so. Greece had
repelled the invading Persian armies and in spite of continuous internal rivalry and warfare was, in intellectual matters, a more or less united civilization. Athens was the center
of the "glory that was Greece."

The city was rich in brilliant native sons and also entertained the cleverest men and women from the rest of Greece.
Herodotus was an Athenian only by adoption and lived but
a few years of his life as one of the jewels in the crown of
Athens. He was born in Asia Minor and spent his last years
in a Greek colony in Italy. He was a citizen of the world,
a great traveler in his time, partaking of the culture not only

of the capital city but of many cities and countries outside Greece. Outside Greece, but not far outside Greek culture, for we must remember that for centuries before the time of Herodotus and for centuries after, long after Alexander had conquered the world, Greece, as a civilization, meant almost

HERODOTUS

all the life that touched on any part of the Mediterranean Sea. The Greek arms which kept Asia out of Europe are not so wonderful as the Greek mind, which, backed by physical prowess, absorbed and in part s u p p l a n t e d every kind of thought and civilization which it encountered.

The theme of Herodotus is the triumph of the Greeks over the invading Persians. He treats the theme in the "grand manner," and though his history is in prose, it has the scope, the dramatic power, and much of the fire of a poetic epic. Because he was gifted with a spacious vision and because he had seen much of the world, he was not vainglorious. If he celebrates the deeds of his countrymen, he also criticizes them shrewdly. And he devotes much of his work to an account of other countries, especially the Persian empire. He appreciates the enemies of Greece, partly

of course because the more splendid the enemy, the more splendid the victory. But the victory is only the climax; Herodotus
is a student of men and peoples, he sees war in its relation to
the rest of life, and he finds the proper time and place to discuss
the arts of peace, commerce, manners and customs. If modern
historians know more than he did, it is largely due to him that

THE PARTHENON

they know so much. We will let them dispute about his
accuracy. We are sure that he was a superb artist who
handled his narrative with immense sweep and movement.
And if, as some who read Greek easily have told us, his style
is even finer than Rawlinson's English version of it, then we
can quite believe that Herodotus is not only the father of
history but the father of narrative prose.

Thucydides, the second great Greek historian, wrote an
account of the conflict which took place in his own time be-

tween Athens and Sparta and their allies, the Peloponnesian
War. He was the first great war correspondent and reporter,
with an immediate sense of fact. He could not correspond or
report in our meaning of the words, for there was no Athens
Herald delivered before breakfast to his fellow-citizens. But
he did take notes on the spot, and his acquaintance with the
leading men of his time gave him access to the "inside" story.
He worked his notes over at leisure after the conflict, and, unlike many who are now trying to write books about the World
War, he happens to be a man of genius. He was an artist.
For all his severe assumption of accuracy, he invented speeches
like a dramatist and put them into the mouths of historical
characters. His major mistake is that he thought the war
between the Greek states the most important thing that had
ever happened to mankind. This was not true in his time
and it seems still less true after twenty-four centuries. For
us the glory that was Greece is the story of peaceful arts, of
which Thucydides says very little. One lesson which the
historian of the present and the future has to learn from the
omissions and false emphasis of the ancient historian is that
the record of killing is not the whole tale; even the terrific
tragedy from which our world has not yet emerged may to
later chroniclers with proper perspective take its place as
only an important episode in the life of the race. Perhaps
the present hour, when we are sick of the reminiscences of
major-generals, politicians, and professional and amateur war
correspondents, is the very worst time to appreciate Thucydides. Yet there is magnificent dignity in his narrative of
battles long ago. All modern historians, even the most
critically analytical, respect him. And thanks to that master
translator from the Greek, Benjamin Jowett, Thucydides is
an English classic.

A few years after Thucydides there lived and wrote a Greek

historian who was a man of action as well as a writer—Xenophon. He was the general in command of the ten thousand Greeks whose retreat he records in the *Anabasis*. As the hero of his own tale he resembles the Roman commander and historian, Julius Cæsar. And there is another point of resemblance which is humorously sad: the first text presented to modern children in their Latin lessons is Cæsar's *Commentaries* on the Gallic War, and the first text in Greek is Xenophon's *Anabasis*. The reason is the same in both cases. Cæsar and Xenophon wrote exciting narratives in simple plain style. Schoolmasters naturally selected them as the easiest examples of languages the complexities of which, in the hands of philosophic and poetic writers, would be baffling to beginners and are probably baffling to most of the schoolmasters. Perhaps we learned to hate Xenophon's Greek too young, but his story is a good one; and it is a curious illustration of the fact that an adventure of a few thousand men centuries ago, if told by the right man, can hold its interest in a world where recently ten thousand men, defeated or triumphant, seemed almost as unimportant as flies. Literature is the written record of life. Yet, strangely enough, there is no exact correspondence between the intellectual magnitude of a book and the magnitude of the facts, events, ideas which it treats. The simplest answer in this case is that Xenophon was an interesting person who knew how to write. We owe to him the most "human" portrait we have of his master, the philosopher Socrates, in the *Memorabilia*. Xenophon was not a profound thinker and his account of Socrates is thin compared with that of Plato, who made Socrates the vehicle of Platonic wisdom, as we shall see in a later chapter. But Xenophon gives us a living picture of the wisest man in Athens and of the actual life that surrounded him.

To pass from Xenophon to Polybius is as if, in English

literature, we jumped from Walter Raleigh's *Discoverie of Guiana* to Gibbon's *Decline and Fall of the Roman Empire,* a leap of about two centuries. Polybius is the most important Greek historian after Herodotus and Thucydides. His voluminous history, of which about one-sixth is preserved, narrates the growth of the Roman empire in the second century B. C. He is a plain practical historian, matter of fact and impartial in his observation of events. He is for historians a most valuable source of information. Rome was becoming mistress of the world, and Polybius, though a Greek, admired the triumph of Roman arms and policies. His aim, however, was accuracy rather than the expression of admiration; for he kept his emotions to himself and was not a literary artist.

The historians who come after Polybius are not of great importance, perhaps because we do not know what they wrote. The remaining fragments, though they are treasured by scholars, have no interest to the general reader. But in the first century of the Christian era we meet a writer who is immensely important in history and in the art of letters, Plutarch.

In Plutarch's *Lives* we have a work of universal genius, a masterpiece which is part of the heritage of all living readers of European languages. Plutarch was a Greek and wrote Greek; but in substance he belongs almost equally to Roman history, for about half of his subjects are Roman. His method is to make parallels or comparisons between Greek and Roman heroes, for example, Alcibiades and Coriolanus, Demosthenes and Cicero. He is not a blind hero-worshiper, and there is not a trace in him of the kind of patriotism which exalts one's fellow-countrymen above the rest of the world. He has a thorough understanding of human character, reasonable and temperate ethical standards without moralistic fustian. More-

over, he has a solid knowledge of outer facts and circumstances that are the background of his characters. Modern
research has corrected him at several points, but has not on
the whole discredited him. And his persons live in modern
tradition as he portrayed them. The reputations of some of
the ancient good and great remain as Plutarch created them.
Some of his portraits were made doubly secure and permanent in English literature because they were the basis, in part,
of Shakespeare's *Cæsar, Coriolanus,* and *Antony and Cleopatra.* This partial dependence (partial because I do not
believe that Shakespeare's knowledge of the classics was
restricted to any one book) was due to Thomas North's translation of Plutarch by way of the French version of Jacques
Amyot. In *Antony and Cleopatra* some of the speeches seem
to be lifted without much change from North. The interest in
Plutarch has been continuous in English literature. A century after North, Dryden was sponsor for a translation; he
supplied a life of Plutarch, but did only a part of the work
on the text. This translation was revised in the nineteenth
century by the English poet, Arthur Hugh Clough, and that
revised version has become the standard for English readers.

It is no paradox to say that the greatest Greek historians
were not Greeks but modern scholars. Since the Italian
Renaissance, which means primarily the revival of interest
in the ancient classics, Greek civilization has been the subject
of almost worshipful study on the part of historians and men
of letters. In the nineteenth century this study was deepened
and sharpened by the scientific spirit which investigated documents and sources. Owing to this spirit and the advantage of
perspective, the modern historian knows some things about the
Greeks that they did not know about themselves. To name
only a few of those eminent in English literature, George

Grote, Benjamin Jowett, J. P. Mahaffy, Gilbert Murray, and J. B. Bury, can tell us more about the life and times of Thucydides than we can get from the Greek master. And we have to omit from our limited and unscholarly sketch even a mention of the works of French, Italian, and German historians. In spite of the efforts of some practical professional educators to strike the study of Greek out of the curricula of schools and colleges, ancient Greece is still alive in the cultivated thought of the present time. The reason for this is that literature, rather than boards of education and trustees of colleges, ordains what we shall read and think about. For example, Grote's *History of Greece,* which experts tell us is full of inaccuracies and has been superseded, belongs to English literature, whatever its place may be in the rigid school of history. I cannot explain to myself or to anyone else why a book, by Gibbon or Grote, Darwin or Huxley, comes over from a clearly bounded technical province of thought into the vague world of literature; the words are all vague and not clearly bounded. Grote has style—whatever that is; he is good to read, good for the ordinary layman. I suspect that if we read Grote we shall be filled with the essential spirit of Greece. And I know that if we read him we shall get a lesson in clean direct use of our language. The same thing is true of the work of Mahaffy, who was—another word that defies definition—an artist. In his *Social Life in Greece* a civilization lives again, or continues to live. A little later than these eminent Victorians is J. B. Bury, professor of modern history in the university of Cambridge. In his *History of Greece* are combined the scholar and the artist. It is an especially happy combination in an historian who writes of the most artistic people that ever lived.

CHAPTER VI

GREEK EPIC POETRY

Then felt I like some watcher of the skies
When a new planet swims into his ken.

—Keats.

EIGHT or nine centuries before the Christian era there may have lived a blind bard who went about among the Greek cities of Asia Minor reciting ballads or versified legends. His name may have been something like Homer. He may have been the author of the *Iliad* and the *Odyssey*. He may have been a person, or his name may stand for a group or school of poets. Many cities claimed the honor of being the birthplace of this mighty legendary poet.

We know nothing about Homer as a person. By the time that Greek history and criticism, in the fifth and fourth centuries, B. C., began to investigate origins and study documents, Homer was as much a myth and a legend to the Greeks as he is to a modern reader. Plato and Aristotle, if we are to judge by the records, knew less about the history of the Homeric poems than we know of Shakespeare. The reason for the relative difference of knowledge is that Shakespeare lived in the age of print and might have seen with his own eyes the pages of type from which modern editions of his work are reproduced. An educated Athenian in the age of Pericles might conceivably have known by heart some version of the Homeric poems without ever having seen a manuscript. And what such a version might have been we have no means of knowing. It may be that in the sixth century, B. C., the literary statesman, Pisistratus, collected the works of Homer and gave them somewhat the form in which we have them. But it is certain that later scholars edited the text upon which our modern editions depend. The whole problem of authorship was raised by the German scholar, Friedrich Wolf, at the end of the eighteenth century, and cannot be finally solved.

This is a question for technical scholars. But there are two or three aspects of it which are of great general interest. First, we are reminded that poetry was originally something spoken or recited. And not only "originally," if that word suggests the primitive and barbarous, but among highly civilized people. For the Homeric poems, with all their mythological machinery, are not childish but grown up, as adult as Dante, Milton, Tennyson or Browning. The *Iliad* and the *Odyssey* are organized with a constructive skill not surpassed by the work of any later poet. Though Homer is antique and his gods no longer rule the heavens, though he was to later Greeks hidden in the mists of the past, yet we must not make too much of a few centuries. Homer is not a musty curiosity. He has survived because he expresses thoughts that we can understand and enjoy and because he is a supreme story-teller.

And we should not make too much of the fact, though it is an important fact, that the works of Homer were oral, addressed to the ear, recited or sung by rhapsodists. That does not wholly account for their superior beauty of sound, if indeed it be superior to the beauty of later poets. For even in our time when every writer thinks of his work in print, the true writer both of verse and of prose writes with his ear, hears what he is saying. There has been a change in the conditions under which literature is recorded and preserved. There has been no essential change in the use of the human senses and imagination which produce poetry and prose. Wordsworth is reported by his neighbors as wandering about the countryside mumbling his verses. Tennyson liked to recite his work to his friends, if not to large audiences. Every poet, the most shy and stage-struck or the most popular and theatrical, recites his verses, in the very act of composing them. In this respect Homer, when he "smote 'is bloomin' lyre," winks back at us, not quite in the sense that Mr. Kipling intended, but in the sense that Mr. Kipling was actually exemplifying when he chanted that verse to himself.

So Homer is a very modern poet; he lived, in the brief recent part of the life of the human race which is recorded in literature, only a day or two ago. That is our short answer to two of the biographical questions which really concern literature, how it is made and how it is related to us. There is a third question: Must there not have been some single commanding individual genius and master, whether or not his name was Homer, who created, or recreated from what material we do not know, such solidly unified and consistently phrased stories as the *Iliad* and the *Odyssey?* For they are unified and consistent, no matter what flaws and breaks in continuity an inquisitive scholarship has discovered. With respect to all these questions Matthew Arnold's essay *On Translating Homer* is most satisfactory. I have no doubt, though I do not know, that later scholars have corrected Arnold on many points. He asked to be corrected; his dog-

matic manner was only a crust over a sensitive inquiring
spirit. Though, as a rule, the best thing to do is to go direct
to the original (that is, for us, a translation) and to ignore
intervening critics, yet I believe that a good way to approach
the poems of Homer is to read Arnold's essay. It is two

ACHILLES BANDAGES THE WOUND OF PATROCLUS
(From an Antique Vase)

things for us readers of English, an introduction to a master
and itself a masterpiece of English prose.

But, to go directly to our poet, what is the *Iliad?* The
theme is the final incident in the siege of Troy by the Greeks.
The action occupies only a few days. But in the swift nar-

rative there are recalled the story of the nine years of war
that have gone before and the cause of the war; indeed a
large part of Greek mythology is implicit in the poem. The
immediate episode is the wrath of Achilles, the best fighter
among the allied Greeks. He is angry at his chief, Agamemnon, because he is obliged to give up a captive girl who has
fallen to his lot as part of the spoils of war. So he quits the
fight and sulks in his tent. Wherefore the battle goes against
the Greeks. But the bosom friend of Achilles, Patroclus, is
killed, and Achilles, with another kind of anger, goes back
into the combat to avenge his friend's death, and kills the
Trojan prince, Hector.

This of course is only a faint outline of part of the back-
bone of the poem. To get an impression of its real substance,
of its nervous vigor and beauty (it is as athletic as one of its
own god-like heroes), we need not be Greek scholars. We
are wonderfully fortunate in our English translations, though
Matthew Arnold, who knew Greek profoundly and was, besides, a fine poet and critic, found fault with all the accepted
English versions. The translation by George Chapman, a
contemporary of Shakespeare, is in a swinging long line of
fourteen syllables. He takes liberties with the text and puts
in words for which there are no corresponding words in
Homer. But the effect of it all is spirited and poetic. No
wonder that two centuries later it inspired the young poet,
Keats, to write the splendid sonnet *On First Looking Into
Chapman's Homer,* from which are taken the two lines at
the head of this chapter. And we may understand the enthusiasm of Chapman himself, who begins his preface: "Of
all books extant in all kinds, Homer is the first and best."

A hundred years after Chapman, Alexander Pope published
his famous translation, which won immediate popularity and

remains the most readable rendering of Homer in English verse. It may be that the scholar Bentley was right in saying: "A fine poem, Mr. Pope, but you must not call it Homer." Perhaps Pope's rhymed couplets are too sharp and glittering to represent the sustained flow of Homer's hexameters. But Pope's version is a fine poem, and it probably seemed even finer to readers in the eighteenth century than it does to us. The version which I recommend to readers who are not comfortably at home in Greek, is the prose of Leaf, Lang and Myers. That version in clear simple English, rhythmic in its way, untroubled by the difficulties of verse, and preserving the essential poetic metaphors of the original, reads like a first-rate novel; it is no very serious violation of critical terms for us to regard (and enjoy) the *Iliad* in prose as an historical romance.

The *Odyssey* is closely related to the *Iliad*. The two poems may be considered as adjacent sections of the vast epic legend of gods and heroes, other parts of which may or may not have been cast into narrative verse. In manner the *Odyssey* and the *Iliad* are much alike, and if they are not expressions of the genius of some individual poet they are expressions of the genius of a race. The *Odyssey* concludes the story of the siege of Troy, its capture by the trick of the wooden horse; and then narrates the travels and adventures of Odysseus or, as we have it in the Latin form, Ulysses. While he is on his long and round-about journey home, his wife, Penelope, is surrounded by suitors who try to force her to infidelity and take advantage of her young son, Telemachus. She remains faithful and is rewarded by the return of her husband who outwits and kills the suitors.

There is no more thrilling story in the literature of the world. In its essential plot it seems even stronger and finer than the *Iliad*. For the *Iliad* is a series of celestial intrigues and hand-to-hand combats which are as repetitious as the exploits of the knights of King Arthur or as modern prize fights. The career of Ulysses embraces the world and touches all the primary emotions and activities of man. Moreover, Ulysses is a more splendid hero than Achilles. Though some of our modern "moral" considerations are irrelevant, alien to the Greek spirit, it is artistically pertinent to point out that Achilles is disloyal to his companions and in the end defeats a better man than himself.

The triumph of Ulysses is wholly satisfactory. He has wit and patience, something more than a strong right arm. And his feats and encounters have a breathlessly rapid variety of interest. He is a man or a superman, and such he will always remain among the great characters of fiction.

It is true that mythological characters have a double meaning. Ulysses may represent a sun god, and Penelope may represent the spring to whom the god returns, routing the forces of winter (the suitors), or she may be the moon from whom the sun is separated and to whom he returns with the new moon. The interpretation of myths and symbols is a fascinating subject on which we can barely touch; lay readers will find a delightful approach to that wonder world in J. G. Frazer's *Golden Bough*. But if we take the Homeric legends at their face value without going very deep under the surface we have in them the finest examples of swift moving tales of adventure; we accept and enjoy Ulysses as we do Tristan and Robin Hood. Ulysses was a favorite subject of later poets. In Virgil Ulysses is a crafty villain, for Virgil's hero is a Trojan. Dante in a marvelous passage in the twenty-sixth canto of *Inferno* almost out-Homers Homer in a few lines which describe the death of Ulysses. Tennyson's *Ulysses* is the most virile and one of the loveliest of his early poems.

As in the case of the *Iliad* so in the case of the *Odyssey* we English readers are very fortunate. Chapman's version in ten syllable heroic couplets is a little "tighter" and more solid than his *Iliad*. Pope and his collaborators made a vivid readable translation. But here again we are happiest in point of accuracy, facility and sheer enjoyment if we read a prose translation, that of George Herbert Palmer. Another fine translation is that by Butcher and Lang. If I put a good deal of stress on translations (there is a word more about them in the biographical note at the end of this volume) it is because through translation the thoughts of the world have passed from nation to nation and from race to race; also because translation can be a fine art, and in rendering the classics the English have practiced the art with much skill.

Around the name of Homer and his tremendous epics are grouped some minor poems, the *Homeric Hymns,* short prologues or introductions to epics or long narrative recitals. The authorship of them is as obscure as that of the great epics, but they have something of the tone of the major poems. These are the first few lines of Shelley's translation of the *Hymn to Athena* (protecting and titular goddess of Athens and so "town-preserving maid") :

> I sing the glorious Power with azure eyes,
> Athenian Pallas! tameless, chaste, and wise,
> Tritogenia, town-preserving maid,
> Revered and mighty; from his awful head
> Whom Jove brought forth, in warlike armour drest,
> Golden, all radiant!

A poet as fabulous as Homer is Hesiod, the reputed author of *Works and Days,* a didactic poem of which we have about eight hundred lines, and the *Descent of the Gods,* a poem of about a thousand lines, dealing with mythology. Of the poems ascribed to Hesiod most have been lost, and we do not know any more about him than we do about Homer. But there seem to have been many centuries in which the Greeks regarded Hesiod as the equal of Homer, and we know that the supreme Latin poet, Virgil, took lessons from the Greek master. For us there is little enchantment in the Hesiodic advice to farmers and sailors in *Works and Days;* and the *Descent of the Gods* is pale beside the splendor of the Homeric poems. Hesiod, like many others whom we mention or pass by, is part of the history of literature but not vividly important in the living, the *active* library of the world, which tingles with interest. There are several Greek epic poets whose names are recorded but whose work has vanished. Do we suffer from the loss or is there a cleansing justice in the rude hand of time?

CHAPTER VII

GREEK LYRIC POETRY

In the fair days when God
By man as godlike trod,
And each alike was Greek, alike was free . . .
—*Swinburne.*

N Greek literature, as in all other literatures, some form of song, words mated to music, was among the earliest modes of artistic expression. Undoubtedly there was behind the Homeric epics, those massive narrative structures, a kind of balladry. Yet so far as we know by what survives, the highest development of the lyric poem was later than the development of the epic. This is not a mere matter of dry dates, but a most interesting question in the growth of the human mind. At first men talk about things and events external to themselves, they recite tales of gods and heroes, that is, their poetry is objective. As they grow more civilized, perhaps more complicated in their emotions, they sing of their own souls, they become subjective. A lyric is a cry, whether laughing or tearful, of the individual heart. This inward, personal meaning of lyric is magically expressed in Shelley's *Ode to the West Wind:*

Make me thy lyre, even as the forest is.

The word lyric is derived from the name of the musical instrument which the Greeks borrowed from some earlier people and on which they strummed an accompaniment to sung or recited verses. It was a thin and primitive instrument, to our ears quite inadequate to the magnificent, varied, sonorous words which we can still hear in Greek poetry. Some Greek lyric verses seem as inappropriately superior to a lyre as Shelley's *West Wind* or Keats's *Nightingale* would be to a mandolin. This suggests the whole problem of the relation between words and music. In the case of the Greek lyric poets we can only guess at the relation; for though we have some of their musical instruments we have no satisfactory records of their musical notation and do not know how rich and elaborate their melodies and harmonies may have been. It is probable that a people who wrought so superbly in words and marble also created a supremely sophisticated music. But we do not know. Words, marble, and musical instruments, survive; but the sound made by musical instruments and the human voice has perished forever.

Lyric poetry was a distinct, special division of Greek verse, and the Greek critics, as acute and precise critics as ever lived, have made all the distinctions clear. One of those critics would be puzzled to read in the advertisement of a modern opera that the "lyrics" are by Jerome Smith and the music by Victor Robinson. Yet that advertisement is in its way true to the history of the word as we use it. And the history of a word almost always includes the truth about the fact. We feel as lyric any sequence of words that sings, whether or not it is intended to be accompanied by musical instruments or uttered by a voice which changes pitch according to a definite scale. Our use of the word includes "lyric" prose. And for our purposes we may disregard the fine distinctions and call

all poetry lyric which is not epic or dramatic. Of course there are lyric lines in Homer, Virgil, the dramas of Shakespeare. And of course a lyric may be sung, accompanied by a flute or a symphony orchestra or not accompanied at all, merely read with the eye and heard by the ear which is somewhere inside the head.

Now here we meet two great losses. The first is minor, one which we may be able partially to correct for ourselves: we seldom find anybody, even a professor of Greek, who knows how to read Greek verse aloud in a way to give a sense of its beat and vowel value. The second loss is irreparable: most Greek lyrics have disappeared from written literature and we know the poets only by fragments. Some poets have been wiped out, not by the judgment but by the mechanical accidents of time: we know their names only because a writer whose work has survived has mentioned them, or imitated them.

Two of the most tantalizing collections of fragments are those of Alcæus and Sappho. That Alcæus was a great poet we know from the testimony of his admiring imitator, the Latin poet, Horace, who was a sound critic and who knew thousands of verses by Alcæus and other Greeks which have been lost. A large chapter in the story of literature, as, indeed, in the whole story of the human race, is a negative chapter; the imagination is teased by the thought of vanished intellectual temples and the buried tombs of poetic kings. And queens. For one of the earliest of the great Greek lyric poets was Sappho, who in the sixth century, B. C., was acknowledged head of a school of poetry in Lesbos. The few verses of hers which we have are but shreds and patches of the queen's mantle, but they show her quality, her passion, her sharp sense of the joy and pain of love. In Greece her reputa-

ALCÆUS AND SAPPHO

tion was almost as exalted as that of Homer; she was called
"the tenth Muse," which was probably more than a mere
poetic compliment; and she became a romantic legendary
heroine. The most famous story about her is that because she
was repulsed by Phaon whom she loved, she leaped into the
sea, but it is not quite clear whether she was killed. In all
likelihood she was a woman of genius and passion, like George
Sand and the divine Sarah Bernhardt. One form of verse
which she invented, or brought to perfection, is named after
her. The Sapphic measure was used by the Latin poets,
notably Horace. The best way for us to get a sense of its
shape and rhythm is to quote one stanza from Swinburne, who
was a supreme master of all forms of verse and was as full
of the Greek spirit as a modern man can be:

> All the night sleep came not upon my eye-lids,
> Shed not dew, nor shook nor unclosed a feather,
> Yet with lips shut close and with eyes of iron
> Stood and beheld me.

The Alcaic measure, perfected by Alcæus, and imitated by
other Greek and Latin poets, does not seem to *go* in English,
but a fair example of it is the following from Tennyson, who
knew how to manipulate English meters and probably had
as good a sense of ancient meters as any modern poet. His
Alcaics are, appropriately, a poem to Milton.

> O mighty-mouth'd inventor of harmonies,
> O skill'd to sing of Time or Eternity,
> God-gifted organ-voice of England,
> Milton, a name to resound for ages;
> Whose Titan angels, Gabriel, Abdiel,
> Starred from Jehovah's gorgeous armouries
> Tower as the deep-domed empyrean
> Rings to the roar of an angel onset.

RUOTOLO 32

HOMER

If all the best verse of Greek poets had been preserved, what a library we should have! Of the poems of Solon, the wise man and lawmaker of Athens in the seventh and sixth centuries B. C., there remain about three hundred lines which seem to be rather instructive than beautiful. And this is true of the verses of Theognis of Megara, whom we know in a few hundred lines. These poets with their stiff moralistic injunctions are representative of one side of Greek character. They are called elegiac, because of the structure of their verse, a technical matter into which we need not go. The Greek would not have known what "elegy" means to us in Gray's *Elegy Written in a Country Churchyard*. And aside from questions of form, Theognis was far from making elegies over the dead, or weeping over the short and simple annals of the poor. He hated the poor and their poverty. He was a stalwart aristocrat; it is a pity we have not more of his valiant lines.

A poet who enjoyed among the Greeks a reputation almost as shining as that of Homer was Archilochus, who seems to have been a master of elegiac verse and to have invented the sharp iambic satirical verse, somewhat analogous perhaps to the stinging ten-syllable lines of Dryden and Pope. But the river of time has drowned the fire of Archilochus and we can only surmise from a few extant lines what was the "rage" which Horace admired and what was the magnificent form which Horace and other Greek and Latin poets imitated.

Anacreon, whose verse, as in the case of most of the other Greek singers, we know only in broken snatches, played upon the themes of love and wine, in a graceful manner, lighter and less passionate than that of Sappho. His delicacy and neat turn of phrase made him much admired by the Greeks and by modern poets, and he had imitators who wrote *Anacreontics* which were ascribed to him for many centuries. It is to these poems that modern imitators and translators usually refer rather than to the genuine Anacreon. But some of the *Anacreontics* are lovely enough to be worthy of the master.

Such lyric poems as those of Sappho and Anacreon are intensely personal, the expression of the emotion of the individual, the cry of grief, pain, joy, laughter, pity, which the poet feels as his experience. A broader type of lyric is the choral poem, made to be sung, as the word implies, by a chorus and expressing the common emotions of some group, such as hymns and pæans to the gods, odes in praise of victors and heroes. Such poems are necessarily stamped with the peculiar genius of the poet, but they are in substance outside the individual, phrasing the religious and social life that surrounds him. This kind of lyric therefore approaches the poetic drama and resembles the chants of the dramatic chorus, though a dramatic poet may never have written an ode and a master of lyric poetry may never have tried to make a drama.

Of the choral lyric poets (there must have been hundreds whose songs are now forgotten) the three greatest are Simonides of Ceos, Bacchylides, and Pindar. If we think of them as living about 500 B. C., a century after Sappho, that is as near as we need to come in our intentional disregard of exact dates.

Simonides perfected the encomium, a poem in praise of a great man, the method of which is to recall for flattering comparison some hero of the past; thus the legendary story is preserved though the immediate subject of the poem may have been forgotten.

Bacchylides is an illustration of the strange luck that governs the reputation of a poet after he is dead. His poems were lost for many centuries, and then a few of them were found in 1896 in Egyptian papyrus, ragged and incomplete. Books which record the adventures of human beings sometimes have curious adventures themselves! The genius of Bacchylides and much of the spirit of Greek victory-poetry are illustrated by an ode in celebration of a horse which won the race at the Olympic games. The Greeks took their athletics even more seriously than do modern college boys, for the athletic contests were involved not only in patriotic motives (as when American crews row against English crews on the Thames) but in religious motives which are outside our experience. In praising the horse, the poet is praising the owner, Hiero, ruler of Syracuse. But the value of the poem is that the mythological part tells of the meeting of Heracles and Meleager in the nether world, and that is the only place in Greek literature where the story appears. At the festivals in honor of the gods, the great festivals at Olympia and Delphi and other cities, Greek competed with Greek in every form of prowess from wrestling and running races to music, poetry, sculpture, philosophic discourse. So that though some of the philosophers thought that too much honor was paid to mere athletes, a complaint which we have heard from scholars in our own time, the public then, as now, overruled them, and it was an honorable thing for a poet to celebrate the victor in a horse race or a chariot race in a dignified ode.

The greatest of the writers of odes of victory is Pindar. He was happy not only in his genius, but in his posthumous fortune, for about a fourth of his work remains, several complete odes celebrating victories at the Olympian, Pythian, Isthmian and Nemean games, and several hundred fragments. The ode thus became almost exclusively associated in modern times with the name of Pindar, though among the Greeks he was no more distinguished than several other poets.

An ode was actually sung by a chorus to a sort of circling dance. One stanza was accompanied by a movement from right to left, that was the *strophe* or "turning"; with the next stanza the movement was reversed, the *antistrophe;* during the third stanza, the after-song, *epode,* the chorus stood still. And this triplicate unit could be repeated as many times as the poet wished. The ode became an important and beautiful form in English poetry, though it is looser in structure than the Greek and has little in common with the substance of the Greek. Shelley's *West Wind,* Keats's *Nightingale* and *Grecian Urn,* Wordsworth's *Intimations of Immortality,* Swinburne's *Birthday Ode* to Victor Hugo, Tennyson's *Duke of Wellington*, are all odes in the modern sense. They resemble their Greek ancestor in one essential respect, the dignity and emotional seriousness of the themes. An interesting example for Americans, though not a highly inspired poem, is Lowell's *Commemoration Ode.* An example which adheres more closely to the Greek form is that addressed to Queen Anne, on the occasion of Marlborough's victories, by the brilliant William Congreve. He was the first to point out that the true Pindaric ode is regular and accurate in structure, and not a wilful irregular arrangement of long and short lines, such as had been called *pindariques* by the poet Cowley in the seventeenth century. But Pindar's beauty does not lie wholly in his form; it is also in the boldness and loftiness of his thought. He was an artist with a feeling for all the arts, a feeling not peculiar to him, since it is characteristically Greek, but by him exquisitely phrased. For example, he recognized the kinship of poetry and sculpture and said in words whose beauty is not altogether lost in translation: "No sculptor I, to fashion images that shall stand idly on one pedestal for ever; no, go thou forth from Ægina, sweet song of mine, on every freighted ship, on each light bark."

We think of Athens as the intellectual leader of Greece, and so it was for several centuries, chiefly the fifth and the fourth, B. C. But Greek civilization extended from Asia Minor to Sicily and Southern Italy, and the arts flourished in many cities and provinces. It is significant that seven cities claimed to be the birthplace of Homer. Pindar was born near Thebes, Bacchylides and Simonides on the island of Ceos, Anacreon in Teo in Asia Minor, Alcæus at Mytilene in Lesbos, and so on. Poets and artists from other Greek states were attracted to Athens and went there if they could, either for a short time or to settle as citizens, much as a French writer will try to go sooner or later to Paris, or an Englishman to London, though Athens never was a populous political and commercial capital like the great modern cities.

When Alexander the Great conquered the world, all the Greek cities lost their power, though they could not immediately lose their individual and local characteristics, and literature gradually weakened in several ways. It was no longer the natural expression of the people through the lips of genius. The whole world spoke Greek and literary men wrote for each other, a wide and learned audience, but all alike, no longer the intense and varied populace. Literature became less and less the voice of life and more and more a matter of books, of mutual imitation, and self-conscious artifice. The chief literary center, Alexandria in Egypt, founded by the conqueror at the end of the fourth century, B. C., soon had a population of three hundred thousand, and partly on account of the vast library which the ruling Ptolemies built up, attracted scholars and artists and poets. The rulers at Alexandria and at Pergamum and other cities old and new certainly tried to foster art and learning. And learning flourished, philosophy and criticism. But something had happened to art, especially to poetry.

There is no exact way of explaining why Alexandrian poetry (Alexandrian refers to the period, not the city) lost the savor and vigor of the older Greek. For one thing the new poets wrote their poems to be read, that is, addressed to the eye, whereas the older poetry was made to be recited and sung, addressed to the ear. And it may be that Greek genius had said all that it had to say and was not able to renew itself in fresh thoughts and forms.

One poet did have something fresh to say in an original manner, that is Theocritus. He brought the pastoral to such perfection that the name of this important form and his name are identical, like the almost monopolistic identity of the ode with Pindar. The pastoral is, as the word implies, a poem about shepherds, their loves, their superstitions, and the natural scenery in which they live. The dialogues and songs of the shepherds are so graceful and poetic that critics of a later and even more artificial time doubted whether crude peasants could have had such fine sentiments, but we know that the folk-song of so called common people is imaginative and often lovely in phrase and rhythm. As a matter of fact Theocritus derived his idylls (the word means "little images") from the actual shepherds who sang and piped on the green hills and under the blue skies of Sicily as their descendants do to this very day. Though he shaped his material with sophisticated art and was himself an aristocrat, what makes him vital and sincere poet is the reality of his material and its relation to the lives of simple people. His rustic poems are his best; when he turns from the bucolic to the conventional epic theme he is not the natural poet of Sicily but the bookish poet of Alexandria. His successors, Bion and Moschus, are memorable for two poems, Bion's *Lament for Adonis,* and the *Lament for Bion* by Moschus; these represent the pastoral idyll in its character of threnody or chant for the dead, and in that character the pastoral is at its noblest in the many modern imitations.

For the pastoral became a tradition in all modern languages. Virgil's *Eclogues* are imitations of Theocritus, the rather servile work of a young poet who has not yet found himself, but with a charm of their own and increasingly admired as the reputation of Virgil's mature poetry spread and solidified. Virgil, of course, exerted more power over the romance nations and England than any Greek poet, and it is partly due to him that bucolic poetry multiplied. Much of the pastoral literature of modern nations is insincere and as silly as those idle people in the French court who used to dress as shepherds and shepherdesses in silks and laces! But much pastoral poetry is perfectly genuine, because poets do love the countryside, and if a poet call a pretty English girl Chloe, well, she is just as fragrant as if he called her Tess or Annie.

The pastoral developed in four ways. The short idyll or eclogue of the Theocritus-Virgil type continued to be a favorite form with the poets for many centuries. The literature of Elizabethan England swarms with "Affectionate" Shepherds, and "Passionate" Shepherds, all kinds of shepherds. Some of the English eclogues are lovely and natural. The most famous are the twelve in Spenser's *Shepheards Calender*, one for each month of the year, consciously imitative of the classics but full of English spirit. In the eighteenth century John Gay in the *Shepherd's Week* deliberately anglicizes the eclogue and sets out to describe "the manners of our own honest and laborious ploughmen, in no wise sure more unworthy a British poet's imitation than those of Sicily or Arcady."

The second development of the pastoral was the expansion of the little dialogue into a complete drama. The best known example in Italian is Tasso's *Aminta*. In English the best examples are Ben Jonson's *Sad Shepherd,* which smells of the English woodland, and John Fletcher's *Faithful Shepherdess* inspired by Tasso's *Aminta,* and Greek or pseudo-Greek in the setting and the names of the characters and the mythology. And we must not forget the *Gentle Shepherd* in the Lowland Scottish dialect by Allan Ramsay, a poem of genuine simple beauty with living characters.

A third development was the prose romance, or the romance in which prose and poetry are combined as in the *Arcadia* of the Italian, Sannazaro. On this Philip Sidney based his *Arcadia* written in an embroidered style far above the speech not only of rustic people but of any people except literary courtiers. The prose pastoral that we care for is simply the romantic novel which deals with country folk, like the romances of George Sand in France, and of Thomas Hardy in England. They probably owe nothing to the tradition of Theocritus, but they belong in the same world because their sheep and shepherds are real.

The fourth development and the most loftily poetic is exemplified in Milton's *Lycidas* and Shelley's *Adonais*. The poet lamenting a dead friend figures himself and his friend as Greeks. In *Adonais* there is little touch of the pastoral; Keats, the dead hero, is not directly represented as a shepherd, but as a poet mourned by

All he had loved and moulded into thought,

and the Greek disguise is only in the name. But in *Lycidas* Milton carries out the pastoral symbolism. He and his friend, King, who were friends at college

> were nursed upon the self-same hill,
> Fed the same flock, by fountain, shade, and rill.

A dirge for the dead in any form of verse is artificial, but there is something especially artificial in expressing sorrow for an English friend under a Greek mask. Milton of course did it magnificently and Matthew Arnold in his *Thyrsis* showed himself the learned Greek scholar that he was. But I doubt if we shall care much for any later specimens. Our taste for that kind of poetry has grown dull, except for great examples of it in the past; it will surely never come back into modern literature.

One of the most precious books of extant Greek poetry, and that means of all poetry, is the *Anthology,* a collection of short poems by many authors from the sixth century B. C. to the fifth or sixth century A. D. These poems, little odes, little idylls, epigrams, brief love lyrics, all the moods of humanity succinctly phrased, give us a deeper look into the heart of Greek life—or some corners of that heart—than the great epics and dramas and historical records.

The *Anthology* was begun by the poet Meleager in the first century B. C. He put together poems by about forty poets, including many of the great lyrists of the preceding centuries, and called his collection the *Garland,* a wreath of flowers, which is what *anthology* means. This work became very popular and was imitated and added to by later anthologists until finally, ten centuries after Meleager, Constantinus Cephalas (of whom nothing else is known) made a sort of anthology of anthologies, plundering previous collections and making additions of his own. The history of this anthology is a fascinating chapter in the long tale of books. A monk named Paludes in the fourteenth century made a new edition. He omitted many good things from the work of Cephalas and added other things, some good, some mediocre; and this Paludean anthology became the standard text for a long time. Meanwhile Cephalas was lost and forgotten, until in the early part of the seventeenth century a young student discovered a manuscript of Cephalas in the University of Heidelberg. This manuscript, rescued from oblivion, was to have still further adventures. During the Thirty Years' War when no perishable thing was safe in Germany, it was sent to the Vatican. Then at the end of the eighteenth century when the French conquered and looted Italy they took the manuscript to Paris whither scholars flocked to see it.

The value of the *Anthology* cannot be overestimated. It preserved many poems which without it would have perished. Not only are the thousands of single flowers exquisite (some, it must be confessed, are but artificial paper) but the collection as a whole covers the entire range of feeling and experience. It reveals, though we know so little about the individual poets, the development of Greek poetry from early morning vigor to twilight decadence. Can we find in any other literature (except possibly Chinese) such a long continued, many-voiced choir? The Greek, not any one Greek, but the race, knew how to say anything that a human being has ever thought or felt (I mean, of course, fundamental human facts, not details that have come into life since Greece crumbled, ideas peculiar to modern civilization). The Greeks were expressive, articulate, outspoken people. They could drive a poisoned two-edged epigram into a human enemy and with proudly curled lip and philosophic brow contemplate the last enemy and friend, Death—a favorite subject in the *Anthology*.

The English poets have made excellent versions of many of these perfect little poems. I quote one example, a poem by Callimachus, a poet and scholar of the third century B. C., and one of the librarians of the great library of Alexandria. The translation is by an English poet and scholar of the nineteenth century, William Cory.

> They told me, Heraclitus, they told me you were dead,
> They brought me bitter news to hear and bitter tears to shed.
> I wept as I remembered how often you and I
> Had tired the sun with talking and sent him down the sky.
>
> And now that thou art lying, my dear old Carian guest,
> A handful of grey ashes, long, long ago at rest,
> Still are thy pleasant voices, thy nightingales, awake;
> For Death, he taketh all away, but them he cannot take.

CHAPTER VIII

GREEK DRAMA

Many the things that strange and wondrous are,
None stranger and more wonderful than man.
—*Sophocles.*

WHEN anything terrible happens, battle, murder, or sudden death, we call it a tragedy. If a novel or a play ends "unhappily," it is a tragedy. How does it happen that the word "tragedy" is derived from the Greek word for goat? To us the goat seems a rather ridiculous animal. The answer is that Greek tragedy, the great poetic literature, had its origin in a sort of folk-play or pageant in honor of Dionysus, god of fruitfulness. Some of the performers in the festival pageant were dressed as satyrs, half man, half goat. The primitive satyr-drama was developed by "literary" poets into highly elaborate plays. Of course this development was a slow growth, occupying centuries, we do not know how many, probably more centuries than there were between Shakespeare and the earliest known mystery plays.

The first of the three greatest Greek tragic poets, of whose work we have several entire plays, is Æschylus. Of the seven

extant plays three form a trilogy, the *Oresteia,* which is the
only Greek trilogy that survives. Æschylus wrote seventy
tragedies, and it is likely that the lost plays contained some of
his best work. In depth and magnitude the genius of the first
great tragic poet has never been surpassed. His subjects, like
those of most Greek drama, are
religious or mythological, dealing with the power of the gods
to punish men for their crimes
and for the sin of pride. Behind
the gods looms that sinister
super-god, Fate, from whom
there is no escape. The Greek
view of life embraced certain
joyous elements, and some of the
wisest of the Greeks, Socrates,
for example, looked at things
with a smile, if not with exuberant gayety. But the fundamental
philosophy of the tragic poets

ÆSCHYLUS

was somber and as sternly moral as the Old Testament.

We do not know just what were the devices of Greek stage-
craft at the time of the greatest dramatists, for there is no
trace of a theater of the fifth century B. C. The mechanics
must have been elaborate, for in the *Prometheus Bound* of
Æschylus the chorus of ocean nymphs floats in the air until
Prometheus bids them come down. Probably there was not
much acting in our sense of the word, for the effect of the text,
as we read it now, is that of recited narrative with lyrical
choruses rather than the conversation of modern plays which
implies action in immediate view of the spectator. Only two
or at most three principal actors were allowed on the Greek

PROMETHEUS

stage, and their recitative was accompanied and interpreted by the chorus. The chorus was endowed with an impersonal knowledge of the will of the gods superior to that of the distressed and groping tragic hero; and chorus and hero argue the case in poetic dialogue.

The best way for us to approach Æschylus is to read the translation of *Agamemnon* by Robert Browning and the translation of *Prometheus Bound* by Mrs. Browning. Readers of English poetry will of course know Swinburne's splendid *Atalanta in Calydon,* which Professor J. P. Mahaffy (there is no better authority) says is "the truest and deepest imitation of the spirit of Æschylus in modern times."

The second great tragic poet of Greece was Sophocles, who was a generation younger than Æschylus. It was the custom of the poets to compete for prizes, and in one contest in which Æschylus was a competitor Sophocles, twenty-eight years old, won the prize. From that time on he enjoyed almost unbroken success until his death at the age of ninety about 400 B. C. He wrote more than a hundred plays. Seven have survived. His themes are traditional and are linked with those of Æschylus. The Greek dramatists, like Shakespeare and other modern poets, did not pretend to originality in the invention of plots; they vied with each other in treatment. Sophocles advanced the art of the drama in point of theatrical effectiveness, rapidity, directness, sense of suspense and climax. It is a commentary on the universal dramatic appeal of Sophocles that translations or adaptations of his *Œdipus the King, Œdipus Colonus,* and *Antigone,* have been successfully produced in English, German, and French. Mendelssohn wrote the music for *Antigone,* and in recent years Richard Strauss wrote an opera of which the text by Hofmannsthal is based on the *Electra* of Sophocles. In an English translation, preferably the prose of R. C. Jebb, or the verse of E. H. Plumptre, the Sophoclean dramas hold one by their sheer narrative excitement. What they must be with all their original harmonies only those who really hear and feel Greek can tell us. The story of Œdipus and his mother Jocasta is profoundly terrible, and Sophocles handles it with dramatic irony which must have been stunning to a Greek audience.

TRAGIC ACTOR
(From antique statue)

They were familiar with the story and knew that Œdipus was doomed; but in the play Œdipus does not know his fate and in pride and blindness stumbles toward it unconsciously. There is no finer dramatic situation than that in all literature.

Euripides, the third great tragic poet of Greece, was a few years younger than Sophocles, and for half a century the two poets were rivals before the Athenian audiences. Fate, that dreadful shapeless shadow that lurks behind the Greek world and ours, has been kinder to Euripides than to his fellow-dramatists, because eighteen of his ninety plays have been preserved. Euripides was the romantic among the Greek dramatists, which means simply (the word "romantic" has been tortured to death in modern criticism) that he made much of the motive of love.

This motive was not unknown to the other Greek poets; for was it not the elopement of Paris and Helen that launched a thousand ships and caused the Trojan War? But Euripides made the passion of love, and other human passions, the dominant motives. People are more important than gods, and even the gods and mythological personages speak the living speech of men. Euripides knew Athenian society, which had grown sophisticated, philosophical and sceptical, which no longer believed in the gods, and he knew that the way to hold an audience was to play on the universal emotions which we all feel, the passions that are in the blood, independent of religion. Medea, the sorceress, who murders her children to spite Jason, retains the externals of her traditional mythological character and flies off in a winged chariot. But in her words, in her heart, she is a tormented woman, as real a woman as Lady Macbeth.

In *Hippolytus,* Phædra, who kills herself because her stepson does not return her love, is a character fit for a modern melodrama. The heroine of *Iphigenia among the Taurians* and *Iphigenia at Aulis* is a charming creature; Euripides loved a lovely girl as heartily as any latter-day novelist. It is easy to understand why he had more influence on the romantic-classic drama of France and Germany than any other ancient poet. In spite of his human interest, the masterpiece of Euripides, the *Bacchae,* deals wholly with the gods, with the punishment inflicted by Dionysus on King Pentheus who opposes the Dionysian worship. It is wildly magnificent. One needs very little knowledge of Greek mythology to be thrilled by it in Gilbert Murray's translation.

The worship of Dionysus, which was the origin of tragedy, was also, oddly enough, the origin of comedy. Tragedy represents the serious aspect of the ceremony, and comedy its laughter, revelry, and tipsy merriment. The great comic dramatist of Athens was Aristophanes, who flourished in the last half of the fifth century B. C. The old Athenian comedy was not only an entertainment but a vehicle of satire and protest against political and social vices; it had somewhat the function which belongs in modern times to sharp editorial writing and the political cartoon. Imagine a combination of E. L. Godkin, Thomas Nast, W. S. Gilbert, Mr. Dooley,

MEDEA

George Ade, Will Rogers, and Art Young,—and you have something like a modern analogy to Athenian comedy, to its leading genius, Aristophanes. These local contemporaneous allusions are perfectly appropriate to the spirit of Aristophanes. For he was local and limited by his immediate environment. Few of his plays, however witty, could interest modern spectators, because we could not get the jokes on the wing; those jokes were for Athenians, and their point is lost to us without explanatory notes—which kill the fun of them. But the general humorous conception of some of the plays comes through to us. Of the eleven extant plays, two are attacks on the Athenian politician, Cleon, and demagogy. One, *The Clouds,* is aimed at the current philosophies and is a wicked caricature of Socrates. *The Frogs* is a literary criticism of Æschylus and Euripides. Two plays are a plea for peace with Sparta. The most brilliant of all the plays is *The Birds,* a satire on Athens and indeed on the whole human race; the idea of the birds building a city in the clouds is delightfully fantastic. And it is poetic; Aristophanes was a lyric poet as well as a laugher at the foibles of men.

Aristophanes left no successors; evidently no other writer dared or cared to imitate him. Greek comedy, the New Comedy, turned from that local political and public satire of which he was the past master to the comedy of manners, of intrigue, of farce, of merriment at the expense of the ordinary foolish human being—which we all are. The chief dramatist in the New Comedy is Menander, a kind of missing link, great in his influence, though we have only fragments of his plays, discovered within the last thirty years. From him the Roman dramatists, Plautus and Terence, derived substance, form, and spirit; and in turn modern dramatists, Molière and Shakespeare, learned lessons from the Latin playwrights. We cannot say that Molière and Shakespeare would not have been great comic dramatists if Menander and his contemporary, Philemon, had been strangled in their cradles; the would-have-beens of history are insoluble puzzles. But certainly those

Greek comedians *did* come down to us through later dramatists
and in a way are alive on our stage.* The Greek tragic poets,
as we have seen, are alive there, too, by direct adaptation, especially in the French classic theater and the somewhat later
German classic theater. Racine and Goethe go directly to
Greek subjects. The English have done excellent translating
in a bookish way, but I cannot think of a single actable play
in English comparable to the neo-Greek dramas of Racine
and Goethe. That vigorous practical play-maker and profound scholar, Ben Jonson, probably knew more about the
Latin Seneca than he did about the Greek tragic poets. But
Seneca knew the Greeks. The descent is devious, like all
genealogy. But there is an unquestionable thread, or chain,
of connection between the modern theater and those half religious revels and ceremonies in Greece hundreds of years before the great Greek dramatists were born.

* Since we are on the subject of comedy, I think it is a fair and pertinent joke to
remind ourselves in this age of bobbed hair that one of Menander's comedies is the
Girl Who Gets Her Hair Cut Short. But in Menander's comedy the cutting of the
hair is a punishment inflicted by an angry lover.

CHAPTER IX
GREEK PHILOSOPHY, ORATORY AND OTHER PROSE

All men by nature are actuated with the desire of knowledge.
—*Aristotle.*

IN the library of the world there is, there can be, no more profound book than a good history of Greek philosophy, unless it be a book which includes modern philosophy too! The Greek mind delighted in speculation and investigation into the causes of things and the processes of the human mind. Probably the roguish Aristophanes was the only cultivated Athenian who took no stock in metaphysical arguments. Most educated Greeks absorbed and emitted philosophy like the air they breathed. The proof of this is that much of the prevailing instruction in philosophy, the passing of wisdom from master to pupil, was not a formal school-room business but was casual and conversational. If Aristotle's sentence, quoted at the head of this chapter, seems too favorable an account of the average human mind—when we think how many people seem utterly lacking in real intellectual curiosity—the answer is that he spoke as a Greek and a member of the leisure classes who were privileged to think.

In two thousand years the human race has made a little progress in thought. Plato did not know so much about the movement of the spheres as the most commonplace student of astronomy in one of our observatories, and modern physics is no longer concerned with the four elements into which the ancients analyzed the material world. The study of psychology, the functions and habits of the mind, has gone far beyond anything that the most learned Greek even dimly conceived. The physical basis of philosophy has shifted and developed and no doubt has been immensely strengthened and enriched. Nevertheless the Greek mind meditated on all the essential problems of philosophy, thought them through and through; and sometimes when we dip into Plato and Aristotle, we feel that for all the advantage we have in knowing modern philosophy (much of which depends on the Greeks) we have not only not made much progress, but have not begun to catch up with the ancient lovers of wisdom.

Plato and Aristotle sum up the ideas of philosophers who preceded them, make enormous original contributions, and are the foundation of most of the important philosophies down to the present day. Let me say, parenthetically, that philosophy is everybody's affair and not the private monopoly of a few highly trained specialists. We are all philosophers more or less ignorant or wise, guessing about human life and the universe in our own way or parroting the guesses of others. The philosopher is simply the wise man who thinks more deeply and coherently than most of us are capable of thinking. He straightens our ideas out for us, whether we agree with him or not. The philosopher often seems to smother his thoughts in difficult technical words and so to befog us rather than clarify us; but that is because the problems of life are complicated and involved. On the whole the professional philos-

PLATO

PLATO.

opher is a help and an inspiration even when he is somewhat puzzle-headed. There is no department of literature in which the amateur can play with more pleasure than in what is called philosophy. And let us remember that, as Mr. George Santayana, one of the finest of modern thinkers, has recently said, philosophy is found in the poets and novelists often in purer form than in the professional philosophers.

That is a long parenthesis. Let us return to our Greeks. Before Plato there were two or three thinkers who hit upon great ideas. We can barely hint at them. Heraclitus conceived of life as a continuous change; nothing is what it was a moment ago, nothing is what it will be the next moment. He thought that the essential element is fire, which condenses to liquid and to solid, which dissolve again into fire. Empedocles developed the theory of the four elements, fire, air, water, earth, an idea that prevailed in physics until modern times. He also had a rudimentary notion of evolution and the "survival of the fittest." Pythagoras, or the school that took his name, advanced the sciences, mathematics and astronomy; the differences between the various substances are all a matter of number. Well, it was only yesterday that physicists found out that one substance differs from another according to the rate of vibration of the electrons that compose it. It is too bad that these imaginative old Greeks cannot visit a modern laboratory and see their primitive intuitions verified by scientific tests.

Early Greek philosophy advanced to the point where the teaching of it was a recognized paid profession, and the teachers were called "sophists." Then in the fifth century B. C., contemporaneous with Sophocles and Euripides, there appeared on the streets of Athens a noble and original thinker, the great philosopher who never wrote a book—Socrates. He spent most of his life talking with people, rebuking the pretensions of the wise and encouraging the young to seek truth for themselves. His method was humorous and ironic. He sometimes made positive direct assertions, but he usually arrived at his conclusions by asking questions. His assumption of ignorance was not merely a whimsical pose, a dramatic attitude. He was fundamentally serious; he believed that he was commanded by an inner voice, or "demon," to teach. He was beloved by those who understood him, but his radical

THE SCHOOL OF SOCRATES

ideas, his unpatriotic remarks about the state, his irritating methods of argument, and his indifference to the conventions of life made him enemies. He was accused and convicted of corrupting youth and of introducing new gods. The accusation, of course, was false and the whole trial was a piece of political chicanery. Socrates accepted his sentence like a true philosopher and spent his last days talking with his friends about immortality. One of the bitter jokes that humanity plays upon itself—Socrates appreciated the wry humor of it —is to kiil the good and the brave. It is no irreverence to compare the fate of Socrates with that of Jesus. One difference is that Socrates was seventy years old, had lived his life and said all that he had to say, whereas Jesus was a comparatively young man when he was crucified.

To learn the ideas of Socrates we have to turn to his most illustrious pupil, Plato, who uses Socrates as the spokesman of his thoughts. It is impossible to tell, and it makes no difference in the tale of human wisdom, how much of the philosophy of the dialogues of Plato is Socrates and how much is Plato. The Socrates-Plato partnership embraces the supreme wisdom of Greece. The literary form is delightful; it is the give-and-take of conversation, question and answer, living, human, and dramatic. There are about twenty Platonic dialogues, and they touch on almost every aspect of human thought. Socrates, of course, is the chief character, into whose mouth Plato puts his own favorite ideas. But Socrates does not have it all his own way. With amazing serenity and fairness Plato phrases the opinions of the other characters, so that all sides of a question are brought to light. And some questions are left open, as they must always be in an honest philosophic mind. "The germs of most ideas, even of most Christian ones, are to be found in Plato." That was the opinion of Benjamin Jowett, whose translation of Plato is an English classic and whose introductions to the several dialogues are masterpieces of literary criticism.

It is impossible to give here even an inkling of Plato's many ideas. But we can suggest two. One is the favorite notion of Socrates that virtue is knowledge and vice is ignorance. The belief that man misbehaves because he does not know any better is today widely current and is as good an explanation of sin as has ever been offered. It is consonant with the teaching of the man who in the hour of his death said: "Forgive them, for they know not what they do." Another thought, central in Plato's metaphysics, is that the real world is idea, and material individual things are merely reflections of the idea. If you love a beautiful person or a beautiful flower, what you really love with the highest part of your intellect is the idea of beauty and not the single specimen of it. This is a rough and inadequate statement of the doctrine of Platonic love, a notion that has been erroneously narrowed to the question of friendship between a man and a woman. Plato's thought was much broader than that, as we shall see in a moment when we say a word about the *Symposium.*

The most attractive of Plato's dialogues for the reader who is not interested in technical philosophy are the *Republic* and the *Apology* and the *Symposium* or *Banquet.* The *Republic* is not only an account of an ideal commonwealth but an analysis of the soul of man and of the nature of justice; in the ideal commonwealth the king will be not the politician nor the rich man but the thinker, the philosopher, just as in the perfect man the mind is supreme over all the other elements of human nature. The *Apology* is a beautiful and touching account of the trial and last days of Socrates. Whether the speeches of Socrates are what he actually said or whether they are in large part the invention of Plato, the artist and poet, makes little difference. The effect is dramatic and noble. The splendid conclusion is that "no evil can happen to a good man in life or after death."

The *Symposium* is on the whole Plato's most charming literary performance. The theme is love in all its aspects developed by a variety of characters, by Socrates, of course, who as usual has the last and wisest word, and by the young and brilliant Alcibiades who became so important in Athenian politics. It is here that we find the true account of Platonic love, a term amusingly misunderstood and abused in common parlance. The essential thought, barely stated and so not quite true to the subtle development in the dialogue, is that love loves beauty, loves the idea of which the beloved object is only one image or manifestation. A poetic expression of the Platonic ideal love is to be found in Shakespeare's sonnets, which, however, contain much else. In the *Symposium* there is every element of wisdom and delight, character-drawing which makes Plato almost a dramatist, humor, which puts the salt of good sense in his most intricate ideas, and exquisite phrasing, the phrasing of the true poet. Probably all modern philosophers, of whatever school, would agree that Plato is the supreme glory of their profession.

Aristotle, Plato's greatest pupil, shaped the course of European philosophy for two thousand years. Up to the seventeenth century he was *"the* philosopher." His teachings informed the official philosophy of the Christian Church—which was founded four hundred years after his death! His authority became so rigid that modern philosophers like Francis Bacon rebelled against it and asserted the right to independent investigation; which was really true to the spirit of Aristotle himself though not to what scholars and pedants had made of him. For Aristotle was a free spirit with a curious inquiring mind, essentially scientific, seeking to know what the facts are. He parted company with Plato, whom of course he revered, on one great crucial problem of philosophy. Plato, dreamer, mystic, artist, poet, believed that the eternal reality is abstract idea, and that things are but the images of it. Aristotle, more prosaic and endowed with hard-headed common-sense, believed that things are about what they seem to be, though we may misunderstand them, that you and I and stone and wood are actual substances. Generalities like Man, Nature, Beauty have no real existence except in the mind which uses them for purposes of classification.

The fundamental difference between Aristotle's conception of the world and Plato's has been one of the chief problems of philosophy down to the present day. It has not been settled and never will be settled except to the satisfaction of philosophers who take one side or the other. If Aristotle were alive today he would probably be with the pragmatists, or an experimenter in the physical sciences—though this will be immediately denied by those who disagree with pragmatism. Certainly the most eloquent account of Aristotle, or any other philosopher, that I ever listened to was from the lips of that great idealist, Josiah Royce.

To Aristotle we owe accidentally the word "metaphysics" as the general term for fundamental philosophic principles. Aristotle himself called the subject "first philosophy," but one of his editors put his treatise on the subject *after* (that is, in Greek, *meta*) his treatise on physics. Hence "metaphysics." Aristotle knew all that was known in his time and he set out to arrange the whole world of wisdom, first principles, natural history, ethics, politics, literary criticism. With the increased diversity and specialization of knowledge no modern philosopher would attempt so much, and therefore no modern philosopher has such a colossal unity, not Kant, nor Hegel, nor Spencer. It may be that Aristotle's metaphysics has been supplanted by the work of later thinkers, and he has not Plato's literary art to keep his speculations everlastingly fresh to the mere reader of literature. The *Ethics* and the *Politics* and the unsurpassable book of literary criticism, the *Poetics,* will give to the ordinary reader who has no technical equipment for philosophy a sufficient glimpse into Aristotle's mind. The last book has a redoubled vitality in the edition, with the accompanying essay, of S. H. Butcher. Bernard Shaw in his delicious comedy, *Fanny's First Play,* pokes fun at a critic who has a too servile respect for Aristotle's views of the drama. But after all the centuries that intervene, including the brilliant critical thought of the nineteenth century, Aristotle's *Poetics* stands solid and essential; whoever knows that book cannot go far wrong in his literary judgments—even of the latest novel.

After Aristotle there were two great schools of thought which dominated the Greek and Roman world, the Stoic and the Epicurean. These schools did not supplant Plato and Aristotle; on the contrary, they drew much of their wisdom from the two great masters. Stoicism and Epicureanism were practical philosophies peculiarly fitted to intellectual men of the world, in a world which was expanding and becoming cosmopolitan. Aristotle's most famous pupil, Alexander the Great, had conquered every land that was of any interest to a Greek and had founded the city of Alexandria in Egypt. This city, as we have seen, became the center of Greek culture, though Athens never quite stopped beating as the heart of Greek civilization. When Alexander's empire crumbled and the seats of the mighty were transferred to Rome, the vanquished Greeks became the teachers of their Latin conquerors; and the Romans, who were less inclined to pure speculation than the Greeks, naturally absorbed and developed the more practical philosophies which have to do with every-day conduct.

The Stoic philosophy has given us a common word. When we say that a man is stoic or stoical, we mean that he bears pain with calm fortitude. That idea is true to the spirit of the ancient Stoic philosophers, but it suggests only part of their teachings. They taught not only bravery in bearing pain, but also the suppression or control of pleasant emotions. For the Stoic the Wise Man is one who does not let his feelings run away with him. The aim of life is wisdom, reason; and the supreme happiness is virtuous conduct.

Two of the most famous Stoics were the slave, Epictetus, and the noble Roman emperor, Marcus Aurelius. Epictetus lived in the first century of the Christian era. In his youth he was a slave, but he was subsequently freed, and became a missionary teacher and preacher. Like Socrates, he taught by word of mouth, and we owe the preservation of his thoughts, the *Discourses,* to one of his disciples. He overcame poverty and ill-health by renouncing all worldly ambition. He believed that true philosophy is to understand the ways of nature and to be resigned to the will of the gods. He was not unlike some of the bare-footed saints of the early Christian church, and he taught, somewhat in the spirit of St. Paul, that we are all members of one body, and that for the individual to realize himself he must try to realize the good of all men. But it was not until much later, just when is a complex problem in the history of thought, that Greek-Roman ethical ideas and the new heretical Christian ideas reconciled their differences and discovered their resemblances. And then for centuries the scholars who keep Greek and Roman philosophy alive are Christian priests and monks!

So it need not surprise us to find that the wise and gentle Roman emperor, Marcus Aurelius, was hostile to the Christians, who were teaching ideas which seem, at this distance in time, quite in harmony with his. The oppositions of schools of philosophy are part of the human comedy and of the human tragedy. Marcus Aurelius was an emperor; he believed in the sacredness of the Roman state, and the Christians were a nuisance because they cared nothing for the Roman Empire. But oddly enough, in the first Christian century Epictetus and other philosophers, from whom Marcus Aurelius derived many ideas, were exiled from Rome because they were "liberals" opposed to the tyranny of the emperor Domitian. Marcus Aurelius was no tyrant, but a very Lincoln in devotion to his task. It was a difficult and bitter task, vexed by pestilence, famine, and wars, which he hated as sincerely as the most thoroughgoing pacifist and non-resistant of our day. In Stoicism he found support and consolation, the philosophy of duty, frugality (unusual virtue in a Roman emperor!), resignation, self-control. His book of *Meditations,* which he called by the fine direct title *To Himself,* is a small volume of maxims and moral counsels written to brace himself up and help him forward with his work. His philosophy is not a systematic description of the universe, but the sort of book, the expression of a character, which we all understand when we say that a man takes life "philosophically." "Life," says the emperor somewhat sadly, "is more like wrestling than dancing." But toward the end he quotes his master Epictetus: "No man can rob us of our will." That is the heart of Stoic philosophy, without its speculations. But why do we put a Roman emperor in a chapter on Greek philosophy? Because the Roman gentleman with Latin characteristics, problems, and affairs, thought and wrote Greek. Later the gentleman of all western European countries thought and wrote Latin (if he could write at all!). Perhaps a close parallel is to be found in the fact that the educated Englishman of the twelfth and thirteenth centuries spoke not as an Englishman, but as a Frenchman. The geographical boundaries of thought are not determined by customs-house officials. And this idea would have appealed especially to a Stoic, or to any other Greek philosopher. "We are made for one another," says the Roman emperor, Marcus Aurelius. And the Jewish Christian, Paul, said something very like that!

Epicurus and his followers were, to some extent, opponents of the Stoics, and also of the more highly developed philosophies of Plato and Aristotle. Epicurean philosophy is generous and humane, not so puritanical as the Stoic (we may be taken to task for injecting the modern word, "puritanical" into Greek philosophy). The Epicurean had a very sound psychology; he knew how the human being is made, that man obeys his desires, though he never reaches the goal. The Epicurean emphasized the right of "life, liberty, and the pursuit of happiness." He believed that the senses are the primary source of knowledge. For this reason his name, or the name of his philosophy, was strangely distorted in popular usage: an "Epicure" is a man who likes good food! Nothing could be more false to a great teacher, whose life, so far as we know, was moderate and temperate. He taught the pleasures of duty and simplicity as well as of the senses. He knew human nature and walked with his feet on the earth, somewhat sceptical of philosophers who walked with their heads in the clouds. For English readers the essential nobility of that school of thought is best expressed in *Marius the Epicurean* by the English critic Walter Pater, a beautiful book. In modern times not only technical scholars but artists and poets have revived and rediscovered the great Greeks.

It is possible to overpraise the Greeks, to become idolaters of all things Hellenic, as were many modern men of letters, for example, Swinburne, Matthew Arnold, Walter Pater. The critical judgment should keep its balance and seek the best in all periods and all peoples. And yet it is impossible to overpraise the Greeks, who developed every art and every science, except certain sciences which are modern.

One of the literary arts which reached a high degree of skill and power, in all the Greek communities but especially in Athens, was oratory. Oratory is literature if the spoken words committed to paper have a *readable* eloquence. Much oratory vanishes, like the art of the singer or the actor with the silencing of the physical voice. The spiritual or intellectual voice sometimes persists. Edmund Burke seems not to have impressed the British parliament or to have had great oral power. But his speeches and orations have an imperishable place in English literature. Other orators who held the attention of cynical politicians and of the gaping multitude, Gladstone, for example, are flat and uninspired in cold print. Still others seem to have been gifted with vocal effectiveness and with literary eloquence that can survive the test of the printed page. The Greek orators brought the art to a high degree of perfection, for their political fortune depended on it to an extent inconceivable in our day of the newspaper and the *Congressional Record,* which prints speeches never delivered at all! One of the great orators of Athens had a silent tongue, Lysias, who was not a lawful citizen, was therefore disqualified from speaking in the courts, and so devoted his gifts to writing speeches for others. That is, he was a professional logographer (speech writer). One exception is his spoken oration against the tyrant Eratosthenes who was responsible for the death of the brother of Lysias, Polemarchus. Lysias served his clients in a dignified business-like way, bearing somewhat the relation to them that a modern lawyer, expert in drawing briefs, might bear to a barrister with a good voice and skill in persuading judge and jury. A contemporary of Lysias, Isocrates, was also a logographer, committing his work to writing and not appearing as a public speaker. He was a teacher of rhetoric and oratory, perhaps the most distinguished during the fourth century B. C. He lifted oratory from the ordinary subjects which had engaged Lysias to magniloquent themes, treated in the grand manner, eloquence for its own sake. But his work is more than mere declamation, he is sound and sincere in his praise of Athens and his exhortations to her to take the brave course against Persia and the generous course toward the other Greek states.

DEMOSTHENES

The greatest of all Greek orators was Demosthenes. That may mean that he was the supreme orator of all time. The tradition of his oral power is clouded by foolish legends, for example, that he improved his diction by putting pebbles in his mouth—no man practicing the art of speech would do anything so obstructively s t u p i d. But there is no doubt that his eloquence held his audiences, and the orations that survive are prose of the highest quality, in clearness of organization, variety of images and sonority of diction. His most famous orations are those directed against Philip of Macedonia, who was conquering the rest of Greece and laying the foundations of the empire of his son Alexander.

The vigorous passionate attacks of Demosthenes on Philip have given us the generic name for that kind of oratory (written or spoken)—philippic. Demosthenes was a practical politician as well as an artist in words, and he did as much as a talker could do to guard Athens from the superior power of arms and the man from the north. His most splendid oration is that *On the Crown.* It had been proposed that in recognition of his public services the city of Athens give Demosthenes a golden wreath or crown. His political enemy and rival in oratory, Æschines, a tool of Philip, objected. Whatever the merits of the case, there is no doubt that Demosthenes swept his opponent off his feet and wrote himself down (we can only guess what the spoken effect may have been) as a great master of prose, the fervid vigor of which is not lost in translation.

Milton, who was immersed in Greek, inserted his classic learning into *Paradise Regained,* in some magnificent lines which have nothing to do with his story—the literary scholar triumphing over the narrative artist:

> Thence to the famous Orators repair,
> Those ancient, whose resistless eloquence
> Wielded at will that fierce democraty,
> Shook the Arsenal, and fulmined over Greece
> To Macedon and Artaxerxes' throne.

The history of later Greek literature and language is fascinating but we can barely touch on it. Greece, that is Attic Greece with Athens at the center, was conquered twice, by Macedon and by Rome. In both conquests the vanquished was intellectually dominant: Athens and her pupil-provinces ruled the world of thought. During the whole period of classic Latin, the educated Roman spoke and wrote Greek as a matter of course. Then about the fourth century, owing both to the political supremacy of Rome and to the intellectual power of the Roman Church, Latin became the dominant language among educated people and Greek almost disappeared for ten centuries, to come to life again in that splendid rebirth of learning called the Renaissance.

Of the later Greek writers there is one man of genius who is great by virtue of his own creation and perhaps even greater by his influence on modern writers. That is the satirist, Lucian, an original, witty man, better than that, a profound humorist, the Swift, Voltaire, Mark Twain of his time. He lived in the second century after Christ. The vicissitudes of time have left us a good deal of his work, which has been translated into English, and is as joyously fresh and readable as anything in Greek literature. The *True History,* an account of a journey to the moon, and of the fight between the people of the sun and the people of the moon, is a piece of imaginative fooling, suggesting Rabelais, Swift, and Jules Verne. It is likely that Swift's *Gulliver* took a lesson or two from Lucian, though of course Swift's genius stands on its own stout legs. Lucian lived in the clear light of scepticism; he believed in nothing, though he evidently had a great respect for Plato and Socrates; he shot his keen shafts at the gods of tradition, and at the philosophers, and in an earlier time he might have shared the fate of Socrates. In *Alexander* he flays a mountebank who set up an oracle which was known throughout the Greek and Roman world. To Lucian all religion was superstition and all philosophy, or most of it, sophistical playing with words. But Lucian, whatever his beliefs, was a great imaginative artist. Those who read Greek easily—or pretend to—speak of the charm of his style. Th charm, the wit and civilized intelligence of his thought, come through to us in translation.

As Greek literature faded, poetry went out of it and the vigor of its philosophy—the supreme gift of the Greek mind —became but the impotent repetition of sophists, professional school-teachers who did not contribute an idea to the thought of the world.

There were, however, in the twilight of Greece, two ideas of literary and intellectual importance. One was the novel. The other was the junction of Greek thought with Christianity. The Greek novel, or romance, does not amount to much; no man of real talent happened to take hold of it; poetry crumbled into prose. But its importance is greater than its merit. It had some effect on Roman and medieval literature and perhaps helped to shape the tales of adventure which have persisted down to the last novel printed yesterday. The most charming example is *Daphnis and Chloë,* written by Longus about two centuries after Christ. The other Greek romances depend for their interest wholly on exciting incidents. *Daphnis and Chloë* comes nearer to the modern novel in that it has emotion. The two foundlings are brought up together by the shepherds, and the gradual development of their childish affection into mature passion gives to their later adventures something of the sentimental glow of *Paul et Virginie.*

Very important is the fusion of Greek thought with Christian, and many philosophers who had an influence on the Church were Greek in spirit and language. Fundamentally Christianity is Hebraic, and its chief exponent, Paul, called himself Hebrew of Hebrews. Later with the universal triumph of Rome Latin became the official language of the Church. But in the early centuries, as we can see in the Greek version of the Bible, the language if not the thought of Greece prevailed in Christianity. Paul must have been brought up on the Greek Bible, and probably preached in Greek, for that seems to have been the language that every literate person understood. An important Greek writer who deliberately injected Greek thought into Christian was Origen, a preacher and editor of the Bible. He belongs rather to religious history than to the art of letters. So also do Athanasias and Basil who lived in the fourth century. Christian literature did not ripen and flourish until ancient Greece had ceased as a political and an intellectual power. But that power, let us remember, had been dominant, though not exclusively important, for more than a thousand years, and the revival of Greek is the most important *literary* fact in the last five centuries. In a thousand years of activity and after a thousand years of almost complete oblivion, Greece was, and is, the intelligence of the world. It is not necessary to read Greek easily—few people do—but it is necessary, or highly desirable, to get from later civilizations and languages some of the best Greek thoughts. The Greek had many failings, but no other race in recorded history had such a faculty to express in all possible ways, in words or marble, the horror and the beauty of this world and the world beyond and the humorous pathos of us human beings who populate a small corner of the cosmos.

CHAPTER X

ROMAN HISTORY AND HISTORIANS

I came, I saw, I conquered.

—*Julius Cæsar.*

T HE man of words is not always, not often, the man of affairs. The maker of records, the phraser of life, is usually a timid person who could not lead a regiment or face a group of politicians in debate. But in literature, as in life, no rule holds good. It sometimes happens that the man who does things can say things. Two supreme examples of the double genius are Napoleon and Julius Cæsar. Cæsar made history and wrote it. His *Commentaries* on the Gallic War and on the Civil War (between Cæsar and Pompey) are clear, simple, and sincere narratives.

On account of the simplicity of the substance and the style the *Gallic War* is used as an elementary text-book in the study of Latin; so that it has probably been more widely read (if that school-room grind can be called reading) than any other Latin book. Many of us learned to hate it in our youth, as we came to hate some English masterpieces which we were required to parse and otherwise mutilate. But the mature reader who turns to Cæsar's works, either in the original or in a good "trot," will find them immensely interesting, swift, vigorous stories.   The *Gallic War* is the basis of half our knowledge of the northern provinces of Rome, which have since become great modern nations, and the *Civil War* is an

JULIUS CÆSAR

indispensable document for the understanding of the internal affairs of Rome.

The purpose of Cæsar's writing was to justify himself in the eyes of the Romans, but he understood as artist and politician the value of moderation, and he made his case without palaver or boasting and without serious misrepresentation of fact. The magnitude of his fame is indicated by the adoption of his family name as the common name for emperor, not only in ancient Rome but in Germany and Russia. His death at the hands of Brutus and other liberal or envious patriots is the supreme example in history (even more dramatic than the life of Napoleon) of the irony of human greatness. For English readers the tragedy of his career and the power of his character are best expressed in Shakespeare's play. Cæsar has fascinated modern historians, who in turn fascinate the lay reader. Among the most eloquent accounts are those in the *History of Rome* by the German, Theodor Mommsen, and the more recent *Greatness and Decline of Rome* by the Italian, Guglielmo Ferrero. Both of these works are in English.

Cæsar's writings are personal memoirs, his own adventures amid events which were greater than himself but which he partly shaped. A somewhat similar modern example is the *Memoirs* of General Grant. And in our day it is impossible to count the autobiographies, recollections, apologies, and defenses by generals, admirals, and diplomats who played a part in the World War of 1914-18.

The first great impersonal, or objective, Roman historian was a contemporary and supporter of Cæsar, Sallust. He had been a man of affairs and had grown rich as governor of Numidia, an African province of Rome. After the death of Cæsar, in 44 B. C., Sallust retired to his magnificent villa and lived the life of a gentleman and scholar. He was a sound historian, employing secretaries to study and compare documents for him, and he was an artist with a sense of style and a gift for dramatic narrative. The two complete works of his which survive are the story of the conspiracy of Catiline (the subject also of Cicero's famous oration), and the history of the war between the Romans and the Numidian king, Jugurtha. The books of Cæsar and Sallust are only episodes in the long history of the Roman empire, and the Roman empire is only an episode in the long tale of human life. But these two fragmentary historians give vivid glimpses of the expansion of Rome, to the north in Cæsar, and to the south, across the Mediterranean, in Sallust.

In the next generation after Julius Cæsar and Cicero and Sallust we cross the line into the Christian era. The Roman empire was the world, an empire in fact and in form, governed by the splendid Cæsars, the first of whom was Augustus. The literary period is called Augustan, just as the literary period in England which includes Shakespeare is called Elizabethan. The foremost historian and the greatest master of Latin prose in the Augustan age was Livy. He attempted to tell the whole story of Rome from the beginning down to his own time. The title of his work was something like *Books of History From the Foundation of the City*. It was a tremendous task which he almost finished. About a fourth of his work has survived, enough to place him, in the almost unanimous judgment of modern historians, among the greatest chroniclers. He made the prose epic of Rome, as Virgil made the verse epic, and his style has rich poetic color.

The Rome before Christ which lives in history is very largely the Rome which Livy created or re-created from earlier historians. He was pessimistic about his own times, as historians and philosophers often are, and his patriotism took the form of looking back with regretful admiration at the past. We find the same attitude in recent writers who think, for example, that nothing good has happened to humanity since the Renaissance, or, for another example, since the Forefathers made the American Constitution. It is not a critical attitude, but it makes for eloquence and dramatic interest; the man who does not admire the past of his race or nation is not a born historian. And Livy was just that, a born historian, of wide vision and industrious learning, who absorbed and made superfluous the lesser Latin historians before him and laid the foundation for all historians of Rome who have come after him. He is accessible to us in cheap readable translations. Not only the special student but the unlearned browser in history will enjoy him.

In the second half of the first Christian century and the beginning of the second lived Tacitus, the third great Latin historian. To his *Germania* we owe the earliest account of our Teutonic ancestors who lived two thousand years ago. Tacitus, like Cæsar, had a great respect for people who were to the cultivated Roman primitive barbarians. Indeed one reason why the Romans dominated the world was that for all their predatory ruthlessness they had on the whole a generous philosophic understanding of other races and nations. Moreover Tacitus heightened the virtues of the German tribes, their simplicity and honesty, in order to point a moral for Roman society, which was extravagantly luxurious. Especially interesting to English readers is his biographical eulogy of his father-in-law, the Roman governor of Britain. He also wrote the history of his own century. Of this work considerable fragments remain, and are the basis of our knowledge of the early Cæsars, good and bad—mostly bad. His genius consists in his ability to depict character and the terse vigor of his phrases. He is a stern moralist, unsparing in his accounts of the crimes of the emperors, but like most noble Romans of his time he believes in the empire and in the essential virtue of Roman character. "I believe," he says, "that the highest function of history is to let no worthy thing go

uncommemorated." The spirit of Tacitus, like that of most
ancient historians, is moralistic, patriotic, artistic, and this
spirit, for better or for worse, has not altogether disappeared
from the work of modern historians, even those who insist on
impartial study of documents, search for fact, and critical
judgment.

For modern readers the history of Rome is written not in
the original Latin chroniclers, but in the work of historians of
our own race and time who have studied the Latin sources,
extracted their essence and told the story over in their way,
in our language. The great English historian of Rome is
Edward Gibbon, whose *Decline and Fall of the Roman Empire* is a masterpiece of English literature. Later students
have corrected him at many points partly in the light of documents which have been discovered since Gibbon's work was
published in the last quarter of the eighteenth century. Gibbon knew all that in his time could be known about Rome
and he put his knowledge together so solidly that one of the
most recent critical scholars has called him "the greatest historian who ever dealt with the fortunes of Rome." Gibbon
came as close to the Roman spirit as it is possible for a modern
student to come, and his approach was the more intimate because his early education was both English and French. His
first work was written in French, and it is said that there are
traces of the influence of the French tongue in his English
style. However that may be he is one of the glories of English
prose. He was a pagan, a recluse who lived in his library,
and yet a man of the world, with a more than English vision,
scornful of such a sacred English institution as Oxford University! His un-Christian, that is his pagan, Roman attitude
toward Christianity roused much controversy among people
who had been brought up to believe that the chief sport of

Roman emperors was making martyrs of Christians. If he had biases and prejudices—as every man has—they have been corrected and balanced in the notes and introduction to the text of the *Decline and Fall* edited by one of the most profound and sane of recent historians, J. B. Bury of the University of Cambridge. Gibbon's history begins in the second century A. D. Those who wish to get a connected complete view of Rome will find nothing better than the *History of Rome* by the American scholar, Professor Tenney Frank.

CHAPTER XI

LATIN EPIC POETRY

O courteous Mantuan spirit, whose fame still lasts in the world, and will last as long as time.

—*Dante.*

IT was the artistic and patriotic ambition of Roman writers to create a literature as great as that of Greece. This ambition was never realized in drama, but it was approximately realized in poetry in the work of the preëminent Latin poet, Virgil. He not only perfected and crowned the work of earlier Latin poets but was for centuries "the" poet of Europe, as Aristotle was "the" philosopher. The classic culture of Europe through the Middle Ages was Latin and not Greek, except as the Latin had borrowed and absorbed the Greek, and Virgil was, and is, the most splendid voice of Rome. Oddly enough, the Christian world made him a kind of saint, seer, and magician, subject of superstitious legend; and Dante in the thirteenth century chose him as his father and guide. He deserved his enormous reputation, however distorted, and except for some niggling criticism at the beginning of the nineteenth century, all men of letters, poets and critics, have regarded him as the greatest of Latin writers, and as one of the five or six supreme poets of the world.

More than a century before Virgil, the poet Ennius had written the *Annales,* a long narrative poem which seems to have been something like a national epic and of which the remaining fragments, a few hundred lines, show dramatic intensity and poetic power. But the national spirit had not solidified, and what is more important, the national language had not reached its highest development. Ennius adapted the Greek hexameter to the Latin language, and Virgil perfected the hexameter, which Tennyson called "the stateliest measure ever moulded by the lips of man."

The first important work of Virgil is the *Eclogues* or *Bucolics,* pastoral poems of country life and legend imitated from the Greek of Theocritus but full too of Virgil's love of nature and of the actual north Italian farm-land where he lived. The *Eclogues* alone might have made Virgil one of the national poets of old and of new Italy (even with the passing of Latin as a popular spoken language) ; for the Italian landscape and the Italian spring have not changed, and no poet has felt them more sensitively than Virgil. His humanity and sympathy and charm give life to the somewhat artificial and obsolete shepherds and gods and redeem the immaturity of this early verse. The true poets announce themselves at once even in youthful work. About one of the *Eclogues* there is a strange superstitious story, absurd on the face of it, but important in literary history, because it accounts in part for the respect paid to Virgil by Christians. A vague account of a child who was to be born and to usher in a reign of peace was interpreted as a prophecy of Christ! In uncritical times when valuable works were being neglected or destroyed, it was fortunate that Virgil's reputation was in part preserved by a misunderstanding.

The *Eclogues,* fine as they are in spots, are little more than an artificial literary exercise in preparation for the *Georgics.* The *Georgics* are genuine nature poetry, "a song of the husbandry of fields and cattle, and of trees." It may well be that Mæcenas, the rich patron of poets, wishing to promote a sort of "back-to-the land" movement, encouraged Virgil to celebrate rural life. At any rate it was a theme in which Virgil's genius was happily at home, even more happily and naturally than in the *Æneid.* He loved the country as profoundly as did his Greek master, Hesiod, and he knew farm-life at first hand. His scenes are as fresh today as they were two thousand years ago and his nightingale still sings, lovely as the nightingale of Keats.

The *Æneid* was to some extent a patriotic duty. The real hero of it is not the mere man, the faithful Æneas, but the eternal city of Rome. Earlier poets had established the legend, which has no basis in fact, that Rome was founded by heroic wanderers from fallen Troy, and Virgil takes this idea as the skeleton of his theme. Since Æneas must make a long and devious journey from Troy to the country of Latium, there is abundant adventure on the way, as exciting as that in the *Odyssey;* and behind the "arms and the man" there is the conventional celestial machinery of the gods and fate guiding the hero, the individual, and the great city to high destinies. In our time when poetry is only a pleasant artistic plaything it is almost impossible to realize the reception which the Romans gave the *Æneid.* It expressed all that was ideal in the Roman state. Because of its subject and its unrivaled use of the Latin tongue it dominated Latin literature henceforth.

Virgil did not live to know what a great thing he had done. The poem was published after his death, and the story goes that he was so dissatisfied with his work (it is a feeling that

RUOTOLO.32

VIRGIL

VIRGIL.

every conscientious and delicate artist knows) that he wished
the poem destroyed, and that it was saved by his friends and
the command of the emperor Augustus. As the emperor is
the final personal hero of the poem, the subject of a great eulo-
gistic passage, he had especial reason for preserving the work
of his most distinguished subject. If Virgil had lived he
would have been crowned as second only to the emperor. As
it was his tomb became a religious shrine. And no poet ever
better deserved such homage.

Let us read the *Æneid* in the plainest translation, if we are
so unfortunate as to have no ear for Latin verse, in the honest
prose of John Conington. And what have we? Primarily a
story, which one needs to be neither Roman nor scholar to
enjoy. The only parts of the story which fail are the battle
scenes—a glorious failure! Virgil had to put them in because
they belong in his narrative of struggling and conquering
Rome. But his gentle soul is not made for battles; he has
almost none of Homer's dashing delight in a conflict. He
is more philosophic and humane than Homer—we will not
stir up the foolish question which is the greater poet, for
all great things are independently, incomparably great—and
his theme in the introduction to his poem is the effort, the
bravery, the difficulty that went into the founding of Rome.

Virgil in the very act of celebrating the glory and greatness of Rome feels the "tears of things." He is a romantic in
every sense of a word which has been worried to death, and
which came from Rome! And he is a romancer. The Romans did not have (except possibly in the work of Petronius
Arbiter, of whom we shall say a word later) anything like
our novel, and their sense of romance, their love of a love
story, expressed itself and found its satisfaction in drama and
poetry. To the literature of romance Virgil has added one

of the great stories, the story of Dido. The love of Dido and Æneas is only an episode in the career of the hero; it is the final tragedy in the life of the woman, and that is true to human nature, which is the basis of all literature, novels or mythological epics.

Because Latin dominated later European literatures, and because Virgil is the commanding genius in Latin literature, he has been a vast power in English poetry (in the times almost past when English poets read Latin as a matter of course), and he has tempted many men of talent to translate him. Dryden's translation is an English classic like Chapman's *Homer* or Pope's. In the nineteenth century the amazing William Morris, who could rip off a hundred lines of poetry before breakfast and design a tapestry before lunch, made a spirited translation in swinging long lines somewhat like Chapman's *Homer*. If Matthew Arnold had written an essay on "Translating Virgil" like his essay on Homer, he would probably have laid a severe hand on Morris, and on all other translators. I take most pleasure in the prose translations, those of Conington and J. W. Mackail. Mackail knows Latin like a second mother tongue, and he writes excellent English. Conington's introductory essay not only reviews previous translations of Virgil, but throws light on the whole vexed problem of translating poetry from one language to another.

Poets are but human beings; but if there is any truth in the fancy that they are inspired, the words of Dido about Æneas may be applied to their creator: "I do believe that he has the blood of gods in his veins."

CHAPTER XII

LATIN DRAMATIC, PHILOSOPHIC, AND LYRIC POETRY

What has this bugbear death to frighten men?
                    —*Lucretius*: Dryden's translation.

THE dependence of Roman thought on Greek is obvious in all forms of literature. In the drama the dependence is so close that most Latin plays are little more than clever adaptations. In the Latin versions the scenes and characters at least in name remain Greek. We should have a somewhat similar situation if all the plays given in New York were borrowed from the French and retained the French proper names and the Parisian setting with some American types and jokes thrown in. Dramatists, even those of great talent, have always been the most cheerful literary thieves. Molière and Shakespeare and his contemporaries borrowed from the ancients, and the playwrights of modern nations have lifted from each other with or without acknowledgment. It is difficult for us to tell just how funny and true to life the comic dramatists, Greek or Roman, seemed to their fellow-countrymen; humor, especially if it has local touches, is a perishable commodity, and I suspect that **no**

modern reader, even the most intimate student of the classics, is shaken with laughter by the mirth of the two most eminent Latin comic playwrights, Plautus and Terence. Plautus, who lived about two centuries before Christ, illustrates one of the few principles which our fragmentary book hopes to suggest, that is, the continuity of literature, the fact that a minor man as well as the towering genius passes thought along from generation to generation. Plautus got many ideas from Greek comedies, especially those of Menander, most of which have been lost, and so through him we get a glimpse of what those comedies were. And as later dramatists, French, Italian and English, took plots from him, he is more important than himself. About twenty of his plays survive. One of them, the *Menæchmi,* is of especial interest to us, for it is the basis of Shakespeare's *Comedy of Errors.*

Terence, who succeeded Plautus, wrote a more finished style, still closer to the Greek, with a servility of imitation which is the death of art. But we can remember at least one great line in a play called *The Self-Tormentor*:

> I am a man: I regard nothing human as alien to myself.

We do not know why the Romans did not do better work in the literature of the theater (the we-don't-knows of literature are part of the pleasure and profit of studying it) ; if they imitated the Greek theater, they also imitated other kinds of Greek literature and revealed really original genius. Perhaps they were too much interested in gladiatorial combats and other spectacles to develop the legitimate stage— somewhat as our stage is threatened, though by no means destroyed, by base-ball and the moving-picture. A more unanswerable question is why second-rate or third-rate work, like the tragedies of Seneca, were so much respected by modern poets. They are as dull plays as a great or almost great man ever wrote. Ben Jonson, Shakespeare's most learned contemporary, in the verses prefixed to the first folio collection of Shakespeare's plays, refers to Seneca as the equal of Æschylus and Euripides. That may have been a joke— and we must keep our eyes and ears open for the jokes of literary men. Shakespeare was certainly joking when in *Hamlet* he makes that pathetic old ass, Polonius, advise the players: "Seneca cannot be too heavy, nor Plautus too light."

Seneca was a bad dramatist, but he was an important philosopher in the Stoic school. And he needed all his courageous philosophy; he was the tutor of the erratic emperor Nero, rose under him to wealth and eminence and then was commanded to commit suicide.

The Roman mind, under Greek tutelage, was philosophic. In one Roman mind philosophy and Latin poetry met and made a masterpiece—the mind of Lucretius, when it conceived the *De Rerum Natura* (*Of the Nature of Things*). It is a superb poem, almost prophetic in the depth of its plunge into the substance of life. Philosophic ideas find their natural vehicle in prose, though much early Greek philosophy is in verse. Lucretius is one of the few poets of all time who have succeeded in embodying philosophy in verse which is not mere metrical prose but has the magic of real poetry—of great poetry. Ages before modern science he foreshadowed the atomic theory and the evolution of man from mysterious beginnings. Fortunately we have his poem complete, and it is the most majestic and eloquent Latin verse, next to Virgil, that has come down to us. We have an excellent English version of Lucretius by the American poet and scholar, William Ellery Leonard. Lucretius summed up Epicurean philosophy with added glimpses and visions of his own.   Readers who think ancient philosophy dry and musty will find Lucretius surprisingly alive, and their way to him, and so to the heart of some of the best Greek and Roman thought, will be lighted by the essay of the modern philosopher, George Santayana, in *Three Philosophical Poets*.

A contemporary of Lucretius was Catullus, a brilliant young poet (he died at thirty, the Keats or Shelley of his

time) who was not interested in the "nature of things" but only in his own nature and emotions, his loves, his friendships, his hatreds.   He adores, abuses, and immortalizes his lady-love, Lesbia.   In him are combined heart and art.   His passion is genuine, poignant, lyrical with the human cry, but controlled by exquisite command of verse.

To suggest Catullus we might think of him as an Elizabethan writing sonnets like those of Philip Sidney or Shakespeare, or, later, the vigorous lyrics of Burns, or the equally vigorous and more lovely lyrics of Shelley.   The Latin readers after him, both Roman and modern, felt the sting, the loveliness, the perfection, natural and technical, of his verse.   If you had asked such poets as

SLAVE

Tennyson and Swinburne who was to them the first of Latin poets, they might have said, thinking of relative fames, Virgil; but in their hearts they would have said, Catullus.

After Catullus, but still in the splendid century just before Christ, lived Horace, the wittiest, most widely read, most often quoted and translated of all Latin poets.   Horace had nothing of the passion (real or literary) of Catullus. He was cool, collected, intellectual, serious underneath but with his tongue in his cheek, very serious in his careful turning of phrases and meters. Take life as it comes and live serenely is his philosophy. It is no wonder that men of the world have liked him and that the somewhat cynically cultivated gentlemen in the British Parliament of the eighteenth century brightened their oratory with his lines. The solemn politician, Gladstone, and the clever manipulator of light verse, Eugene Field, (and his journalistic progeny) have been admirers and translators of Horace. We may get a taste of the spirit of Horace from a stanza, translated by an unknown modern poet, of his ode to his patron Mæcenas.

> Self-secure and free from sorrow,
>   He who says, "I've lived today!"
> God send rain or shine tomorrow,
>   Naught can steal the past away.
> What has been no power can spoil.
>   Fortune in her saucy game
>   Seldom deals two hands the same,
> Tireless in her wanton toil
> Each in turn to aid and foil.

Horace was much more than a clever versifier, an elegant gentleman who liked to drink wine with his patron. He was a profoundly serious poet with a great variety of moods, satirical, reflective, pathetic. And to all he adapted with almost unfailing ease his terse, rhythmic, imaginative style. English readers can find him at one of his finest lyric moments in Milton's translation of the exquisite ode *To Pyrrha.* Horace was a master of the theory as well as the practice of poetry; his *Art of Poetry,* a brief and apparently casual letter, had an immense influence on modern literature, in

Italy through the poet Vida, in France through the poet and critic Boileau, and in England through Boileau's more than original imitator, Pope. It may be that with the more expansive and less disciplined ideals of the romantic movement which swept Europe in the nineteenth century, Pope's brilliant *Essay in Criticism* has not the authority that it once

BRAGGART

enjoyed and that the Horatian spirit no longer has the power which it held for nearly twenty centuries. But whatever our changes of taste and theories of poetry we shall not find any better expression than Horace gave to the ideal of devotion to art. The man Horace is as great as the artist. His personality shining through his verse is delightful, at once dignified and humorous. He grows steadily in power, in insight, in serenity and wisdom, in command of the ultimate right phrase. The Latin lyric did not die with Horace, but continued to flourish for several centuries. It did not, however, in any one poet attain anything like the variety and vigor of Horace.

But about this time, contemporary with Horace, though a little younger—the time is just before the Christian era—there was an interesting group of poets, the elegists. As I said briefly, apropos the Greek elegists, the word originally seems to have had nothing to do with the substance of the poem but to have designated a form. Verse forms are out of our province, if only because, though they constitute a fascinating subject, we have not space for them or for many other matters of literary technique. But because it tells us so much in little I will quote Coleridge's specimen of an elegiac couplet:

> In the hexameter rises the fountain's silvery column;
> In the pentameter aye falling in melody back.

That "elegy" came to have the meaning which we give to it, a threnody or lament for a dead friend with praise of his virtues (Tennyson's *In Memoriam* is an "elegy" as we feel the word) is apparently due to the fact that the elegists happened to take death as their theme. But by no means all. The first and oldest, Gallus, who did much to naturalize the Greek form in Latin, wrote not of death but of love. His success set the fashion and for a time elegiac poets outnumbered all other kinds of literary men. The greatest of the elegists are three, Propertius, Tibullus, and Ovid.

Propertius was a precocious poet, mastering his Greek models so thoroughly as to be an original poet at the age of twenty (a few years later he was dead). Love is his theme, and his Cynthia became one of the celebrated heroines of poetry. The lover-poet himself was, as Mackail has pointed out, the forerunner of the sentimental, self-pitying, somewhat neurotic boy who is such a familiar figure in the romantic verse and fiction of the nineteenth century. Students of English literature will be interested to look at the poet Gray's imitations from Propertius.

Propertius seems to have had some of the faults as well as the divine vigor of youth, and the Romans, who were becoming more and more critically Greek in their standards, complained of his defects, which seem to have been due to haste and impetuousness; we cannot tell now for the surviving manuscripts are broken and incomplete. The more exacting Romans admired another young elegist, Tibullus, whose clarity and delicacy of form fit perfectly with his tenderness and loveliness of thought. He has not half the power of Propertius, but power is only one element in lyric poetry. Tibullus, too, was a young man in love with love, and inclined

PARASITE

to tears over the cruelty of his mistress. But they are honest tears, and the hard-hearted Delia is as real as the lady-love of a poet ever can be. There is a general rule (subject to exceptions) which will illuminate our reading of much love poetry. The poet is celebrating, not a Celia, or Cynthia, or Julia, or Jennie, though he may have had tragic or comic experiences with actual flesh-and-blood women. He is celebrating the passion of love, expressing the women or goddesses of his imagination. Mary, Mabel and Jane may have existed; there may have been a dark lady behind Shakespeare's sonnets. But the real Mary, Mabel, the real dark lady are in the brain of the poet.

The most popular of the elegiac poets, certainly the best known in modern times, is Ovid. He wrote: "Tibullus was the successor of Gallus, Propertius the successor of Tibullus, and I myself was fourth in point of time."

He was an aristocrat, a member of the brilliant society that surrounded the imperial court, until for some reason that is not clear he incurred the displeasure of his royal master and was banished from Rome. It is possible that the emperor punished the poet for his *Art of Love,* but it is somewhat doubtful whether that amusing and delightful poem, though it is not a book for a Sunday-school library, could have shocked the cynical and maturely intelligent world of which Ovid was a product and an interpreter. The *Art of Love* is an honest book, hard and glittering, lacking in most of the spiritual and romantic aspects of love and therefore not likely to appeal to the weak and the innocent. Professional men of letters have always liked Ovid for his sincerity, his vivacity, his imagination. His imagination is at its best in the *Metamorphoses* in which he put together many of the Greek and Græco-Roman myths. This was the great source-book of ancient legend for modern poets, the Italians of the Renaissance, Shakespeare and his contemporaries, and English poets of the eighteenth and nineteenth centuries. If he could have foreseen his posthumous importance he might have been less bitter in his exile. Perhaps Ovid never wrote a stunningly great line; better Latinists than I seem to have failed to find one; but he was a born story-teller and a poet of really extraordinary facility. His work as a whole had an incalculable influence on the literature of modern countries, unsurpassed even by the influence of Virgil. The English poets from Marlowe to Dryden—and later—are full of Ovid, not only because he told the traditional tales of antiquity so clearly (other poets had made those tales familiar), but because in his *Art of Love* he handled a somewhat forbidden subject not like a moralist but like a scholar, a poet, and a gentleman.

After the Augustan period (let us omit exact dates and think of the period as about the beginning of the Christian era), Latin poetry goes from good to mediocre and then from mediocre to stupid. But the process is not continuous cr in any way logical. Literature does not move in curves that we can plot on engineers' or geographers' paper. Neither does life, which is the stuff of literature. Latin poetry declined, but the decline, like that of the empire itself, extended through several centuries in which there were genuine if not great poets.

Among the poets of the first Christian century is Seneca's nephew, Lucan, a brilliant young orator whose *Pharsalia,* a chronicle in verse, was much read in its time and throughout the Middle Ages, who through his effect on Corneille had a lasting influence on French classic poetry, and who is of especial interest to English readers because Marlowe made a brilliant translation of the first book of *Pharsalia.* An important figure in this century was Statius, a voluminous epic poet, who was by many considered superior to Virgil, and whose *Thebaid* was so highly valued by the English poets, Pope and Gray, that they translated some passages, which have a mild elegance, but seem to lack the divine fire.

There are two poets of the Silver Age, the first century of the Christian era, who in their kind are not decadent from previous poetry but are supreme masters; they are the satirists, Martial and Juvenal. The Roman mind was at home in the satiric mood and indeed invented the type of poetry which conveys that mood. Horace had given a fine literary quality to satiric verse, but satire was only one side of his genius, and his satire became urbane and gentle. Martial and Juvenal, especially Juvenal, hit harder, and the corruption and scandals of the times gave them plenty of material. All times and all places afford abundant material to the satirist, but satire is a very nice art which not all poets possess. The English have it in high degree. The Elizabethan and Jacobean poets wrought it into a terrific broadsword. Dryden put a finer point on it, and Pope made it a flexible rapier. All this English satiric verse owes something directly or indirectly to the Romans, and more to Juvenal than to any other Latin.

Martial's *Epigrams,* though of very uneven quality, have one invariable merit; they draw Roman life as he views it, its gross faults seen and set down sincerely and faithfully; and the form, even when it is crude, is compact and expressive. Ever since his time the true epigram has borne the stamp of his genius. Juvenal, a man of more bitter nature than Martial, is like the older satirist in his relentless realism, in his hatred of sham and hypocrisy, of tyranny and assumed superiority. He says of his work: "Indignation makes the verse." His real or alleged coarseness is simply the coarseness of life, for which the honest man who holds up the mirror is not responsible. In his mastery of words, his power to suggest, to carry the concrete image to the second and third degree of allusiveness, Juvenal has no superior. Dryden translated five of Juvenal's *Satires,* and his hack assistants did others. Dr. Johnson's two imitations are probably true to the spirit of Juvenal; for Johnson was a great scholar, though he was not a born writer of verse.

We cannot follow the course of Latin poetry into the dusk of the Middle Ages. That it faded gracefully can be seen in the Latin Anthology, which is not, like the Greek Anthology, a natural growth edited by native poets but is a collection made by a modern scholar of poems found in earlier collections or in the works of individual poets from Ennius to the year 1000 A.D. One of the loveliest poems in the collection is the *Vigil of Venus,* a song for the spring festival of Venus the Mother. The author is unknown, and the date of composition can only be conjectured. All we know is that the festival for which it was written expresses the finer aspects of the Roman imagination, which borrowed from the Greek, and that the author was a true singer. It is a beautiful note on which to take leave of the Roman poets. Latin poetry died. Latin prose lived on as an active language for many centuries.

CHAPTER XIII

LATIN PROSE

What is base never is expedient, not even when you obtain what you think to be useful.

—Cicero's *Offices.*

N the first half of the century before Christ there lived and wrote and spoke a man who was in his time and for centuries after the dominant figure in Latin prose—Cicero. He was politician, historian, orator, philosopher, critic, moralist, advocate. And he was more than all that; he made the standard Latin prose of the sixteen or more centuries that followed him. Good Latin after him was Ciceronian, though, to be sure, much of the Latin of medieval churchmen and philosophers was far away from the elegant classic Roman. There is no other man, so far as I know, in all literature whose individual style imposed itself on almost every writer who ventured to use his language for artistic effect. When he was killed by one of the brutal flukes of Roman politics his head was cut off. The wife of Mark Antony thrust a hairpin through the tongue. But that tongue continued to speak for hundreds of years.

Because Cicero is so rich in quotations and allusions he is he source of much of our knowledge of the literature that preceded him. For example, the finest passages of Ennius that are preserved to us we owe to Cicero who quoted them as passages of poetic power. His philosophy, which is Academic, with a strong leaning toward the Stoic on its ethical side, is highly moral and so made him acceptable to Christian writers, including St. Jerome and St. Augustine. And he was the model of eloquence and elegance for many writers of English down through the eighteenth century. So that we all have a touch of Cicero in us, whether we know it or not. It has been held against him that he was not a deeply original man, that he was derivative, a plagiarist, and a mere phrase maker; and it is true that many of the political and legal issues which were the occasions of his speeches are deader than those which awakened sonorous echoes in the halls of Congress last year. Who of us that has labored over the famous oration against Catiline did not grow weary both of the conspirator and the orator? Nevertheless, if Cicero was a phrase maker, he was a skillful one; and that after all is what literature is, phrase-making, whether the impulse behind the phrase be shallow or profound. He was a great letter-writer, and his familiar epistles not only are pleasant to read but give valuable intimate details of the life of his times. They are the immediate inspiration of the letters of the younger Pliny, which are invaluable little essays on life and nature; and all the best letter-writers in English in the eighteenth century, when letter-writing was a fine art, were in some measure pupils of Cicero.

After Cicero, and in spite of his influence, Latin prose is said to have degenerated. But there are some lovely colors in the twilight of the classics. The *Satiræ* of Petronius, who was a friend of the emperor Nero, is very amusing and is important as a picture of Roman life. In the fragment which has survived we have the only thing in Latin literature which resembles a modern novel. It is a laughing and honest picture of society, or of one section of it. As that society was dissolute and gross, the picture is not altogether edifying. A recent English translation of it caused a flutter among the timidly moral. But Professor Mackail of Oxford, a sound authority on Latin and English literature, justly compares Petronius to Shakespeare and Fielding. And let us reiterate one principle on which this brief survey of literature is based—namely, that any intelligent person can read anything ever put on paper without the slightest moral damage. And unintelligent humorless people are safe because they will not read literature or will not understand what they try to read.

CICERO

Petronius approximates the novel of manners and customs, that is, of daily life, what in our time is called realism. A century later appeared the *Golden Ass* of Apuleius, which contains the story of Cupid and Psyche, a most charming romance. If that story were used as a school text-book instead of the works of the great Cæsar and Cicero and the intolerably dull fellow, Nepos, we should all have grown up with a greater affection for Latin. As it is, we depend for our translated knowledge of Latin upon modern writers. The story of Cupid and Psyche lives for us in William Morris's

Earthly Paradise, and the *Golden Ass* is the source of episodes in *Don Quixote, Gil Blas,* and the *Decameron.*

The joyous and fanciful creation of Apuleius is a bright island in a rather dull river. For Latin became the official language of schoolmen and churchmen, some of whom were men of genius, but whose ideas were expository, religious, and philosophical, not artistic.

Many writers are important in history, in philosophy, in religion, who are not literary artists; and many writers who are rogues and rascals and do not care which way the old world turns are simply born artists with the magic gift of words. A man who was not a great artist but who did almost as much as Cicero to establish classic literary Latin was Quintilian, a critic and rhetorician whose book on oratory tells us more about Latin literature than any other work by a Roman. He was almost the only successful teacher in the world who, after twenty years of practical experience, wrote a book on education. In an age of competition when there were no university professorships to keep a studious man in a high seat Quintilian by sheer merit held his place at the head of his profession. In spirit he resembles, though he does not equal, Aristotle. For let us understand this clearly, though it is one of those odious comparisons and dubious generalities of which we should be wary: the Latin mind was in most departments of thought inferior to the Greek.

A product of the Ciceronian tradition as fostered by Quintilian is the correspondence of the younger Pliny, a friend and avowed follower of Tacitus and a favorite of the Emperor Trajan. His uncle, Pliny the Elder, a distinguished naturalist and man of affairs, gave him every advantage of education and social position and helped to make him a pedant and prig

His letters are important for the light they throw on the social and political life of the times. But from the point of view of literary art their value is not first rate.

As the Christian church conquered Rome, Rome with its language conquered the Church. Latin is to this day the language of the Catholic Church, and for many centuries, when many languages were being developed, Latin was the mother tongue of wisdom, the first thing which an educated man was supposed to know and *did know*.

Latin persisted because Rome was the world and because Rome became Christian. All learned works for more than a thousand years, works devotional and works secular, were written in Latin. And though Christian Latin probably lost some of the elegance of classic Latin, there were masterpieces written long after the end of old Rome. For a few illustrious examples: St. Augustine's *Confessions* and *City of God* in the fourth and fifth centuries; and about the same time St. Jerome's Latin (Vulgate) version of the Bible; in the thirteenth century the philosophic and theological books of St. Thomas Aquinas, which are the work of a profound mind and became the standard philosophy of the Roman Church. And learning was not confined to monks and priests. A secular philosopher like Spinoza wrote Latin as a matter of course.

In our day a man may be very highly cultivated and not be able to "construe" a sentence from Cicero or Virgil. As a formal literary exercise the classics, Greek and Latin, are on the wane. But Latin got into our blood in spite of ourselves. For it is incorporated in almost every modern western European language—the romance languages, French, Italian, Spanish, and that magnificent eclectic thief which we try to speak and write, English. French is modern Latin preserving much of the form and spirit of the ancient language. English is to some extent Germanic in form and part of its vocabulary is Germanic but a rich part is Latin. The advice, often repeated, to use "good strong Anglo-Saxon words" is utter nonsense. Most of the common roots of speech (those that relate to physical processes that we share with the animals) are Anglo-Saxon, but the moment we leave them for human relations, that is, civilized life, the words necessarily become Latin. We walk, start, stop, breathe, sleep, wake, talk, live and die—all Anglo-Saxon; but advance, retreat, approach and retire, inspire and animate, confer and discuss, compare, refute, debate, perish or survive, to say nothing of the vocabularies of business, commerce, finance as well as of government, diplomacy, and the professions, are Latin. We can no more get along without words of Latin origin than we can live without a head on our shoulders. It is true that English has been effectively, even beautifully, used by writers who have not studied Latin. But it is also true that most of the great modern writers have had at least a schoolboy's acquaintance with the classics, a little knowledge of Greek and Latin meanings, of the root-sense of words. No doubt much of the old-fashioned schoolroom drill in the classics was dry and fruitless, and there were many unimaginative pedants who could read Latin verse at sight and yet never learned to think clearly or to write their own language skillfully. Nevertheless, those who are trying to banish from the schools even the poor smattering of Latin that the ordinary pupil can get are rendering no service to education. Macaulay defined the true scholar as a man who reads Plato with his feet on the fender. This defines not only the scholar but the lover of literature who reads for pleasure; and the sense of pleasure, not the solemn obligation of self-improvement, is the real motive for reading. Whether or not

Macaulay's ideal scholar exists in this world, there is still an audience to whom the classics speak in translation. Let us not call Latin a dead language; it has a double immortality, in its modern linguistic children and in its imperishable patrician self. Rome is still the eternal city.

PART II
THE MIDDLE AGES

CHAPTER XIV

GERMANIC, CELTIC AND ROMANCE ORIGINS

There is no more interesting or important revolution than that by which the language of the people in the various European countries gradually pushed aside the ancient tongue and took its place, so that even scholars scarcely ever think now of writing books in Latin.

—*James Harvey Robinson.*

THE Eternal City, its language, literature, and religion dominated much of Europe down to recent times. In the Middle Ages the Empire of the Cæsars was reconstructed on a German basis in the Holy Roman Empire, which as Voltaire wittily but not quite accurately said, was neither holy, Roman, nor an empire. The Pope at Rome was often the unifying personality as head of the universal Church, who presided not only over the spiritual life but over the temporal affairs of the many countries and principalities of Europe; and at least one great and strong man, Hildebrand, Pope Gregory VII, was a supreme monarch with kings under his thumb.

So that Europe did not quite cease to be Roman through those long centuries which we call the Middle Ages, or the Dark Ages. What were the Middle Ages? In conventional history the period is about a thousand years from the middle

of the fifth century to the middle of the fifteenth. The men
of the Renaissance, the humanists who rediscovered the
classics, felt in their enthusiasm that they belonged intellectually with the Greeks and the Romans, and that everything
between themselves and the ancient world was "middle" and
most of it was dark. But they were not sound historians, they
did not understand the centuries that immediately preceded
them, and the suggestion of contempt which they put into the
word "medieval" and which still persists betrays a profound misunderstanding of the story of European civilization.

There were dark streaks in those ten centuries, and the
period was middle in a sense. But there were flashes of great
brilliancy and there was a continuous subdued light which
never expired. The vitality, joy, artistic enthusiasm of the
Middle Ages was triumphant over ignorance, superstition,
incessant warfare, and hard physical conditions. Moreover,
we must remember that human thought, human life, is not an
interrupted process but an unbroken progress for better or
for worse. No part of the intellect of mankind came definitely
to an end or underwent a sudden change when in the fifth
century Odovaker, the German, deposed the last Roman emperor and became ruler of Italy. We do not know by the
clock when the Renaissance began to glow over the horizon.
History does not divide into clean-edged sections; all periods
are indistinct and blurred on the margins. The fourth century flows into the fifth, the fifteenth into the sixteenth. And
let us remember also that the racial, linguistic and geographical sections of human activity and thought are not sharply
divided, that no people, or nation or province in Europe developed alone independent of its neighbors.

The supreme artistic genius of the Middle Ages is expressed
not in literature, which is the special subject of our study, but

in architecture and the allied arts. The Gothic cathedrals, if they do not dwarf the modern man at least rebuke his arrogance when he takes a condescending attitude toward his medieval ancestors.

Of medieval literature the richest part from an artistic point of view is the poetry, epic, romantic, lyric. The prose is of incalculable importance for history, for philosophy, for theology. But our medieval ancestors sang and spun their yarns in various metrical forms. Even works of information they put into crude verse. Up to the thirteenth century the Germans never thought of prose as an artistic medium. And in England there is little good prose until after Chaucer; the spoken language was long in developing a literary standard.

The main divisions of medieval literature in respect of race and language are German (including Scandinavian and English), Celtic, French, Spanish, Italian. These literatures borrowed from each other, and a fair account of their interdependence would require a long course of study in comparative literature. It is enough to note the very important fact that in the "dark" ages when the petty states were constantly at war and peaceful communication was tediously slow, ideas flowed to and fro over Europe and little streams starting in obscure corners swelled into main currents. As we do not know in many cases which of the various forms of a story is oldest in germ or in full development, we may approach this voluminous body of medieval literature at will from any of the main literary divisions of Europe.

First a word about the characteristics common to all these divisions. Most of the romances, epics, legends, ballads deal with the exploits of knights in battle and in love. They fall into groups or cycles clustered about some real or fictitious king, Alexander the Great, Cæsar, or Charlemagne, or Arthur.

The adventures resemble and repeat each other, encounters with dragons, the rescue of distressed damsels, the defense of innocence and the punishment of evil-doing. The mythological machinery is a mixture of pagan and Christian. The ideal knight of romance is a Christian, as indeed was the flesh-and-blood knight who fought for his lord and went on crusades to the Holy Land. The social and ethical code was that of chivalry, which to some extent actually existed and for the rest was a poetic dream. The ideal and practice of chivalry flourished well into the Renaissance and are exemplified by the Frenchman, Bayard, the good knight without fear and without reproach, and by the Englishman, Sir Philip Sidney. In the stories some of the adventures are rather "tall," and Cervantes in *Don Quixote* ridiculed them with immortal laughter. The Spanish romances like the very popular *Amadis of Gaul,* Spanish in treatment though probably French in origin, were especially extravagant, and we can rejoice in their absurdity—and read Cervantes.

The Latin sources of medieval romance consisted of broken down and distorted versions of the classic legends. Only a few priests and scholars knew the classics, and their knowledge was imperfect. A whole cycle of stories grew up about Æneas and Dido and the rest ("matter of Troy"), which would have puzzled Homer and Virgil. Ovid, a good story-teller as we have seen, and an expert in the art of love, was a sort of handbook authority for the elaborate courtly love which was one of the pastimes of gentlemen and ladies. Alexander the Great became a demi-god and a feudal king whom the most admiring Greek would not have recognized.

The Celtic contribution to medieval romance is of two sorts: First there are the great poetic stories in verse and prose which are part of the literatures of Ireland, of Scotland, of

Wales. These stories exerted some influence on the later romantic literature of the continent but not much on the early literature; they are known to English readers in modern translations such as Macpherson's alleged Highland Scots *Ossian* and Lady Guest's Welsh *Mabinogian* and the more recent work of the leaders of the Celtic revival. The Celtic literature contained an immense body of poetry and romance which was for centuries shut off from the rest of Europe.

The other Celtic contribution, early and radical, is the "matter of Brittany," the source of many French romances, principally the Arthurian cycle. The French province of Bretagne in northwestern France is just across the channel from England. A part of the English (or British) coast, Cornwall and Wales, is still Celtic, and long ago it was all Celtic. After the Saxon invasion many of the original British fled across the channel. They became French in customs and language but they retained many of their Celtic stories which go far back of any written record. Now one of two things happened (it makes little difference which) : either these Celts in the north of France gave the stories to French writers, or the Celts who stayed in England gave the stories to Norman-English writers who took them over to France. However that may be, the whole group of stories associated with the name of Arthur is French in its first extant literary form. Whether Arthur was a real king or a creature of legend we do not know. If he was a real man he was a Celtic king, an enemy of the English. That he is represented as a great conqueror extending his conquests as far as Rome is due to the influence on the Arthurian legend of the legends of Alexander and Charlemagne.

The stories of Arthur and his Table Round went back across the channel to England in French and in translation from the

French. The earliest mention of Arthur in English is in a poetic chronicle of the thirteenth century, the *Brut* of Layamon, which was based on a French versified chronicle by a Norman poet of Jersey named Wace; this, in turn, derived from a Latin chronicle by Geoffrey of Monmouth which purports to be a history of the British. If Layamon contains more fancy than fact, so much the better for literature; here we find not only Arthur and the wizard Merlin but the germ of the plot of Shakespeare's *King Lear*.

The Arthurian story after many developments in French comes into English literature with a great variety of episodes and in a style which we can read with pleasure in *Le Morte d'Arthur* compiled from French romances by Sir Thomas Malory in the second half of the fifteenth century. There had been several English metrical romances dealing with the adventures of the great knights, Lancelot, Launfal, or Gawain, but Malory's work is *the* Arthurian story for English readers and is the source and inspiration of the many versions which modern English poets have essayed. The most popular version of the Arthurian tales in modern English poetry is Tennyson's *Idylls of the King*. Tennyson makes Arthur a very English king, almost suggesting a silk hat instead of the iron helmet and missing a good deal of the Celtic and fairy flavor of the older stories. Nevertheless, despite a tendency in recent criticism to underrate Tennyson and for all the objections raised by Swinburne, who had drunk deeper than Tennyson of the waters of the Middle Ages, the *Idylls* contains superb passages and is a masterpiece of English poetry.

The stories grouped round the name of Arthur are many, some overlapping the others, some taken from legends not originally associated with Arthur. First there is the story which chiefly concerns him, his marriage to Queen Guinevere,

PARZIFAL

her infidelity, her love of Lancelot, the downfall of the court
and Arthur's death at the hands of the sinister Mordred.

The second and most poetic is the story of the Holy Grail,
an interesting example of the fusion of Christian legend with
stories which in their earliest form could have had no contact
with Christianity and some of which perhaps antedate the
Christian era. The Grail is the vessel in which the blood of

Christ was preserved; it is the symbol of perfection, and only the knight of Christ-like purity is permitted to look upon it. Lancelot's virtue is stained and he fails. According to different versions the successful heroes are Gawain, Galahad and Perceval. Perceval is the pure knight in the French and German forms of the story; he is the Parzifal of Wagner's opera.

The third great story associated with the Arthurian legend, but an independent tale complete in itself, is that of Tristan and Iseult. This story is evidently Celtic in character and setting, for Iseult is an Irish princess and King Mark who sends Tristan to bring her to his court is king of Cornwall. The story was one of the most popular of medieval romances and was known in almost every part of Europe. Readers of French will find the story exquisitely retold by Joseph Bédier in *Tristan and Iseult.* Swinburne's *Tristan of Lyonesse* is glowing and melodious. In Wagner's opera the story is set to the most gorgeous love music ever written.

A knightly hero who rivals Lancelot in popular legend is Gawain, who though associated with Arthur is himself the center of a group of romances, and in the earlier stories is more important than Arthur. One of the best of the English stories, which is beyond question ultimately Celtic (probably Welsh) and has no known French original is *Gawain and the Green Knight,* a lively tale, swifter than the usual leisurely medieval pace, and an excellent example of early English alliterative verse.

It must not be thought that all medieval English literature owes its substance and inspiration to Celtic and French. It had a strong Germanic side which came from its Saxon parentage. The English Saxon was, however, much less imaginative than his Celtic and French neighbors and lagged behind them in the arts. His language as a literary vehicle had a hard struggle to survive in a world where scholars spoke Latin and gentlemen spoke French. It did survive, however, and the beat, the pulsation, the accent, the tone, the feeling of English verse is Germanic to this day, though the prosody of the ancient verse is quite different from that of modern English. Anglo-Saxon as a distinct language disappeared, and we read it as a foreign tongue, as foreign as its kinsmen, Dutch and German. Its literature, as much as has come down to us, is not rich but deserves to be remembered.

The longest, best sustained example of Anglo-Saxon poetry is *Beowulf,* an heroic tale, much below epic proportions, and of about the same stuff intellectually as hundreds of knightly adventures found in the legends of all countries. It must have been composed after the German invasion of Britain under Hengist and Horsa in the fifth century and before the year 1000, which is the date usually assigned to the oldest extant manuscript (in the British Museum). Though the language is Anglo-Saxon, the hero and the scenes are Scandinavian and German, which indicates that there was probably a continental original, perhaps a recited tale of great age before it was committed to writing. Some of the episodes are like those in the Icelandic saga *Grettir the Strong* (of the Icelandic literature we shall say a word presently). Beowulf is a mighty warrior of course. He goes to the defense of a neighboring king whose royal hall is attacked by a terrible monster. Beowulf kills the monster and the monster's mother and later kills a dragon, whose fiery breath and venomous teeth cause the hero's death. We have here good fairy-tale stuff, perhaps the oldest specimen of its kind in all extant European literature. It is not a masterpiece, but its intrinsic value is genuine. There are several translations of it into modern English. William

Morris, always in love with things ancient and medieval, made a vigorous version. One of the best is by the American poet and scholar, William Ellery Leonard.

There are other anonymous Anglo-Saxon poems, *Widsith* and *Deor,* which are important to the literary historian as indicating, if nothing else, the extent of Anglo-Saxon literature, much of which must have been lost. One short poem of real beauty is the *Seafarer,* the first, in existence, of that great line of English poems of the sea which is not yet extinct with John Masefield.

Two religious poets are Cædmon and Cynewulf. We are not sure just what they wrote or when they lived. But Cædmon, apparently in the eighth century, made versified paraphrases of Genesis and Exodus. It has been suggested that a passage in Cædmon's Genesis was known to Milton; and a story of Cædmon is worth telling because it gives a bit of the color and feeling of the time and because it introduces that noble old Saxon, the venerable Bede, who belongs to English literature only because King Alfred translated his *Ecclesiastical History.* The story is that Cædmon, a servant of a monastery, had to leave a festive gathering because he could not sing and play the harp as it was passed round. In his sleep a stranger appeared and bade him sing the beginning of created things, and there came to his lips verses that he had never heard.

Cynewulf is pretty certainly the author of three of the sacred poems grouped as *Christ,* for he wrote his name into them by an acrostic device. And he was probably author of four Lives of Saints which have passages of considerable dramatic and narrative power. Poetry has always been the handmaiden of religion. Cynewulf holds a high place artistically and spiritually in a long tradition of religious verse, and in him (it does not always happen to the most pious religious poets) the singer drew real poetic inspiration from his faith.

The first to commit our grandmother tongue to writing and give it literary form were poets, perhaps because poetry is a fitter vehicle than prose for high themes and perhaps because prose, the language of reason, develops later than poetry, the language of emotion. There was, however, a considerable body of Anglo-Saxon prose, among the most interesting of which is the work of Alfred the Great, who ruled beneficently in the last third of the ninth century and tried to educate his people not only in the law but in the arts and philosophy. He translated from the late Roman philosopher Boethius and perhaps had a hand in the *Chronicle,* which is the most important prose document in Anglo-Saxon and the source of much of our information about England from the middle of the eighth century to the middle of the ninth. The book, valuable both to history and to literature, has been translated into modern English.

Anglo-Saxon, "Englisc," decayed as a distinct language about the time of the Norman conquest, but not wholly on account of that conquest; and it was more than a century before Middle English took shape. In that middle period the twelfth, thirteenth and fourteenth centuries, prose is still laggard and what remains for literature is the poetry, the metrical romances and some other poems more indigenously English and less indebted to Celtic and French sources. Two of quite different nature are worth remembering—and worth reading: *The Pearl,* a poem on the death of a young girl, which has real pathos and beauty; and a swinging narrative, *Havelock the Dane,* which is, perhaps, as the title suggests, of Scandinavian origin. By the time that Middle English develops into the language which is instantly recognizable as ours, though still somewhat archaic, the Italian Renaissance has arrived, and it is dawning in England in the superb poetry of Chaucer.

Now let us cross the channel to England's great neighbors, France, Spain, and the German states.

CHAPTER XV
MEDIEVAL FRENCH LITERATURE

Herein may be seen noble chivalry, courtesy, humanity, friendliness, hardiness, love, cowardice, murder, hate, virtue, and sin. Do after the good and leave the evil.

—*Caxton*: Preface to Malory's *Le Morte d'Arthur*.

MEDIEVAL France was divided in language and literature (as in geography and politics) by a line drawn east and west below the middle of what is now modern France. The southern part was less than the northern in area—and less in literature. For the literature of the north prevailed, and the language and literature of the south declined and exist today in the work of a society of poets who preserve and cultivate Provençal as an act of patriotic devotion. The best known of the modern Provençal poets is Frédéric Mistral. In the Middle Ages this southern literature, Provençal, flourished prodigally and during the twelfth, thirteenth and fourteenth centuries that sunny land, with its Spanish neighbors to the west and its Italian neighbors to the east, had the most colorful and charming civilization in Europe.

The poets were the troubadours, so called from the word

that means to find or to invent (the French word *trouver* and the second part of our word "treasure-trove"). The troubadour was not in the great period of his art a wandering minstrel in grand-opera costume, strumming a guitar, but a gentleman, knight, noble, even king, who cultivated verse and music as elegant accomplishments. The rank of troubadour was jealously exclusive; only one who had proved his talent as a composer was admitted; but it was democratic in that a man of low social degree could win the coveted title. Noblemen who were not poets themselves patronized the arts of verse and song, kept troubadours in their courts and entertained troubadours from other courts. Besides the troubadours there were the *joglars* (in French *jouglers;* it is our word "juggler") who were professional entertainers, not as a rule creative poets, but skilled in song and in the recitation of ballads and romances.

The theme of the troubadours was lyric love. The songs, many of which have been preserved, are sometimes simple and touching and close to the natural song of the people, sometimes highly elaborate and sophisticated, the poets vying with each other in inventing new verse forms and giving original turns to the old forms. The troubadours were also the composers and preservers of the longer narrative poems, and to them is due in large measure the wide dissemination over Europe of the great cycles of romances. We have the names and some biographical knowledge of more than a hundred Provençal troubadours. The art depended on the prosperity of feudal courts. When in the thirteenth century the nobles of the south were ruined by war, the poetry of the troubadours waned and flickered out in northern Spain and Italy.

A more lasting and continuous life was granted the poetry (and prose) of the north of France; for that is the French literature which dominated Europe for centuries and which has an unbroken tradition for more than a thousand years down to the latest lyric by a young French poet. The northern counterpart of the Provençal troubadour was the *trouvère,* who early developed a more professional and less amateurish attitude toward his art than his southern brother, and who— this is most important from a literary point of view—was more interested in narrative, in story, in life, than in music. The result was that while the south remained for centuries the land of song the north became the land of narrative romance, though the French lyric blossomed early and never died, and the Provençal singers made excellent narratives.

The first French poetry to come to vigorous fulfillment is the *chanson de geste.* The words mean "song of deed (or ad- venture)", and the subject is the exploits of some knight or royal hero; it is epic in spirit and substance, often intensely national and patriotic in feeling, the true *chanson* dealing with French history ("matter of France"). Other stories are cen- tered about vague giants of the past like Alexander the Great and the mythical heroes of Homer and Virgil ("matter of Rome"). Others deal with Arthur and his knights ("matter of Brittain"). These *chansons* and metrical romances in verse and later in prose, which fill huge volumes, satisfy or partly satisfy the natural hunger of people for stories, exactly the same hunger that is fed today by thousands of novels (that is, something *new*) and millions of magazines. Much of this medieval yarn spinning is to us rather tedious, and unless we are scholars to whom every old scrap of paper is precious we are willing to forget most of it or never look at it. There are, however, a few masterpieces in the hundred *chansons* that we possess. One is the *Chanson de Roland.* Roland was a real historic person, a knight of Charlemagne, killed in the retreat

through the Pyrenees after Charles's army had been defeated
in Spain. Roland, the impetuous soldier, refuses, until he and
his followers are hopelessly overcome, to sound the horn which
shall summon Charlemagne to the rescue. Roland and his
cousin Oliver die together, and at the last (it is a pretty touch)

ROLAND AND FERRAGUS

Roland the pure throws down his gauntlet to God. The
chanson, with much other early French poetry, was not redis
covered until about a hundred years ago, since when it ha
been edited many times and translated into modern French an
English. The Roland story in countless versions persiste
through the Middle Ages and well into the Renaissance. U

was immensely popular in Italy and was the subject of Ariosto's masterpiece *Orlando*. It did not apparently take hold in England until the story had become weakened and prosaic. The great French-English cycle was not that of Charlemagne, but as we have briefly glimpsed in the preceding chapter, the Arthurian legend.

Of early French poets who contributed true genius to this collection of stories two are important, Marie de France and Chrétien de Troyes. Marie de France lived most of her life in England, a dependent perhaps at the court of Henry II, where the culture was French and the queen Eleanor was a Provençal princess. In the *lais* of Marie we meet Tristan and Launfal, in a rather short form and with the spirit and flavor of a fairy-tale. She was a true poet, perhaps naïvely unconscious of how finely she was telling her tales. Perhaps, on the other hand, she knew her business with a very grown-up and professional wisdom; modern scholars incline to the opinion that early poets were not really early but had a very rich background and centuries of forerunners which they felt and knew with a vitality which modern investigation cannot recover. There are translations and paraphrases of the *lais* of Marie. For English readers interesting free versions of some of the *lais* are those of the nineteenth century poet Arthur O'Shaunessey.

A poet of great individual merit and of first importance in the long development of the Arthurian story is Chrétien de Troyes, who lived at the court of Champagne in the second half of the twelfth century. His *Knight of the Lion* (Iwain), *Eric and Enid,* the *Knight of the Cart* (charette), one of the Lancelot stories, *Tristan,* and *Percivale,* are the flower of early French narrative poetry and the foundation of the later prose romances which we find in Malory's translation. Chrétien also had a great influence on German literature, as we shall see in the next chapter.

Besides the romances relating to Arthur and other heroes there are three kinds of poetry in which are specimens—amid much waste—of fine imaginative talent. One is the fabliau, or fable, a beast-tale, such as has never ceased to be popular from Æsop to the last bunny story with which we read our modern baby to sleep. A loosely related collection of these animal tales is the Romance of Reynard the Fox. A good English example of a Reynard story is Chaucer's *Nonne Preestes Tale,* where the fox is not as usual ingeniously and wittily triumphant, but loses his game as in Æsop's fable. The great fable-maker of later French literature is La Fontaine, who draws not from his French ancestors of the Middle Ages (who were indeed not rediscovered until the nineteenth century) but from classic sources and from his own keen satiric imagination. The old fabliaux are simple animal tales not intended as a portrait of society but with some humorous lights on human character like the tales of our own Uncle Remus.

Another type of poem is the allegorical, moralistic, or didactic, in which the characters are abstract virtues and vices, Love, Hate, Envy, and so on. The great example is *The Romance of the Rose,* a long poem the general theme of which is the art of love, gallantry with a refreshing breeze of satire. The people of the Middle Ages, for all their sober chivalry and social rules and magnificent gestures, liked to laugh. *The Romance of the Rose* is in its seriousness and solemnity, its humor and its honest portrayal of the times a work of first importance. It is probably the only unified poem written by two poets not in collaboration but in succession. The earlier part was written by William of Lorris in the first half of the thirteenth century, the second part two generations later by Jean de Meung. He was a poet of real power, and the subject, which is much more than love, sums up most of the social thoughts of the Middle Ages. And Jean de Meung looks ahead. One of the wisest of French critics, Professor Lanson, says that the work of this poet expresses what is to germinate and grow, it contains the future. For it is life, the life of the people. A fragment of *The Romance of the Rose* was translated by Chaucer; but scholars doubt the authenticity of other parts of the translation ascribed to him. The poem struck and held for three centuries the fancy of the Middle Ages and is a revelation of many aspects of the medieval mind and of universal humanity. Of its historical importance there is no doubt. As for the pleasure it affords—that is another question. The modern reader does not relish as keenly as did his medieval ancestor a long moral allegory even when it is enlivened by humor or when it is supremely poetic as in a greater example, Spenser's *Faërie Queene*.

A third important division of medieval poetry is the lyric which flourished in great abundance and variety. The writers, most of whom are unknown though the names of a surprisingly large number have come down to us, belonged to all grades of society. There was the scholar who mixed his melody with learning and helped to give dignity and form to the literary language. There was the nobleman who patronized the art and practiced it himself. In those days even the kings were singers; among the royal bards was Thibault IV of Champagne, and with him we may remember several other monarchs who had the gift of song, Richard I of England (the "Lion-Hearted") and James I of Scotland, and Alfonso X of Spain ("The Learned"). More prolific than the poetic aristocrats and not less skillful were the common people whose popular songs (*chansons populaires*) are close to life, as are the folk songs of all countries, and express the elementary emotions, grave and gay, frivolous and passionate.

A great book of the fourteenth century which may fitly be grouped with the romances of chivalry is Froissart's *Chronicles,* for this work, which is the history of "France, England, Scotland and Spain" for almost the whole of the century, is more exciting than romance; it is a great portrait of the times. Froissart was a tireless traveler, who looked at the world with unfailing curiosity and recorded what he learned from others and what he saw himself. The vivacity and freshness of his style and the self-evident honesty of his substance make him one of the important historians (Thomas Gray called him "the Herodotus of a barbarous age") and also a master of the art of narrative. The chronicle became part of English literature early in the sixteenth century through the translation of Lord Berners. Froissart was a minor poet of considerable skill. But his century was an age of prose, and not until the next century did the French lyre make magic sounds. The influence of Froissart on French prose made for sanity and, though his details are disordered, for that clarity which for centuries was to be the great merit of French *prosateurs.*

Intimately related to the literature of medieval France, especially to the southern part, the Provençal, is the literature of Spain. The national heroic poem which corresponds to the French *Chanson de Roland* is the *Poem of the Cid.* The Cid was a real person, who fought mightily against the Moors. His name was Ruy Diaz de Bivar and his title Cid is the Spanish form of the Arabic word for lord. Like Roland and other half historical characters the Cid became the subject of legendary exploits. The wise Cervantes makes one of his characters say (the comment belongs to literature as much as to history and should be borne in mind as the true word for much medieval romance): "There is no doubt there was such a man as the Cid, but much doubt whether he did what is ascribed to him." The Cid was one of the great favorites in European literature outside Spain and is the subject of a tragic masterpiece by the French dramatist Corneille.

A medieval Spaniard of authentic record but of almost incredible achievement is the Castilian King Alfonso the Learned, of the thirteenth century, who fought the world with one hand and made literature with the other. He was intellectually monarch of all he surveyed, he gave shape to Castilian verse, wrote or supervised works on all the arts and sciences and welcomed to his court the artists and singers of France, especially the troubadours who were suffering from the political upheavals in Provence. The Spanish troubadours were never so thriving as those of France, for Spain was a poorer country. But they produced an enormous quantity of lyrics and ballads of all moods and all degrees of merit from doggerel to exquisite verse. The unmistakable rhythms of Spanish tunes found nowhere else in the world except in countries now or in former times under Spanish influence must go back to the Middle Ages and color Spanish lyric verse. Today Spain, the least modern of modern countries, preserves at least in outward show something of the medieval spirit. The Spain of the Renaissance will offer us a bright subject for a later chapter.

CHAPTER XVI

EARLY GERMAN AND SCANDINAVIAN LITERATURE

To us in ancient story wonders great are told
Of heroes rich in glory and of adventures bold.
—*The Nibelungen Lied.*

IN spite of many diversities of politics, race and language the European countries of the Middle Ages were not intellectually isolated one from another. Ideas passed between them not with telegraphic speed but with great rapidity if we take a long view of the time element in the history of thought. The artisans, really fine artists, who wrought the wood and stone of the cathedrals traveled all over Europe, to any city where a building was under construction. And priests and scholars who all spoke Latin were at home in any country. A literary ambassador was sure of courteous treatment wherever he went; politicians often met mysterious or violent deaths, but there are few recorded cases of foul play (though there were plenty of personal brawls) to men whose primary interest was poetry and who did not meddle in practical affairs. Not only did the upper classes foster the singer and give him shelter; the common people flocked to hear him and listened to his tales of war and chivalry and fairyland. No wonder that so many tried to qualify for the profession of *jongleur* when a dinner and a night's lodging could be bought for a song.

In no country was the poet more honored than in the German countries, especially the southern parts, Bavaria and Austria. Under the influence of the Provençal troubadours there grew up the tradition of the Minnesang (love song), courtly love with an elaborate code of etiquette. The German Minnesinger was more robust, sincere, less stagey than the Provençal. He took his art with high seriousness and developed in two centuries, the twelfth and thirteenth, a great body of lyric verse, much of it conventional, some of it the expression of true poetic genius, and the foundation, together with more naïve popular song, of the German *lied,* both melody and words, in which the Germans are supreme. The Minnesinger was usually a knight of the lower order, and the main theme of the Minnesang was adoration for a mistress so far above him socially as to be forever beyond his reach. Sometimes such a lady existed in the wife of the knight's lord; sometimes she was a creature of his fancy. The motive of the young lover and his chaste devotion to the unattainable queen runs through much medieval and Renaissance poetry. It was a great game, half theatrical, but often inspired by genuine passion and expressed in beautiful verses.

The greatest of the Minnesinger was Walther von der Vogelweide who excelled in the art of verse but, more important, broadened and deepened the lyric and gave it an emotional intensity which is strangely modern, which is not the courtier strumming to his lady but the poet uttering his heart. Modern poets value him greatly and feel that he is closer to us than most of his contemporaries. His poem *Unter der Linden* (which has nothing to do with a famous avenue in Berlin!) makes him an older brother of Heine. The lady of the lyric is not a dame of high degree but a simple girl of the people, and the pathos is sincere.

Early in the thirteenth century at the Thuringian court Walther von der Vogelweide met Wolfram von Eschenbach. It was the encounter of the two most vigorous and original poets in Germany. Wolfram was a Minnesinger. He was more than that, he was the poet who gave shape to the epic romance *Parzifal,* the finest version of the legend of the Holy Grail. The story came to him from France, a part from Chrétien de Troyes, a part from other French sources. Wolfram was a more robust poet than Chrétien, with a broader sense of narrative and dramatic values. He was sometimes crude and obscure partly because German as a narrative vehicle was less highly developed than as the vehicle of a "mouthful of song." Wolfram, like other poets who lived in their own world of romance, became a romantic figure in later romantic tradition and he has sung to millions who never read a line of his poetry in Wagner's *Tannhäuser* which shows the Minnesinger as competitive artists, not unlike the poets and dramatists of Greece who contended for the prize. That the historical Minnesinger Tannhäuser may have lived too late to have looked upon the not very venerable face of Wolfram makes no difference. In romance all time is true and standard, and in the veracious history of literature it is the spirit and not the calendar that counts.

A contemporary of Wolfram and Walther and forming with them a great triumvirate in German medieval verse, is Gottfried von Strassburg, who wrote the finest of the epic romance of Germany—or of Europe. His *Tristan* is based on French sources, but in strength of expression, unity of conception truth to human character (which is no more spoiled by the machinery of love potions and other superstitious devices than *Macbeth* is spoiled by witches) it is superior to anything known in French and is the standard version from which all later Tristan stories derived, including Wagner's opera. The relation of the Tristan story to the Arthurian cycle we have already touched on.

An epic cycle purely Germanic in source, development and final expression is the *Nibelungenlied,* the greatest monument of medieval German poetry. The poem in the Middle High * German form dates from the thirteenth century and is a compilation by an unknown poet, or perhaps more than one, of many heroic tales and myths more or less closely related. The sources can only be guessed at. It is safe to assume that the tales were told long before the age of written literature. The story or series of stories is familiar to the modern world outside Germany in the universal music drama of Wagner. It is of little moment whether Wagner reshaped the story to fit a nineteenth century symbolism peculiar to himself and his age. The essential stories are almost the same, with variations due to the individual story-teller and the accidents of long traditional recitals and repetitions. The central figures are Siegfried and Brunhild, demigod hero and goddess who is a very feminine queen. Siegfried is the Sigurd of a version of the story which comes from the Icelandic and the story of that story is a romance in itself.

The Norsemen, the Scandinavian cousins of the Germans

---

* "High" in this phrase has nothing to do with intellectual elevation. It is a simple matter of geography; the high dialects or, better, divisions of German, being those found in Southern or Central Germany. We have the phrase, or the converse of it, in "low" countries, the Netherlands, that is, countries down stream. "Middle" is also a matter of time, adopted more or less arbitrarily by scholars to indicate the period between "old" and "modern." We have something like the same use of the word in English; Middle English is somewhat between old English and modern and covers about three centuries.

and the English, made many voyages of discovery, conquest and piracy in the known and the unknown seas as far as America. In Normandy, Northern France, in Sicily and Southern Italy they left their blood but gave up their language (except a few traces) adopting the speech of the people they

SIEGFRIED

conquered. In Iceland, that lonely island where they had no people to overcome and where they were shut off from many of the turmoils of Europe they developed a civilization of dignity and beauty which fused with that of their Celtic neighbors of Ireland and Scotland and the western islands. From these Icelandic people we have inherited a literature obscure in its origins and related nobody knows just how to the literature of Germany but of unquestionably close kinship.

Our Viking ancestors were a mighty race of poets as well as warriors. We have but sparse records of the lives of their singers, but are fortunate in the songs. In the thirteenth century a poet and scholar named Snorri Sturlason made a collection of tales called the younger Edda. The word Edda has a fairy-tale flavor for it means great-grandmother, suggesting that the stories were told to children by the most original and garrulous of tale-tellers. The second Edda, called the elder, consists of many poems which even the Icelanders seem to have lost (unless they kept them as an oral tradition) until a learned bishop of the seventeenth century rediscovered them. Fragments of these poems came into English literature in the eighteenth century when Bishop Percy and Thomas Gray and others became interested in northern poetry. The full glory of the Icelandic story blazed in our language only fifty years ago when William Morris made his version of *The Story of Grettir the Strong* and *The Story of the Volsungs and the Nibelungs*. These *sagas* (the word means story) are the now familiar tales of Siegfried (Sigurd) and other heroes. We all know, as we know Cinderella and Jack the Giant Killer, how Siegfried welded the magic sword and killed the dragon and of the love of Brunhild and her sorrow and how she killed Siegfried. The Volsung saga may not be as Morris called it the "grandest tale that ever was told," but it is a grand tale, more vigorous perhaps in the Scandinavian than in the German which has the romantic color of the Middle Ages. Wagner's version which is available in not very poetic English translations is interesting aside from his colossal music. A critical interpretation by Bernard Shaw called *The Perfect Wagnerite* is suggestive and brilliant, but some of it might have surprised Wagner.

The *Nibelungenlied* is great in its own right and can stand as a magnificent monument of the genius of the old German people. But its eminence is due in part to the flatness of the surrounding country. Germany produced almost no literature of memorable value until the Reformation when we meet the meistersinger and the strange priest, poet, rebel and Puritan, Luther. The meistersinger were the direct heirs of the minnesinger. They were less spontaneous, more academic in the forms of their verse and in the rules of their organization, but they carried on the tradition of the German lyric, which has not yet ceased.

CHAPTER XVII

DANTE

The central man of all the world, as representing in perfect balance the imaginative, moral, and intellectual faculties, all at their highest, is Dante.

—Ruskin.

O period of history begins or ends in any certain year. Human life (and the literature that records it) flows along through shallows and rapids, with windings and subterranean disappearances. Chronological divisions are merely conveniences to mark approximately where we are in our course; they do not help us much in actual navigation but are only surveyors' stakes on the shore. The terms, "medieval" and "modern" are of no value unless we keep them flexible, and they crumble if we try to dam the stream of life at any given point. The use of "medieval" as a condescending term of reproach, implying that something before, "ancient," or something after, "modern," was necessarily finer is an utter misconception of human history. The supreme genius transcends all artificial sections of time, for he is universal; and why he is born at a particular moment in the stream of life has never been explained and never can be.

Dante was born in the thirteenth century and lived into the fourteenth. He was a few years in advance of the official dated "Renaissance," but he was a renaissance in himself. His native city was Florence, which in his time and for two or three centuries after him was a center of literary and artistic activity equaled only in the golden age of Athens. Dante, however, did not compose his masterpiece in Florence. For in the bitter political strife of the time he was on the losing side and was exiled from the city; he found refuge in the houses of wealthy patrons in several Italian cities, especially Verona and Ravenna.

The *Commedia,* commonly called, though not by Dante, the *Divine Comedy,* is a dream journey through Hell, Heaven, and Paradise. It is the one work in all literature which on a vast plan achieves perfection; in an account of it superlatives become mere positives. It cannot be classified as "epic" or grouped under any other known form, because there was nothing like it before and nothing written since is at all comparable to it. Dante made it, substance, form, and language; and though no man invents anything without drawing upon minds that have preceded his, the *Commedia* is the original creation of an individual intellect.

It is no inconsistency to say that Dante created his material and at the same time summed up all the wisdom of the world of his age. As he goes to "view the dead," he has all history and biography behind him, and he retells or suggests in wonderfully compact verses the stories of sinners of all degrees, of the almost good, and of the blessed. It is these stories which give the poem its extraordinary human interest, especially in Hell, for sinners have more dramatic careers than saints. Dante's treatment of sinners is puritanically severe, sometimes terrible; the torments of his under-world are both physical and spiritual. Yet the ruling emotion is not vindictive punishment but compassion. Dante relives the sufferings of the sinner and the ecstasies of the happy. The emotional power of single passages, for example, the famous fifth canto of Hell, the story of Paolo and Francesca, is unsurpassed in narrative poetry. And, more wonderful, this power is sustained throughout the poem and is involved in a rational plan, an allegory of the entire universe of humanity and God. The end of the dream pilgrimage is a vision of deity and the merging of the individual will in "the love which moves the sun and the other stars."

Dante's avowed purpose was to open that vision to us all, to lead us out of wretchedness to blessedness. He did not succeed in that, even for the people of his own vexed time —it is a task beyond the power of a poet and, if one may judge by observable results, beyond the power of the Master whom Dante imitated and followed. He did succeed as a poet, as a maker of loveliness. He left many theological and philosophic tangles (because life is tangled) which six centuries of scholarship have tried in vain to straighten out. We, as readers, can take Dante at his face value, with a minimum of explanatory notes, as in Norton's translation, and enjoy the superficial beauty, which contains much of the essential and profound beauty. Dante piles meaning upon meaning, but the main course of his little bark, as he calls it, is clear. Much of the argument of critics as to whether Beatrice, who guides him to Paradise, is a real woman or a compound symbol only serves to veil her fair face and is not the poetic veil that Dante intended.

The magnitude of Dante's conception is no more wonderful than the form which he gave it. His structure, viewed as a technical achievement, is a miracle of composition; in shapeliness and continuity it is not approached by any other poem. The *Commedia* consists of three sections or canticles, Hell, Purgatory, Paradise, each containing thirty-three cantos, with an introductory canto at the beginning of Hell, making a hundred in all. The cantos are about the same length, a hundred and forty lines more or less. The stanza unit is the *terza rima,* the "three rhyme." Here is a specimen of the *terza rima* in English, the last ten lines of the fifth canto of Hell, translated by a modern poet, Walter Arensberg:

> When we had read how one so amorous
> Had kissed the smile that he was longing for,
> This one, who always must be by me thus,
>
> Kissed me upon the mouth, trembling all o'er;
> Galeot the book, and he 'twas written by!
> Upon that day in it we read no more."
>
> So sorely did the other spirit cry,
> While the one spoke, that for the very dread
> I swooned as if I were about to die
>
> And I fell down even as a man falls dead.

Each stanza of three lines is linked to the one before it and the one that follows it, until the last line shuts the sequence and ends the canto. The middle line of each terzina, or triplet, rhymes with the first and third lines of the next. Dante sustains this form unbroken through his hundred cantos. And his handling of the form, which he invented, is not mere metrical virtuosity; he found in the *terza rima* the natural vehicle for the multitudinous variety of his thoughts, narrative, descriptive, epigrammatic, philosophic

PAOLO AND FRANCESCA

and the means of weaving the whole into a texture from which no thread can be dropped. A negative proof of his mastery is that after he had established the *terza rima* as a conventional form of verse many poets tried it and not one succeeded in managing it with his dexterity and power. It was his creation, and it remains his uniquely personal mode of expression.

He was original not only in his stanzaic form but in his diction, his language. In a time when men of learning wrote Latin as a matter of course he took the popular Tuscan dialect and made it a literary language, so that, with later modifications, it became what is now classic Italian. Italy had, and still has, many dialects, some of which have their own literature, popular or deliberately artistic. That the Tuscan dialect (that is, the speech of Florence and the surrounding cities and country) prevailed over all the others as the correct, official language of the educated is due almost wholly to Dante, though it is possible that without Dante the culture of Florence and her neighbors would have set the standard for the whole boot-shaped peninsula. Dante's guide through Hell is Virgil; the younger poet greets his master as the one from whom he took the "beautiful style." It is true that Virgil had a great influence on Dante and on all the scholarly poets of "middle" and "modern" Europe. Yet if ever a poet made his beautiful style himself that poet was Dante.

In the fine sonnet which Longfellow prefixes to his translation of the Inferno, he compares Dante's poem to a cathedral. It is a just and noble image suggesting the splendid solidity of the structure. But there is a difference for the beholder between a stone masterpiece and a literary masterpiece which consists of a series of words. As we approach and enter a cathedral, its massive splendor overwhelms us immediately,

DANTE

no matter how much time we may later devote to studying the details. A poem can have no such sudden effect; it must be read from first line to last if we are to get the total impression of it. Dante imagined his poem like a sphere, the universe, and if we take a sphere to pieces it ceases to be a sphere. Nevertheless I recommend that the casual reader, in violation of Dante's plan and the totality of his logic, dip into the *Commedia* and find for himself here and there an interesting passage, for example, the fifth canto of Hell, and the twenty-sixth canto. I find more in Longfellow's image of the cathedral than he intended: when I go into St. Peter's at Rome I stand long in contemplation of Michelangelo's Pietá, which is only a detail of decoration and does not help to hold up the immense dome. Well, that is not a scholarly way, but it is a very human and delightful way to enter Dante.

English readers who do not know Italian can find Dante's substance and spirit (though the magic of his verse is necessarily lost) in several translations. The best is the prose of Charles Eliot Norton. Besides his translation of the *Commedia,* Norton made an excellent version of an earlier work of Dante's, the *New Life,* which is the story of Dante's young love for Beatrice and is an inseparable introduction to the longer poem. Early in the nineteenth century Henry F. Cary translated the *Commedia* into blank verse, and this rendering became an English classic. Longfellow's translation, also in blank verse, is good, faithful, but slow and lacking in fire. Those who have a slight acquaintance with Italian will get great pleasure from the three little volumes of the *Commedia* in the Temple Classics, in which the Italian is printed on the left-hand page and an almost literal English translation on the right-hand. Dante is a "hard" thinker and his thought is subtle and involved. But at least in its surface meanings his Italian is not too difficult for us to follow. He meant to speak to all men, for he was as arrogant as a religious prophet about the value of his message. If we are to judge by the increasingly enormous number of translations, commentaries, and biographies in all languages, his work is approximating the universality which he proudly hoped for it.

PART III

MODERN LITERATURE BEFORE THE NINETEENTH CENTURY

CHAPTER XVIII

THE ITALIAN RENAISSANCE

The metaphor of Renaissance may signify the entrance of the European nations upon a fresh stage of vital energy in general, implying a fuller consciousness and a freer exercise of faculties than had belonged to the medieval period. —*John Addington Symonds.*

As for the claim that the Renaissance delivered men from that blind reliance upon authority which was typical of 'medieval' thought, that is a fallacy cherished by those who themselves rely upon the authority of historians, blind to the most ordinary processes of thought.
—*James T. Shotwell.*

FEW years ago Mr. J. P. Morgan bought a medieval manuscript for a sum of money which would have made the unknown copyist and the obscure author f a b u l o u s l y rich. When Giovanni Boccaccio, who was born during the life-time of Dante, visited the library of a famous monastery he found that the manuscripts were mutilated, that the monks tore out leaves and sold them to the superstitious as magic charms. The world is as brutal as it ever was; perhaps it has never been more ferociously destructive than it is today. Yet we have in the nineteen-hundreds a respect for learning, or for the symbols and documents of learning, that makes us different from the people of the nine-hundreds. A change, a light, or

an increase of light did come over the face of Europe in the
fourteenth and fifteenth centuries. The light came first in
Italy, so that *Renaissance* is Italian in fact, though French in
form. And part of the light came from the kind of interest
which Boccaccio had in those monastic manuscripts, so that
the Renaissance is indeed a Revival or Rebirth of Learning.
There happened, also, to be men of genius who found the light
and gave it brilliancy and direction.

BOCCACCIO

One was Petrarch, who was a generation younger than
Dante and whose fame in his own time and for two centuries
later surpassed that of Dante. He was crowned poet
laureate at Rome and enjoyed all the honors that his contemporaries could give him. For us he lives by his lyrics,

he was an apostle of culture, a "humanist," that is, a preacher of civilization, which to him was Greek and Latin civilization.

Much more human, if not humanistic, is Boccaccio, the first great master of Italian narrative prose, and, as many critics think, the still unrivaled master of the short story. He was, like his friend Petrarch, an enthusiastic scholar, collecting and copying manuscripts and encouraging the study of Greek. He knew better than most of his contemporaries the greatness of Dante and wrote a biography of him. He was also a prolific poet. But all his other achievements are overshadowed by the incomparable *Decameron*. This collection of a hundred tales is well described by the title which was given to an English translation of it in the seventeenth century: "The Model of Mirth, Wit, Eloquence, and Conversation." The range of the stories is extraordinary, from buffoonery to the most delicate pathos. Some of the stories are trivial and some are too improper to be published in a modern family magazine. But not one is guilty of the greatest sin in literature, dullness. The entire *Decameron*, like other great things in literature, may be read with delight and a sound conscience by anybody who has brains enough to know his right hand from his left. Boccaccio invented some of the tales, remade others that were current anecdotes, and took others from old French *fabliaux*. The *Decameron* became part of universal European literature, and English poets from Chaucer to Keats borrowed from it. Yet it remains intensely local in time and place, a picture, or series of pictures of the Italian of the fourteenth century.

Boccaccio's easy flexible prose is the medium of a joyous art. In the next century Machiavelli forged Italian prose into a keen instrument of exposition and analysis. He was

a politician and man of affairs as well as an artist in words.
In the Italian Renaissance the various activities of the intellect were not mutually exclusive. A man could be a poet
and a statesman. A sculptor wrote poetry, went to war, and

sat in the city council. Lo-
renzo di Medici, the tyrant
of Florence, who was a few
years older than Machia-
velli and whose c a r e e r
Machiavelli studied, was
not only a patron of the
arts but a man of letters.
Machiavelli, having seen
the world as ambassador to
foreign courts and having
scrutinized the govern-
ment under which he lived
and suffered, set out to
solve the problem of the
state, and in the *Prince*
wrote the first realistic examination of political society. He tells what in
point of fact a ruler must

MACHIAVELLI

do in order to succeed. The word "Machiavellian" came
to mean unscrupulous cunning in politics. That is because
Machiavelli told the truth without hypocrisy, without pre-
tending that government is or can be wholly honest and
beneficent. He believed government to be necessary and
was far from being an anarchist. He was seeking not a
Utopia but the plain principles of organization and control.
The *Prince* is a great and original piece of thinking, and
though it has some local and obsolete details its main

thoughts are still fresh. Writers on politics, especially those who palaver about morals and the honor of nations may misunderstand it, but practical politicians and diplomats, who have lately made a bloody mess of the world, know in their secret hearts that Machiavelli gives a faithful account of the way things work. His book is in its implications dangerously sincere, scientific in spirit and method; and though Machiavelli was a conservative who in a measure justified tyranny and laid down its laws, to give his name to political chicanery is only like naming a disease after the physician who discovers it.

Our hasty survey deals with literature, but literature is only one of the arts, and the arts are only part of life. In the Renaissance, as I have suggested, there was a unity of knowledge which we in our crowded compartments of thought cannot equal. While Machiavelli was meditating upon the state he might have met in the streets of Florence or in a company at the palace of the Medici the most robust genius of them all, Michelangelo. This sculptor and painter belongs to literature, because not content with chisel and brush he also wrote poetry, putting some of his surplus energy at the age of sixty into sonnets! A few years later another sculptor, Benvenuto Cellini, with his fascinating *Autobiography,* added to Italian prose and to the joy of the nations. It is the self-portrait of a romantic, swaggering, conceited man, whose beautiful bronze Perseus still stands in the Loggia dei Lanzi at Florence to prove that he had a right to be conceited.

The writers and artists of the Renaissance were both romanticists and classicists. The distinction is not absolutely sharp. A very beautiful combination of a tale of chivalry and something like a classic mode of narrative is the ro-

ARIOSTO

mantic epic of Ariosto, *Orlando Furioso*, which became the most popular of the many romances of the fifteenth and sixteenth centuries and won for its author the title "Divine Ludovico." We have to take its merits somewhat on trust, for there is no translation of it that has permanently endeared it to English readers. The version by John Harington published at the end of the sixteenth century was known, like many French and Italian romances, to the Elizabethan poets. Orlando is of course the Roland of French story, the chief peer of Charlemagne.

The most brilliant Italian poet of the sixteenth century was Torquato Tasso. His *Jerusalem Delivered* is a story of the crusades, of the capture of the Holy Sepulcher by Godfrey of Bouillon. The poem is of almost epic proportions, and the subject had for Tasso and his contemporaries a religious elevation which we no longer feel. For us the value of *Jerusalem Delivered* seems to be about

TASSO

equal to that of Scott's novel, the *Talisman*. But we must yield to Carducci, the Italian poet and critic of the nineteenth century, who calls Tasso the heir of Dante. Tasso wrote his great poem and many other things when he was a young man. Before he reached middle age he became an invalid, partially insane. He thus pathetically represents the history of his time. For after him dusk fell upon the Italian Renaissance. The metaphor is rather pretty than logical. For the Renaissance never died. It lives by its works; they are there in marble and bronze and paint and words. It spread to other countries. And even in Italy though poetry faded thought survived, perhaps the more vigorous because of the political darkness, in the philosophic prose of Giordano Bruno and Galileo Galilei. These men are both more than technical philosophers: by their style they belong to literature. There is a story that when the ecclesiastical authorities compelled Galileo to deny that the earth moves round the sun, he rose from his penitential knees and exclaimed, "Eppur si muove!" ("nevertheless it does move!"). The story is probably not true. But the saying is a perfect maxim to hold in mind when one thinks of astronomy or life or that part of life which is literature.

CHAPTER XIX

FRENCH PROSE BEFORE THE NINETEENTH CENTURY

Bookes have and containe divers pleasing qualities to those that can duly choose them.

—Montaigne.

FRENCH prose of the sixteenth century is dominated by two of the most original and delightful thinkers in all literature, Rabelais and Montaigne. Rabelais lived in the first half of the century and Montaigne in the second half. The two men were of quite different temperaments, Rabelais jocose and hearty, Montaigne gravely smiling and reflective; and there seems to be no evidence that Montaigne knew the work of his great predecessor. Montaigne was a bookish classicist, somewhat scornful of things purely French. But together they created French prose, so far as individuals create anything they had a great influence on English essayists and satirists and the tradition which they established survives eminently in such a modern writer as Anatole France.

There are two rare things in literature: a writer of verse who is a poet, and a humorist who is funny. Rabelais is funny. The difference between one kind of humorist and another has been the subject of serious philosophic and psychological essays. We can suggest the problem, not the solution, by examples. Jonathan Swift, who undoubtedly knew Rabelais, makes you shiver, his humor is almost tragic, he never makes you laugh aloud. Dickens and Mark Twain, profoundly serious men, who understand the bitterness of life, make you giggle and shriek with merriment and a jolly sense of absurdity. So does Rabelais. He is a wise man and a gigantic laugher. In his novels, which are loosely united, he sends forth into the world of fact and the world of fancy his gigantic hero Gargantua, and Gargantua's son, Pantagruel, and the most attractive character in the book, the amiable good-for-nothing, Panurge. In their adventures they encounter and pass in review the whole of the life of the time, all seen in broad burlesque, but true as only a comic vision of humanity can be true. All sorts and conditions of men, especially the learned professions, priests and lawyers, come in for a sound spanking. Rabelais had been a monk and was later a physician, and he had no respect for gowns and degrees. As in all good comic writing there is under his riotous fooling a fundamental seriousness. His laugh at the "furred law cats" is a laugh with a sting, and it would be risky to read it aloud before a meeting of a Bar Association. His irreverence offended some of the more narrowly devout spirits of his own time and both his irreverence and his coarseness are out of tune with the finest sensibility of our time. But his huge laugh, as Gargantuan as his gigantic hero, puts prudery out of countenance; he is a cure for hypocrisy and for the blues, if those diseases of mind and soul can be cured. He has a prodigious vocabulary, some of which he invented, and he piles up images and analogies almost too rapidly and abundantly. He is fortunate (or we are fortunate) in his English translators of the seventeenth century, Urquhart and Motteux, who reproduced his rushing fullness, his grotesquely farcical phrasing, and so enriched the English language. Some of the richness we are not allowed to avail ourselves of in polite modern usage; it is uproariously amusing but a little too vigorous. The translation of Urquhart and Motteux is an English classic and has been many times reprinted. An edition published by Chatto & Windus of London contains illustrations by Gustave Doré which are as spirited as the text. In Morley's Universal Library is an expurgated edition for those who need to have literature cut and prepared for them. I believe that Rabelais can be swallowed whole without deleterious effect by anyone who has a sound stomach and a sane mind. Coleridge, a man of delicate literary feeling and fine ethical judgment, said: "I could write a treatise in praise of the moral elevation of Rabelais' work which would make the church stare and the conventicle groan, and yet would be the truth and nothing but the truth." But Rabelais requires no such treatise. He is essentially wholesome; and—what is more important—he is screamingly funny.

"Be frolic now, my lads, cheer up your hearts." This is the message and the mood of Rabelais. Montaigne cares nothing for frolic lads, but communes quietly with his own nature and his books. The essay is the only form of literature whose parentage and date of birth are certainly known. The origins of the drama, the lyric, the short story, the novel fade vaguely into the past; no one man of genius stands forth clearly as father and inventor of any of these types. The essay alone has a recorded date, before which it was not, after which it everlastingly was. When in March, 1571, Michel de Montaigne retired from a noisy world to the tower of his castle and began to talk to himself about himself, the essay was conceived; and it was born exactly nine years later when the first edition of the *Essais* was published. The first essayist was the greatest. There have been distinguished essayists in all languages since Montaigne and long before, if you think, for example, of the discourses of Aristotle and Cicero as "essays." But Montaigne from his solitary tower of refuge is still in command, is the acknowledged captain. "I speake unto Paper, as to the first man I meete," he says, and in another place, "my selfe am the groundworke of my booke." No man ever spoke unto Paper to better purpose about a greater variety of subjects from a more substantial groundwork. The Index of the *Essays* is almost encyclopedic in its range. Montaigne had digested his library, made it his second nature and he had also examined his own character with intimate curiosity and impersonal detachment. He is a sceptic, doubtful about his own age, but generously credulous of the reports of human nature at its best. His contradictions are the contradictions of life and of the same observer of life in different moods. "I am no philosopher," he says, and that is true if philosophy means a reasoned system of thought. But he is a philosopher if philosopher means a lover of wisdom. He suffers harassments and physical pain with ironic fortitude, without a grouch. He is the great exemplar of what a modern artist, Joseph Conrad, has called the sigh that is not a sob, the smile that is not a grin. "The world," Montaigne says, "is nothing but babbling and words," and then he himself goes on "babbling."

It is glorious talk. The standard English translation is that made by John Florio in the early part of the seventeenth century. Florio was a polyglot, of Italian origin, a teacher

of French and Italian at Oxford.   His cosmopolitanism made
an English masterpiece of Montaigne who saw the whole
cosmos from his egotistic tower.   And Montaigne, the solitary
philosopher, became for English readers, as for his own countrymen, the best companion in the world.

No reader would think of calling Rabelais or Montaigne
obscure, and they do not seem old-fashioned to Frenchmen
who have been brought up on them.   But they are, each in his
own way, a little free and easy, like the prose writers of early
Elizabethan England.   As French prose grew into the seventeenth century there was a gain in clearness and regularity
and formal logic.   Calvin, who was almost exactly contemporary with Rabelais, had shown his power in sustained lucid
discourse, which was perhaps transferred to his French from
his Latin style.   His *Institution of the Christian Religion* is
a work for special students and his manner is forbiddingly
cold, but the excellence of his writing rescues him from theology and claims him for literature.   Early in the seventeenth
century Jean-Louis Balzac did for French prose somewhat
the same service (if it was a service) that Malherbe performed
for French verse.   The aim was correctness, polish, accuracy
of rhythm as well as of thought.   And that ideal prevailed,
for most of the great prose writers of the "great century,"
the classic age, went to school to Balzac whether they knew
it or not.   The French Academy was founded, and it was the
official judge and exemplar of purity of style.   It cannot be
said that the newer and narrower standards of oratorical elegance and Ciceronian perfection did any harm to French prose
for the century was rich in writers of genius, and genius can
learn lessons from the pedagogue without having its spirit
cramped.   We may remember that in England somewhat later
and in part due to French influence there was a similar move-

RABELAIS

ment toward restraint, dignity and sound phrasing. But the English nature, as compared with the French, has always been inclined to disregard rules and go its own way.

It is difficult to decide in the case of some thinkers whether they belong to literature or to a special department of philosophy or science. The discursive reader does not have to make the decision, for he can wander among books wherever his interests lead him—and that is the best way to read. But in a book about literature, like this rapid survey, we have to draw the line broadly between what the French call "beautiful letters" and works which, however important, are not part of general literature. A briefly inadequate sketch of philosophy alone, without a glance at drama and fiction and song, would fill a larger volume than this. When we try to draw that broad line we shall make blunders of judgment and be guilty of loose and doubtful definitions. Let us grope toward a rough principle of division by way of some examples. Plato, a philosopher, is a literary artist of first importance. So is Francis Bacon. So is Schopenhauer. Other thinkers of immense genius can be omitted arbitrarily from a purely literary view; for example, Abelard, Thomas Aquinas, Kant, Hegel. I cheerfully agree to any disagreement with these examples. They suggest at least what I am blindly driving at.

There are two French philosophers of the seventeenth century who tower not only as technical thinkers but as masters of the art of French prose: Descartes and Pascal. Descartes taught philosophy to speak French as Bacon taught philosophy to speak English. Hitherto most learned discourses were in Latin, and both Descartes and Bacon wrote much of their work in the traditional learned tongue. Descartes's *Discourse on Method* in French is a brilliant specimen of order, clarity, and logic, qualities which we have come to take for granted as the commonplace virtues of French prose. We cannot discuss the philosophy of Descartes. Let us leave that to the philosophers. But we can suggest one central idea, an idea that makes it appropriate that he was born a year or two after Montaigne died. He believed in reason, in the power of human thought; his philosophy begins in the famous phrase: "I think, therefore I am." His thought is so precisely, so luminously phrased that he became a model for all succeeding French thinkers, even those who disagreed with him. His principal works have been translated into English and other languages and belong to the literature of the world.

Descartes was a rationalist and believed that the origin of all truth that we can know is inside us. Pascal, who lived a generation after Descartes, distrusted human reason and thought that truth lies outside us, to be found by faith. He belonged to the heretical party of Jansenists, who tried to reform the Catholic Church from within and attacked the Jesuits. It is an old controversy of fading interest to us, but it was the occasion of Pascal's *Provincial Letters* and *Thoughts,* which have the supreme distinction of making theological argument and religious meditation humanly delightful. Pascal is a master of aphorism, of the sentence which contains matter for a whole chapter. His passionate eloquence is expressed in perfect style. He writes: "When one sees the natural style one is astonished and delighted; for one expected to find an author and one finds a man." He would have pleased Montaigne, whom he admired, as he did please Voltaire who wrote of Pascal's *Provincial Letters:* "All kinds of eloquence are contained in this book."

The most fertile and energetic writer of prose in the classic period was Bossuet, a man of gigantic energy, who in the midst of an industrious life as teacher, priest and bishop, made himself the head of French letters of his time. And he achieved his position, which he holds to this day in the minds of students of French literature, not by work which we usually think of as forms of literary art, but by sermons, multitudes of controversial papers and orations. In this form he was an artist and his orations belong to the great eloquences though oratory is a form of literature for which time has little respect. It may be that Bossuet is always an orator in method and effect, whether he is at the funeral of an English queen or attacking the abuses of the theater or confounding the Protestants or setting forth the true Catholic doctrine. He is not a dull preacher but a man of great force of character and command of the art of expression. He is learned without pedantry, a churchman without bigotry; he is a hard hitter but he does not strike unfairly. And though he is capable of the grand gesture and the sonorous phrase he is on the whole simple, sincere, master of many moods and tones from the sublime to the familiar.

Another oratorical clergyman, of less power than Bossuet, was Fénelon, archbishop of Cambrai, a gentle soul whose writing was incidental to his professional labor and to the development of his ideas on education, morals, and religion. It must be remembered by readers who have not felt the spirit of the Catholic countries that in the great centuries of the church men of intellectual power naturally went into the priesthood. That is why we find cardinals as prime ministers and clergymen of all degrees who contributed to the great secular library of prose and poetry, just as we find Italian painters clad not in the smock of the studio but in the gown of the monastery. The world cherishes the artist and the man of letters long after it forgets some of the religious motives that occasioned their masterpieces. Fénelon believed, and expressed his belief in

Maxims of the Saints, that we should forget ourselves in relation to God and think of Christ as the redeemer of humanity, not as the redeemer of this particular sinner. Bossuet attacked the idea and Fénelon's book was condemned by Rome. But both priests live in literature and the merits of their dispute do not greatly excite us. The Pope, Innocent XII, deserves a line in a literary record, for in condemning Fénelon he said with humorous wisdom that Fénelon erred by loving God too much, and Bossuet by loving his neighbor too little. Fénelon did love his fellow men. In a sort of parable, *Télémaque*, he sketched a fanciful Utopian state of society in which are foreshadowed some of the dreams of the eighteenth century liberals and democrats.

Not all the prose of the seventeenth century was the work of learned clerics. There were brilliant prose writers among the laity. One was La Bruyère, a lawyer and man of the world, whose *Characters* portray actual and typical French people of the time. It was originally based on the work of the Greek philosopher Theophrastus. But La Bruyère went beyond the lesson of his master. His fine sword often cut deep and many of his contemporaries were offended. But his interest was the study of human beings, which interests us, and he was not a mean observer of his fellows. His maxims and epigrams are clever and searching, a model of pellucid French.

Another writer of maxims, less gifted than La Bruyère but shrewd, is La Rochefoucauld. He was a witty man somewhat disillusioned by practical failure. He is not cynical, but his underlying thought (or one of his many thoughts) is that all the motives of the human being can be reduced to some form of self-interest. His maxims keep their point after two centuries of repetition. What he says may not be part of the wisdom of the ages but it is well said. For example: "We all have enough strength to endure the misfortunes of others."

In the "great century" women played a great part in politics and letters. Their education was in many ways restricted; in other ways they were remarkably free, and a woman who used her wits became a power in the land, no matter what the official pedagogues had taught her. Many of the salons over which great ladies presided had a vital influence on letters, and several women, all of course of the upper classes, made their mark in literature.

One of the most charming is Mme. de Sévigné, the queen of letter writers. Her early life was darkened by grief and disappointments, but she had a strong heart and a cool head and bore her sorrows with fortitude and good humor. The letters are simply the gossip of a highly cultivated woman who lets her pen run on the daily affairs of life and sometimes on public affairs and literature. But she does not write with her eyes shut. She watches her substance and her style carefully, as a lady would watch the stuff and style of a gown. Her letters reveal much of the life of her day in aristocratic circles and disclose an admirable clear mind and honest character.

Another woman with an extraordinary gift of expression was Mme. de Maintenon, who rose from obscure and painful circumstances to be the wife of King Louis XIV. The marriage was never publicly announced but everybody knew about it. For thirty years Mme. de Maintenon had the practical privileges (and difficulties) of a queen; she managed some of the great monarch's affairs with good sense, though she never interfered with his government. Her letters are among the important political and social documents of the time. At her house she conducted a private school and she wrote wisely on the education of girls. She was a born teacher with a positive genius for understanding the motives of the young and expressing them.

Mme. de Sévigné and Mme. de Maintenon did not intend to be literary artists, but their natural genius took them, without their suspecting it, into the company of important writers. A less important writer, but one who was primarily an artist, was Mme. de La Fayette, whose novel *The Princess of Clèves* is perhaps the first honest novel that a woman ever wrote. More than that, it is one of the founders of the revolution in fiction which substituted for fatuously impossible adventures simple situations and for extravagant style the natural language of life. Mme. de La Fayette had not power to go very far but the later French novel owes something to her quiet sense of truth as it does to the sparkling *Characters* of La Bruyère.

It was in the eighteenth century that the novel developed, went forward, though not very far, while some other forms of literary art fell away from the old traditions. Most of the great thinkers were expounders, essayists. It was an age of reason or was such on its serious side in spite of wildness and frivolity, and it may be that the gain in good sense helped at once to destroy the bloom and perfume of poetry and to put salt and sanity into fiction. The first novelist of the new era is Le Sage, a writer of many plays and stories but chiefly known for his masterpiece *Gil Blas*. This is a picaresque or vagabond novel of adventure based on Spanish types and laid in Spanish scenes, but it is more than that, it is thoroughly French in feeling and style, and still more, it is universal in its humanity. The interest is not, however, the inside of humanity, the deeper emotions, but the outer experiences. Gil Blas goes through many adventures with great rapidity, having no time to rest and reflect but plenty of time to prepare for the next adventure and to give a lively account of it. The book went all over Europe and was almost more important in England than in France; for it had no successors in its own country, whereas across the channel it influenced its translator, Smollet, and a much greater artist, Fielding.

A romance which took a permanent place in literature, the only work by which its author is remembered, is *Manon Les-*

ROUSSEAU

caut of l'Abbé Prévost. This little story is the first which in subject and tone gives us the feeling of what we mean by a novel. The love story is pathetic, passionate, the motives are perfectly realized, and the writing is simple, direct, and without apparent artifice. After two centuries of novel writing the world still has an honest tear for the tragedy of Manon.

The strength of the eighteenth century was not in its fiction or its poets but in its thinkers, Montesquieu, Voltaire, Rousseau, Diderot, who expressed themselves in various fashions, but principally in some form of philosophic exposition or essay. They were all rebels in some way against the existing social order, and each in his way made some contribution to the vast body of ideas that led to the French Revolution.

MONTESQUIEU

Montesquieu, who was only less famous in his own time than Voltaire, was a liberal reformer, not a dreamer of the type of Rousseau, not a revolutionist but, as we should now see him, a conservative aristocrat with no delusions about the rights and virtues of his own class. He began with his *Lettres persanes,* which satirized the follies of church, state, society, and literature. It is a witty book with much wisdom under its light tone. He became in his later work much more serious, a profound student of history and law, and one of the forerunners of the science of politics. He wrote *Considerations on the Grandeur and Decadence of the Romans,* a work which was undoubtedly known to Gibbon, whose culture was largely French as that of Montesquieu was partly English. But Montesquieu has a fault which later historians of equal genius, including Gibbon, would have avoided or not allowed themselves to commit so often: he generalized too facilely from single facts to principles. So that the philosophic historian quarrels with him but can, with the lay reader, be stimulated by his suggestions and enjoy his clarifying examination of the causes of events in history. After all he belongs to the breed of Gibbon and Taine, the great masters of historical generalization, and he has the supreme merit of being readable, his style carrying him through a multitude of ideas. His *magnum opus* is *The Spirit of the Laws,* a treatise on jurisprudence, forms of society and government, studies of manners and customs in ancient and modern countries, a thousand matters which in our day would be jealously divided between at least ten kinds of professor.

It was felt even in that time, when men were free to assume authority on many subjects, that knowledge is divided and that the way to truth is to assemble the wisdom of the best minds. This was the basic idea, largely due to Diderot, of *l'Encyclopédie,* a repository, which grew to many volumes, of all that was then called science and much besides. The best French thinkers contributed, and so did some who were less than best. The editing of this work is Diderot's great monument. But his own essays make him one of the foremost men of letters and original thinkers in literature, and they are somewhat like the encyclopedia for they range in merit from works of genius to hasty commonplace and cover an extensive variety of subjects. Perhaps not one of his essays is a master work; but each of them is significant, suggestive. He touched every subject with a renovating vitality; and the fearless independence of his mind, his willingness to see everything in sight, is shown in all his work from the early famous *Letter on the Blind for those Who See* to his *Essay on Painting,* which Goethe thought magnificent, and throughout the many expressions of his fundamental philosophy. That philosophy was Nature. Like many of the thinkers of this time he found that Nature contained and explained everything, and She became the poetic feminine substitute for Him, the God of tradition. Diderot's Nature is not so soft and sentimentalized as Rousseau's; it is more reasonable and less poetic. The art of Diderot is not at its highest in what is usually called his masterpiece, *Le Neveu de Rameau,* a fantastic satire, which Goethe's translation introduced to Europe; Diderot's genius is in his rapid, individual discourse, the best example of the conversational style of an "inspired journalist."

Diderot's Nature was something different from that of Buffon; for Buffon was a naturalist, a professional biologist, who studied plants and animals and minerals, described them and classified them. He was not a modern biologist working in field and laboratory, but a man of great imagination, who tried to find and express the order of nature. The order that he found has been revised, even destroyed, and obviously a million facts have been discovered of which Buffon was ignorant. But his order remains because it is the order of a seer with great synthetic power who made a real unit of the universe and who preserved the multitude of created things not in a frigid system but in a living style. His *Natural History* is a literary monument, whatever science may finally make of it. It was Buffon, man of science, who in his inaugural address before the French Academy, *Discourse on Style,* gave a lesson to men of letters.

Buffon was placid in his contemplation of Nature. His Nature had no occasion to say to him, in Emerson's phrase,

VOLTAIRE

"Why so hot, little man?" Many writers of the time, most of those who are still interesting and hosts who have been forgotten, were constantly hot, or pretended to be, and wrote much, perhaps too much, in a polemic mood. The chief of polemic writers, whose versatility, however, embraces much besides polemics, is Voltaire. His life fills three quarters of the eighteenth century. He tried every literary mode, drama, poetry, satiric fiction, history, criticism, familiar correspondence. And he had so many contacts with life that he is the epitome of his time. He is like Dr. Johnson in one respect, that the story of his life is more interesting than any of his own works. He fought ecclesiastical and political power, and was a guest of Frederick the Great of Prussia. He passed into tradition as a mocking anti-Christ, but it was not Christ that he attacked, or even current Christianity so much as intellectual tyranny. By his wit he baffled his enemies and critics in his own time and he perplexed critics of later times, including Thomas Carlyle, who seems to have lost his sense of humor when he wrote his famous essay. But we must read that essay for Carlyle as well as for Voltaire. Of Voltaire's voluminous work what interests us is the prose, that agile, limpid transparent prose which every later French writer has admired even if he has despised Voltaire's thought. Much, but not all, of Voltaire has been translated into the principal languages of Europe. The serious side of his many-sided mind we can read in his *Life of Charles XII*. His comic satiric vein is best exemplified in *Candide,* a burlesque of optimism, in which Dr. Pangloss, despite the misfortunes which he and his pupil suffer, insists that "all is for the best in this best of possible worlds." The vivacity and variety of Voltaire's mind, as well as the strength and weakness of his character, are best seen in his letters; there is no more entertaining letter-writer in all literature.

Voltaire was a rationalist endowed with swift wit and inexhaustible humor. His younger contemporary, Jean Jacques Rousseau, who had an even greater influence on thought and on the course of history, was born without humor but with a strong sense of pathos and beauty. He was a sentimental rebel against the social order of his day and became the prophet of the French Revolution; of course neither he nor any other man of thought or action made the Revolution, but Rousseau eloquently phrased many of its motives, and his thought spread beyond the Revolution through the romantic literature of Europe. Rousseau's ideas are in part out of date and in part still far in advance of our practical world. His *Social Contract* is an exposition of an impossible state of society without foundation in economic fact, but it still shines in the dark library of political discussion. He believed that the human being is naturally good and that the corrupt and false organization of society spoils him. He thought that the individual must sacrifice his liberty for the general good. "The greatest good to the greatest number" is an ideal that has not lost all its meaning. Rousseau's democracy was a combination of a kind of back-to-nature movement, a return to a state of innocence, and a conception of the good old days of Greece and Rome which is not sustained by the facts of history. It is the function of an emotional writer like Rousseau to be suggestive and stimulating rather than accurate and logical. His belief that we are born pure led to his theory of education which is developed in a sort of novel, *Emile,* the main principle of which is that the child should be left free and not trammeled by the false learning of its elders—a fine idea, not quite practical, but the spirit of it survives in all liberal systems of pedagogy down to Dr. Montessori. Rousseau was the inaugurator of the sentimental, picturesque novel in *Julie or the New Héloise,* in which is expressed his passionate love of human nature and of external nature; he was the first writer of fiction to join the landscape to the heart—a conjunction which after him became a commonplace and often tiresomely and pathetically fallacious. Rousseau's ideas about people and things, his objective observations were and are of great importance. But his most interesting book is that about himself, his *Confessions,* written toward the end of his life when his mind had not lost its power but when his sensitive and eccentric soul was unbalanced. Some of the facts may be doubted—for no autobiography can tell the whole truth— but it reveals the character of the man.

CHAPTER XX

FRENCH POETRY AND DRAMA BEFORE THE NINETEENTH CENTURY

Love reads out first at head of all our quire
Villon, our sad bad glad mad brother's name.
—*Swinburne.*

BEFORE the fifteenth century the lyric poets had developed a great variety of measures and verse forms, and had made them artificial conventions which too often had no feeling, no pure poetry. But the forms were ready for the poets to use and fill with life—whenever the poets should arrive. They came in the fifteenth century, several with the real gift of song, three who stand above the rest: Charles d'Orleans, Villon, and Clément Marot.

Charles, Duke of Orleans, if not a new kind of voice in poetry, is certainly a true one. In his verse form and his thought he is a medieval nobleman, but he feels what he sings and though he has not great passion he has charm, his gallantry is natural, and his Spring is real. The duke, who was prisoner in England, is not a memorable figure in history but the poet who sings from the British coast his homesickness for France will not be forgotten.

In strange contrast to the elegant duke is the next poet after
him, and a much greater poet, François Villon. He was a
vagabond and a thief, his neck was more than once in danger
of the hangman's noose, but he must have had a winning personality, for he found a patron who sent him to school. All
that we really know about him is that he put his personality
into the set forms that had been shaped by the court poets of
the preceding centuries and he gave those conventions a
vitality they had not had before and perhaps have not had
since. This is Swinburne's version of the *Ballade* which Villon wrote when he thought that he and his companions were
to be hanged next day:

> Men, brother men, that after us yet live,
>   Let not your hearts too hard against us be;
> For if some pity of us poor men ye give,
>   The sooner God shall take of you pity.
>   Here are we five or six strung up, you see,
> And here the flesh that all too well we fed
> Bit by bit eaten and rotten, rent and shred,
>   And we the bones grow dust and ash withal;
> Let no man laugh at us discomforted,
>   But pray to God that he forgive us all.
>
>
> If we call on you, brothers, to forgive,
>   Ye should not hold our prayer in scorn, though we
> Were slain by law; ye know that all alive
>   Have not wit alway to walk righteously;
>   Make therefore intercession heartily
> With Him that of a virgin's womb was bred,
> That his grace be not as a dry well-head
>   For us, nor let hell's thunder on us fall;
> We are dead, let no man harry or vex us dead,
>   But pray to God that he forgive us all.

The rain has washed and laundered us all five,
  And the sun dried and blackened; yea, per die,
Ravens and pies with beaks that rend and rive
  Have dug our eyes out and plucked off for fee
  Our beards and eyebrows; never are we free,
Not once, to rest; but here and there still sped
Drive at its wild will by the wind's change led,
  More pecked of birds than fruits on garden wall.
Men, for God's love, let no gibe here be said,
  But pray to God that he forgive us all.

Prince Jesus, that of all art lord and head,
Keep us, that hell be not our bitter bed;
  We have nought to do in such a master's hall.
Be ye not therefore of our fellowhead,
  But pray to God that he forgive us all.

For anything as poignant in French poetry as that and other poems of Villon we have to come down to the nineteenth century. Modern English poets have been attracted by his spirit and his poetic form and have rendered him with great skill, as in this dexterous example from Swinburne. A fine humanly critical account of the poet is that in Robert Louis Stevenson's *Familiar Studies of Men and Books,* and a delicious short story based fancifully on Villon's life is Stevenson's *A Lodging for the Night.* Stevenson's essay on Charles D'Orleans is also delightful.

With Villon we leave behind rather definitely medieval French poetry and in his successor and editor, Clément Marot, we meet a graceful poet who leads us well into the sixteenth century and has a modern flavor. His best verse is distinguished by a light touch, the use of every-day words and a loosening of the tightly elaborate forms. He thus became the first of the writers of *vers de société,* rhymes on slight themes, pretty but not silly, and simple, yet difficult to do because there is no embroidery to cover the slightest flaw in the texture. Readers of English verse will find a perfect master of this sort of poetry in the nineteenth century Englishman, Austin Dobson. Marot is admired by all modern lovers of skillful and unaffected verse, which may not be great but

VILLON

is immensely pleasing. For a time he was overshadowed almost to extinction by the rise of a new group of poets, stronger and more serious, whose purpose was to purify the French language and to imitate the classics. They were part of that general movement which we call the Renaissance and they learned their lessons not only from the classics but from Italy,

importing into French the Italian sonnet. They called themselves the *Pléiade* in imitation of a group of seven Greek poets.
They broke away, as far as they could, from old French poetry,
and so in the very act of refining and perfecting their language
they parted company with an important part of French life.
They resolved that French should be as fine as Greek, and
they almost succeeded in making it so, at the same time making
it artificially rigid; they established French classic verse which
persisted into the nineteenth century, when writers of "free
verse" and other rebels broke it up. The two important figures
in this sixteenth century cluster of seven stars are Joachim du
Bellay and Pierre de Ronsard. Their poetry determined the
shape of French verse, even though they went out of fashion
for almost two centuries. Moreover their work spread into
our literature, a wave of the Renaissance which splashed into
England. Spenser translated du Bellay's *Antiquities of
Rome,* and evidently these French poets were known to the
poets of Elizabethan England. They were experimenters in
form, too much concerned with the rhetoric of poetry and
blind to the merits of native French verse. But they were not
lacking in humanity and honest emotion. Let anyone who
thinks French verse is cold and formal read du Bellay's *Epi-
taph on a Little Dog.* It is in tone and feeling like nineteenth
century poetry. If the lyric verse of the sixteenth century
seems stiff and pseudo-classic, it has immensely greater freedom in the expression of genuine emotion than the verse of the
next two centuries, which became frigidly accurate, all brain
and no heart. The man who did as much as one man could
do to give French verse its icy shapeliness was Malherbe, poet
and critic, whose great influence is inconceivable when we
look back at his almost lifeless verses. The modern spirit

looks through that icy sheet of plate glass to the warm humanity of Villon, of Charles D'Orleans, of Clement Marot.

At this point let us make one or two observations apropos French poetry which will help us to understand all modern poetry. Verse with its rhymes and meters and stanzas is an artificial shaping of words. But verse is also a natural thing; people sing because they must, and song comes from the lips and throats of multitudes who would not understand a word of a learned work on the theory of prosody. There are thus two sources of poetry, the popular and the literary, the spontaneous and the deliberately artistic. The two things are not sharply separated or antagonistic; there may be the most cunning and skillful art in folk-song and there may be the very accent of life in the lines of a highly "literary" and elaborate poem. Perfection consists in the combination of what we call nature and what we call art (both very vague terms). The danger is that form, with which poets of course are greatly concerned, may become formalism and may stiffen and strangle ideas or refine the life out of them. This happened to French poetry. The editor of the *Oxford Book of French Verse* says: "The passion for order ... this phantom bestrides Pegasus behind the poet." That is why so much French verse, though exquisitely made, leaves us cold. The same tendency to rigidity is observable in Italian poetry after Dante, who made the supreme alliance of plain vernacular speech and intricate construction. English poetry, the greatest poetry in modern literature (this is not linguistic patriotism, for all European critics would consent to the "greatest"), has always been free, flexible, varied, true to the natural rhythms of living speech and at the same time of solid structure and with polished surfaces. During one period, the eighteenth century, literary manner got the better of matter

in English verse. But that was a temporary triumph, some·
what due to the influence of French. Toward the end of the
century English poetry regained its native freedom and has
never lost it in these hundred and fifty years; so that "free
verse" is no novelty in English, however startling, outrageous,
or beautiful any individual specimen may be. In German
the tradition of popular song persists unbroken, even through
the classical period, in which Goethe is the giant. The German adapted to his tongue the Greek-Latin hexameter of
Homer and Virgil and he became the most profound student
of the classics in all Europe. But his lyric poetry remained
German and its genius was united in holy artistic wedlock
with German music. There is a similar union in Russian,
Hungarian, and other languages, but we shall have to accept
that on faith or on authority, for we can hear the universal
bride of music, but the ears of most of us are deaf to the male
tongue of the languages. Everybody finds the poetry of the
language in which he was brought up the most natural and
beautiful, and every language must be beautiful when it is
sung by a real poet. But there are distinctions which are
interesting in themselves and which help us in an approach
to any literature. Remembering that these distinctions are
not very sharp, we may say that English poetry is its own
music, for England has had few first-rate composers, and
that it is both popular and literary; that German poetry is
sublimated by German music and has kept its popular feeling
and form. so that it is a democratic art, even in the hands of
a most learned and deliberate poet; that French poetry is
almost always deliberate and literary, with a cool care for
form. A French poet, though he may be a rebel in thought
and may intend to be an innovator in expression, preserves a
certain shapeliness and fidelity to convention. In a way this

is a limitation, but in another way it is an essential element in the beauty of French verse, and it is related to the clearness and neatness which are characteristic of French prose.

The tendency to formalism appeared early in French poetic drama, and continued down to the present time. The sources of French drama, and indeed of all western European drama, were two (much as in the case of lyric poetry), the literary or bookish, that is Greek and Latin, and the popular. The popular drama consisted of moralities, miracles and mysteries, very simple dialogues on subjects ranging from Bible stories to naïve buffoonery. (I shall say a word more about these early plays in connection with English drama, which had somewhat the same development as the French, in Chapter XXV). French dramatists in the sixteenth and seventeenth centuries all but ignored these early plays of the Middle Ages and devoted their energies largely to adapting and naturalizing classic drama.

The first great tragic poet in French is Pierre Corneille, whose life covered almost the whole of the seventeenth century. He wrote more than thirty comedies and tragedies, some of which were instantly successful, have held the French stage down to the present day, and largely determined the course of French poetic drama. Corneille was much more than an imitator of classic drama, though several of his plays are drawn from ancient sources. His most popular play, the *Cid,* is based on a Spanish original and the hero is the half-fabulous, half-historical Spanish chieftain, whom we have met among the heroes of medieval romance. Corneille's play has been translated into every modern European language. In its own time and country it made a great stir, and rival poets and critics, including the great Cardinal Richelieu, attacked it. The attacks failed because people liked the play.

I suspect that the vitality of that drama has not much to do with its exemplification or violation of classic form and consists not in the nobility of Corneille's style, but is due to and identical with the fact that it is ripping good romantic melodrama. And I suspect also that many other great plays and stories which have been buried beneath a heap of criticisms and annotations simply shake their shoulders, stand up and command us by primitive emotional strength. Corneille has all the gifts that make the writer of high tragedy. His plots have order, dramatic situations, action. His grasp of character is firm and he is a profound student of human nature, especially the internal conflicts, the clash of wills. Moreover he has the final art of the poet, the grand manner, which he sustains with remarkable power, though he sometimes writes commonplace verses, as does Shakespeare. Above all, he makes verse sound natural as the speech of living people. In *Cinna,* in *Horace,* in *Sertorius,* in *Rodogune* we have dramatic poetry of the loftiest tone. The French public early accorded him the welcome he deserved, applauding plays that now seem less than his best, and his dramas have held the stage for more than two centuries. Since the classic drama of Corneille we have the rich romantic drama which has more fire and color than the well reasoned plots of Corneille and we have the realistic drama which is closer to life. Much of the classic drama has withered and not all of Corneille is worth reading. But the best of him is imperishable.

The successor and younger rival of Corneille was Jean Racine. His subjects were Greek and Roman, as in *Andromaque* and *Phèdre*, and Biblical, as in *Esther* and *Athalie*. He has been praised for the excellence of his style, which to the native French ear is passionate, emotional, though it seems to us rather cold. But beneath that coldness we can find, even through the still colder medium of an indifferent translation, the secret soul of Racine, his knowledge of human nature. His people are not Greek, not Hebrew, not even French; they are the stuff of which we are all made, as truly as the characters of Shakespeare or Ibsen. Racine's ideal was perfection of form and phrase and he realized his ideal in five or six of his greatest plays, a compact unity of construction and an elegance (in the highest sense of the word) of diction which no French poet from Corneille to Claudel has excelled. He was an acute critic and in the prefaces to his plays he sets forth without modesty or boasting his creed, wrecked by the romantics and demolished by modern dramatists but absolutely sound for classic drama. His ideal as expressed in the preface of *Britannicus* is a simple situation without too much matter, which never departs from the natural to plunge into the extraordinary, which goes step by step toward the end, sustained by the interests, feelings, passions of the characters. It is customary to compare Racine with Corneille, which is as useless as comparing Ben Jonson with Shakespeare or Tennyson with Browning. But it is worth while to note that Corneille is the more vigorous and independent genius, Racine the more careful, delicate, disciplined.

It may require some effort for an English reader to find the secret of French tragedy. French comedy shines round the world and enlightens the most ignorant of us. Contemporary with Corneille and Racine was Molière, the greatest comic dramatist in all literature. He is French and of the seventeenth century, but he belongs to the timeless and nationless breed of laughers which includes his countrymen, Rabelais and Anatole France, the Spaniard Cervantes, and our linguistic kinsmen, Shakespeare, Fielding, Bernard Shaw, Mark Twain.

Molière was, like the Shakespeare of tradition, an actor and theatrical manager, and his plays are not only readable but actable—the French theater has never neglected them. In literature he has a unique and commanding place. He ridicules the human race by drawing its typical foolish figures. It has been said that Molière's figures are too typical, gen-

MOLIERE

eralized caricatures. His hypocrite is all hypocrite and his miser is all miser. But Molière knew that characterization on the stage must be swift and definite, and he made his outlines broad but close to life. The lines are so firm that their essential shape can be preserved in translation, though much of the wit of the dialogue may be lost. Tartuffe, the villain-hero of the play, is of the same race as Dickens's Pecksniff; Monsieur Jourdain in the *Bourgeois Gentleman* was certainly born on the same planet as Sinclair Lewis's George F. Babbitt. Molière directed his shafts against pomposity, pedantry, hypocrisy, greed, and other major vices, and also against the minor, innocent vices, simple stupidity and futility. Some of his shafts are sharp, even poisoned, and he made many enemies. He has been called a moralist, a philosopher, a social reformer. Perhaps he was all that. I think he was primarily a play-maker, trying to write entertaining shows. It has been said that a comedy is a farce by an author who is dead. A good deal of Molière is farce, some of it still fresh and funny. His masterpieces strike deeper than farce, and are comic criticisms of life.

The comic spirit expressed itself, outside the drama, in the work of Molière's friend, La Fontaine. The *Fables* of La Fontaine are the finest examples of that form of story in which human creatures are represented in the guise of our fellow-creatures, the beasts and the birds. It is an old kind of story, going far back of *Æsop's Fables* to the time when men believed that "animals" could speak. In familiar folk tales and fairy tales, for example, the *Uncle Remus* stories of Joel C. Harris, which are based on traditional negro myths, the animals speak and act "like folks." A recent writer, Kenneth Grahame, in *The Wind in the Willows* has charmingly portrayed in little beasties their upright two-legged brothers. Stories of animals with or without regard to human nature have always been popular and will be until the last child grows up and all stories end. The animal-fable, which we know in the Æsop of our childhood, is a short story leading to a moralistic maxim. La Fontaine transmuted the prosy fable into delightful verse. He draws human traits with delicate humor. No other French poet has been more often reprinted or more widely read, for children enjoy the lively tales and adults enjoy the shrewd comment on humanity and the cleverness of the verse.

Over all these dramatists and poets was a presiding genius who had more authority than any other critic from Aristotle to Matthew Arnold—that is Boileau. He is a superbly arrogant genius, aware of the finest literature of his time and of the past and satirically hostile to his weaker contemporaries. He recognized immediately the beauty of Racine and the wit of Molière. His genius, translated into values most familiar to us, is Horace and Alexander Pope. His *L'Art Poétique* is based on the *Ars Poetica* of Horace, as certainly as Pope's *Essay on Criticism* and *Rape of the Lock* are based on Boileau. But Boileau, like Pope, stands solidly on his own legs, a distinct, vigorous personality, generous, just and keen, though somewhat narrow and school-masterly. I find no magic in his verse; to my non-French ear it is cold and sharp as an icicle. And as for his alleged wisdom, well, Gautier's *L'Art* and Verlaine's *Art Poétique* seem to me to contain a thousand times more of sense and beauty than Boileau's famous poem. And when he says:

Laissons a l'Italie
Des tous ces faux brillants l'éclatante folie

he does put his finger on a certain weakness in Italian verse of the seventeenth century. But we wonder whether he ever did or could read Dante. Our French poetic critic is provincial both in time and in geography.

In the eighteenth century there were two or three writers of comedy whose laugh is still vital and hearty. After Le

Sage, whom we have met as a great master of the humorous novel and whose acid dramatic satire, *Turcaret,* holds a high place in the literature of the comic stage, there came a strange genius, Marivaux, who cannot be placed in the rational, orderly, too well criticized succession of French authors. His novel *Marianne* is a leap toward modern realism, modern, yet ancient psychology, what happens in the human breast. Marivaux's plays, notably *The Game of Love and Chance,* have wit and grace and a somewhat wilful originality: he did not like to say things as other people had said them, he hated adjectives and nouns that had been mated too long and he disunited some old hard-and-fast unions. He is one of the most original men in literature, a delight to all French critics even when they point to his defects, and his fantastic style, too metaphorical and eccentric, has given to the French language a curious word: *Marivaudage,* which, though quite different in substance. may be compared to *Euphuism* in English literature.

Marivaux's great but erratic genius never made him a favorite of the French public and he is almost unknown outside France. A later dramatist has been a joy forever to the whole world, Beaumarchais, whose *Barber of Seville* and *Marriage of Figaro* have probably made more people laugh than any other plays in the world, not excepting *Charley's Aunt.* The delight of these comedies has been manifolded by the music of Mozart and Rossini. Figaro is one of the supreme comic characters of literature. If authors meet in some corner of Heaven I like to think of Beaumarchais and Sheridan talking about plots and planning some foolish trick on gods and men.

CHAPTER XXI

MODERN GERMAN LITERATURE BEFORE THE CLASSICAL PERIOD

> I cannot and will not recant, because it is neither safe nor prudent to do anything against conscience. Here I stand, I cannot do otherwise. God help me. Amen!
>
> —*Luther at the Diet of Worms.*

MANY men of action have been also men of letters, for example, Sir Walter Raleigh and the Portuguese poet, Camoens. The only man in history who was the strongest individual force at once in practical affairs and in the literature of his nation is Martin Luther. It is impossible to separate one side of a man's character from another or any part of life from the literary expression of it. We cannot tell to what extent Luther's power in religion and politics was due to his command of words, or explain how far the fact that he became a German national hero accounts for the other fact that the German of Saxony, as developed by him, became the basis of modern literary German for the entire nation. It is the literary fact that chiefly interests us. The only thing in literature that at all approximates such a one-man dominance of the language and literature of a country, or a loosely related group of countries, is Dante's imposition of Tuscan, and his particular style of Tuscan, on the literature of Italy. From the literary point of view (which, let us remember, is historically not a complete view) it is Luther's translation of the Bible that gives him his

LUTHER

authority and importance. The German Reformation of the sixteenth century was not wholly a revolt against the abuses of the Church and it was not wholly theological. But it was intensely German, and Luther saw that one way to bring his forces together was to give his people a version in their own tongue of the Bible, which before had been in the ancient languages and so the exclusive possession of the learned, scholars and priests. His motive was somewhat like that of the earlier English translators of the Bible, to give the people the fundamental document on which all Christian religious dispute turns. To be sure, many of the people could not read and could not afford to own a book, but they could understand their language when it was read to them. Later the prose of German scholars and philosophers became notoriously complicated, involved, and difficult even for born

Germans. But Luther's *Gemeindeutsch* (common German) remains to this day the backbone of popular German prose. Luther was not by first intention a literary artist. He wrote for practical purposes; the dubious story that he threw his ink-pot at the devil is symbolically true, but it was the ink, not the pot, that he threw. He was, however, like many of his contemporaries from prince to peasant, acquainted with simple music and was noted for his skill in playing the lute; and he was brought up on the revival hymns of the fifteenth century, which were in tune and phrase like many English hymns (the music is often borrowed from the German). Luther wrote some of the strongest German hymns, the words certainly, and probably the music. The most famous of his hymns is *Ein Feste Burg Ist Unser Gott* ("a fast stronghold is our God"). This vigorous, compact German has never been well translated into English and probably cannot be. Thomas Carlyle, an idolater of German genius, failed to get Luther's meaning. The line: *Mit unsrer Macht ist Nichts gethan,* means simply that our human strength is nothing without God, as the next lines carry on the idea. Carlyle's version: "With force of arms we nothing can" is a misinterpretation of the original and is very bad English verse. This is perhaps a minor detail in our brief survey, but it illustrates the difficuty of translation, a very important problem in the story of literature.

Luther and the Reformation did not absorb all the intellectual life of Germany in the sixteenth century. Secular poetry flourished, in the great gilds of the *meistersinger* (mastersingers) which were composed of artisans and tradesmen as well as of gentlemen and knights. They carried on the traditions of the *minnesinger* (love-singers) of the twelfth and thirteenth centuries. Their art was very serious; to attain the rank of *meistersinger* a candidate had to prove his ability to invent both words and melody, and his success was as momentous as being knighted or receiving a university degree. The spirit of the *meistersinger,* the poetry and the comedy, is preserved in Wagner's opera. The most celebrated poet

HANS SACHS

was Hans Sachs, of Nuremberg, a contemporary and adherent of Luther. Sachs was a cobbler, but to be a cobbler in that time did not mean to be less than a gentleman and a scholar. It was for all its monarchs and petty nobles as democratic a period as has ever been. The artisan was no slave of a

machine but an independent worker and was a member of
very powerful gilds. It is well within the range of general
fact, though it may not be true as a specific detail, that a
shoemaker became Lord Mayor of London in the fifteenth
century, as the story is told in the merry comedy, *The Shoemaker's Holiday,* by the Elizabethan dramatist, Thomas
Dekker. Hans Sachs was a prolific writer of prose and verse,
much of which has become a permanent part of German
literature. But more permanent than the work of any one
man was the effect of the whole movement; thousands of
disciplined amateurs among the common people, burghers
and craftsmen, made songs, and those who could not create
at least got the echoes and rumors of poetry. There is a
profound relation between this popular art and the fact
that German children of all classes learn as a matter of course
the elements of poetry and music. The most commonplace
German sings and plays Bach and Schumann, and reads
Goethe and Schiller. For when the great German musicians
and poets arrived their countrymen were able to understand
and enjoy them.

But the arrival of great genius in Germany was postponed
until the eighteenth and nineteenth centuries. The seventeenth
century, which was so brilliant in France and England, was
a time of darkness in central Europe. The Thirty Years'
War which lasted until 1648, and even then was not finished,
devastated Germany, depressed the mature and slaughtered
the young. (Who knows how many boys killed in a war
might have proved to be men of talent?) The light of the
Renaissance which blazed over the rest of Europe faded out
in Germany and resulted in little else than dull pseudo-
classicism or uninspired imitations of the literature of neighboring countries. Thought did not cease: fortunately it never

does cease even in periods of despair. Toward the close of
the Thirty Years' War there was born the first of the great
German philosophers, Leibnitz, whose rationalism prevailed
in the eighteenth century among professional thinkers both
in his own country and in France. But the art of letters in
Germany, though it did not go out, was dim for a hundred
years until the revival which we shall try to sketch in Chapter XL.

CHAPTER XXII

SPANISH AND PORTUGUESE LITERATURE BEFORE THE NINETEENTH CENTURY

O most incomparable author! O happy Don Quixote! O famous Dulcinea! O facetious Sancho Panza! Jointly and severally may ye live through endless ages for the delight and recreation of mankind!

—*Cervantes.*

SPAIN is to us a country of romance, of hot blood, dark eyes, picturesque costumes, and thrilling adventure. This character has been attributed to it not by impressionable tourists but by Spanish writers, even by some of the excellent modern novelists. But the Spaniard with all his pride and chivalry and handsome manners, and perhaps as a corrective reaction against them, is endowed with a glorious sense of humor. At the beginning of the seventeenth century Cervantes wrote *Don Quixote*, which is the greatest comic novel in literature. Even Rabelais does not rival Cervantes (there is of course no question of rivalry between men of genius who are doing different things), for Rabelais writes a vast burlesque with gigantically absurd heroes, and Cervantes writes of persons who are conceivably, undeniably, true to life. His grotesque knight, Don Quixote,

249

whose mind has been turned by reading too many tales of chivalry, goes forth to find adventures like those in the stories. He mistakes windmills for giants and quiet inns for mighty castles. His prosaic squire, Sancho Panza, comments on these adventures and misadventures with plain good sense. It is the comic clash between dreams and reality. The sympathies of Cervantes, and so of the reader, are largely with the dreamer. Don Quixote is an old fool, but he is a likable old fool. He is a good man gone wrong. The animus of Cervantes is directed against the cause of Don Quixote's aberration. He says at the end of the book that his sole object was "to expose to the contempt they deserved the extravagant and silly tales of chivalry."

If that was his sole purpose, then he builded better than he knew. Chivalry died a natural death and so did most of the tales of chivalry. Cervantes made a story which is as broad and varied as life itself and which delights people who know nothing or care nothing about the romances which he scorns. Its vitality is deeper than burlesque or parody. Cervantes may have set out on the narrow winding lane of ridicule, but he found himself on the highway of humanity. He is in love with his two fools, in a paternal, not a sentimental, way. After the publication of the first part of the book, a cheeky rival wrote a sequel, and this spurious work so enraged Cervantes that he wrote the genuine second part. It is better than the first—a rare thing in the history of sequels. He pretends that his story is taken from the authentic records of an author named Cid Hamete, and the quotation at the head of this chapter is addressed to this fictitious original. If it is Cervantes praising himself, the praise is deserved! *Don Quixote* was translated into every language in Europe. The standard English version is by Motteux, the translator of

DON QUIXOTE

Rabelais. It is one of the great books of all time. Don Quixote and his faithful squire meet in their travels all sorts and conditions of men, and in them Cervantes portrays the life of Spain. But these people are more than Spanish. They are ourselves; mad knights and shrewd matter-of-fact philosophers are still abroad in the world.

If Cervantes had not written *Don Quixote* he would have an honorable, an amusing place in literature as the author of plays and stories. In the same way Chaucer would be historically a very important poet if he had not written *The Canterbury Tales*. But when a man overwhelms himself with a towering masterpiece he may sleep quietly beneath it with all his other little works beside him.

In the time of Cervantes Spain was at the height of her power, political and intellectual. Before Cervantes died Velasquez, the foremost Spanish painter, was born. The intellectual and artistic supremacy continued well into the seventeenth century. The political supremacy was terminated by an event which took place in 1588, when Cervantes was forty years old, the defeat of the Invincible Armada by the English fleet. One of the Spanish sailors was a young man, Lope de Vega, who was to become the founder of the Spanish theater and the almost absolute monarch of Spanish literature of the seventeenth century. None of his works has intrinsic value in literature outside Spain, certainly not in English literature, though he had some influence on Elizabethan drama. But he is one of the glories of Spanish literature, and the man himself is tremendous; he wrote more than a thousand plays, or, if that figure be an exaggeration, so many that no Spaniard pretends to have read them all. In addition he wrote many non-dramatic works. Perhaps the reason that no single work stands out as a specimen of his genius is that he wrote too

CERVANTES

CERVANTES

much. But we must pause long enough in our story to salute a man who could write a three act play in twenty-four hours!

The man who filled the Spanish theater for almost the whole of the seventeenth century was Calderón. He was the authentic successor of Lope de Vega, but perhaps less a man of the professional stage than a poet. There was a type of play in Spain, religious in motive and allied to the English and French miracle play, the *auto*. A dramatic procession moved through the streets with fantastic but reverent garments to be received by the king or the bishop. Of this type of play Calderón was the acknowledged master. He also wrote the romantic fabulous play, such as *Magico Prodigioso* and was admired by the German and English poets of the so-called romantic period—we can identify them by great names— Goethe, Shelley, and half a century later, FitzGerald, the poet of the *Rubáiyát*. It is mostly sword swinging over and by people who have been wronged, that point-of-honor stuff which was the detritus of the old chivalry over which Don Quixote drove his crazy horse. The Spanish still clung to it and so did Victor Hugo. It is good grand opera material but it takes a fine musician and a real poet to pull it to true tragic heights. Calderón did. And so did Corneille. And so did Hugo.

At the end of the peninsula Spain has a neighbor and kinsman, Portugal, a small nation, but in the sixteenth century a great maritime power. Camoens, the prince of Portuguese poets, was one of the sailors who dared the great sea in little ships, and he knew by experience the perils and sufferings of his hero, Vasco da Gama, the Portuguese navigator who first turned the Cape of Good Hope and so discovered the route to India. From the adventures of that splendid and brutal old pirate (who died in the year that Camoens was born, 1524) the poet made an epic so splendid that it has not been obscured by the fact that Portuguese is one of the little brothers among European languages. The great epic of Camoens, the *Lusiads* (Lusitania is the legendary name of Portugal), is more than the story of Da Gama and even

CAMOENS

more than the story of Portugal. It is the romance of discovery, of the struggle with the sea and the conquest of strange lands. It is the most powerful poem of the sea after the *Odyssey*. If Columbus had been a poet this is the kind of poem he might conceivably have written. There is a vigorous translation made in the nineteenth century by Richard Burton, who, like Camoens, was both a man of letters and a traveler and adventurer. When the Spanish occupied Lisbon and made Castilian the official language, it was the work of Camoens which saved his native tongue from destruction and inspired his countrymen to resist the invader and preserve their nationality. The pen may not be mightier than the sword but it sometimes helps to determine the fate of nations.

CHAPTER XXIII

ENGLISH LITERATURE BEFORE THE AGE OF ELIZABETH

Chaucer is the first great poet who has treated Today as if it were as good as Yesterday.

—Lowell.

UCH English literature before Chaucer belongs rather to history than to art, though the impulse that created it may have been artistic. We can read some of it with interest but not much of it with pleasure. Suddenly —there is no way of accounting for it—appears a great and delightful poet. Chaucer is a palm in a desert, or rather, a towering pine in the midst of underbrush. Chaucer's culture was French, like that of all English gentlemen of the fourteenth century. The court of his king, Richard II, spoke French and was somewhat contemptuous of English. Chaucer translated from the French and borrowed generously from Italian. But his language is English. It is not quite modern English; a little study is necessary to get his vocabulary and the accents of his verses and the rich values of his vowels. All attempts, even by so clever a man as Dryden, to render Chaucer in the idiom and measure of later English have

failed. Chaucer's masterpiece, the *Canterbury Tales,* is a
collection of stories drawn from many sources, assembled
under a unifying situation. The tellers of the tales are
pilgrims on their way to Canterbury—it was a holiday excursion rather than a pious journey. The tales are admirable,
but finer than any of them is the Prologue which describes
the company. The knight, the parson, the prioress, and
the rest are drawn each in a few perfect lines. There is

CANTERBURY PILGRIMS

in all literature no more neat and clear characterization. The
persons are varied, chosen from all walks of life, so that the
group is a picture in miniature of England of the fourteenth
century. The tales reveal all the moods of narrative, from
grave tragic adventure to gay comedy.

If Chaucer had not written *The Canterbury Tales* he would have a high place in English poetry for his other poems. *Troilus and Criseyde*, the theme of Shakespeare's play, is interestingly told, but it is not a very thrilling story, in Chaucer or in Shakespeare, or in Boccaccio's *Filostrato*, from which Chaucer borrowed it. The finest of Chaucer's "minor" poems is *The Book of the Duchesse*, a lovely miscellany drawn from all sources, his reading and his dreams thrown into a loose yet very shapely unit. All Chaucer's verse is worth reading and most of it delightful; and there is at least an archeological interest in his prose, notably his translation of the philosopher Boethius, whom the thinkers of Chaucer's time and for a thousand years before him held in higher respect than we do —for we have never read him.

Chaucer is so eminent in a barren period that he makes us forget, and then remember, two of his contemporaries, men at opposite poles of thought and language, Gower and Langland.

Gower was a good conventional versifier. He wrote French, Latin, English, and was immensely respected in his time. His *Confessio Amantis* contains some good lines but is formal and dull, and nobody reads him but scholars. The authentic tribute to him is the line of great Chaucer, at the close of *Troilus and Criseyde*:

> O moral Gower, this book I directe
> To thee

Chaucer, a great artist, knew his contemporaries, and we accept his judgment. But time has bleached the color out of Gower. He has no thrill, no melody for me, but the most casual wanderer in English poetry will take a look at a few lines selected by Ward or some other anthologist.

Much more vital is a strange poet, Langley or Langland, who wrote the *Vision of Piers the Plowman*. We know nothing of the author, but there must have been a vigorous individual behind this unique and original poem. It is a loosely constructed dream-allegory of Heaven and Hell and the life of Christ. The rough alliterative verse, suggesting the older poetry rather than that which was to come, has little of the urbanity and grace of Chaucer, but it is good verse, imaginative, dignified, sincere.

For a century after Chaucer English poetry was commonplace, partly because there was no first rate genius among the poets and partly because they had to wrestle with a language that had ceased to be the language of Chaucer and was not yet the language of Shakespeare. The art of versification had to be learned anew. The loveliest lyric notes came from the north, from Scotland, in the poems of Henryson, Dunbar, Douglas and King James (though the verses ascribed to him are of doubtful authorship). They are all disciples of Chaucer, but they are not imitators, and their individuality is enriched by their Scottish vocabulary, which has always retained its freshness and natural vitality.

CHAUCER

If the fifteenth century is not rich in literary poetry it is the great age of the popular ballad. Most of the best versions of English and Scotch ballads which have come down to us are evidently in the language of the fifteenth century, though it is impossible, and unnecessary, to determine exact dates, and though many of the ballads probably existed in earlier versions. We know nothing of the authors. As a piece of verse does not make itself, probably any given version of a ballad was put into final shape by some individual. But the origin is obscure as that of a fairy-tale. There were professional ballad singers or reciters who may have altered familiar poems to suit themselves. Even the later custom of printing and peddling single ballads did not insure permanence of form. The subjects of the ballads are simple love stories, more or less mythical adventures like the famous Robin Hood cycle, celebration of some actual event, a battle or the death of a hero like *Sir Patrick Spens*.

The ballad is closely related to the epics and romances which flourished in the Middle Ages and handles much the same material in shorter form. The great manuscript source of ballads is the Percy folio from which Thomas Percy in the eighteenth century took his *Reliques*, a book which played a great part in the romantic revival. The ultimate collection is the monumental work of the American scholar, Professor Child. Besides the popular ballad, which we think of as spontaneous, there is the deliberate literary imitation like Coleridge's *Ancient Mariner,* Oscar Wilde's *Ballad of Reading Gaol,* and Swinburne's many fine experiments with the form. But the flavor of a literary masterpiece like *The Ancient Mariner* is as unlike that of a traditional ballad as champagne is unlike Scotch ale. Even Walter Scott, who probably knew scores of ballads by heart, never quite caught the accent in his own verse. Nevertheless, the ballad has had a great influence on sophisticated poetry and has a charm which every true poet has felt.

The poets of the early part of the sixteenth century are

chiefly interesting as heralds of the dawn of the great age of Elizabeth. Two of the most important of the singers of songs before sunrise were Thomas Wyatt and Henry Howard, Earl of Surrey. Wyatt imitated and translated the sonnet of Petrarch, which has ever since remained a favorite form with

THOMAS MORE

English poets, and he also experimented with other metrical forms. Surrey, who was younger than Wyatt, wrote smoother verses and in a translation of a book of the *Æneid* gave English literature its earliest example of blank verse, the ten-syllable line of Shakespeare and Milton. There is always something admirable about the pioneer, the discoverer. But Surrey was not a great poet. The great poets (after Chaucer) were still to come.

If Wyatt and Surrey were not great poets they brought a fresh note into English verse and they brought it from Italy. A young Englishman after leaving the university always visited Italy, and we have only to say Milton, Shelley, Keats, the Brownings to remind ourselves that Italy has been for centuries close to the heart of English poetry. Not only Wyatt and Surrey but the other minor poets included in *Tottel's Miscellany* show the Italian influence. This Miscellany is a milestone in the history of English poetry. In that age gentlemen wrote verse as a polite accomplishment and circulated manuscript copies of their productions among their friends. An enterprising printer would get possession of a sheaf of these manuscripts and publish a collection, without much care as to order or authorship. To Tottel and other miscellanies we owe the preservation of many verses which might have been lost—as no doubt many were lost.

Among the minor poets of this age who are memorable because they are forerunners and pioneers is Gascoigne. His *Steel Glass* is the first satire in English verse and is by no means a contemptible beginning. A better poet is Sackville, who wrote part, the only truly poetic part, of *The Mirror for Magistrates*, sad stories of the death of kings. It is the deepest, most finely cadenced poetry between Chaucer and Spenser.

Much of the English prose of the fifteenth and early sixteenth centuries is to our ears more antiquated than the poetry. Real poetry seems to be timeless, whereas prose grows stale and out of fashion. But in this period are several prose writers whose vitality triumphs over any difference of idiom between their time and ours. Toward the end of the fifteenth century there was one man of talent, Thomas Malory, of whose *Morte d'Arthur* we have already spoken. It is a translation from French romances, rather loosely put together as a whole, but well told in the several episodes and written in a style which sounds to us only slightly archaic.

English literature early enriched itself by liberal translations and adaptations from foreign languages. One of the earliest and most industrious translators was Caxton, the father of English printing, a man of scholarship and good taste. He realized that Chaucer had "embellished and ornated" English

and in imitation of the master by studying his French originals
Caxton also ornated English and had a lasting good influence
on our prose. He translated twenty books and printed on
his own press, the first in England, at least fifty more. One
of the books that he printed and sponsored is Malory's *Morte
d'Arthur.*

About the time that Malory was making his translation
there was born one of the noblest of Englishmen, Thomas
More, "the blessed." More's masterpiece, *Utopia,* has a capital place in English literature, though it was written first in
Latin and not translated into English until after More's death.
It was also translated into the other principal European
languages, and the title of it became the universal common
noun for any ideal state of society. In setting forth the virtues of a perfect commonwealth, he necessarily attacks the
vices of his own time—which were evidently much like the
vices of our time. If the principles of More's state have not
been put in practice, neither have the best ideas of Plato's
Republica nor the best ideas of any philosophic statesman. It
is one of the ironies of history, by no means unusual, that
More, who was the finest spirit of his time, should have been
beheaded for no other offense than that he was too upright
and honest for the age of Henry VIII. The man is more important than the writer. He was the first of the English humanists, the equal in learning and character, though not in
literary genius, of his Dutch friend, Erasmus. The function
of the humanist was not to be an artist in his own language
but to spread the light of the classics.

Religious controversy and homilies are seldom of interest
to the general reader. It is a proof of the genius of Cranmer,
first Protestant archbishop of Canterbury, that the beauty of
his style has preserved substance which, if less eloquently

phrased, would long since have perished. His rhythms are quite modern; he seems at least a hundred years later than the period in which he lived. Aside from his importance in the history of the Reformation he is the foremost artist in English prose before the age of Elizabeth.

Less eloquent than Cranmer but equally endowed with force and sincerity is another bishop, Latimer. He, too, is an important figure in the history of the Reformation and it is largely on that account that his sermons survive. But they are worth reading for their style, which is direct and vigorous; its strength is due to its freedom from anything "parsonical" and to the use of homely illustrations taken from life, not from books.

This chapter may well be closed with a note on Ascham, who in a practical sense did inaugurate the age of Elizabeth, for he was Elizabeth's tutor. His best known book, *The Schoolmaster*, is the first important treatise in English on education, and though the problems have been threshed over many times, it still has passages that are not outworn. Ascham is a bit of a pedant, a scholar but not an artist. One thing suggests the measure of the man: he thought the *Morte d'Arthur*, which has afforded innocent pleasure to more people than any other prose of the time, a harmful book!

CHAPTER XXIV

THE AGE OF ELIZABETH: LITERATURE OTHER THAN DRAMATIC

Foole, said my Muse to me, looke in thy heart, and write.
—*Philip Sidney.*

N the middle of the sixteenth century were born Philip Sidney, Edmund Spenser, Walter Raleigh, and others whom we cannot even mention, for now English literature begins to blossom so profusely that we cannot count the flowers. Philip Sidney was a poet with his pen and a poetic figure in his life and death. His magnificent gesture on the battlefield when, after having received his death-wound, he gave his last drop of water to a dying soldier, is worthy of Roland, or any other knight of fable. However much or little fact there is in the story of Sidney's love for Stella, who was married to another man before Sidney realized his passion for her, at least it is a good romantic story and inspired him to write the first fine sonnet sequence in English, *Astrophel and Stella*. The emotion of his verse sounds genuine, and the appearance of sincerity is all that counts in literature. Not all; the ability to use words counts too. Sidney mastered the sonnet and made it a natural, or naturalized, form of English poetry.

If *Astrophel and Stella* did not directly inspire Spenser's sonnet sequence, *Amoretti*, it had some influence on the greater poet, and even on the supreme Shakespearean cycle. But it should be remembered that sonneteering was the fashion. The gentleman and the professional poet learned to make a sonnet as they learned to use their swords. Some of the sonnets are formal and merely graceful exercises. Some have the true accent of passion. But whether the love that is celebrated is for a certain lady we do not in most cases know as definitely as we do in the case of Sidney. The dark lady of Shakespeare's sonnets is an unsolved mystery. Second only to the sequences of Spenser and Shakespeare and, to my ear at least, quite as beautiful, are the sonnets of Drayton, who, outside the drama, left a larger body of genuine poetry than any other poet of the period except Spenser. There are few finer, more deeply human love-sonnets than the one that begins:

> Since there's no help, come let us kiss and part.

Another poet who made splendid sonnets is Samuel Daniel. Such sonnets as the one that contains the lines

> When yet the unborn shall say, *Lo, where she lies!*
> *Whose beauty made him speak, that else was dumb!*

place him in the company of Shakespeare.

Sidney was called by Drayton, "That Heroe for numbers, and for prose." His prose consists of two works, *The Countess of Pembroke's Arcadia* and *An Apology for Poetry*, which was appended to the *Arcadia* and is the more important. It is fine prose, simple and musical, and it is one of three or four essays that are the foundation of English criticism. It was an answer to an attack on drama and poetry by Gosson, called *The School of Abuse*. These pamphlets are very illuminating

as showing the state of literature and the real struggle that
poetry had before it finally triumphed over all criticism and
went in the right direction. An essay that should be mentioned
with the *Apology*, and was perhaps influenced by it, is
Webbe's *A Discourse of English Poetry*. More instructive

SIDNEY

even than Sidney is *Putten-
ham's Art of English Poesy*,
the most important critical
work of the period. But Sidney's essay is the best prose
and he who died so young was
father of them all.

It is interesting to turn back
from the prose and verse of
this old young father for a
glance at the *Arcadia*, which
is the work of a clever amateur, an idle, artificial, affected
thing, though it has charming passages. The *Arcadia* is one
of several romances which the taste of the time approved, far
beyond the borders of the world of reality and palatable to
us only when taken out of prose and turned into the poetry
of fairyland, as Shakespeare turned Lodge's fantastic *Rosa-
lynde* into the magically romantic *As You Like It* and as
Lodge himself in the songs came near to the magical. There
is a kind of extravagance which poetry carries naturally but
which is an intolerable burden upon prose. A capital example
is Lyly's *Euphues*, whose strained artificial manner is to us
ridiculous; yet when a touch of that manner tinged the verse
of the time it did no harm, but was often an appropriate
decoration.

Those who say that euphuism—Lyly's book gave us a common noun—had an evil influence on Shakespeare's style simply do not understand poetry or the problems of style. Euphuism was in the air, and no single author was responsible for it. It was as natural for an Englishman to use a highly elaborate fashion of speech and to practice ingenious turns of phrase for the pleasure of the queen or some other lady as it was for him to wear a lace ruff, pink silk breeches, an embroidered cloak and a bejeweled sword. This briefly explains why the poetry is noble and stately, too often toplofty, and the prose too often flimsy and grotesquely embroidered—that is, the prose of romance, for the expository prose is sober, dignified, and sound. It is all illustrated in a small way in the *Arcadia* and the *Apology*. The prose argument is firm, fluent and sane, first rate criticism. The lyric bits are charming. The rest is dangerously near to nonsense, a wedding cake with a china shepherdess on top.

But there were to be live shepherdesses in English poetry, and the pastoral, at which we glanced in an earlier chapter, was to become so natural that we almost forget that the English countryside never heard an oaten pipe or the voice of Amaryllis and that Herrick's Lost Shepherdess was named Eliza. It was a great moment in English poetry when in 1579 Spenser published *The Shepheard's Calender*. It announced the arrival of a poet of the first order, and the succeeding "sundrie short poemes" confirmed the announcement. It often happens that the lesser poems of a great poet who has made a colossal masterpiece are lost in the shadow of it. This is not true of Spenser—or of Milton. It is fitting to name them together, for whatever else they are both are unrivalled lyric poets.

The lyric poet is a man of short breath, though he may express the universe in four lines. The greater poet, if there really is a greater, measured in terms of long and short, works out a broad plan or plot, and then fills in his scheme with all kinds of lyric loveliness. Spenser is the first English poet after Chaucer who had a splendid conception and the skill to execute it. *The Faërie Queene* is an elaborate allegory planned in twelve books, of which Spenser finished only six. Each book narrates the exploits of a knight who symbolizes one of the "morall vertues," holiness, temperance, chastity, and so on. Perhaps our interest in allegorical romance is not as profound as it should be, and the *Faërie Queene* is too long; it fills two volumes of Everyman's Library and four hundred closely printed pages in the Globe Edition, so that it does not comply with Poe's rule that a poem should be of such length that we can read it at one sitting. It is a colossal performance, admired by most of Spenser's contemporaries and by all poets since his time. Charles Lamb called Spenser "the poet's poet." One reason is that poets appreciate his fertility and power of composition; the poem is written in the Spenserian stanza which he invented, and in the hundreds of stanzas, though the substance may at times be dull, he never technically breaks down. The other reason is that Spenser had the supreme poetic gifts, melody, rhythm, image. Those who cannot read the *Faërie Queene* through (and nobody does except the poet, the scholar, and the proofreader) may open to any canto at random, and they will light upon verse of gorgeous texture, like old tapestry. The "aged accents and untimely words," for which he was chided in his own time, only add to the richness of the color.

To be a supreme lyric poet in an age which has such a wealth of song is to be great indeed, for in the Elizabethan and Jacobean period and throughout the seventeenth century (the first period flows into the next without a break) there are so many lyric voices that one can hardly listen to them all. What is the secret of that wealth, that freshness, that almost bewildering variety which not even the immensely rich nineteenth century quite equalled and to which indeed the poets of the nineteenth century returned for sustenance and inspiration? If we open any of the anthologies or miscellanies of the time, for example, *England's Parnassus, The Choicest Flowers of Our Modern English Poets,* published in 1600, and *England's Helicon* of the same year, we come upon exquisite bits, some by poets whose names are not familiar. Or if we turn to any of the dramatists, even to plays by secondary men, we find that all poets who wrote for the stage could sing. Better still, perhaps, for a "lyric feast" (the words are Herrick's in his poem to Jonson) let us open a modern anthology in which a discriminating editor has culled the best or some of the best, for example, Professor Schelling's *Elizabethan Lyrics* and the companion volume, *Seventeenth Century Lyrics,* Arber's *English Garner* and Bullen's *Lyrics from Elizabethan Song-Books.*

The obvious common characteristic of the Elizabethan poem, which is truly lyric and not epic or dramatic or satiric or epigrammatic, is that it sings itself, and in point of fact some of the lyric poems must have been sung, certainly those that are found in the dramas. Others were written to traditional melodies. Still others were composed to new tunes, in some cases the poet being master of the lute as well as of the pen. The most distinguished example of poet-musician is Thomas Campion, whose *Four Books of Airs* contain both words and music, all the words and most of the music by Campion. Every one of his poems has a singing quality that almost makes the tune audible, even when one has only the words and not the music. It is strange that this perfect singer thought little of his songs, strange too that he advocated unrhymed verse, and stranger still that he sank into complete oblivion until modern scholars rediscovered him.

The prince of song, acknowledged by all the other poets, was Ben Jonson, of whom we shall say a word more when we come to his plays. The famous song which everybody knows

Drink to me only with thine eyes

is but one of scores of poems remarkable not only for their beauty of form and exactly right choice of words but for the dignity of feeling, the restrained vigorous passion. It may be that Jonson's immense erudition makes his tragedies somewhat heavy, but in his song he carries his learning on powerful and graceful wings and his voice is not of the owl but of the skylark. His devotion to the classics had a wholesome effect on his verse and on the verse of all the tribe of Ben that followed him, for he was not a slave to the ancients, he mastered them for his own use and benefit. Horace, Catullus, Martial influenced him, were his models. Like some later poets, Arnold and Tennyson, he knew the Roman poets, believed that their symmetry held a lesson for English verse. Elizabethan verse was in danger of being eccentric and Jonson with his great authority helped to keep it regular but not stiff, normal but not conventional, clear but not commonplace.

A friend of Jonson's who holds a high place in English verse is Drummond, whose madrigals and sonnets are graceful, refined and full of feeling. What could be better than his sonnet to a Nightingale, which I think Keats must have read?

The finer characteristics of Elizabethan England and of all western Europe in the sixteenth and seventeenth centuries were intellectual curiosity, a love of adventure, and boldness in experimenting with new ideas and forms of expression. Those were, indeed, as Tennyson calls them, "spacious times." Men were surprisingly versatile. Walter Raleigh, explorer and captain, was one of the finest of the lyric poets, and when he was shut up in the Tower of London, he amused himself for the twelve years by writing his *History of the World*.

The Elizabethan lyric has every possible mood known to the human soul and it is so splendid that we ought to end these few imperfect paragraphs about it on a note of joy, with one of the tender love songs. But the age was full of tragedy in life as well as on the stage, and it is fitting to quote Raleigh's somewhat sad *Conclusion,* especially as he was in thought and action as representative as any one man could be of that varied age.

> Even such is Time, that takes in trust
>   Our youth, our joys, our all we have,
> And pays us but with earth and dust;
>   Who in the dark and silent grave,
> When we have wandered all our ways,
> Shuts up the story of our days;
> But from this earth, this grave, this dust,
> My God shall raise me up, I trust.

One of the most independent and original thinkers was Francis Bacon, the founder of modern English philosophy. Whether he was also a poet is a problem into which we cannot go here. His best known book is the *Essays*, in which he has compressed all that there is to say on fifty subjects, a hundred subjects. He seems to have read all the wisdom in the world and boiled every idea down to its essence. In a famous letter he wrote, "I have taken all knowledge to be my province," and if he had written nothing else but the essays he would have proved his title. His style is epigrammatic, fluent, rich in analogies, and informed by a kind of plain common sense that distinguishes it from much of the too fantastic prose of the period. But the *Essays* are only a small part of his writings in Latin and English. His most important work is the *Novum Organum,* a fragment of a vast philosophy which he planned but could not carry out.

FRANCIS BACON

No man could. He thought it possible—this was his only great mistake—for a man to learn the whole truth about the universe and organize this knowledge in final form. His great contribution is his experimental method and his revolt against the authority of the schools. For centuries Aristotle and his disciples had ruled almost all speculation; they first accepted principles and then proceeded to argue about particulars. Bacon reversed that; he said we must find out the particular truths and from them reason toward the general principles. This method of thought is called induction and resembles the method of Socrates. The spirit of this mode of inquiry created a revolution in the thought of Europe and prevails in modern science. It was Bacon's *New Atlantis* that led to the founding of the Royal Society which has been a powerful influence in the progress of science. No man did more than Bacon for independence of thought, for the establishment of the right and duty of the individual to make his own researches. In the *Advancement of Learning* he says: "Men have withdrawn themselves too much from the contemplation of nature, and the observations of experience, and have tumbled up and down in their own reason and conceits." And again: "Whereas the more constant and devote kind of professors of any science ought to propound to themselves to make some additions to their science, they convert their labours to aspire to certain second prizes; as to be a profound interpreter or commentator; to be a sharp champion or defender; to be a methodical compounder or abridger; and so the patrimony of knowledge cometh to be sometimes improved, but seldom augmented." We have taken some long steps since Bacon, but his comment is still a rebuke to some current scholarship.

Much of the richness of Elizabethan literature was due to the translators who went not only to the classics but to contemporaneous European literature. We have already mentioned Florio's *Montaigne,* Thomas North's *Plutarch,* and Chapman's *Homer.* Translation today is as a rule none too good in point of style, but it is supposed to be fairly faithful to the original; there is a kind of literary honesty required even of a hack translator. The Elizabethan translator had no such idea. He took all kinds of liberties with the original, used it as so much material to handle as he pleased, and with true English independence had no respect for the intellectual rights of a foreign author. The result is that the Elizabethan versions of foreign classics are intensely English, not so much translations as naturalizations and so almost a part of the native literature. And that literature was growing apace.

CHAPTER XXV

ELIZABETHAN DRAMA BEFORE SHAKESPEARE

If all the pens that ever poets held
Had fed the feeling of their masters' thoughts,
And every sweetness that inspired their hearts,
Their minds, and muses on admired themes;
If all the heavenly quintessence they still
From their immortal flowers of poesy;
      .   .   .   .   .   .
If these had made one poem's period,
And all combined in beauty's worthiness,
Yet should there hover in their restless heads
One thought, one grace, one wonder, at the least,
Which into words no virtue can digest.

—*Marlowe.*

 NGLISH drama springs from two main sources, the popular and the literary. The popular forerunners of Shakespeare are the miracle plays of the middle ages. The miracle plays were simple dialogues based on Bible stories, such as the story of Abraham and Isaac and the birth of the Savior. They were actually performed in the churches with all reverence. But the actors, whether priests or laymen, introduced secular ideas, even comic ones, and ecclesiastical authority forbade them inside the church. The people enjoyed them and continued to play them in public places. The guilds, or trades unions, took them up and prided

themselves on the excellence of their performances. The groups of plays that survive are named for the towns in which they developed, Chester, York, Coventry. It is probable that the other name for these plays, "mysteries," has nothing to do with the sacredness of the subject but comes, both in English and in French, from the word "mistère," which means a trade, because the players were craftsmen. However that may be, here was the beginning of dramatic dialogue, the trained actor and primitive stagecraft. Besides the miracle plays, and a little later, there were the morality plays, in which the characters are allegorical abstractions. Some of these have real literary quality. A good example is *Everyman,* which was revived on our stage a few years ago and proved very effective.

It is true that most of the liturgical plays, versified Biblical episodes in crude dialogue, and the moralities which have for their characters abstractions, Sin, Hate, Pride, Folly, and so on, and the interludes, which are wholly secular entertainments, often farcical jibes at human nature—all these preliminaries to the great drama have little poetic quality. Their interest is historical, archeological. Yet it is an interest not to be neglected. As Saintsbury says with emphatic italics, "The modern drama *did* arise out of the Miracles. The Miracles *did* pass into the Moralities. The Moralities *did* pass into modern drama." But if one may modestly pit one's ignorance against vast and venerable learning, I venture to say that Saintsbury goes too far when he says: "Though the imitation of the ancient classical drama, and its performance in schools and universities, coloured, shaped, generally influenced the modern drama most momentously, this drama no more arose out of them than Spenser rose out of Virgil, or Hooker out of Cicero."

At any rate, even the earliest crude specimens of English drama which have anything like the modern play form were written by university men who may be supposed to have had a glimpse of the classics. The earliest "legitimate" English comedy, *Ralph Roister Doister*, was written about the middle of the sixteenth century by Udall, headmaster of Eton and a graduate of Oxford. The play is English in substance, crude slap-stick humor, but there is a dramatic outline and continuity which suggests the descent upon English shoulders of the classic robe. The diction is English doggerel of little merit.

Another farce, coarse and cheap, heavily funny, is *Gammer Gurton's Needle*, by John Still, a Cambridge graduate who became Vice-Chancellor of his university. It is thoroughly English in its rough laughter but it has a construction which is as old as the classics and was new to English.

The first English tragedy in regular form, the Senecan, is *Gorbuduc*, reputed to have been written in whole or in part by Sackville, whom we have met as an early lyric and narrative poet. It is a dull play in stodgy unilluminated verse. But it has an approach toward shape, progressive action, and sense of character.

All these plays are but groping experiments, and so are others in the early years of the great queen's reign, and so too, rudimentary and dull, are most of the plays before Marlowe. But immediately before Marlowe and surrounding him is a group of dramatists, who were also lyric poets, pamphleteers and miscellaneous writers, the so-called University Wits, Lyly, Greene, Nash, Peele, Lodge, and Kyd (who went to a public school if not to a university). The merit of these men, except Marlowe, is not great and it suffers diminution because we see them through the blazing glory of the mature Elizabethan drama.

Lyly, whose euphuistic prose is so conceited and false, loses much of his vice and increases his virtue when he turns to romantic drama. *Endymion* and *The Woman in the Moon* are (to euphuize) of fine fancy if not of immortal imagery. Shakespeare evidently knew them, and it is not without significance that Jonson in the memorial verses prefixed to the Shakespeare folio groups Lyly, Kyd, and Marlowe.

Peele is at his best in two plays, *The Arraignment of Paris*, a pastoral court masque which contains some lovely lines, and *David and Bethsabe*, a really dramatic rendering of the Bible story with many passages of poetic beauty.

Greene's best play, *Friar Bacon and Friar Bungay*, is a mixture of the supernatural, of horse-play and love story, a combination to be found in much higher form in Marlowe's *Faustus*. More interesting than Greene's dramas are his pamphlets, notably his *Groat's Worth of Wit Bought with a Million of Repentance*, which contains the famous left-handed uncomplimentary reference to Shakespeare as "Shakescene."

Lodge is very much more important as lyric poet and pamphleteer than as dramatist, and Nash, a clever pamphleteer, barely touched the drama.

Kyd in *The Spanish Tragedy* gives an early example of the tragedy of blood, full of rant and murder; in other words, roaring melodrama.

Dwarfing all these and himself undwarfed by even the greatest, Shakespeare or Milton, is Marlowe, the first great tragic poet in our language, a fierce, insolent spirit, who accomplished miracles of beauty in the short twenty-nine years of his life. He wrote four plays, in all of which the theme is human ambition and love of power, the will of man to penetrate the baffling mystery of the universe. His best play is *Faustus,* based on the old legend of the magician who sold his soul to the Devil in return for a brief period of unlimited power. This is the story which Goethe wrought into his complicated philosophic poem, *Faust*, and is the subject of Gounod's perennially popular opera. In Marlowe's play the tragic hero is the poet himself, rebellious against human bondage and striving toward infinite knowledge. The play contains much fustian, but it also contains passages on Marlowe's "admired themes," some of the most magnificent verse that has ever been written in English. Blank verse, even in the hands of Shakespeare, cannot be more sonorous. When Mephistophilis summons Helen of Troy, Faustus speaks the famous lines:

> Was this the face that launched a thousand ships
> And burnt the topless towers of Ilium?
> Sweet Helen, make me immortal with a kiss.

And when Faustus asks:

> How comes it then that thou art out of hell?

Mephistophilis replies:

> Why this is hell, nor am I out of it:
> Thinkst thou that I who saw the face of God,
> And tasted the eternal joys of Heaven,
> Am not tormented with ten thousand hells,
> In being deprived of everlasting bliss?

Faustus is Marlowe's masterpiece. But the three other plays are as characteristic and are crammed with fine things. *Tamburlaine the Great*, his first arrogant challenge to the world of poetry, is a rhetorical pageant, young with a Byronic youth. Here indeed are what the prologue promises, high astounding terms, Marlowe's mighty line, as Jonson called it. The barbaric splendor of it pushed one stage further would break and flutter into mere theatrical trappings. But Marlowe is in command of his great natural power. *The Jew of Malta*, with its terrible cruelty, is a good specimen of the tragedy of blood and it shows most clearly Marlowe's one shortcoming—the lack of wisdom, which may be due to passionate youth, complete indifference to human character, or ignorance of it. When in *Edward II* the facts of history and of actual character subdue him he is somewhat ill at ease, there are not so many magnificent lines, but the play is dramatically and humanly his best.

Marlowe was a great lyric and narrative poet. He would be remembered for his *Hero and Leander* alone, in which is the line that everybody knows, though not everybody knows that he wrote it:

> Whoever loved that loved not at first sight?

Neither Marlowe nor any other one man created blank verse or suddenly made English tragedy. But there is truth in the opinion of Swinburne that "He is the greatest discoverer, the most daring and inspired pioneer, in all our poetic literature. . . . After his arrival the way was prepared, the paths were made straight, for Shakespeare."

CHAPTER XXVI

SHAKESPEARE

Sweetest Shakespeare, Fancy's child.
—*Milton.*

IN 1623 was published the most important book in English literature, the first folio collection of Shakespeare's plays. (We need not except the Bible from our superlative, for that is not primarily creative English literary art.) There is a mystery about this folio and its author. It is a mystery unsolved and too complicated to argue about in our short space; we will merely suggest the problem, because it is important or at least interesting in the story of English literature. Who was Shakespeare? We know very little about him, as we know very little about many other men of genius. The Shakespeare of traditional biography was born in Stratford in 1564, was married at eighteen to Anne Hathaway, went to London when he was about twenty, became an actor, was known when he was about thirty as poet and playwright, enjoyed an increasingly prosperous career as author and theatrical manager and owner, and retired to Stratford when he was about forty-five, and died there in 1616. About the middle of the nineteenth century some sceptical persons raised the question whether a man without university training, or at least abundant opportunity to read, could have written the plays which show profound learning and a highly cultivated knowledge of literature. The answer, not yet widely accepted by scholars, was that Shakespeare was only a pseudonym, or "blind," for Francis Bacon. We cannot trace the intricacies of the argument. The gist of it is that the Baconians insist that the actor from Stratford could not have done the work and Bacon could. The Shakespeareans insist that Bacon, as proved by his prose writings, could not have done the plays and poems and that Shakespeare not only could but in point of fact did.

Let them argue. We have the work, the sonnets and the plays, which are, taken as a whole, the highest word in English poetry. The sonnets may have great biographical significance, but much of the disputation as to what they mean and who was the object of Shakespeare's abusive love has served less to reveal their deeper value than to obscure their surface beauty. We can sympathize with the view of Browning, who during his lifetime suffered from too many commentators, that Shakespeare did not use the sonnet to unlock his heart; "If so the less Shakespeare he!" Sequences of love sonnets were a convention in Shakespeare's time. Many poets wrote them, as we have seen, and some very good ones. A poet writes as a poet, not as a lover; and the only question is how beautiful a sonnet can he make? Surely there is no difficulty in understanding the loveliness of such a sonnet as the following, which expresses a mood that any man might have but that only a true poet knows how to express:

> When, in disgrace with Fortune and men's eyes,
> I all alone beweep my outcast state,
> And trouble deaf heaven with my bootless cries,
> And look upon myself, and curse my fate,

Wishing me like to one more rich in hope,
Featured like him, like him with friends possest,
Desiring this man's art and that man's scope,
With what I most enjoy contented least;
Yet in these thoughts myself almost despising—
Haply I think on thee: and then my state,
Like to the lark at break of day arising
From sullen earth sings hymns at Heaven's gate;
   For thy sweet love remember'd such wealth brings
   That then I scorn to change my state with Kings.

Shakespeare's plays, as assembled in the first folio, are
fourteen comedies, ten histories bearing the names of English
kings, and eleven tragedies. We do not know with any cer-
tainty, or care with much enthusiasm, about the order in which
they were written. We are not even sure of the general principle that the weakest are the earliest; an artist, even one who
does not live to be senile, may do strong work when he is
young and may sometimes in the course of his life fall away
from his highest standard. That is a question about which
professional students of Shakespeare do not agree, and it need
not trouble us. Here are the plays, and "the play's the thing."

As you run superficially over the history of the Shakespearean dramas one practical fact that strikes you is that more
of them have held the stage continuously to the present time
than the work of all other Elizabethan dramatists put together,
that through all the changes of fashion and taste in three hundred years, if he has never at any moment been the most popular, he has never been forgotten and has never lost his appeal
to audiences or to ambitious actors. The great actors of the
nineteenth century, like Edwin Booth, Henry Irving, Mod-
jeska, and Salvini, made their most notable triumphs in
Shakespearean characters. Within the last generation we have
seen performances, more or less successful, of the *Comedy of*

Errors, Midsummer-Night's Dream, The Merchant of Venice, As You Like It, Twelfth Night, Richard II, Henry V, Romeo and Juliet, Julius Cæsar, and *Hamlet.* In Germany Shakespeare is constantly played, and, we are told, played very well. The importance of this is that the dramas which contain the most beautiful English poetry are effective "shows," as they were probably intended to be. In Shakespeare's time people had not such easy access to books as we have, and the theater was a relatively more important vehicle of ideas than it is today.

The fundamental quality of most of Shakespeare's plays is that they have good plots, entertaining stories. He took his plots wherever he could find them, from older plays, Italian stories, English chronicles, Plutarch's *Lives,* and his invention consists in the skill with which he made a story over and covered the skeleton with the living flesh of his language. Some of the plots are slight and conventional; and practical playwright though he may have been, with ability to manage his story, it is in the characters and the diction, the poetry and the humor of the speeches, that his genius shows itself supreme. There is hardly one of the plays, even the most trivial, which has not lines of that peculiar beauty which we know to be Shakespearean. But we must remember that this poetic style is in some measure due not to the genius of an individual but to the genius of the age; several of the other poets wrote lines quite Shakespearean. And Shakespeare, whoever he may have been, was not a god; he often fell below his best, and wrote many weak scenes and slovenly verses. So that in the case of plays doubtfully ascribed to him we are all at sea when we try to affirm or deny the authorship on the ground of the merits or defects of the style.

Perhaps the reason that we recognize the peculiar beauty

of passages in Shakespeare is that we know in advance that
Shakespeare wrote them.   Yet who else has his verbal magic,
which age cannot wither nor quotation stale?

The lines of Prospero in the wonder-play, the *Tempest:*

> Our revels now are ended. These our actors,
> As I foretold you, were all spirits, and
> Are melted into air, into thin air;
> And like the baseless fabric of this vision,
> The cloud-capped towers, the gorgeous palaces,
> The solemn temples, the great globe itself,
> Yea, all which it inherit, shall dissolve
> And like this insubstantial pageant faded,
> Leave not a rack behind. We are such stuff
> As dreams are made on, and our little life
> Is rounded with a sleep.

The words of Cleopatra when she is dying from the bite of
the poisonous asp:

> Peace! Peace!
> Dost thou not see my baby at my breast,
> That sucks the nurse asleep?

Almost all of *Hamlet,* including passages which modern
stage versions omit.   In the perfection of the phrasing, the
pertinence of every line to the character and the situation
Hamlet is Shakespeare's best, an unrivaled masterpiece.

Macbeth's words on hearing of the death of the queen:

> She should have died hereafter;
> There would have been a time for such a word.
> Tomorrow, and tomorrow, and tomorrow,
> Creeps in this petty pace from day to day
> To the last syllable of recorded time;
> And all our yesterdays have lighted fools
> The way to dusty death.

HAMLET

And so one might go on quoting beyond the covers of this book. Other poets can say certain kinds of things perfectly. Shakespeare can say anything. The range of his thought is enormous, corresponding to the great variety of his characters. He utters the ideas and emotions appropriate to clown and to king, to the amusing rogue, Falstaff, and to the perplexed and unhappy Hamlet, to witty Portia and to tragic Lady Macbeth. There is no essential human emotion or experience from farcical fooling to terrible suffering, which Shakespeare has not touched with a sure hand. His one splendid fault is abundance. When a situation suggests an idea, the poet runs away with the playwright and turns the idea in many aspects. This is one reason why the acting versions in our impatient time are so severely cut. For example, Macbeth, after murdering his sleeping king, would in his terror have said:

> I heard a voice cry, Sleep no more!
> Macbeth does murder sleep.

Shakespeare sends him on into a lyric on sleep, with six magnificent metaphors, too much for a man in his state of agitation. It was probably not to such a glorious passage, but to weaker ones that his great rival and admirer, Ben Jonson, refers, when he expresses the wish that Shakespeare had blotted a thousand lines. However it was Jonson who wrote of him, truly:

> He was not of an age, but for all time!

CHAPTER XXVII

OTHER ELIZABETHAN DRAMATISTS

Souls of Poets dead and gone,
What Elysium have ye known,
Happy field or mossy cavern,
Choicer than the Mermaid Tavern?
                                    —*Keats*.

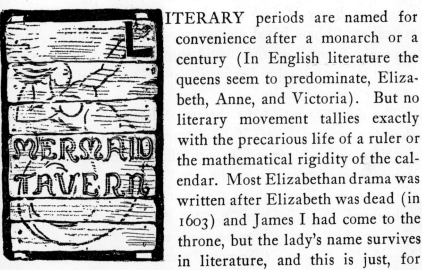 ITERARY periods are named for convenience after a monarch or a century (In English literature the queens seem to predominate, Elizabeth, Anne, and Victoria). But no literary movement tallies exactly with the precarious life of a ruler or the mathematical rigidity of the calendar. Most Elizabethan drama was written after Elizabeth was dead (in 1603) and James I had come to the throne, but the lady's name survives in literature, and this is just, for she is herself a great poetic figure. The Elizabethan drama was at its height in the first quarter of the seventeenth century. There were giants in those days besides Shakespeare, and many secondary dramatists of talent. Readers who have neither disposition nor opportunity to turn to the complete editions of these many dramatists will find their best plays selected in the admirable Mermaid Series.

Those who wish only a taste of the best passages will find them in Charles Lamb's *Specimens of English Dramatic Poets Who Lived about the Time of Shakespeare.*

One of the stalwarts of the time was George Chapman, but he is remembered less for his plays than for his translation of Homer. Chapman was not a born dramatist, but turned to the drama because it was the "going" thing among all forms of literature, much as in our time men of various literary gifts try or would like to try the novel, whether or not the novel is their best vehicle. Chapman's comedies are rather heavy. One does not get from the cynical *All Fools* even such a laugh as is sometimes provoked by the rough humor of Jonson. His tragedies, *Bussy D'Ambois* and the sequel, *The Revenge,* are tragedies of blood based on contemporaneous history. There are magnificent lines and turgid stupid lines. Chapman was by nature a philosophic reflective poet, a mighty genius but of most uneven quality.

The man nearest to the throne of King Shakespeare was Ben Jonson, or rather, if Shakespeare joined the poets of the time at the Mermaid Tavern, the meeting place of wits, it was Jonson who sat at the head of the table and ruled the company. Throughout the seventeenth century his reputation and authority were greater even than Shakespeare's. The one of his plays to choose, if we choose only one, is *Every Man in His Humour* ("humour" meaning mood or character, as in "good-humour," "ill-humour"). It holds up to ridicule the foibles of his time and is a vigorous important "comedy of manners." If any proof of its vitality is needed, outside the play itself, we may remember that Charles Dickens chose it as the first drama to be given by his company of players. Jonson was a scholar as well as an observer of the human comedy, and his scholarship shows in his tragedies, *Sejanus* and *Catiline*. The learning is not pedantic, and the sense of tragedy is profound. If in character and magic of language Jonson's Roman plays are not equal to Shakespeare's, that is only to say that Jonson is not Shakespeare. One Roman play neither Shakespeare nor any other poet but Jonson did or could write, that is *Poetaster*, in which the poets of the age of Augustus—Virgil, Horace, Ovid, Tibullus—discourse in a style that seems a translation of them, but is Jonson's creation. And there is a double meaning to it, for under the Roman guise are some shrewd stabs at Jonson's contemporaries, Dekker and Marston. What Milton calls Jonson's "learned sock" contained a foot with a kick in it.

BEN JONSON

Jonson's greatest comedies are *Volpone or the Fox, Epicene or the Silent Woman* and the *Alchemist*. The method in all Jonson's comedy is to make a character stand for a single motive, a "humour," Avarice or Cunning or Arrogance. Of all Jonson's comic figures the one that is most rounded and overwhelmingly credible is Sir Epicure Mammon, in *The Alchemist,* still a "humour" as the name indicates, but in the talk and action a magnificent swaggerer as convincing as Falstaff.

Jonson was a prolific writer of masques, a form of entertainment exceedingly popular in the first part of the seventeenth century, and yet not popular in one sense, for they were very expensive and were made possible only by the lavish extravagance of the court and the nobility. They were a sort of vaudeville, or perhaps more like our modern "follies revue," dancing, song, spectacle. The architect, Inigo Jones, supplied the "stage craft," which was often very elaborate, and the best composers furnished the music. Their interest as a whole must have depended on the presentation. What remains for us is the great number of beautiful lyrics. The most learned man of his time, except perhaps only Bacon, and a man reputed to be rough and swaggering had a touch as delicate as the flutter of a butterfly's wings. No briefest note on Jonson could omit mention of his prose, compact muscular and meaty. The little book of detached notes on men and things called "Discoveries" is a golden treasury of penetrating wisdom. On his tomb in Westminster Abbey is written, 'O Rare Ben Jonson."

Jonson is full of self-contradictions because there are so many sides to his genius. His lyrics are delicate and tender. His humor is rough and hard. A much more genial humorist (not to speak of Shakespeare) is Jonson's collaborator, friend, and enemy, Thomas Dekker. The way the Elizabethan dramatists worked together, quarreled, lampooned each other on the stage, drank and made up, is in itself a vast comedy or series of comedies. Dekker's best play is the *Shoemaker's Holiday,* a rollicking picture of London life and character interwoven with charming romance. We spoke of this merry play in connection with Hans Sachs, the German cobbler poet. Dekker's shoemaker is not a poet, but he is a humorist whom Sachs would have enjoyed.

Thomas Heywood's masterpiece is *A Woman Killed with Kindness,* in which a wronged husband punishes his wife by pardoning her, as the title suggests. It is genuinely pathetic and honest, and in modern times we should say that the "psychology" is true. In diction it is one of the simplest, least ornate of Elizabethan plays. It might succeed on our stage as well as any play of Shakespeare, and the motive of it probably recurs in nineteenth century drama, in which men do not always take revenge by the crude methods of pistol and dagger. When Lamb called Heywood "a sort of *prose* Shakespeare" he meant, as he goes on to explain, that Heywood's characters are naturalistic, of everyday life but that he had not Shakespeare's magical power to make us believe in anything under the sun or beyond the sun.

In writing of Elizabethan dramatists it is natural to compare all the others by the standard of Shakespeare, to try to determine which one of the many men of genius was the closest second to the master. It is not a very subtle method of criticism even when practiced by the poet Swinburne who adored all things Elizabethan. But it is a fair way of suggesting values. The second best writer of tragedy is John Webster, whose *Duchess of Malfi* is terrible, heart-rending. There are scores of these Italian or pseudo-Italian blood-and-thunder plays. Most of them are little more than versified melodrama. A few rise to poetic heights. One is Shakespeare's *Othello*. Another, two centuries later, is Shelley's *Cenci*. Another is Webster's *Duchess of Malfi*. In this play emotion is so powerful that it bursts verse and meter, as in the line which Ferdinand speaks when he sees his dead sister:

Cover her face; mine eyes dazzle: she died young.

There is no better characterization of Webster than Lamb's phrase: "That wild solemn preternatural cast of grief which is so bewildering in *The Duchess of Malfi*." Webster's other great play, *Vittoria Corombona*, in which a beautiful woman brings death and disaster wherever she goes, would be morbid with its brooding on death and decay, were it not elevated to a plane of poetic dignity as high as Greek tragedy or the noblest of Shakespeare.

The other competitors for the place at Shakespeare's right hand are Beaumont and Fletcher, inseparable collaborators until Beaumont's death. They wrote tragedies and comedies, and what distinguishes them seems to be the consistent excellence of their work rather than any single great stroke of genius which excites terror or laughter. They were by birth and training highly civilized gentlemen, and the merit which Dryden found in them (he was an excellent judge) was that "in them the English language arrived to its highest perfection." The range of their work is great. Of the fifty plays that they wrote (whether alone or in collaboration with each other or in col-

JOHN FLETCHER

laboration with other dramatists we can only guess) representative serious plays are *Philaster* and *The Maid's Tragedy,* which are romantically unreal and yet pathetic, human, exquisitely poetic, and finely constructed, quite faultless, viewed as plays. Only Jonson and Shakespeare knew as much, or more, about the business of play-making. A good example of their comedy is *The Knight of the Burning Pestle.* When presented a few years ago by students of Yale University it made the audience laugh heartily—and what better proof could there be of the lasting freshness of its fun?

A minor dramatist, much of whose work is inseparable from his collaborators, is Marston. An interesting example of collaboration is *Eastward Ho*, written by Jonson, Chapman and Marston. It is worth recording, even in so brief a note as this, that when for a supposed insult to the Scots Chapman and Marston were clapped into jail, Jonson voluntarily went with them. Marston had a considerable reputation in his own time as a satirist, and he has a bitter and misanthropic power. But his satires now are tough reading and none of his plays rises above the second rate; the sword may carve fine art, the bludgeon never. Compare his treatment of the misanthrope in *The Malcontent* with the same type in Jonson and Molière, and Marston's shortcomings will be evident at once.

In the voluminous work of Middleton there is at least one masterpiece, *The Changeling*. The peculiar strength of his genius lies in domestic tragedy as distinct from heroic. In this, in his every-day humanity, he is like Heywood. At his worst he is commonplace. At his best he is excellent and if he were not, like Dekker and other professional dramatists, always writing in a hurry, he would be still finer. His *A Trick to Catch the Old One* resembles and equals Jonson in the portrayal of "humours." *The Witch* has a special interest because it may have suggested the witches in *Macbeth*. In two plays Middleton flies from realism to poetic romance. *The Spanish Gipsy* lives in the magic world of *As You Like It*. *A Fair Quarrel* is an intensely dramatic piece filled, as Lamb says, with "admirable passions."

The sunset of the Elizabethan drama (and it is still Elizabethan, though it is past the reign of James into the reign of Charles) was glowing and brilliant. Shakespeare and Jonson were dead. But who shall say that Massinger and Ford and Shirley were not worthy successors? Massinger is remembered chiefly for an excellent comedy, *A New Way to Pay Old Debts*, which held the stage well into the nineteenth century, the principal character, Overreach, being a part that appealed to many actors. Massinger was a poet without the grand passions, but as Lamb pointed out, on that account free from violence of style, equable, serene and enjoyable.

Ford is the most tearful and melancholy of the dramatic poets, tender to the verge of sentimentality and slightly artificial and forced in the aching situations. But he searches the soul with a very modern analysis of emotion and he phrases exquisitely, a true poet though a rather pallid one for all the red blood and piling up of corpses. The very titles of his plays suggest his mood, *The Lover's Melancholy, The Broken Heart, Love's Sacrifice.*

Shirley is already in the twilight. But it is a pleasant, even beautiful, twilight, though Dryden thought it dull. When Shirley tries tragedy, as in *The Maid's Revenge*, he reminds us that the drama is declining. When he writes comedy (and he wrote many comedies) as in *The Lady of Pleasure*, he reminds us of the kind of drama that was to come later, the Restoration comedy. But that was to be a good many years later, after much history had been made. In 1642 the Puritans closed the theaters and the Elizabethan drama was at an end.

CHAPTER XXVIII

ENGLISH LYRIC POETRY OF THE SEVENTEENTH CENTURY

Gather ye rosebuds while ye may,
Old Time is still a-flying.

—Herrick.

ALMOST all the Elizabethan dramatists were lyric poets and their plays are studded with gems of song. If they could not make the jewel themselves they had the wit to steal it and put it in a new setting. And there were plenty of jewels. Great, or rather, big, constructions, the epic, the drama, the novel, rise and fall. The lyric poem in English literature is perpetual, a multitude of flames that never go out. The flames never go out, but they do change color, sometimes almost imperceptibly, one tone blending with another. Those who are interested in classification may find in the seventeenth century lyric three divisions. The first is of the generation when great Ben Jonson is still alive and active and wielding an authority greater than that of any other man of letters in English literature. Also an authority of a different kind was Donne, utterly unlike Jonson, Donne the vague, the introspective, the metrical rebel, Jonson the classicist, in precept and practice, careful of form, though not bound by it. As the century advanced, the "sons of Ben,"

who were also in a less direct, less conscious way the sons of
Donne, lost something of the vigor of Jonson's scholarship,
though they kept the outward show of it, and they could not
attain the subtle power of that strange inimitable poet, Donne,
but were somewhat corrupted by his most obvious faults,
his twisted metaphors, violations of syntax, far-fetched conceits. The "metaphysical" school, as Dryden called it (and
Dr. Johnson borrowed the word) deserved much of the abuse
which the next century directed against it.

Then came the third period when poets sought clarity,
sanity, regularity. We have reached Dryden and are on the
way to Pope. The reactions of literature are like a pendulum,
though not so regular, not so definite. But the revolt of the
age of Pope against the age of Donne is almost exactly counter-
balanced by the later rebellion of Wordsworth and Coleridge
against the rigidities and restrictions of Pope and Johnson.
We who live on this side of the great romantic period are
inclined to discover all the gold and jewels of Donne and his
successors and to think that Pope's well moulded metal is
not so precious. This is a mistake from the point of view
of criticism, from the point of view of pure amateurish enjoyment. Every poet, every artist should be appreciated, judged,
treasured for the best that *he* did in *his* kind, no matter what
other artists before him or near him or after him may have
done. And of excellent specimens of two different kinds who
shall say, who need say which is the better?

And so, though these literary genealogies, these historic
sequences are part of our story which aims at a sort of continuity, the way to get a poet is to go directly to him with
the briefest word of orientation. The most vivid way to write
this chapter would be to give the names of the poets and a few
of their finest verses, for their song is their story.

One of the deepest most original English lyrists is John Donne, a poet whose obscurity and mysticism have kept him from being better known. In his youth he wrote love songs and satires. Later he became a famous preacher and turned his poetic passion into religious verse. In the seventeenth century religious poetry had a fervent beauty which is seldom found in English poetry since that time. English hymns and other forms of devotional verse are pious rather than poetic. Even in the nineteenth century with its multitudes of poets I doubt whether until we come to Francis Thompson we shall find anything comparable in poetic expression of religious emotion to Donne's:

HYMN TO GOD THE FATHER

Wilt Thou forgive the sin where I begun,
   Which was my sin, though it were done before?
Wilt Thou forgive that sin through which I run,
   And do run still, though still I do deplore?
When Thou hast done, Thou hast not done;
     For I have more.

Wilt Thou forgive that sin which I have won
   Others to sin, and made my sins their door?
Wilt Thou forgive that sin which I did shun
   A year or two, but wallowed in a score?
When Thou hast done, Thou hast not done;
     For I have more.

I have a sin of fear, that when I've spun
   My last thread, I shall perish on the shore;
But swear by Thyself that at my death Thy Son
   Shall shine as He shines now and heretofore;
And having done that, Thou hast done;
     I fear no more.

I believe it is a mistake to say that Donne did not understand metrical art and that his poignantly beautiful passages are struck out by the heat of passion through a crabbed and defective meter. He knew what he was about. His inverted accents and broken rhythms are intentional and cunning. He could, when he chose, write as regularly as Jonson, as in the lovely lines beginning

> Sweetest love I do not go
> For weariness of thee.

A clergyman of much gayer nature than Donne's was Robert Herrick, past master of the little lyric which is greatly delightful. He wrote many as good as the following, which I choose because of its excellence but which does not represent his merrier humorous vein.

TO DAFFODILS

> Fair daffodils, we weep to see
>   You haste away so soon;
> As yet the early-rising sun
>   Has not attained his noon.
>   Stay, stay
>   Until the hasting day
>   Has run
>   But to the evensong;
> And having prayed together, we
>   Will go with you along.
>
> We have short time to stay, as you,
>   We have as short a spring;
> As quick a growth to meet decay,
>   As you, or anything,
>   We die
>   As your hours do, and dry
>   Away
>   Like to the summer's rain;
> Or as the pearls of morning's dew,
>   Ne'er to be found again.

Herrick was the greatest son of Ben. As Swinburne prettily says, he had to lay but an idle, reckless hand on the instrument which the master had so carefully tuned and the very note of lyric poetry "responded on the instant to the instinctive intelligence of his touch." If Jonson is his father, then Horace and Catullus are his great-grandfathers. He writes odes and marriage hymns like the Latin lyrists, addresses a dozen fictitious mistresses, is thoroughly pagan and at the same time a sincerely devout Christian, turns an epigram too foul to quote on a modern page and then writes a song of unearthly fragility. The American writer Aldrich called him a great little poet. It is a good phrase, but in certain moods one would strike out the "little."

Carew, a disciple of Donne, to whom he wrote a stately elegy, but whose faults he avoids, is, like Herrick, a lover of flowers, also a lover of wine and women, and the third of the Lutherian trilogy is evident in his work. His verse is supple, melodious and light. His touch is still Elizabethan, the imagery of an age already fading, and he looks forward to that clever, nonchalant almost colloquial *vers de société,* of which the greater master is Prior, who gallantly bestrides the seventeenth and eighteenth centuries.

Mr. Saintsbury, with rueful enthusiasm, complains that the poets of this period are so numerous and so attractive, and their attractions so often consist of fine little bits, that we are in danger of being seduced into dwelling on them with disproportionate emphasis. In this crowded survey, where many writers of merit are not even mentioned, we cannot linger long with the post-Elizabethan choir. It is painful to pass so swiftly over the three religious poets touched in the following scanty paragraphs.

The gentle and pious poet, George Herbert, wrote, it seems

to me, no single striking poem, but is uniformly sweet for all his fantastic "conceits," which are not to our taste but with him were sincere. Of more strange and haunting beauty

GEORGE HERBERT

are the verses of Henry Vaughan, with his "bright shoots of everlastingness." You know that you have met a poet when you come upon lines like these:

> I saw Eternity the other night
> Like a great ring of pure and endless light.

In Richard Crashaw we find the combination, or conflict, characteristic of the age, of the secular and "pagan" and the religious. Crashaw wrote the delicious lines beginning:

> Who e'er she be—
> That not impossible She
> That shall command my heart and me.

And he also wrote the magnificent poem on Saint Teresa, which chants, full organ:

> O thou undaunted daughter of desires!

Of the Cavalier poets, so called because they happened to be gentlemen on the king's side in the Great Rebellion, two

SIR JOHN SUCKLING

are memorable, Suckling and Lovelace. Suckling's love songs have a jaunty charm; they are the lyric laughter of the man of the world, but quite free from the cynicism which was to come with the Restoration. The best of them are neatly made and without too much of the intellectual "conceit," which spoils a good deal of the really lovely and skillful verse of this time. Typical of his best is the well-known song:

> Why so pale and wan, fond lover?
> Prithee why so pale?

Much of Suckling, including the dramas, is quite unreadable.

And unreadable also is most of the work of Lovelace. But two or three of his poems are perfect in their way: *On Going to the Wars*—

> I could not love thee, dear, so much,
> Loved I not honor more

And *To Althea from Prison*—

> Stone walls do not a prison make,
> Nor iron bars a cage.

In that century, so strangely continuous and yet so sharply broken in two by war, the younger brother of Herrick is Marvell. Their kinship lies in their simple love of nature, birds and insects and flowers. If Marvell's *The Mower to the Glow-Worms* were printed by accident in a volume of Herrick, nobody would feel it out of place:

> Ye living lamps, by whose dear light
> The nightingale does sit so late.

Marvell is the supreme poet of gardens—

> Annihilating all that's made
> To a green thought in a green shade.

And *The Mower Against Gardens* is left-handed praise of them. He has a wide range. His *Young Love* is charming, suggesting Prior's *To a Child of Quality*, written half a century later. His *Ode upon Cromwell's Return from Ireland* is stately and impressive and probably as near the Horatian spirit and manner as anything in English.

A poet immensely overrated in his own time and perhaps underrated in ours is Cowley. He was in his day more famous than Milton, who to our eyes so hugely overtops him as to make him almost invisible. But he is far from contemptible. His "pindaric" odes have at least ingenious and skillful structure and his rhymed couplets with their monotonous see-saw would seem much better if the so-called heroic couplet had not been handled in the next generation more powerfully by Dryden and more deftly by Pope. Cowley was one of the men who mark or, rather, make the transition from the metaphysical age to the age of reason, and it is no wonder that he seemed to his contemporaries a new and wonderful phenomenon. But he missed the strength of the kind of poetry that he was leaving, which was indeed withering, and he did not attain to the goal toward which, without his realizing it, all English poetry was moving.

Another transition poet is Denham, whose work is only of historic interest in the development of the rhymed couplet. And such also is the interest of the work of Waller, who is, however, the most adroit manipulator of the couplet in his day. He is a clever versifier and he had a sort of practical instinct which told him that the new kind of verse was to be "the thing." Like the Frenchman Malherbe, he liked to regard himself as the authentic born voice of classicism. His couplets are shriveled and crackling. But there is a touch of real poetry in two of his lyrics, *Go, Lovely Rose* and *The Girdle*.

If these transition poets got rid of the pseudo-metaphorical brambles in which the old poetry was getting tangled, they also left behind the wild flowers and the honey bees. But one great poet kept much of the glory of the old, its dramatic power, its lyric beauty, and at the same time was the never superseded master of the new. That is Dryden. And a still greater poet who belongs almost wholly with the old, with Spenser, with Shakespeare, with Jonson, is Milton.

CHAPTER XXIX

MILTON

Milton! thou shouldst be living at this hour.

—Wordsworth.

 ILTON'S life extends over three-quarters of the seventeenth century, and he was, as we see him now, the giant of his time and the chief English poet after Shakespeare. His biography is more important and more interesting than the biographies of most poets, because it is involved with the history of his age. To be sure, every poet is affected by the world he lives in and is the child of his time, and some poets have taken their part in practical affairs. But Milton's life might be made the basis of the spiritual history of the seventeenth century. In his youth he is a brilliant scholar and precocious poet, an Elizabethan in spirit. His first appearance in print is a eulogistic poem prefixed to the second folio of Shakespeare in 1632. He writes the exquisite short poems, *L'Allegro, Il Penseroso,* and *Lycidas.* If he had died then he would hold a high place among English lyric poets. At the outbreak of the Civil War in 1642 he took the side of the rebels, turned his back on the muse for twenty years and devoted his energies to pamphlets in behalf of liberty. He became blind partly as a result of his labors as

Cromwell's secretary for foreign languages. When the Commonwealth fell and the monarchy was restored he was saved from the scaffold by his friends and by the fact that officialdom was after bigger game than a poor poet. He went into retirement and spent the rest of his life in the composition of his masterpieces, *Paradise Lost, Paradise Regained,* and *Samson Agonistes.* His career thus falls into three periods corresponding to the political history of the century: the twilight of the Elizabethan age, the Commonwealth, and the Restoration of the monarchy.

The early poems of Milton show no sign of youthful fumbling; he discovered his lyric genius at once. The *Hymn on the Morning of Christ's Nativity,* written when he was twenty-one, is magnificent, and announces the poet who was later to turn the Christian theme into an epic. *L'Allegro* is full of the joy of life:

> And young and old come forth to play
> On a Sunshine Holiday,
> Till the live-long daylight fail,
> Then to the Spicy Nut-brown Ale.

Which reminds us that Puritanism was not necessarily hostile to earthly pleasures. And Milton himself is proof that it was not in its early stages the enemy of art, or freedom of thought. It was originally a movement to purify the church and correct obvious abuses. It had its fanatical side which is caricatured in Macaulay's famous dictum that the Puritans objected to bear-baiting not because it hurt the bear but because it pleased the people. The Puritan opposition to the theaters, which resulted in their being closed and attendance at any performance being made a crime, was not antagonism to dramatic art but moral revolt against an institution which had, in point of fact, become rotten. Milton loved the theater, as is shown in the lines:

> Then to the well-trod stage anon,
> If Jonson's learned Sock be on,
> Or sweetest Shakespeare, fancy's child
> Warble his native Wood-notes wild.

It was possible for a man to be an artist and a lover of life and at the same time be a Puritan. There was a strong element of Puritanism in Spenser and in Sidney. And they would not have sympathized any more than would Milton with the narrow-minded ignorance into which Puritanism developed. To Milton and to other poets of the seventeenth century religion was not a painful austerity but a solemn delight. The following lines from *Il Penseroso* remind us that he was himself an organist, trained in music by his father:

> But let my due feet never fail
> To walk the studious cloister's pale,
> And love the high embowèd roof,
> With antique pillars massy proof,
> And storied windows richly dight,
> Casting a dim religious light.
> There let the pealing organ blow
> To the full-voiced quire below,
> In service high and anthems clear,
> As may with sweetness, through mine ear,
> Dissolve me into ecstasies.

The strongest of Milton's early poems is *Lycidas,* a lament for the death of a friend. It is one of three great threnodies in English literature; the other two are Shelley's *Adonais* and Tennyson's *In Memoriam.* The masque, *Comus,* which was written for a private entertainment, shows Milton's close

relation to Elizabethan drama. If he had lived a generation
earlier he would undoubtedly have been a dramatist, as he
showed that he could be in *Samson Agonistes,* written toward
the end of his life.

Paradise Lost is the one epic poem in English which has
the dignity of the classic epics. And though its subject is
biblical, it resembles the classics, rather than Dante's *Commedia,* with which it is usually and somewhat futilely compared. Milton takes the story, which is told in a few words
in the Book of Genesis, and elaborates it into twelve books
of stately blank verse. The essential subject is Hebraic-
Christian; the English is so sound that it has become the
acknowledged standard of poetical diction; but the structure,
the method, multitudes of the metaphors and allusions are
pure pagan. Eve is more lovely than Pandora, and the "great
Creator" of Adam and Eve lives on the same page with
"Jove's authentic fire." Since everybody knows the story and
there is no question about the plot, and our aim is only to
enjoy Milton's verbal splendor, I suggest that the first four
books well read are enough, and that *Paradise Regained* has
not the sonorous beauty of *Paradise Lost.* This is heresy, but
it has the authority of no less a scholar than Charles Eliot
Norton, who thought that two books of *Paradise Lost* were
sufficient to give us a sense of the whole. But we cannot omit
the opening of the third book, which is the blind poet's invocation to Celestial Light. And there are glorious passages
in every book. Except for some dull lines, due to the nodding
of genius and the fact that Milton was utterly lacking in
self-critical humor, he sustained his "grand style" to the end.
It is for the style that we read *Paradise Lost,* for interest in the
theme is not so keen nowadays as it was when people believed

MILTON

it to be gospel truth. To us Milton's originality, aside from the phrasing, is his development of the character of Satan, who is the real hero of the poem. Adam and Eve are only

ADAM AND EVE

victims, and God and the angels are shadowy. Satan is splendidly vivid, the prime mover of the entire action.

Milton's final masterpiece is *Samson Agonistes*. Did ever poet leave this earth with a more lofty valediction? He dramatizes his own blindness in the blind Samson. It is the nearest approach in English to a Greek tragedy, and it ends on a serene note:

> Calm of mind, all passion spent.

Milton was one of the important prose writers of his time and a vigorous controversialist and pamphleteer. The age was hot with argument, some of which has grown cold, and some of which is blurred by bad temper. But some of his essays or speeches still have light, and one is imperishably incandescent, the *Areopagitica,* on the liberty of printing, which is the manifesto for all time of those who believe in freedom of speech. "Who kills a man kills a reasonable creature, God's image; but he who destroys a good book kills reason itself, kills the image of God." After nearly three hundred years we are still asking Milton's question: "What magistrate may not be misinformed, and much the sooner, if liberty of printing be reduced into the power of a few?" There is poetic truth in Wordsworth's lovely line:

> Thy soul was like a star and dwelt apart.

But in point of fact Milton was for the twenty central years of his life in the thick of the conflict, and he is distinguished among all English poets for his insuperable intellectual strength.

CHAPTER XXX

ENGLISH PROSE OF THE SEVENTEENTH CENTURY

The whole Creation is a Mystery, and particularly that of Man. 'Tis
opportune to look back upon old times, and contemplate our forefathers.
—*Thomas Browne.*

ONE great difference between poetry
and prose is that poetry keeps
fresh and timeless whereas prose
from one age to the next tends to get
stale or quaint or out of date. If a
modern poet wrote a sonnet, a really
good sonnet, like one of Milton's, it
would smell as sweet as a loaf of
bread just out of the oven. But a
man who should use a style like Milton's in an argument before Congress
or a labor convention would be an
incomprehensible fool, even more
foolish than those who now argue in
the style of our time. Between us and the prose writers of
the seventeenth century lies or shines the clear prose of the
eighteenth century. A taste for seventeenth century prose is
an acquired literary taste, but it is worth acquiring, especially
when Charles Lamb invites you to try. One of Lamb's
favorites is Robert Burton, whom he calls a "fantastic great
old man." Burton's *Anatomy of Melancholy* is one of the

least melancholy books ever written; it is a great compendium, an anthology of the author's reading in a thousand ancient books, full of fanciful conceits and eloquence, all strung together by a temperament which is almost as original and charming as Montaigne's, but not so serene and philosophic.

A more reflective and philosophic temper, endowed with a strange eloquence, is that of Thomas Browne. His *Religio*  *Medici* (Browne was a physician) and *Urn-Burial* are profound meditations on life and death, sententious and dignified, but never stupidly solemn, and written in English that is both majestic and whimsical. For most of that modern psychology which is associated with the name of Freud one would not willingly exchange Browne's reflections on sleep and dreams. "We term sleep a death; and yet it is waking that kills us, and destroys those spirits that are the house of life." An indication of

SIR THOMAS BROWNE

Browne's serene detachment is the fact that there is not a sign in any of his work that he was living through the Great Rebellion. He is, unlike Milton and most of his other contemporaries, above the conflicts of Church and State.

Two men of great literary gifts, Jeremy Taylor and Thomas Fuller, are less known than they should be, because their writings are mostly in the form of sermons, and the lay reader, whatever his profession of faith and however willing he may be to listen to a preacher on Sunday, does not enjoy reading sermons. But Taylor's *Holy Living* and *Holy Dying* have a literary quality which takes them out of the pulpit; and Fuller's worldly wit in his *Holy and Profane States* and his *History of the Worthies of England* endeared him to Lamb and Coleridge, which is recommendation enough.

If people do not, as a rule, like to read about religion and morals, they do like to read about fishing. Izaak Walton's *Compleat Angler* has enjoyed continuous popularity among amateur fishermen and among lovers of literature who never cast a fly. There is more in the book than fishing; Walton is a very delightful fellow, and it is a pleasure to sit on the bank beside him and listen to his talk. Besides his masterpiece he wrote charming short biographies of Donne, Herbert, and others.

A great thinker of the period, the most eminent philosopher between Bacon and Locke, was Thomas Hobbes. Most of his work lies outside our range in the region of technical philosophy, and he had not the charm of style which transforms philosophy into literary art. But one of his books, *Leviathan,* belongs to literature. It is the first sympathetic account in English of the state or commonwealth, and by arousing sympathy or opposition it influenced all later political philosophy. The main idea is that the state is supreme, the monster, or "leviathan," that swallows the individual; and that is a fair account not of what states or governments ought to be but what in point of fact they always have been. If Hobbes has not charm of style, he is perfectly readable, and he owes some of his vigorous clarity to his life-long study of Thucydides.

The style of most prose writers of the seventeenth century is not such as we would write if we could, though much of it is eloquent and beautiful, and Lamb and Coleridge and other writers in the nineteenth century took lessons from it. But in the second half of the seventeenth century appeared a writer whose prose in structure, rhythm and vocabulary we should be glad to imitate. That is Dryden.

CHAPTER XXXI

ENGLISH LITERATURE OF THE RESTORATION

In verse the twilight of an elder age;
In prose the day-break of a modern page.

—*Anon.*

THIS chapter might well be called the "Age of Dryden," for it is less important that a Stuart king regained his throne than that Dryden was there to celebrate the event. He is so eminent or his contemporaries are so less than eminent that his name is in literature the name of the period. Periods, let us remember, blend with each other, and life does not live nor literature write by the calendar. Young Dryden recognized and admired old Milton, and old Dryden by perfecting the rhymed couplet was the grandfather of eighteenth-century poetry. The first line of the couplet that heads this chapter is not quite true, for Dryden was a real innovator in verse as well as in prose. The reason he seems faded or "twilit" is because we see through and behind him to the older drama and poetry which with all his genius he could not quite equal. His genius was vast and manifold. He wrote lyrics, satires, plays, and critical prose.

His lyrics have the quality of the age that was passing, and

not until many years later do we find in English poetry anything as musical and majestic as the *Song for St. Cecilia's
Day* and *Alexander's Feast* with its familiar line:

> None but the brave deserves the fair.

Dryden's rhymed couplets are vigorous and flexible, and he
used the form for a great variety of subjects, heroic tragedy
and his annihilating satires, which are not the highest poetry
but contain some of the wittiest lines in our literature. There
is a deadly accuracy in his use of words, for example the word
"deviates" in the following couplet from *MacFlecknoe,* in
which he belabors a poor poet:

> The rest to some faint meaning make pretence,
> But Shadwell never deviates into sense.

Dryden's plays were more interesting to his time than to
ours; and to us, who are blind Shakespeare-worshipers, it
seems almost cheeky that he should have tried in *All for Love*
a new version of the story of Antony and Cleopatra. But he
succeeded in making a very fine play; whether it is inferior
to Shakespeare or better does not matter; it is good in its own
right.

Dryden was our first great critical essayist, and what he
wrote about drama is more interesting than his dramas. His
Essay of Dramatic Poesie and other papers are epoch-making
in English criticism and English prose style. His time and
the century after him were an age of prose, and he was the
first master of it.

Most of Dryden's contemporaries in the drama are to us
hardly more than names. Nothing goes out of date so quickly
as comedy, and the change of taste in two centuries has been

more than enough to send most plays of the Restoration to oblivion, where only special students plunge to fetch them to the light. But one young dramatist of the day had the perennial wit which preserves even a light "society" play. That was William Congreve, whose dramatic dialogue has

DRYDEN

an untarnished brilliance. His *Double Dealer* and *The Way of the World* are clever as sin. To the Puritans, who were still strong and were shocked by the licentiousness of the theater, all the drama of the Restoration seemed sinful; to us it seems simply clever and sometimes funny.

Most literary artists, and other artists, have been men of culture who have enjoyed the advantages of education—whatever that rather broad term may include. While the erudite Milton was making his last great verses and the witty men of the world were making sparkling and somewhat naughty dramas, popular religion expressed itself in the unlearned

BUNYAN

genius of Bunyan. *The Pilgrim's Progress* was published in 1678, the same year as Dryden's *All for Love*, four years after Milton's death. It is doubtful whether Dryden ever heard of Bunyan, and it is reasonably certain that Bunyan never read a word of Dryden or of any other gentleman-scholar of his time. Bunyan belonged to the people, to a world that was ignorant of most secular literature or held it in abhorrence. But that was a vastly populous world and in it Bunyan found a larger audience than that reached by any mere literary man. *The Pilgrim's Progress* became a second Bible, and it was from the first Bible, also from common speech, that Bunyan learned his style. It is a good style for his purpose, colloquial and direct in structure and ornamented by Biblical phrases. The theme is a dream-allegory representing the struggles and final triumph of the Christian life. On the whole it is a successful allegory, in that it carries its message on the back of a readable story. The religious interest has waned, but the naïve literary art abides. People who have not ...e slightest interest in the career of the Christian soul can read *The Pilgrim's Progress* with pleasure.

In the story of literature some of the most interesting episodes are accidents. Bunyan was an accident, aiming at religious truth and arriving at literary immortality. A more extraordinary accident is the *Diary* of Samuel Pepys, which was not intended for publication and was not discovered and deciphered until the early part of the nineteenth century. It has been as much enjoyed in the last hundred years as any great work of art of the time of Pepys. It is garrulous gossip of the most inconsequential kind, but without knowing it or in the least intending it Pepys gives us a record of big and little things and makes the great composite picture of his period. That Pepys and Bunyan and Dryden and Congreve are children of the same age—well, the bed of thought is wide, and strange children lie together in it.

CHAPTER XXXII

ENGLISH PROSE OF THE EIGHTEENTH CENTURY

By far the greatest man of that time was Jonathan Swift.
—*Carlyle.*

THE eighteenth century in English literature is an age of prose, not because the poetry is very bad but because the prose is very good. The supreme master in the first part of the century is Swift. *Gulliver's Travels* is a classic which every boy enjoys, delighted by Gulliver's adventures with Lilliputians, who are so small that Gulliver is a giant among them, and with the giants among whom Gulliver is a pygmy. The mature reader knows that Gulliver's ship is loaded with vitriol, that the book is a devastating satire on the human race. The account of the country of the Houyhnhnms, where horses are the real people and human beings, Yahoos, are their filthy servants, has a savage power unequaled in English literature or any literature. The secret of the power is that there is no visible sign of anger, no raising the voice; the tone is cold, restrained, ironic, varied only by some flashes of fooling when Swift's sense of the ridiculous gets the better of him.

There is, however, little laughter in Swift's humor; and he almost never laughed himself. His life was embittered by his inordinate pride (to which he had a right!), by the fact that he was not promoted to a high position in the church, and by the knowledge that he had some form of insanity, which probably kept him from marriage. But it was not only personal grievances which made him "hate and detest that animal called man." He saw with a strange combination of cool vision and hot rage what foolish creatures we are, and he lashed us unmercifully. Yet not unmercifully, for there is a deep vein of pity and compassion under his superficial hardness. And he had a strong affection for his friends. As he said, he loved Tom, Dick, and Harry, but he hated mankind. Yet he used his pen often in the service of mankind, especially in behalf of justice to the Irish, whom he affected to despise but who adored him. His *Modest Proposal* that Irish children should be eaten is by its very brutality a terrific attack upon the brutality of the English. *A Tale of a Tub* is a satire on the weaknesses of the three branches of the church, the Roman, the English, and the Calvinistic. Though on account of the subject it is less interesting to us than *Gulliver,* it is Swift at his best, and he was quite right when he exclaimed in his old age, "What a genius I had when I wrote that book!"

The *Journal to Stella* is as important for the detailed history and gossip of the time as Pepys's *Diary* is for the period just before. And it reveals Swift in all his moods. Yet it is a mysteriously reticent book, and we have never been able to learn from it or from other sources just what were the relations between Swift and beautiful Stella (Esther Johnson). We are not concerned with inquisitive chatter about the private lives of great writers; by their works we shall know them. But an understanding of Swift's life is necessary to an understanding of his writings. And misunderstanding of the man results in misunderstanding of his genius, as in Thackeray's brilliant but mistaken essay. A satisfactory life of Swift has not yet been written, and perhaps it never will be written. His work is intensely personal and practical; no man's work is more intimately related to his character, even in *Gulliver* and the *Tale of a Tub,* which are narratives projected outside himself. His biography is therefore more worth study and investigation than those of most literary men. The more we study him the more we shall come to believe that he bore intense suffering with fortitude and that his cold ferocity covered a generous and affectionate nature. What he hated was not mankind but sham, and he was himself the most honest of men. This honesty had a direct effect on his style which is plain and downright, without affectations or embellishments, surpassed in beauty by more poetical writers but unrivaled for its naked athletic power.

In contrast with the hard vigor of Swift are the ease and urbanity of Joseph Addison and Richard Steele. Their joint work (with other contributors) is the *Spectator.* It was a small daily paper, consisting of a short essay and some brief advertisements and announcements. In those days there was nothing like the modern newspaper, and the English gentleman found at his breakfast table not the *Times* but, while it lasted, about two years, the *Spectator* with its neat little essay on manners, morals, books, religion, character. Addison and Steele (Addison especially) were moralists, whose aim was to entertain and at the same time teach refinement and good taste. And their humor was genuine, both spontaneous and deliberately critical and philosophical. One of the best papers is Addison's on wit and humor, which begins with the sage remark: "Among all kinds of writing, there is none in which authors are more apt to miscarry than in works of humor, as there is none in which they are more ambitious to excel." The contributors to the *Spectator* seldom miscarried, and their smiling wisdom is still fresh, because the foibles of society have changed very little (in spite of Mr. Spectator's efforts to correct them), and because the essays are touched with an inimitable light seriousness. Dr. Johnson thought that to learn to write well we should give our days and nights to Addison. The learned Doctor was temperamentally too heavy to profit by his own advice, but it is good advice. Perhaps we cannot take Swift for a model; he is too big for us. The *Spectator,* the major contributions of Addison and Steele and the papers by lesser men who caught the manner of the masters, are a well, or a pellucid stream, of English undefiled. Some of the essays are the best criticism between Dryden and Lamb, for if Addison's likes and dislikes are not ours (they are, of course, *his*), he knew how to get the core or essence of a writer and phrase it in a few words. In the de Coverley papers, which describe the placid life and innocent adventures of a good old country gentleman, we have the most important element of the novel, character and social background. The other important element, plot, is lacking, for the episodes are fragmentary, loosely related essays scattered through the *Spectator.* Sir Roger simply lives and dies, and he is one of the most real people in English fiction.

It was Mr. Spectator's avowed ambition to "have brought philosophy out of closets and libraries, schools and colleges, to dwell in clubs and assemblies, at tea-tables, and in coffee-houses." That meant philosophy in its widest, most general sense, perhaps its wisest sense. There is one technical philosopher of the time who belongs to literature because he knew how to write. Whether George Berkeley is a great philosopher is a question which we will leave to the philosophers; his debatable idealism is outside the scope of our inquiry. But that he was one of the great masters of English prose is beyond debate. Most English and German philosophy is turgid and difficult to read. Berkeley's *New Theory of Vision* and *Principles of Human Knowledge* and all his works are clear as plate glass.

The good Bishop Berkeley is serene, reflective, and perfectly restrained in argument. Daniel Defoe, who was engaged in controversy all his life, lacks the finesse of Berkeley and Addison and Swift, but his vigor is unequaled and keeps many of his pamphlets alive, even after the subject has become a dead issue. It is not, however, as a pamphleteer that we remember Defoe, but as the author of *Robinson Crusoe.* This is probably the most widely read story in the English language and we have only to name it to remind ourselves of its merits and of the joy it gave us in childhood. In maturity we enjoy it even more because we appreciate the skill of it. Most novels and tales are the story of the individual in society, in the midst of men. *Robinson Crusoe* is the story of the individual in solitude, and its heroism is the quality that we all admire and few of us have, self-reliance. Defoe had a curiously realistic imagination. *Robinson Crusoe* is said to be based on the experience of a sailor named Selkirk. The impression of actuality is, however, due not to any possible foundation in fact but to Defoe's ingenuity in inventing details which seem like fact. If we question our memories we shall find that we have always believed that the story of Robinson Crusoe was *so,* that the startling discovery of the footprint in the sand is not an invention in the no-man's-land of fiction but rather an event like Columbus's discovery of America. It is the same sense of detail which gives life to

ROBINSON CRUSOE AND THE FOOTPRINT

the *Journal of the Plague Year,* a book of more limited interest than *Robinson Crusoe* but of fascinating vividness. During the plague year Defoe was a small boy and could have known nothing by personal experience of that terrible time, but the book sounds as if he had been through it all. In *Captain Singleton* we are in Africa (which Defoe probably never saw) and the *Memoirs of a Cavalier* is so much like history that it deceived Lord Chatham and many less instructed readers. The minor writings of Defoe have been elbowed aside by *Robinson Crusoe,* but they are enough to make the fortune of a lesser man. If he were alive today he would be making Mr. H. G. Wells and others look to their laurels and he would certainly be a star reporter and newspaper correspondent. Defoe is our first great realistic novelist, a "dime-novelist" at his lowest, a genius at his best. His interest is in adventure rather than in character; his people are real in externals, in action, but he cares very little for their souls.

The first English novelist to get inside the heart, especially of woman, is Samuel Richardson. A century before him the dramatists had studied and portrayed character, and the vivid delineation of people in poetry goes back at least as far as Chaucer. All the material for the novel and indeed the finished treatment of it in short form is present in Boccaccio, whom all literary Englishmen knew in translation. Prose romance with impossibly heroic heroes goes back to the Middle Ages. But the English novel, as we know it, begins, if anything has a beginning, in the eighteenth century, and Richardson is the father of it. *Clarissa* is our first great novel of sentiment, the interest of which is not so much in the plot or adventure as in the emotions of a woman. There is a plot, a quite simple one, the persecution of an innocent girl by a libertine. It is written in the form of letters, to us a tedious form, and it is one of the longest novels in the language. There is not a spark of humor in it. But the girl, Clarissa, is alive. Her pathetic story became immediately popular not only in England but in France and Germany and had an immense influence on the modern novel. No other English writer before Scott and Byron enjoyed during his life-time such a wide reputation at home and abroad.

An earlier work of Richardson's, *Pamela; or Virtue Rewarded,* which is almost absurd in its sentimental moralism, is important not only because its success encouraged Richardson to go on to his masterpiece but because it inspired the first comic novel of the greatest of English novelists, Henry Fielding. In *Pamela* a poor girl resists the advances of her master, and the reward of her virtue is that he marries her! The story has merits, the chief of which is fidelity to feminine character, its virtue and its practical prudence. It is worth reading for itself and for its significance in the history of the novel. We need not be abashed by great reputations, and *Pamela* is little better than what we should now call pretty good moving-picture stuff.

The goody-goodness of *Pamela* excited Fielding's merriment, and in *Joseph Andrews* he reversed the situation by making a virtuous young man the object of the affections of Lady Booby. If he had stopped there he would have given us merely a laughable burlesque or parody. But he forgot or grew away from his original intention of ridiculing Richardson and wrote a real novel of character and manners. His interest, certainly our interest, is not so much in Joseph as in Mrs. Slipslop and Parson Adams, who is an immortal creation. In *Joseph Andrews* Fielding discovered his method, the peculiar genius which he was to develop in *Tom Jones.*

In writing about books which we admire we use the words "great" and "greatest" too often and too indiscriminately. But there is no other word for *Tom Jones,* which has all the merits that a novel can have and which every virile novelist for a hundred and fifty years has regarded with admiration and envy. It was Fielding who gave shape to the English novel. His introductory essays to the various books are digressions with which a novelist of our time could not interrupt his story; and Fielding enjoyed in the eighteenth century a freedom of expression, necessary to the vigorous candor of his nature, a freedom which the taste of the next century forbade. As Thackeray regretfully says: "Since the author of *Tom Jones* was buried, no writer of fiction among us has been permitted to depict to his utmost power a MAN." But the hand of Fielding is discernible in most humorous English fiction after *Tom Jones.* His characters are not only of eighteenth-century England; they are of today and tomorrow. Fielding himself is a most engaging character, very much of a man, a magistrate honest and just, whose experience with the sinners of this world deepened his sympathy and sharpened his perception. He saw life ironically, but his vision was fair and generous, and his irony was without bitterness.

The eighteenth century might be called the age of laughter as well as the age of prose, for almost every man of letters, except Richardson, was born with a sense of fun. And a sense of fun means a sense of life. A robust humorist of the time is Tobias Smollett, much less of an artist than Fielding, but like Fielding a shrewd observer of people. He was for a time surgeon's mate in the navy, where he learned the character of the English sailor, whom he was the first to portray in all his coarse humor. He is the first of the seafaring writers, the company which includes Cooper and

Marryat, and Joseph Conrad, who, of course, are not so rough as Smollett dared to be. Smollett also knew people as they are on land, and the scenes of his masterpiece, *Humphrey Clinker,* are not on the sea but in Scotland and England. His other best known stories, *Roderick Random* and *Peregrine Pickle* are a trifle too strong for weak stomachs, but they are full of life and action and they were immensely admired by Scott and by Dickens, the latter of whom learned from Smollett something of his art of drawing grotesque but humanly true characters.

A common characteristic of Defoe, Fielding, Smollett, and of Swift, is their vigorous sanity, their stout common sense, at least in the structure and texture of their writing. The humor of Laurence Sterne is brilliant, fantastic, eccentric. *Tristram Shandy* is probably the craziest masterpiece in the world as it is one of the most delightful. The book has no apparent order, but is capricious and whimsical in its leaps from one subject to another. Yet Sterne knew what he was about, and beneath his superficial frivolity is the deepest of all unities, the strong timber of character, Tristram's father and his Uncle Toby, the everlastingly charming, simple-minded old sentimentalist. Sterne wrote with his tongue in his cheek and with a wink which was sometimes a leer. But when he let his tongue go, it is one of most brilliant that ever wagged; and there is no real evil in his eye. The *Sentimental Journey,* is a short, half-autobiographical excursion, Sterne at his best in pathos and humor, not so freakish in style as much of *Tristram Shandy*.

It is possible to dislike Sterne as a later sentimental humorist, Thackeray, did dislike him, and to find fault with the mannerisms which mar his genius. It is impossible not to like those admirable friends, Samuel Johnson and Oliver Goldsmith and to recognize that whatever their shortcomings they carry on the tradition of normal sane prose.

Dr. Johnson is the massive center of the intellectual life of the second half of the eighteenth century, and is the leader and embodiment of the critical standards of his time. A century and a half of criticism with different standards and a finer sense of beauty separate him from us, and he no longer has the authority which his contemporaries almost worshipfully conceded to him. It has been said truly that his best book is Boswell's *Life* of him. If it is the best biography of a man of letters, the reason is not only that Boswell had the right kind of talent and devotion to portray his hero but that his hero was really great. A great man, and a prince of talkers, but not a great writer. For Johnson is the only important man of letters who has left no important work of art. His *Dictionary* is a monument to his industry and learning and the preface to it tingles with his personality; but a dictionary is not art even when the definitions are amusingly original. His once famous fiction, *Rasselas,* is dull. His essays, modeled on the *Spectator,* are heavy, lack the grace of the earlier masters and oddly enough have little of the vivacity of Johnson's best conversation. His *Lives of the Poets,* many of which deal with minor versifiers, are almost dead except as an historical record of his taste and the taste of his time. His verse is negligible. Yet he was a great man, the man whom Boswell has preserved and whom the wisest men of his time loved and respected.

Goldsmith was an artist in everything he touched, except his pot-boiling hack work. The *Vicar of Wakefield,* with its romantic plot and humorous character drawing, has been more widely read and more often reprinted than any other

eighteen century fiction except, possibly, *Robinson Crusoe.*
Probably the only man in the world who failed to like it was
Mark Twain, who thought the episode in which the boy
Moses is cheated at the fair not amusing but painfully pathetic.
Goldsmith, however, knew what he was doing and was aware

GOLDSMITH

of the pathos which underlies the comedy of life. It is not
only the English who have enjoyed the *Vicar.* What Thackeray says is almost literally true: that "with that sweet story"
Goldsmith "found entry into every castle and every hamlet
in Europe." And Goethe speaks of Goldsmith's "lofty and

benevolent irony, that fair and indulgent view of all infirmities and faults."

She Stoops to Conquer, the better of Goldsmith's two plays, has lived on the stage for a century and a half, and it and the plays of Sheridan, *The Rivals* and *The School for Scandal,* are the only dramas of that day which have shown such persistent vitality. It is good comedy whether seen and heard in the theater or read on the printed page. Besides his vein of poetry and his gift of narrative, Goldsmith had the gift, which Johnson lacked, and which had all but disappeared with Addison and his associates, of writing the familar essay. The *Citizen of the World,* in which a Chinese gentleman comments on English life, has whimsical charm and the bite of true satire. In Goldsmith's small sheaf of verse is some excellent grain. His *Deserted Village* is almost all quotable. It is in the conventional tone of the time with an ear turned toward Pope, but it is Goldsmith's own, and Pope himself could not have written it.

Retaliation, in which Goldsmith wittily scores his friends, contains the lines:

> Who, born for the universe, narrowed his mind,
> And to party gave up what was meant for mankind.

The subject of these lines is Edmund Burke, orator and politician, who might better be described as having given up to practical politics what was meant for literature. Most of his speeches and pamphlets are on subjects that are not quite so vital in our day as they were in his. One of them, the speech *On Conciliation With America,* has especial interest to us, and its eloquence and logic are unimpaired by the passage of time and by the immediate fact that English statesmen did not heed its wisdom. Burke held his convictions passionately, and even when he may have been mistaken his sincerity gives the ring of truth to his splendid rhetoric. His images are often poetic and his best sentences have a noble resonance.

A contemporary of Burke who has as lofty an eloquence, though of a different kind, is Edward Gibbon. His *Decline and Fall of the Roman Empire* is the most gorgeously written history in the language. Later historians have added details to his, have corrected inaccuracies and revised some of his interpretations. But he dwarfs them all in the magnitude of his vision, his power to organize facts, and above all to make history fascinating literature.

Gibbon's work is literary art. The work of David Hume lies in that mid-region between *belles lettres* and the kind of writing which is less than beautiful but is enduringly valuable for its substance. His *Treatise of Human Nature,* the ideas of which Hume developed in later essays but never outgrew or surpassed, is one of those crucial books that give direction to the course of thought. It not only gave a new start to Scottish and English philosophy (though Hume's countrymen were slow to recognize him), but was the source of much German philosophy, including two or three of the central teachings of Kant.

Most of the prose classics of the eighteenth century have been many times reprinted. Eighteenth century prose is close to us, and much nineteenth century prose is of course continuous from it. Later English writers have come to be more and more appreciative of the merits of the "Augustan age," not only of the vigorous writers of prose, the giants, Swift and Fielding, but of their lesser brothers, the poets.

CHAPTER XXXIII

ENGLISH POETRY OF THE EIGHTEENTH CENTURY

Poetical expression includes sound as well as meaning; *Musick,* says Dryden, *is inarticulate poetry;* among the excellences of Pope, therefore, must be mentioned the melody of his meter.

—*Johnson.*

FOR more than a century England has had an uninterrupted choir of golden-tongued poets, whose melodies have made us deaf or indifferent to the silver poets of the century before. Their verse, even that of the greatest master, Alexander Pope, seems less melodious to our ears than it did to the ears of Dr. Johnson. Pope's couplets, for all their wit and polished grace, are somewhat monotonous if we read many of them at a time. But in short passages he is within the limits of his form, and his narrow ideas have the perfection of brilliant phrasing. He wrote more proverbial lines than any other English poet except Shakespeare. Of his translation of Homer we have already spoken; that shows his industry and cleverness, and it made his fortune, but it is not an expression of his individual genius, which is incapable of the mighty line. He is at his best in the bright comedy of the *Rape of the Lock* and in the malicious wit of the *Dunciad*, in which he flays his enemies, and in the glittering *Epistles* and *Satires*. His philosophy and his æsthetics are the commonplace of the time but phrased as never before or since, exemplifying his own definition:

> True wit is nature to advantage dressed,
> What oft was thought, but ne'er so well expressed.

If clarity of expression without lyric mystery or depth of thought can make poetry, Pope is a poet just short of the greatest. His imitators were legion, but none succeeded and most are now forgotten. Of the clever poets who are not forgotten two are second only to Pope: Matthew Prior and John Gay. Prior was a master of light poetry, the inventor of graceful *vers de société,* very prince of the witty epigram, and there is charm if not passion in his love poetry. *To a Child of Quality* is simply perfect. Gay is remembered not only for his occasional pieces and *Trivia,* his observations of a man about town, but most of all for his

POPE

Beggar's Opera, a jolly witty piece, which, lately revived on our stage after two centuries, enjoyed a considerable success. It is characteristic of him and of the best poets of the time, especially Prior and Pope, that within their limits they had learned the art of verse and even when they seem most casual and off-hand they write carefully with a neat turn of phrase.

The enchanting lyric of the seventeenth century and of the nineteenth was not within their gifts.

However, the sense of song, something quite different from the shining hardness of Pope, did not die out, though it flickered rather feebly. In the best of the few verses of William Collins is a lyric loveliness which makes him seem to have been a neighbor of Keats rather than of Pope. Collins is too little known, though his name is conventionally linked with that of Gray.

We have only to mention Gray's *Elegy Written in a Country Churchyard* to hear those familiar stanzas running through our memories. Not one of the stanzas but is perfect or has its perfect lines, and the poem as a whole is excellently organized. Gray wrote only a few poems to please himself and his friends; as Dickens said of him, no poet ever entered the company of the immortals with so small a volume under his arm. He was a scholar and a professor of history, versed in art, architecture and music, one of the few men of his day who appreciated natural scenery, and in sympathy with the romantic revival, that is the new or renewed interest in old English ballads and the ancient Celtic literature of Ireland and Wales. The romantic and the classic are combined in the *Bard,* in which a Welsh tradition is cast in the form of a Pindaric Ode. He looks back to Dryden and Milton and forward to the romantic period of Wordsworth and Coleridge, which we shall come to presently. Matthew Arnold thought that the prosaic spirit of the time suppressed Gray and that he did not "speak out." But he probably said all that he had to say, and the prosaic quality of the period has been over-emphasized. It simply happened, nobody knows why, that the poets were not gifted with the highest poetic power.

But they were true poets. The love of nature is expressed in the *Seasons* of James Thomson and in the poems of the gentle and melancholy William Cowper, a broken genius, but a real one. His *Task* has a simplicity and freedom from

BLAKE

rhetoric that are new in the poetry of his day. And he had a delightful humor which shows in his ballad, *John Gilpin,* and even better in his incomparable letters—he is the best letter-writer in English in at least one respect, that he knew how to make the little things of life entertaining and the great things of life sincere.

A new voice in English poetry is that of George Crabbe. In his short stories in verse, in *The Village, The Burrough, Tales of the Hall*, he introduced into English poetry a realism unlike anything that had been there before. Instead of falsified pastorals he depicted actual scenes and living people and so put new blood into literature. He is as genuine as Burns. His fault is that he has not a very fine ear and his phrasing is sometimes hard and prosaic. But he is vigorous, sincere, and he often reveals great power in telling a story.

The two lyric poets of the later eighteenth century whom we most value are William Blake and Robert Burns, men not so far apart in spirit (though Burns probably never heard of Blake) and united certainly by their love of men and of animals. Blake was a painter and engraver as well as a poet, and one side of his art affected the other. He engraved on copper plates by some process of his own the text of his poems and the illustrative designs, and the pages printed from the plates were colored by hand. His reputation both as painter and as poet has steadily increased, and he is one of the gods of the younger poets. We shall see why if we quote his most famous lyric.

THE TIGER

Tiger, tiger, burning bright
In the forests of the night,
What immortal hand or eye
Could frame thy fearful symmetry?

In what distant deeps or skies
Burnt the fire of thine eyes?
On what wings dare he aspire?
What the hand dare seize the fire?

And what shoulder and what art
Could twist the sinews of thy heart?
And when thy heart began to beat,
What dread hand and what dread feet?

What the hammer? What the chain?
In what furnace was thy brain?
What the anvil? What dread grasp
Dare its deadly terrors clasp?

And when the stars threw down their spears
And watered heaven with their tears,
Did He smile His work to see?
Did He who made the lamb make thee?

Tiger, tiger, burning bright
In the forests of the night,
What immortal hand or eye
Dare frame thy fearful symmetry?

Blake's *Songs of Innocence* and *Songs of Experience* contain many lyrics of mysterious imagery and simple harmony. But his mystical symbols are often obscure like those of the religious poets of the seventeenth century, to whom he is closely related, so that he missed popularity during his own life, and the greatness of his genius is now known only to poets and other literary folk.

Robert Burns had the double gift of enchanting the literary and reaching the hearts of the unliterary. Before he died he was the recognized poet laureate of Scotland, a position which he still holds; and he is one of the great lyric poets of English literature, known and sung by millions of us who do not happen to belong to the Scottish branch of our race and language. The Scots division of our language (it is not a "dialect" any more than the speech of an Irishman is a "brogue"!) is perfectly intelligible, with the explanation of a word or two, to any English speaking person in the world. Burns is common property of an empire and two or three republics. His songs, *John Anderson, my Jo, Auld Lang Syne,* and a hundred others are his rendering, his artistic shaping

BURNS

into final form, of verses that, with their tunes, were traditional in Scotland for nobody knows how long before him. But he did more than make over the songs of his people. His original poems, *To a Mouse, To a Daisy,* the *Cotter's Saturday Night, Tam o' Shanter, Jolly Beggars,* no matter how much they owe to earlier Scottish poetry, are in their sympathy, their humor, and their execution, the work of a born poet and a fine artist. He failed only when he tried to write like contemporary eighteenth century Englishmen

then he is stiff, formal and literary in the wrong sense of the word. For he was a Scot. But it is fortunate that English poetry of that period closes with the strong, passionate, pathetic and laughing voice from North Britain. Do I say closes? Rather comes to a climax.

PART IV

THE NINETEENTH CENTURY AND TO-DAY

CHAPTER XXXIV

THE ROMANTIC REVIVAL IN ENGLISH LITERATURE: POETRY

Bliss was it in that dawn to be alive,
But to be young was very Heaven!
                                        —*Wordsworth.*

IN 1798, Coleridge and Wordsworth published the *Lyrical Ballads,* a small volume which contains Coleridge's *Ancient Mariner*, his masterpiece, and at least one of Wordsworth's best poems, *Tintern Abbey*. The book is often called a turning point in English poetry, as if it were something quite new and revolutionary. The romantic elements were not new, and the principles of the famous preface would have been quite intelligible to Dryden a hundred years before. The real novelty is that it introduces two new poets, two very great poets.

Wordsworth wrote an endless amount of poetry, much of which is simply stupid and unreadable, the best of which is touched with divinity. He worshiped God and nature and he felt that there is a vast unity between a star and a daisy. And in noble revenge God or nature or the star or the daisy sometimes got control of his incessant pen and put themselves into his verse. Let us recall a few of his lines as a tempta-

343

tion to read more, but not too much, about as much as Matthew
Arnold includes in his volume of selections.

From the *Solitary Reaper:*

> Will no one tell me what she sings?—
> Perhaps the plaintive numbers flow
> For old, unhappy, far-off things,
> And battles long ago.

The beginning of that perfect sonnet, *Evening on Calais
Beach:*

> It is a beauteous evening, calm and free,
> The holy time is quiet as a nun
> Breathless with adoration

And the beginning of another perfect sonnet, *Upon Westminster Bridge:*

> Earth has not anything to show more fair.

From the *Intimations of Immortality:*

> The cataracts blow their trumpets from the steep;
> No more shall grief of mine the season wrong;
> I hear the echoes through the mountains throng,
> The winds come to me from the fields of sleep.

But it is unfair to quote a fragment from that poem, which
Emerson thought the high-water mark of nineteenth-century
poetry. Wordsworth is not merely a poet who writes a good
line here and there; his best poems are completely good, perfect from first line to last. His less than good verses can be
ignored, even though in discarding them we may miss some
flashes of inspiration. His great plan to philosophize poet-

ically about Man, Nature, and Society, never worked out.
But in some of his shorter pieces, like *Michael,* he is as near
to the common lot and suffering heart of humanity as Burns
or Dickens. And his poetry of nature is so intimate and

WORDSWORTH

delicate that almost every subsequent English writer about
nature in prose or verse, not excepting those who left the
English countryside for wild strange lands, has been a Words-
worthian.

The professed intention of the authors of the *Lyrical Ballads* was that Wordsworth should make the common uncommon, and Coleridge should make the uncommon credible. Coleridge's part of the plan is marvelously fulfilled in the *Ancient Mariner,* that magical ballad, which is credible only because it is magical. The structure and rhythm are based on the old English ballads; the miraculous phrasing is Coleridge's.

> The sun's rim dips; the stars rush out:
> At one stride comes the dark;
> With far-heard whisper o'er the sea,
> Off shot the spectre bark.

His gift for expressing the strange and the eerie is at its best, after the *Ancient Mariner,* in the mysterious story of *Christabel,* which he never brought to a conclusion, and in the fragment of a dream, *Kubla Khan.*

> But oh! that deep romantic chasm which slanted
> Down the green hill athwart a cedarn cover!
> A savage place! as holy and enchanted
> As e'er beneath a waning moon was haunted
> By woman wailing for her demon lover!

Coleridge was an important critic. He taught and inspired his contemporaries, and he was an important liaison officer in the passage both ways between Germany and England of the romantic spirit. His *Biographia Literaria* is a rich book which not only expresses Coleridge's individual views but sums up that whole era of poetry and philosophy.

Walter Scott, a less gifted poet than Coleridge, was an even more powerful influence in popularizing the new poetry. The world has enjoyed his prose romances more than his narra-

tives in verse, and whatever it was that turned him to the
novel, the growing popularity of Byron or the fact that prose
fiction pays better than poetry, was fortunate for literature.
He is among the great novelists; he is not a great poet. But
he had the faculty for writing readable, rapid stories in rhyme,
which could be understood by multitudes of people to whom
the mysterious beauties of Coleridge and Shelley might be
unintelligible. His *Lay of the Last Minstrel, Marmion, Lady
of the Lake,* were immensely successful, and he was the adored
king of romance, when more subtle poets were neglected and
the blazing Byron was admired rather than loved. Most of
us read *Marmion* in school, and we can remember it was one
of the easiest of the real or alleged masterpieces that were
inflicted upon us. That is its merit, ease and clarity; the
tale goes forward without interruption, and the verse, though
sometimes commonplace and monotonous, does not get in the
way. Of Scott's prose we shall say a word in the next chapter.

The heir and competitor of Scott is Byron, who became
suddenly the idol not only of England but of all Europe.
With the publication at the age of twenty-four of the first
two cantos of *Childe Harold's Pilgrimage,* he awoke one
morning, as he says, to find himself famous. *Childe Harold*
is a versified account of adventure and sight-seeing on the
Continent, spectacular, picturesque, vivacious. It is written
in the stanza of Spenser, which is in itself one indication of
the return of romance. Byron's stanza has a speed and fire
quite unlike Spenser's grave elegance. But he is careless in
all his work, priding himself on his ability to turn off verses
without effort. He did improvise with astonishing facility,
and it is surprising how much of his verse is good. He has
nothing like Shelley's devotion to the art of poetry; what
triumphs is his energy, his passion, and his wit. He died of

fever at the age of thirty-six in Greece, where he had gone to fight for the Greeks in the war for independence—a fitting climax of his stormy career, though he would have preferred to die in battle. In his short life he produced a great volume

BYRON

of narratives, dramas, and lyrics, the *Giaour, The Prisoner of Chillon*—a mere list of those that were read and remembered for a century would fill a page—which have many faults but almost never the fault of weakness. His last long work and his masterpiece is *Don Juan,* which he did not live to complete; it contains as far as it goes almost every kind of idea of which Byron was capable, and there were many kinds, humor, satire, human character, description of scenery, and philosophy which was once thought to be darkly pessimistic, but which we can endure quite cheerfully, as indeed Byron rather enjoyed it himself. The fame of Byron in Europe is greater than that of any other English poet, not excepting Shakespeare, and there are signs that in England during the last fifty years his reputation has increased.

Byron's powerful influence was immediate and lasting, partly because his ideas are obvious or at least easy to grasp, and they can be translated, as they were promptly, into other languages. His power is crude and brutal compared with that of Shelley, the most delicate lyric poet of the century. It is foolish to say that one great poet is greater than another. But it is not foolish to recognize their excellences as different. Shelley, like Byron, was part and product of all that intellectual turmoil, that almost futile struggle for liberty, which is the French Revolution. Its fiercer energies had been exhausted or crushed by Napoleonism, and there remained only dreams. Byron laughed somewhat cynically, saw through the whole evil game as did few journalists and statesmen of his time, and made his final practical sacrifice to the cause of liberty.

Shelley dreamed, dreamed of some vague future when men should be free. Fifty years after Shelley's death Matthew Arnold called him an "ineffectual angel." And so he was and so was Arnold himself. All poets and dreamers are ineffectual in the practical world as we learned bitterly in the years since 1914, and as we might have learned from any study of reported history beginning, say, about the year 33 A.D. But poetry soars above the facts. The important thing is that

Shelley *was* an angel and sang like one. He was like his own *Skylark* and he was the lyre that he prayed to be in his *Ode to the West Wind*. There was only one loose string on his lyre, and fortunately he seldom tried to strike that; he was as lacking in humor as Milton. The rest of his lyre rings true and it rings constantly, prolifically. Perhaps the reason that he was drowned at the age of thirty is that the gods could not tolerate a young man who had such inexhaustible song. His longer poems, the *Revolt of Islam* (that is, the revolt of humanity) and *Prometheus Unbound* (that is, the liberation of mankind) are so rich in lyrical passages that one almost forgets in reading them that Shelley had a passionate coherent purpose. And his drama, the *Cenci,* is so crowded with beautiful lines that the dramatic action gets lost—the only respect in which it is inferior to Shakespeare. *Adonais,* the elegy on the death of Keats, immortalizes not Keats but Shelley. Only the greatest of poets could write:

> Life, like a dome of many-coloured glass,
> Stains the white radiance of eternity.

Shelley was ethereal, visionary, and for all his militant love of humanity, dwelt among the stars.

Keats was of the earth, but of the earth at its most beautiful, its colors and perfumes, its youth of the present and the youth of its everlasting antiquity. He sang of gladness:

> A thing of beauty is a joy for ever—

and of sadness:

> She dwells with Beauty—Beauty that must die;
> And Joy, whose hand is ever at his lips
> Bidding adieu.

SHELLEY

It is almost incredible that a man who died at the age of twenty-six should have attained the mastery of form and phrase, the ultimate perfection of the three odes, *To a Grecian Urn, To Autumn, To a Nightingale.* Poetry and music belong to youth, and many poets and musicians have done marvelous things when they were mere boys. Keats reached maturity at a bound. How far he might have gone if he had lived is idle conjecture, and the unfinished *Hyperion* is only a suggestion of the possible direction of his genius. But there can be no lamentations for him. His poems are not juvenile promise; they are complete achievement. There is thrilling justice in Matthew Arnold's comment on the expressed belief of Keats that he would be remembered among the English poets; Arnold says simply: "He is. He is with Shakespeare." It was a full-fledged poet, the peer of the great masters, who wrote this stanza of the *Ode on a Grecian Urn:*

> O Attic shape! Fair attitude! with breed
> Of marble men and maidens overwrought,
> With forest branches and the trodden weed;
> Thou, silent form, dost tease us out of thought
> As doth eternity: Cold Pastoral!
> When old age shall this generation waste,
> Thou shalt remain, in midst of other woe
> Than ours, a friend to man, to whom thou say'st
> "Beauty is truth, truth beauty,"—that is all
> Ye know on earth, and all ye need to know.

Keats died young. Walter Savage Landor, who was born twenty years before Keats and so was almost exactly contemporary with Coleridge and Wordsworth, lived far into the nineteenth century and was known and admired by the new young poets, Browning and Swinburne. He carries one age of poetry into the next and he belongs to both, for he

did not decline in his old age like Wordsworth, but was a
poet to the end of his vigorous life. He is best known—
and he should be better known—for his *Imaginary Conversations,* dramatic dialogues in prose between historic or
legendary persons, which contain the essence of the wisdom
of the ages. Landor's character was belligerent and violent
and like most of the writers of his time he was stirred by the
great upheaval of Europe, which began with the French
Revolution and did not end with the downfall of Napoleon.
Indeed Landor took a more active part in affairs than any
of the other poets except Byron, for he raised and led a regiment against Napoleon in Spain. But his poetry is serene
and pure, of an Olympian dignity learned from the Greeks.
A fitting close to that period of storm and stress is his proud
quatrain, *On His Seventy-fifth Birthday:*

> I strove with none, for none was worth my strife,
>   Nature I loved, and next to Nature, Art;
> I warmed both hands before the fire of life,
>   It sinks, and I am ready to depart.

CHAPTER XXXV
ENGLISH NOVELS OF THE NINETEENTH CENTURY

The life of man is not the subject of novels, but the inexhaustible magazine from which subjects are to be selected; the name of these is legion; and with each new subject the true artist will vary his method and change the point of attack.

—*Stevenson.*

THE English novel, viewed as a whole or a multitude, is remarkable for its immense variety and for the great number of writers who drew with skill and power from the "inexhaustible magazine" of life. In the nineteenth century England produced almost every kind of novel that was ever written, and the different kinds did not at any moment exclude each other. Scott and Jane Austen lived at the same time; Robert Louis Stevenson and Henry James were friends. After Fielding the novel declined for a time, though there were many who tried it with some success. It took on new life with the publication in 1814 of Scott's *Waverley,* the first of his long series of romances, which have delighted millions of readers in all countries. For people who have never been in Scotland, and to some extent for people who were born there, that country is the country of Walter Scott. He knew and loved every corner of it, so that his scenery

is not mere picturesque decoration of the tale but the very
rock and soil from which the tale springs.   His knowledge
of history, which was very rich, furnished his imagination with
brilliant adventure and traditional heroes.   Moreover, he had
an affectionate understanding of the common people.   His

SCOTT

spectacular portrait of Queen Mary Stuart is less wonderful
than his drawing of the simple girls, Effie and Jeanie Deans
in *The Heart of Midlothian.*   And in *The Bride of Lam-
mermoor* we remember not only the melodramatic Ravens-
wood but old Caleb Balderstone.   Scott was endlessly fertile

and abundant, sometimes hasty and careless, but always vital, even when he was ill and overworked. He was a born story-teller who let his plots and his style take care of themselves. He was also (though this sort of comment is aside from our purpose) a very great man; he assumed the debts of his publisher, which he could legally have avoided and wore himself out paying them off. But he never to the end wore out his readers. The small boy with no misgiving and the adult reader, with some critical reservations here and there, can read the Waverley Novels through: *Guy Mannering, Rob Roy, Ivanhoe, The Talisman, Quentin Durward*—the titles open the gate of memory and imagination.

Scott lived in his novels and poems in a big world of romantic action and in his personal life he was the center of a fairly big world, enjoying fame, fortune, and the dubious tribute of being knighted.

Jane Austen, Scott's greatest contemporary in fiction, was a shy obscure woman, who lived in provincial towns, far from the madding crowd, and whose work was not widely known until after her death. Scott knew her novels, and his praise of her is final: "That young lady had a talent for describing the involvements, feelings and characters of ordinary life which is to me the most wonderful I have ever met with. The big bow-wow I can do myself like any one going; but the exquisite touch which renders commonplace things and characters interesting from the truth of the description and the sentiment is denied me."

Jane Austen completed six novels, *Northanger Abbey, Persuasion, Sense and Sensibility, Pride and Prejudice, Mansfield Park,* and *Emma.* Each is perfect, and there is no choosing between them for one who enjoys her quiet irony and her simple delicate analysis of character. There are no heroic

passions nor astounding adventures. *Northanger Abbey* is a
gentle satire on the mystery tale of haunted castles. And in
all her novels the love-making of her young people, though
serious and sympathetic, is subdued by humor to the ordinary
plane of emotion on which most of us live. She was the
founder of the novel which deals with unimportant middle-

DICKENS

class people and of which there are many fine examples in
later English fiction. Her style is easy and effortless, a perfect example of what De Quincey meant when he said that we
should have to turn to the prose of the cultivated gentlewoman
for English uncorrupted by the slang and cant of the world.
  At about the time when Jane Austen's *Pride and Prejudice*
and Scott's *Waverley* were published Charles Dickens was

born. He was the best beloved of all English novelists after Scott. At the age of twenty-five he leaped into fame and prosperity with the *Pickwick Papers,* which contains all the elements, some of them never better exemplified, of his later novels—the drollery, the farce, the animal high spirits, the pathos, the sense of action and scene. He captured the public and dumbfounded the critics. He proceeded through novel after novel to create fantastic characters, which are yet true to life, and to invent disorderly plots, which through interminable pages hold the reader captive. The secret, if anyone can divine the secret of genius, is that Dickens was gifted with a vitality so great that only his abuse of it finally exhausted it. He loved life, he loved to write (he wrote enough intimate letters to fill the time of an ordinary man), and he hugely enjoyed his characters and believed in them. They are a great and populous company, whom our fathers and grandfathers knew intimately. Does the younger generation know them?— Weller, Pecksniff, Snodgrass, Bumble, Swiveller, Pegotty, Podsnap, Cuttle, Sykes, Nancy, Nell, Emily, and all the rest?

His gallery is said not to contain a true portrait of an aristocrat, and so to lack something which is found in Scott and Shakespeare and Thackeray. True, he was limited in his knowledge of the upper world. His world is a mixture of the world of common people and of the vast universe of romance which exists only in the human brain. His best book is *David Copperfield,* which contains all his merits and most of his faults, truth and melodrama, genuine pathos and sentimentality, beautiful writing, as in the storm scene, and too many words everywhere; and through it all that tremendous driving force which never lets even his weakest passages sag below a continuous level of interest. His power over our everyday emotions is unrivalled, for with one page he can make you double up with laughter, and he can make you wet the next page with honest tears. Dickens is all black and white, with some gorgeous splashes of descriptive color. His black is the black of villains who come always to a bad end. His white is lovely girls and brave young men, who come to a good end, earthly prosperity, or die a gently pathetic death. So that though he quite heartily narrates terrible murders and rascalities, it was possible for another great novelist to write of him: "I am grateful for the innocent laughter, and the sweet unsullied pages which the author of *David Copperfield* gives to my children."

That other novelist was Thackeray. Thackeray's early work consists of burlesques, sketches, satires, very brilliant, but now remembered because we remember the later Thackeray. He found himself and became immortally memorable in *Vanity Fair,* a novel "without a hero," as he calls it, but with a heroine, Becky Sharp. Thackeray's "good" women are uninteresting. His women who are less than good (though Thackeray's hand is never heavy upon errant women) are attractive. This is true of Becky Sharp, and it is true of Beatrix, the willful, spoiled girl in *Henry Esmond,* a brilliant historical romance of the eighteenth century. Thackeray's sense of the dramatic romance of times past is as vivid as Scott's, and in *Henry Esmond* he not only works out an exciting plot, but gives the intellectual tone of the age. In *Pendennis* and *The Newcomes* Thackeray views the society of his own day with the eye of a man of the world. Here was human nature studied and portrayed with an honesty equal to Fielding's, though not so broadly outspoken, a knowledge of some classes with which Dickens had no acquaintance, and a wider outlook on the whole comedy of life than Jane Austen's. The stories move in a leisurely, almost haphazard way, like life itself, and it is only when Thackeray interrupts the course of events with moralistic comments that there is any break in the illusion that things happened thus and so. He is skillful in his drawing of young men, Arthur Pendennis, and Clive Newcome, whom he treats with a sort of paternal kindliness, and his older men are even better—Major Pendennis, the perfect man of the world such as Thackeray might have met in a London club, and Colonel Newcome, the fine old gentleman who is almost too pure to be met anywhere on this earth, and who is a living refutation of a notion once current that Thackeray is cynical. He is nothing like that; he is a genial talker from a comfortable arm-chair, who loves humanity and laughs at it. Thackeray's genius, like Fielding's, combines that of the essayist with that of the story-teller. In his lightest papers he wrote well, though often with indolent inaccuracies. In his great scenes, like that in which Esmond breaks his sword and forswears his birthright, and that in which Rawdon Crawley knocks down the old rake Steyne, he is a supreme master of situation and character and of the style which conveys them.

Among the distinguished contributors to the English novel are several remarkable women, of whom Jane Austen is the elder sister—or the spinster aunt. Whether women have succeeded greatly in other forms of art is a question which we need not try to answer. There is no doubt of their achievement in fiction. This is easily explained, if explanation be necessary. The basis of fiction is human character, which a clever woman can understand at least as well as a man. Moreover, the use of words is woman's natural function, as it is her talk which carries the language on to children, and the volubility and keenness of her tongue are proverbial. In our time we take women for granted as literary artists, and of a new novel we ask not the general question whether it is by a woman but the specific question whether it is by May Sinclair or Edith Wharton or Gertrude Atherton. In our grandfathers' time the intellectual position of women was more restricted than it is now. Though other women had written and published before her, Jane Austen's reason for publishing her novels anonymously was probably different from Scott's, and was not altogether individual modesty. The same thing is true of the three sisters Brontë, Charlotte, Emily and Anne, who published their novels under the names of Currer, Ellis, and Acton Bell. Emily and Charlotte were women of forceful genius, and, though their genius remained partly thwarted and undeveloped, each has left at least one masterpiece, Emily Brontë's *Wuthering Heights* and Charlotte Brontë's *Jane Eyre*. *Wuthering Heights* is a work of extraordinary emotional intensity, quite independent of any fiction that had been written before it, and in its "atmosphere," its grim dark poetic color as solitary in English fiction as the solitude of its own scene. *Jane Eyre* is equally original and seems to owe nothing to any nameable predecessor. It is a revolt against the conventional heroine, for Jane Eyre is not beautiful, and she is poor and of obscure family. It was a new thing in English fiction that a woman who was not beautiful should taste the romance of life. Balzac in France had developed that idea in a different way, but it is doubtful if Miss Brontë knew Balzac's novels. The immediate and continued popularity of *Jane Eyre* is in part due to the fact that commonplace women were flattered and consoled by the final triumph of a girl who is neither Cinderella nor Helen of Troy.

Charlotte Brontë's friend and biographer, Elizabeth Gaskell, wrote two books, at least, which are important in English fiction. *Mary Barton,* a story of the working people of Manchester, appealed to a wide audience, and won the admiration of Carlyle and Dickens. It is a faithful picture of the poor, written without Carlyle's indignant thunder or Dickens's sentimental eloquence (as in *Hard Times*). Perhaps because it is quiet, and has no touch of melodrama, and not much plot, its greatness has been forgotten; and perhaps we do not like to read for pleasure the long and far from simple annals of the poor. But we all like to read about the people in *Cranford,* a story or rather a series of sketches of village life. It is a delicious book. In that little world nothing happens and everything happens. It is life in a nut-shell—or in a lady's thimble.

The strongest woman in English letters is George Eliot. Because she has an extensive intellectual interest and the ability to analyze character in terms that are now called "psychological," she has been praised for her virile or masculine qualities. She is, indeed, thoroughly and sensitively feminine. In her first great novel, *Adam Bede*, the men, the good men, Adam and Seth, and the sinful young Donnithorne, are drawn with a firm hand and there is little in the characterization to suggest the sex of the writer. The woman's touch shows in the maternal sympathy for the unfortunte Hetty Sorrel, and in the excellent humorous portrait of Mrs. Poyser, who rubs it into the men with delightful shrewdness. George Eliot's strength is in her characters; she lives with them and suffers with them, baring her own heart as openly as Dickens. She understands simple people like Silas Marner and Maggie Tulliver (in the *Mill on the Floss*) and the more complicated nature of Tito Melema, the handsome scoundrel in *Romola*. Her emotional sincerity and intellectual power—in her later work the intellect tended to smother the emotion—were impeded in their expression by a lack of the sense of narrative, that mysterious sense which is a gift of the gods and which can be the easy flow of Thackeray or the pell-mell rush of Dickens. George Eliot's popularity surprised her, and having won it she never tried to repeat her successes, but went on to the next book as to a new problem. The problems of life sometimes swamp her stories and make her less than an artist, but what we get from her finally is a feeling of humorous and philosophic courage to face the problems.

Another Victorian novelist who was deeply concerned with the problems of life, what's wrong with the world and what to do about it, is Charles Reade.   His zeal to reform prisons and asylums for the insane and all other mismanaged institutions is as passionate as that of Dickens, the difference being that Reade's earnestness is not tempered by anything like the expansive humor of Dickens. Reade's masterpiece is far away from modern England; it is *The Cloister and the Hearth*, a story of the father of the humanist, Erasmus, drawn in part from the *Colloquies* and other writings of Erasmus. It is a superb pageant of the late Middle Ages or early Renaissance, with scenes of great dramatic power, and two scenes that are heart-wringingly beautiful, that in which Gerard first sees his child and that in which the child's mother dies. There is no finer historical romance of any period, and no more glowing picture of the fifteenth century.

A secondary genius of real merit is Anthony Trollope, the most prolific of English novelists. He wrote three or four novels a year for twenty years, and the list of his works is almost past the power of mathematics to enumerate. None of his novels is of first rate quality and none is of less than good second rate quality. The splendid scene or passage in which inspiration rises above commonplace, as in Dickens, Thackeray, Meredith, Hardy, even George Eliot and Charles Reade, is not to be found in Trollope. But the totality of his achievement and the even excellence of his workmanship are amazing, and if he had had one touch now and again of the divine fire he would have come nearer than any other novelist to having written the *Comédie Humaine* of England. His multitude of characters are all alive, town clerks and country parsons, members of Parliament and fox-hunting squires, pretty girls and old women, some of whom he introduces into novel after novel, always keeping the character as recognizable as an old friend. His best books—it is hard to choose from his placid uniformity—are *Barchester Towers, The Last Chronicle of Barset, Dr. Thorne, The Small House at Allington, Framley Parsonage,* and the short novel in which he first found his peculiar talent, *The Warden.*

In fiction (and in other forms of literature) there are three classes of writers worth considering from the point of view of the reader, who may or may not be a competent critical judge but on whom the life of the writer depends. First and most fortunate are writers like Thackeray and Dickens who seize the imaginations of their contemporaries and continue to interest succeeding generations. Then there are those who are widely acclaimed in their own day, fade somewhat as time passes, but are not and should not be forgotten. In the nineteenth century, as in our own time, there is a swarm of readable, once popular story-tellers. We shall have to ask the librarians and the publishers of popular reprints how many people still read William Harrison Ainsworth's *Windsor Castle;* G. P. R. James's *Richelieu; Vivian Grey* and *Coningsby* by the brilliant politician, Disraeli; Bulwer-Lytton's *Last Days of Pompeii;* Charles Lever's swaggering *Harry Lorrequer* and *Charles O'Malley;* Captain Marryat's *Masterman Ready, Mr. Midshipman Easy,* and *Peter Simple* (our

boys are missing much if they do not know those books);
Dinah Craik's *John Halifax, Gentleman;* Blackmore's *Lorna
Doone;* Charles Kingsley's *Hypatia* and *Westward Ho!;* Wil-
kie Collins's *Woman in White;* Margaret Oliphant's *Salem
Chapel;* and the works of other novelists whom our grandfathers admired almost as much as they admired the novels of the
five or six who now seem to us the stars of first magnitude.

The third class of writers, not numerous, since the judgment
of the world is just on the whole, includes those men of genius
who have to wait long for recognition. In 1859, the year of
Dickens's *Tale of Two Cities* and George Eliot's *Adam Bede,*
appeared the *Ordeal of Richard Feverel* by George Meredith.
The book and the author were destined to remain for many
years in relative obscurity, and only a few people of discern-
ment, mostly literary people like George Eliot and Dante Gabriel Rossetti, were aware that a new great genius had arrived in English literature. Today an increasing number of
critical readers know that Meredith holds a very high place
among the novelists of the world. He may never win a wide
audience, because his stories are unhappy in spite of his robust humor; *Richard Feverel* is a harrowing tragedy, without, for the hero, the calm consolation of death. His greatest
novel, *The Egoist,* has a sorry conclusion which requires bravery in one's silent laughter at it; and *Beauchamp's Career* ends
in sad futility. Moreover, Meredith's narrative is confused to
the reader who has a single-track mind by the multiplicity of
his ideas which branch out in every direction. His involutions are like those of Browning (whom in some respects he
resembles, though he is much more subtle), the involutions
of life. Human thought is complicated, and Meredith is
concerned with what goes on inside that strange and inter-

esting creature, Man. But there is no lack of "story"; his great scenes are of thrilling interest. Where shall you find a more moving tale than *Rhoda Fleming* or one more filled with dramatic adventure than *Harry Richmond?* He requires for full understanding a reader who can match his brains against the author's, and for that matter so do Shakespeare and every other man of genius.

With the death of Meredith, in 1909, it seemed to many that the Victorian era had definitely closed. But periods do not begin or close so suddenly. And there lived until 1928 one who was as great as any of the last century, Thomas Hardy. When in 1874 his first successful novel, *Far from the Madding Crowd,* was published anonymously in a magazine, some readers attributed it to George Eliot. This suggests how close Hardy is to the older Victorian novelists. But the simplest reader might have seen that the tragic irony of this book and the fatal capriciousness of the heroine were not the work of George Eliot nor of any other writer that the world had heard of before. Hardy's style is perfectly clear, and his stories move as rapidly as melodrama; so that he had not to wait like Meredith for a small and belated public, though his cold and unhappy philosophy must ever estrange him from the sentimental multitude.

Hardy's most famous novel is *Tess of the D'Urbervilles,* the subtitle of which is "A Pure Woman Faithfully Presented." Tess is a victim of fate, of inexplicable accident, of the weakness of one man and the villainy of another. It is a tenderly cruel story, tender because Hardy treats his heroine with immeasurable pity, and cruel because he arrays all the forces of life against her; Richardson did not abuse Clarissa Harlowe quite so inexorably. The beauty of Hardy is in his

descriptions of nature, which he paints like a graphic artist
(he was a professional architect and draftsman), though the
meaning of nature is sad, blind, insoluble. The comedy of
life is in the peasants with their racy speech and primitive
ideas. The tragedy is man's struggle and passion in an in-
scrutably hostile world. His strongest novel, *Jude the Ob-*

ROBERT LOUIS STEVENSON

scure, carries his pessimism, which is not quite the word for it,
so far that readers who had welcomed *Tess* revolted, and
Hardy stopped writing fiction more than thirty years ago. He
devoted the rest of his life to poetry.

The year before the publication of Hardy's *Jude,* Robert
Louis Stevenson died. In the last decade of the nineteenth
century he was admired by the literary for his excellent style

and by the unliterary for his rip-roaring yarns, of which *Treasure Island* was the first and *Kidnapped* the best. The charm of his essays and letters is so potent that it is almost

GEORGE MOORE

impossible for a reader brought up under his spell to judge the importance of his fiction, but it seems certain that *Treasure Island* is as imperishable as *Robinson Crusoe.*

It seems to me that Stevenson for all his praise of youth,

his gay courage, his scrupulous devotion to art and his immense popularity, was a reactionary, an old-fashioned man, and that while he was polishing his sentences the fine new thing was being done by another artist who also polished his sentences

JOSEPH CONRAD

but had stouter metal to polish, George Gissing, whose *Demos,* *The Unclassed, The Whirlpool* place him among the great English novelists. I will stake my reputation on that judgment and I feel the more secure in it because the interest in

Gissing is increasing rather than decreasing. But it is still too early to know what fate will overtake his fame.

It is equally impossible, until critical time comes to our assistance, to estimate the value of writers of fiction who have flourished in the first quarter of our century, many of whom are still living. The English novel (including the American) is a vigorous institution with many competent members. Perhaps H. G. Wells, himself a brilliant novelist, has the right idea when he says, in effect, that though there may be among the living no emergent giant, yet the game which they are all playing together is bigger than ever. People fifty years from now will be blind to our age and will miss much beautiful work if they do not know the short stories of Rudyard Kipling and his long story *Kim,* the romances of Joseph Conrad, the novels of George Moore, of John Galsworthy, of D. H. Lawrence, of W. Somerset Maugham, of Arnold Bennett (once in *The Old Wives' Tale*), of May Sinclair; and we must add the plays of Bernard Shaw, and we may add the work of a dozen other living artists. After Hardy's death the foremost writer of fiction in English was Joseph Conrad. The story of how this Pole became a British seaman and a classic in British literature is itself a romance. His descriptions of the sea are the most splendid in English, and that means in all, literature. The action of his stories (*Lord Jim; Nostromo; Victory;* the marvellous short stories, *Youth* and *The Heart of Darkness*) is as exciting as melodrama. Underneath is a profound thinker about life and character; and the surface, if the surface can be thought of as separate from the essential texture, is the golden prose of one of the masters of English style.

CHAPTER XXXVI

ENGLISH ESSAYISTS AND PHILOSOPHERS OF THE NINETEENTH CENTURY

How little survives of the wordiest authors!
—Charles Lamb.

IKE every other short definition the title of this chapter is only a convenience, and we shall not let it be a limitation, for we shall say a word about two or three thinkers who were historians or men of science rather than essayists or philosophers. It is the function of classifications to give us our bearings and not to tie us to the sign-post.

Charles Lamb almost defies classification, though all the sign-posts point clearly to him as the most original of English essayists. He derived his rich and whimsical style in part from the prose writers of the seventeenth century, but it was not a patchwork garment that he fashioned, it was something new and uniquely fitted to him. The *Essays of Elia* and Lamb's other papers and personal letters range from delicious fooling and nonsense to the tender pathos of *Dream Children* and the finest, most illuminating criticism. He did more than anyone else to revive interest in the old poets and he appreciated the new poets who were his friends,

Wordsworth, Coleridge, and Keats. A liking for "gentle Elia" and for the books he liked is sure proof of literary taste.

An essayist inferior only to Lamb in charm and critical insight is Leigh Hunt, whose miscellaneous writings are not of capital importance in the literature of the ages, but cannot be overlooked in even the slightest sketch of the English essay. They are preserved by a normal, easy style, a model of sound, natural English. A volume of selections from Hunt's essays is one of those precious little books that can never shake the universe but can refresh a corner of it.

A critic writing fifty years ago would have placed Southey among the poets. But to our taste Southey's verse has lost flavor, and it is almost impossible to realize that he was regarded as forming a sort of triumvirate with Wordsworth and Coleridge, just as it is difficult to realize that Rogers and Campbell were once considered important, and that the pleasant Irish balladist, Thomas Moore, enjoyed a reputation second only to Byron's. Southey's verse surely does not raise him to a place among the immortals. But there is enduring value in his prose. His *Life of Nelson,* whatever its value as history, is excellently written. In this and other serious work he is very careful and writes with an Addisonian dignity. But he had a strong vein of humor, and in a too little known book, *The Doctor*, he lets himself go in all manner of fantastic fooling, which is almost equal to the divine nonsense of Sterne.

Southey was a studious, conscientious, scholarly workman, highly respected in his generation. Lamb was eccentric, whimsical, and beloved. Hunt was agreeable and friendly. William Hazlitt, a more powerful critic than they, was a man of vehement temper who enraged his enemies and estranged his friends. The quarrels of the time are interesting chiefly in that they stimulated Hazlitt and gave added strength to his hot, hard-hitting style. He was a profound and systematic student of English literature, and our first important critic of art (he tried unsuccessfully to be a painter), and his reputation among those who read and those who try to practice criticism was never so high as it is today.

CHARLES LAMB

The reader will find nothing to sharpen his interest in books and to lead him into the thick of literary problems (not dull but exciting ones) better than Hazlitt's *Lectures on the English Comic Writers,* the *Spirit of the Age,* and the amazingly brilliant *Table-Talk.* His lectures on *The Characters of Shakespeare's Plays* and on *The Dramatic Literature of the*

Age of Elizabeth shine through a whole century of criticism and scholarship.

Writers like Hazlitt, whose subjects are mostly concerned with literary criticism (though Hazlitt wrote admirably on other subjects), appeal only to people with a literary turn of mind, for comparatively few people read criticism at all. But everybody likes the story of a man, especially if it is a strange story. Thomas De Quincey is known not for his scholarly essays, but for his autobiographical *Confessions of an English Opium Eater.* The account of the young man's wanderings in London, and his friendship for a waif of a girl is simple and touching. The analysis of the effects of opium is self-evidently accurate; and the dreams are not only poetic, but partially interpreted in a way that looks forward to modern psychology. De Quincey returns like Lamb to the gorgeously rhetorical prose of the seventeenth century. But the swelling undulations of De Quincey's prose that rise and fall like the sea and break into foam and rainbows are his peculiar movements of mind, very beautiful to readers who have an ear for rhythm, but repellent to those who must have their ideas plain and straight.

Readers of the latter sort have always found themselves more at home in Thomas Babington Macaulay, who is so clear that nobody can misunderstand him and so emphatic that it takes courage to disagree with him. His monumental work is his *History of England* which has been read by more Englishmen and Americans than any other history. Its great merits, which the public felt at once, and which expert criticism has not been able to deny, are the lucidity of the explanations, and the dramatic effect with which men and events are drawn. The same virtues characterize his essays, especially those that deal with public men rather than with men of let-

ters. The best examples of his power are not the *Milton*
which made him famous, but such essays as *Chatham* and
Warren Hastings.

During the central forty years of the nineteenth century the
acknowledged head of English letters, outside fiction and

CARLYLE

poetry (and perhaps including them), was Thomas Carlyle
He made his way slowly at first. He tried in *Sartor Resartu*
to capture the ear of England with an amazing combinatior
of German and Scottish philosophy written in the most bi
zarre style since Laurence Sterne. Englishmen were not the
interested in German philosophy, though Coleridge in a bril

iantly fragmentary way had taught them a little about it.
Carlyle's book was not well received except by a few, includ-
ng Emerson in America. Yet it was, and is, a great book, the
tory of a man's spiritual struggles with himself and his ef-
orts to grasp the meaning of society, set forth under the fan-
astic conceit of mankind symbolized by its clothes. It would
iave brought a frown of pleasure to the brow of Jonathan
Swift—if he could have understood the Germanized style.
The main theme of the book, however, is not Swiftian, but
)elongs to that period of troubled doubt in which Carlyle was
)rought up. The period is not yet finished and is perhaps now
)eing repeated in intensified form.

Carlyle's message is the growth of the soul from pessimistic
Legation to indifference and then to affirmative and defiant
ourage. He preached some variation of that message for
orty years. And though few people profit by a preacher's
message, at least the world came to recognize in Carlyle a
onic and inspiring force. His first successful book was the
French Revolution, which is not a critical or documentary
iistory, but a prose epic, picturesque and dramatic. The same
:ind of imaginative force animates his *Past and Present,* a
tudy of the Middle Ages. Carlyle believed in heroes, in
Great Men (as he would have capitalized the words), and in
iis *Heroes and Hero-Worship* and his *Oliver Cromwell* he
eaches us to sit at the feet of the mighty, the noble mighty,
f we are to find salvation. His style and his ideas at their
worst are grotesque and fuddled, and are marred by a kind of
)rivate Carlylean cant which is almost as bad as the current
)opular cant which he denounced. At his best he is magnifi-
:ent as a Hebrew prophet. And through his grim earnestness
:here are glints of shrewd humor.

A disciple of Carlyle in many of his ideas is John Ruskin.

who resembles his master in his austere morality and h
hatred of the prevalent sham and cruelty of the political an
economic world. Ruskin, like Carlyle, was of Scottish bloo
Carlyle was born poor, of peasant stock, and remained poc

MARIE ANTOINETTE

all his life. Ruskin was the son of a wealthy merchant, an
he enjoyed all the advantages of travel and of early trainin
in music and art. He was an expert draftsman, and was th
first English writer on art after Hazlitt who wrote with th

uthority of a man who had practiced with pencil and brush
s well as with pen.   In his *Modern Painters, Seven Lamps of
Architecture,* and *Stones of Venice,* his sense of visual beauty
s transmuted into highly colored prose full of poetic joy in
eautiful things which is half killed by a dull, drab moralism.
Ie taught that art and architecture are an expression of the
eligion and the social habits of the people, and that art must
e pure and devoted and earnest.   This is profoundly true as a
1atter of history, and as an account of the way the artist
vorks, and Ruskin's principles are the final expression of
thical æsthetics.   But it leaves out much of the joy of art,
incerely as Ruskin loves lovely things, and one suspects that
3envenuto Cellini would have laughed at it, Michelangelo
vould have been too busy to listen to it, and the men who
1ade St. Mark's and the Doges' Palace in Ruskin's beloved
°enice would have wondered what this solemn man from the
orth was talking about.

Ruskin grew more and more interested in social problems,
f which his views are best expressed in *Unto This Last* and
esame and Lilies.   He was, with William Morris, the foun-
er in England of a sort of artistic socialism, the ideal of which
°as a society where art would be accessible to everybody and
gly cities and buildings should be impossible.   He was, ex-
ept in form, a poet like Shelley, a dreamer defeated by the
acts of life.   He gave away a good deal of the fortune left
im by his thrifty father, and was always sweet and unselfish,
vith no egotism except that of the man of passionate convic-
ons who wishes his ideas to prevail.   Ruskin learned early
1 life the art of writing, and for fifty years, though he some-
mes lost himself in a multitude of subjects, he never lost his
tyle, or his two styles, one a clear and simple exposition of
Jeas, moral, economic, social, the other a branching, elaborate

eloquent expression of his artistic enthusiasms. In his use o
words he is never grotesque like Carlyle or careless like Thack
eray. Critics have riddled his views of art, and economist
have made havoc of his social theories. Nobody has seriousl
quarreled with his style or denied him a first place among th
masters of prose.

Ruskin hoped that by means of art, religion, and literature
all people might become civilized. His contemporary, Mat
thew Arnold (they graduated from Oxford at about the sam
time), had little of Ruskin's passionate faith in democracy, bu
preached culture for the saving remnant whom he though
capable of it. His outlook on life was limited by an almos
snobbish definition of culture, but his outlook on literatur
was broad, serene, urbane, and humorous. In *Culture an
Anarchy* and other essays he defends the Greek ideal, "Hellen
ism," against the Hebraic ideal, as represented by the too nar
row Christianity of his time. In *Literature and Dogma* h
rescues the Bible from the theologians and Philistines. I
these more argumentative essays of Arnold's have grown
little pale, it is because cultivated people now take for grante
ideas for which he had to make an adroit intellectual fight
No development of criticism can take the bloom from hi
essays on poetry, *On Celtic Literature, On Translating Homer*
on Keats and Wordsworth, for he was himself a poet, if no
a great one, and his real interest was in beautiful letters, no
in the problems of society. If he harped too much on culture
he could not foresee that it would become a tiresome word i
our day through much repetition, and he had an especial righ
to it, for in his time he more than any other English man o
letters *was* culture.

The nineteenth century boiled with controversy about eco
nomic, religious and scientific matters, and the leading men o

letters, Carlyle, Ruskin, Arnold, even the novelists, took a hand in the conflicts or felt the echo of them. And some of the arguers and expositors, who were not primarily men of letters, wrote so well that they are secure in English literature, no matter what their special subject.

John Stuart Mill's *Political Economy* is out of date, and recent events have sent much nineteenth-century economic theory to the waste-basket. But Mill's book is a paragon of expository writing. His *Subjection of Women* is also obsolete in view of the recent emancipation of the sex. But his essay on *Liberty* is everlastingly alive, never more fresh and pertinent than today.

John Henry Newman was the leading mind on the Roman Catholic side of a controversy between the Protestant and Roman branches of the Church, a controversy which stirred all the intellectual life of England in the middle of the nineteenth century, and which is of historical importance. It is only the literary interest of the contest which concerns us, and Newman's contributions have the highest literary value even to those who are indifferent or antagonistic to his beliefs. His *Apologia pro Vita Sua* is a charming intellectual autobiography, written in a flawless style at once simple and subtle. Though his vigorous mind was directed to practical ends, he was instinctively an artist; he was also a teacher, and the slightly humorous passage in the *Idea of a University*, on English composition should be in the hands of every instructor, and of everyone who is trying to learn to write.

Another thinker whose purposes were practical, but who made literature his servant was Charles Darwin. It is not our function to comment on the scientific value of the *Origin of Species* and the *Descent of Man*. We will leave that to the biologists to argue about. We do know that Darwin fashioned

for himself a style perfectly suited to his subject, and that hi
literary power gives immortality to his work, no matter wha
may be the future development of theories of evolution. On
the other hand Darwin's friend, Herbert Spencer, the philoso
pher of evolution, is already threatened with oblivion in liter
ature if not in philosophy because he did not know the art o
writing. If we understand or surmise in the broadest way
without exact definition the distinction illustrated by thes
two powerful friends and colleagues, who were in substantia
agreement, the distinction between the man who can writ
and the man who cannot write, we shall have an inkling o
what we mean by literature.

Of all men of science of the nineteenth century the one whom
literature most securely claims for her own is Thomas Henry
Huxley. He was a professional biologist, the acknowledged
leader in his department of science. He lives in literature by
his miscellaneous essays and lectures, which grew out of the
continuous quarrel between scientific liberty and orthodox
authority. His writings are much more than technical dis
cussions; they are polemical pleas for the right of free in
vestigation and the untrammeled search for truth. *Man'*
Place in Nature and *Lectures and Lay Sermons* are model
of their kind, perfectly clear to the reader who has no scien
tific training, and they had an immense influence on popula
opinion. The only virtue which his style lacks is the Addi
sonian graciousness of Matthew Arnold and Cardinal New
man. But in Huxley perhaps that virtue would have been
a weakness, and the absence of it does not mean that he wa
not always fair and courteous. He went at his subject and hi
audience with a direct aggressive vigor and a cool command
of his material, a remarkable union of scientific knowledge and
literary art.

The pure literary essay, apart from the controversial and practical contests of life, rises to a very high excellence in Robert Louis Stevenson (of whose fiction we have already spoken) and in Walter Pater. Pater was the last word in refinement of style. He wrote little, and he wrote very carefully, and almost everything he wrote is worth reading. His *Appreciations* is a collection of beautiful essays, notably those on Lamb, Wordsworth and Coleridge. For a generation after his death half the young men in England who tried to write criticism were deliberate disciples of Pater rather than of Arnold. On those young men and others the future is still to pass judgment.

CHAPTER XXXVII
VICTORIAN POETRY

I come as one whose thoughts half linger,
Half run before;
The youngest to the oldest singer
That England bore.
—*Swinburne* on Landor.

THERE was no particular time when Victorian poetry began, no particular man who began it. The poets who were born early in the nineteenth century, and were at their prime in the middle of it, are in direct and continuous succession from Wordsworth and Coleridge and Keats and Shelley. The *Oxford Book of Victorian Verse* opens properly enough with selections from Landor, of whom we have already said a word. He lived far into the century, and his death was celebrated by the young Swinburne in the lines quoted above. The generations touch hands.

Perhaps the first significant date in Victorian poetry is 1842 when Tennyson published his *English Idylls and Other Poems*. He had been known to a few admirers, by a small volume published ten years before, as a fresh voice in English song. The volume of 1842 included the best of his earlier pieces, excellently revised, and new poems, *Ulysses, Locksley Hall,* and others, which have become so much a part of common speech and thought that we can scarcely recover the sense of surprised delight with which English readers greeted them eighty years ago. For example, from *Ulysses:*

> I am a part of all that I have met;
> Yet all experience is an arch wherethro'
> Gleams that untravelled world, whose margin fades
> For ever and for ever when I move.

For fifty years after the publication of the *English Idylls,* Tennyson was the prince of English poets both by popular suffrage and by official appointment. And in all those years he was, as in his first volumes, an exquisite lyric poet, varying his song with great skill, and touching as many subjects as can be sung. When he tried to go beyond the lyric to narrative and drama, he was not at his best. After the publication of *The Princess,* a romantic medley, Carlyle, a poor judge, and Edward FitzGerald, a good judge, gave him up for lost. The poem is saved by the perfect songs and by the purely lyrical passages of the narrative. Two quotations will recall the loveliness which redeems the tediously humorless whole:

> Ah, sad and strange as in dark summer dawns
> The earliest pipe of half-awakened birds
> To dying ears, when unto dying eyes
> The casement slowly grows a glimmering square;
> So sad, so strange, the days that are no more.

>   Sweet is every sound,
> Sweeter thy voice, but every sound is sweet;
> Myriads of rivulets hurrying thro' the lawn,
> The moan of doves in immemorial elms,
> And murmuring of innumerable bees.

The *Idylls of the King,* to which he devoted thirty years, ought to have been a great English epic. It is a great subject. Milton, who was the only English poet with true epic power, had once thought of treating it and then abandoned it for his biblical subject. Tennyson had not the narrative power to handle the theme. He sentimentalized the vigorous old romances. His King Arthur is a prig and most of the knights are dim echoes of romance. But there are lovely places in which Tennyson's eye and ear are in harmony. For example, the passage where Sir Bedivere throws the dying Arthur's sword, Excalibur, into the sea:

TENNYSON

The great brand
Made lightnings in the splendour of the moon,
And flashing round and round, and whirled in an arch,
Shot like a streamer of the northern morn.

Such passages—there are many—and the countless lyrics of which he never lost the art to his last valedictory breath, *Crossing the Bar,* are the glory of Tennyson. It is a glory which can be partially obscured by clouds of criticism, but which cannot pass.

Just as in popular thought the names of Dickens and Thack

eray are associated like joint or competitive owners of the
Victorian novel, so the names of Tennyson and Browning are
united in a rival proprietorship of the poetry of the time.
As a matter of fact there is no such antagonistic rivalry or exclusive partnership in the aristocratic, anarchic democracy of
letters. Each man of genius goes
his own way, modified by time,
circumstance, and birth, but un-
alterably himself. Tennyson's
popularity was immediate and
extensive, not because he deliberately courted it but because,
cultivating his art with the utmost care and all the strength
that was in him, he discovered
the supreme gift of making people feel and see and sing with
him. Robert Browning had to
wait long for recognition, because he seemed at first to many
readers obscure and puzzling.
The world had to learn to read

BROWNING

and like him. As late as 1868, when he was fifty-six years old,
he wrote in his massive narrative, *The Ring and the Book:*
"British public, ye who like me not, God love you!" The
public came to him perhaps because he had, when he chose to
exercise it, the lyric genius, direct, passionate, and musical:

> O Lyric Love, half angel and half bird
> And all a wonder and a wild desire,—
> Boldest of hearts that ever braved the sun,
> Took sanctuary within the holier blue,
> And sang a kindred soul out to his face.—

Yet human at the red-ripe of the heart—
When the first summons of the darkling earth
Reach'd thee amid thy chambers, blanch'd their blue,
And bared them of the glory—to drop down,
To toil for man, to suffer or to die,—
This is the same voice: can thy soul know change?
Hail then and hearken from the realms of help!

THE ROUND TABLE OF KING ARTHUR
(From a Miniature of the Sixth Century)

Browning is at his best in a form which he invented, the
dramatic lyric, or dramatic romance, in which an assumed

character sings or tells a story. He wrote a great number of these in many moods and situations: *In a Gondola, The Last Ride Together, Rabbi Ben Ezra, Saul, My Last Duchess, Love in Life.* These are part of the permanent treasury of English song, and it requires no Browning Society to interpret them. Throughout Browning's thought, which is often complex and difficult, there runs one clear idea which has strengthened his hold on the affections of readers who are not cynical or too philosophically critical: that is, the note of courageous, fighting optimism. Just before he died he said the last word about himself:

> One who never turned his back but marched breast forward,
>   Never doubted clouds would break,
> Never dreamed, though right were worsted, wrong would triumph,
> Held we fall to rise, are baffled to fight better,
>   Sleep to wake.
>
> No, at noonday in the bustle of man's work-time
>   Greet the unseen with a cheer!
> Bid him forward, breast and back as either should be,
> "Strive and thrive!" cry "Speed,—fight on, fare ever,
>   There as here!"

Browning's wife, Elizabeth Barrett, was a poet in her feelings and of splendid intellectual power. If she fell short of the highest poetry, the reason is that neither by instinct nor training did she master the art of verse. In a poem published before she and Browning were acquainted she had written:

> Or from Browning some "Pomegranate," which, if cut deep down
>   the middle, ...
> Shows a heart within blood-tinctured, of a veined humanity.

This was the beginning of their romance, one of the happiest in literary history. But she was an invalid and feared that she might be a burden upon him. The poetic expression of her time of hesitation and renunciation is the *Sonnets from the Portuguese,* which are in emotion and imagery, if not in technical construction, as beautiful as any in the language. Browning, who rather scorned the idea of "Sonnet singing about himself," must have known that with this key his wife had unlocked her heart as no Englishwoman had ever before done in poetry:

> Go from me. Yet I feel that I shall stand
>   Henceforward in thy shadow. Nevermore
>   Alone upon the threshold of my door
> Of individual life shall I command
> The uses of my soul, nor lift my hand
>   Serenely in the sunshine as before,
>   Without the sense of that which I forbore—
> Thy touch upon the palm. The widest land
> Doom takes to part us, leaves thy heart in mine
>   With pulses that beat double. What I do
> And what I dream include thee, as the wine
>   Must taste of its own grapes. And when I sue
> God for myself, He hears that name of thine,
>   And sees within my eyes the tears of two.

In 1859 appeared a small book of verse to which nobody paid any attention, and the greatness of which the author himself did not suspect. This was Edward FitzGerald's *Rubáiyát of Omar Khayyám.* It was derived from the Persian, but it was much more than a translation, it was a masterpiece of English poetry. Rossetti and Swinburne discovered it and gradually its fame increased until at the end of the century, after FitzGerald was dead, it became a sort of poetic Bible to young literary folk, and was praised even above its lofty merits; today it is better known and more widely quoted than any other poem in the language of equally fine quality. Its luxurious fatalism, its languid melancholy touched with romantic pessimism, reach some pagan instinct which is in us all and which Occidental poets had not before expressed. And the FitzGerald quatrain is haunting; once it gets into the ear it is there to stay. We need not quote from that poem, for everybody knows it. But to recall its rhythm:

> A book of Verses underneath the Bough,
> A Jug of Wine, a Loaf of Bread—and Thou
>   Beside me singing in the Wilderness—
> O, Wilderness were Paradise enow!

Matthew Arnold, whom we have already seen as an important critic, was a poet of excellent skill, discipline, and taste, whose verse just fails to be great poetry; the divine fire seems to touch the edge of it and then go out and leave it cool as the moon. Perhaps Arnold was too much a critic to let himself go. His loveliest poem is the *Buried Life,* which has a cry of passion. I will not quote that, however, but a more characteristic poem, which in form and substance suggests his perfection and his limitation: the *Austerity of Poetry:*

> That son of Italy who tried to blow,
>   Ere Dante came, the trump of sacred song,
>   In his light youth amid a festal throng
> Sate with his bride to see a public show.
> Fair was the bride, and on her front did glow
>   Youth like a star; and what to youth belong,
>   Gay raiment, sparkling gauds, elation strong.
> A prop gave way! crash fell a platform! lo,
> Mid struggling sufferers, hurt to death, she lay!
>   Shuddering they drew her garments off—and found
>   A robe of sackcloth next the smooth, white skin.
> Such, poets, is your bride, the Muse! young, gay,
>   Radiant, adorn'd outside; a hidden ground
>   Of thought and of austerity within.

This severe view of poetry is true to the spirit of Dante and of Milton in his maturity. But it is uncomfortably ascetic especially when held by a man who talked so much about the Greek spirit. A more joyous and human conception of the muse was that of three poets, slightly younger than Arnold, Dante Gabriel Rossetti, William Morris, and Algernon Charles Swinburne.

ROSSETTI

Rossetti was a painter as well as a poet, belonging to a group who called themselves Preraphaelites and who tried to lead English art away from conventionality to the morning freshness of early Italian painting. Rossetti's pictorial art had some effect on his poetry; the genius which saw life in the terms of a painter, as color and vision, used words as visual symbols. Rossetti's talent had another duality; his father was an Italian, and he was brought up with a perfect knowledge of his ancestral language and literature. It is understandable that he should be the greatest of all English masters of the sonnet, which England had borrowed from Italy. His genius is thoroughly English, derived from Shakespeare, the old English ballads, and his contemporary, Browning. But he brings into English, which is the most flexible and amenable language in the world, something of the sonorous fluency of Italian. His *House of Life* is the most beautiful sonnet sequence after Shakespeare's. The following, called *Death-in-Love* shows Rossetti's pictorial power and the symbolism which is his natural idiom, though it is as old as Dante:

> There came an image in Life's retinue
>   That had Love's wings and bore his gonfalon:
>   Fair was the web, and nobly wrought thereon,
> O soul-sequestered face, thy form and hue!
> Bewildering sounds, such as Spring wakens to,
>   Shook in its folds; and through my heart its power
>   Sped trackless as the immemorable hour
> When birth's dark portal groaned and all was new.
>
> But a veiled woman followed, and she caught
>   The banner round its staff, to furl and cling,—
>   Then plucked a feather from the bearer's wing,
> And held it to the lips that stirred it not,
>   And said to me, "Behold, there is no breath:
>   I and this love are one, and I am Death."

Rossetti's friend, William Morris, was also a painter as well as a poet. Morris was a universal genius like the men of the Middle Ages and the Renaissance whose spirit he tried to bring back to industrial England. His activities were prodigious. He designed wall paper with one hand and wrote a poem with the other, and by way of recreation made speeches on social problems. Somebody has ironically said that if he had not been lazy, he would have composed a few symphonies in Beethoven's best manner.

It is Morris's literary work that interests us here. His *Defence of Guinevere* is one of the most beautiful of the many poetic revivals of the Arthurian romances, of which Tennyson's *Idylls* were most popular, but not the most spirited and colorful. In the *Life and Death of Jason* Morris turned the familiar Greek legend into a metrical romance which strangely blends the ancient spirit with the medieval and with the nervous rapidity of the nineteenth century. It is one of the few long poems which can be read through without a sense of tedium, and it was immediately successful. Morris followed it with the *Earthly Paradise,* twenty-four narratives drawn equally from Greek and romantic sources, the most stupendous undertaking since Spenser's *Faërie Queene,* and carried triumphantly through. The fault of Morris is that he wrote too much, and for all his power, speed, and color, his ability to manipulate English meters, he seldom made the ultimately perfect line of Rossetti, whose two little volumes would be lost in one of Morris's. Nor did Morris achieve the wizardry of his other friend, who was almost as prolific, Swinburne.

SWINBURNE

In 1864 Swinburne at the age of twenty-seven published *Atalanta in Calydon* which he followed two years later with *Poems and Ballads.* His flaming youth, his rebellion and fire were combined with a sophisticated and scholarly command of meters and melodies not equalled by any of his contemporaries and not surpassed by any English poet who had been before him. And all young English poets since Swinburne have been under his spell except those who have broken away from the beauties of meter into free verse, which to him would have been child's play if it had occurred to him to try it. He was master of every harmony, rhythm, cadence, accent into which English words can be combined, and from the oldest materials he devised new measures and stanzaic forms.

And Swinburne's genius is not a mere matter of verbal virtuosity. Nothing could be more untrue to the spirit of poetry than the notion that Swinburne lacks ideas. He has so many ideas that they tread on each other's heels, ideas drawn from his enormous knowledge of ancient and modern literature and from his profound passions. His lyrics often run to great length—no poet could more marvelously sustain his song—and fragmentary quotation from him can give little impression of his sweep and flow, his orchestral fullness of tone. But four lines from the *Hymn to Proserpine* will suggest his music, as one bar may suggest a symphony:

> All delicate days and pleasant, all spirits and sorrows are cast
> Far out with the foam of the present that sweeps to the surf of the past:
> Where beyond the extreme sea-wall, and between the remote sea-gates,
> Waste water washes, and tall ships founder, and deep death waits.

Swinburne is more than a lyric poet with a necromantic charm of language. He is one of the great narrative poets. Of the many revivals of the Arthurian romances his *Tristram of Lyonesse* is incomparably the most rushing and glowing.

A poet hardly less magical than Swinburne, though of more limited scope, is George Meredith, whom we have already

met as one of the foremost novelists of the century. He sings
the praises of earth and of man's communion with nature, and
his poems of love are intensely beautiful in their fusion of
human passion with the loveliness of the world. Of his *Love
in the Valley* Tennyson said that he could not get the lines out
of his head, and it is impossible for anyone to hear those enchanting rhythms and forget them:

> Shy as the squirrel and wayward as the swallow,
> Swift as the swallow along the river's light
> Circleting the surface to meet his mirrored winglets,
> Fleeter she seems in her stay than in her flight.
> Shy as the squirrel that leaps among the pine-tops,
> Wayward as the swallow overhead at set of sun,
> She whom I love is hard to catch and conquer,
> Hard, but O the glory of the winning were she won!

Less magical but more philosophical and searching is the
series of poems, somewhat like sonnets, called *Modern Love,*
which reveal the novelist rather than the singer.

A pure angelic voice is that of Christina, sister of Dante
Gabriel Rossetti. Like her brother she had perfect control of
form, especially of the sonnet, and she shared the medieval
mysticism of the group of which he was a leader. But her
mysticism took the form of religious devotion of the most
sincere and lofty tone. Her love poems are in a mood of nun-
like renunciation. It is customary, though not very illuminating, to compare her with Mrs. Browning. Mrs. Browning's expression was more abundant and vigorous, but she
never approached her sister-poet's ultimate simplicity and
rightness of rhythm and word. The following *Song* is not
Christina Rossetti's masterpiece, but it illustrates the sweet
sadness of her spirit, and it is perfect verse:

When I am dead, my dearest,
  Sing no sad songs for me;
Plant thou no roses at my head,
  Nor shady cypress tree:
Be the green grass above me
  With showers and dewdrops wet;
And if thou wilt, remember,
  And if thou wilt, forget.

I shall not see the shadows,
  I shall not feel the rain;
I shall not hear the nightingale
  Sing on, as if in pain;
And dreaming through the twilight
  That doth not rise nor set,
Haply I may remember,
  And haply may forget.

The last survivor of the elder Victorians is Thomas Hardy, who at the age of eighty-three published a new volume of poetry. He is, like Meredith, a master of the novel as well as a poet, and a score have read his fiction to one who cares for his verse. But his heart, his passionate, pitying and suffering heart, has always been in his verse, and one feels from his short poems and from his tremendous epic drama, *The Dynasts,* that he wrote stories because he could and because there was an external demand for them, and that he wrote poetry in obedience to an internal command. He is the saddest poet in English literature, and sadness is the term for it, not the much abused word pessimism. He is as close an observer and lover of nature as Wordsworth, but he derives from nature almost none of Wordsworth's placid consolation. His verse is excellent, though a little hard, the hardness being rather in the thought than in the cadences. A glimpse of his dominant mood at its most nearly cheerful moment is the

last stanza of the *Darkling Thrush*. He hears the bird sing
of "joy illimited" and then:

> So little cause for carollings
>   Of such ecstatic sound
> Was written on terrestrial things
>   Afar or nigh around,
> That I could think there trembled through
>   His happy good-night air
> Some blessèd Hope, whereof he knew
>   And I was unaware.

A note of sadness runs through most lyric poetry, for poets
know how to turn their sorrows into art, whereas the rest of
us hug our griefs and make them squeak or wail, or what is
better, get no sound out of them at all. No century of English
poetry has so many wistful songs of sorrow—something quite
different from the suffering of great drama, Greek or Elizabethan—as the nineteenth. A man of genius who cannot be
forgotten, a broken genius whose agony was actual and
physical, is James Thomson, author of *The City of Dreadful
Night,* a marred masterpiece, but marvelous. It is impossible
to quote from it, for no stanza means anything without the
rest. Of course Browning's healthy-mindedness was an anti-
dote to the in-growing soul. And younger men struck the note
of vigor and courage; William Ernest Henley, whose "Out of
the night that covers me" has become a more than familiar
quotation; Robert Louis Stevenson, who phrased his confident
virility better in his prose than in his verse; and Rudyard
Kipling, whose athletic poems twenty years ago were on everybody's lips and are not yet forgotten.

As we glance back over the poetry of the Victorian age
we are amazed by its wealth, by the number of poets whom
we have not even mentioned, but who, without their greater

brothers, would make a noble literature: Thomas Hood, the poet of three or four perfect songs, a fine spirit, too much known as a joker and too little known as a poet; Mangan, the Irish poet of *Dark Rosaleen*, born with Celtic magic; Clough, Arnold's friend, whose few lyrics are true poetry if not the very highest; Coventry Patmore, whose verses, such as *The Toys,* bring tears; Sidney Dobell, who wrote the lovely *Even-Song* before "free verse" was ever heard of; Thomas Edward Brown, a Manx poet, much of whose longer work is written in dialect, but whose short lyrics in classic English are striking in thought, in emotion, in original daring, and melodious management of rhythm; and the delightful lighter versifiers, Lang, Dobson and others.

It is impossible even to name all the younger poets living and dead who at the end of the nineteenth century, and the beginning of our own, have carried on the great tradition of English song, and have added distinctive individual notes. Some of them are: Oscar Wilde whose *Ballad of Reading Gaol* is poignantly powerful; John Davidson, an authentic writer of muscular ballads; William B. Yeats, whom the elves endowed with Celtic charm; A. E. Housman, whose *Shropshire Lad* is proof that the magnitude of a poet is not measured by his bulk; John Masefield, master alike of lyric and adventurous narrative; Walter de la Mare, beneath whose delicate fancies are profound depths. The glory of English poetry is not only in the great solo voices, but in a multitudinous choir of lesser singers, each a soloist, since a poet does not sing in chorus. We could make a beautiful anthology of verse by poets who are not even mentioned in our brief sketch.

The name which all living poets would agree may stand as climax of a chapter on nineteenth century poetry is that of Francis Thompson. He was not the last of the great English poets, for there is, and shall be, no last. But we may think of him poetically, if not critically, as a magnificent sunset, and crown his own head with the prodigal imagery of his *Ode to the Setting Sun:*

> O thou down-stricken Day,
> That drawest thy splendours round thee in thy fall,
> High was thine eastern pomp inaugural;
> But thou dost set in statelier pageantry,
> Lauded with tumults of a firmament:
> Thy visible music-blasts make deaf the sky,
> Thy cymbals clang to fire the Occident,
> Thou dost thy dying so triumphally:
> I *see* the crimson blaring of thy shawms!

Thompson was miserably poor and lonely until good friends discovered his genius and rescued him. His ornate and luxurious dreams are an escape from the bitterness of life; poetry is such an escape both for poet and reader. He found his consolation in religious ecstasy, *The Hound of Heaven,* in reverently chaste and elevated poems of love, *Sister Songs* and *Love in Dian's Lap* and in wistfully tender *Poems on Children.* He expresses in *Poppy* that proud consciousness of conferring immortality on his subject and himself which is found in Shakespeare's sonnets. With this quotation our chapter ends, for it phrases the story of poets and the final triumph of the poet's vision:

> Love, love! your flower of withered dream
> In leavèd rhyme lies safe, I deem,
> Sheltered and shut in a nook of rhyme,
> From the reaper man, and his reaper Time.
>
> Love! *I* fall into the claws of Time:
> But lasts within a leavèd rhyme
> All that the world of me esteems—
> My withered dreams, my withered dreams.

CHAPTER XXXVIII

FRENCH PROSE OF THE NINETEENTH CENTURY

After the picturesque but prosaic romance of Walter Scott there remains to be created another romance, more beautiful and more complete. That is the romance at once drama and epic, picturesque but poetic, real but ideal, true but grand.

—Victor Hugo.

Everything has always existed and everything has always co-existed. Romanticism has had its fools, and it has had its wise men.

—Remy de Gourmont.

The French Romantic School may therefore, without exaggeration, be called the greatest literary school of the nineteenth century.

—Georg Brandes.

THE romantic period of French literature corresponds in time and somewhat in spirit to the romantic revival in English literature, and both are related to the ideas involved in the French Revolution. The English movement was, in spite of Brandes, very much stronger than the French, and it flourished earlier and more abundantly because in England there happened to be born men of literary genius greater than any in France. The time (let the year 1800 stand diagrammatically as the center of it), stirred English thought, and the English poet was there to respond. French thought was depressed, and there was not until later any literary man

in France comparable to Scott and Byron, not to speak of
Keats and Shelley, of whom France never heard until years
after their death. From the French thought of the eighteenth
century the clear acid intelligence of Voltaire disappeared
as a literary influence, though his individual fame persisted.
The controlling force was the sentimental romanticism of

CHATEAUBRIAND

Rousseau, converted into
religious emotion and in-
tellectual reaction by
Chateaubriand, w h o s e
Génie du Christianisme,
published at the begin-
ning of the century, was
the most influential new
book in France. It is a
defense or praise of Christianity, not in terms of
argument or theology,
though there is plenty of
that, but in terms of color
and beauty and symbol·
ism. The worst of it is
bad preaching, the best of
it is stained glass and a
cathedral organ. One episode, the story of *René,* is the romance of the searching, yearning, sorrowful young soul, who
became popular and populous in the fiction and poetry of all
Europe. Shelley's *Alastor* and Goethe's *Werther* are expressions of the same idea—not directly borrowed, for the idea
was in the air of the time. Carlyle's rather gruff answer to
it all was in effect: "Young man, stop mooning and go to
work."

In the fiction of our day we have these pathetic dissastisfied boys, but we have taken to sending them to doctors called psychoanalysts, who may or may not be wiser than Chateaubriand. "Everything has always existed." His note of melancholy is not so impressive to English readers as it was to the French of a hundred years ago; for English romance had been acquainted for two centuries with a sad sceptical boy named Hamlet, and English fiction about the year 1800, though there was plenty of current nonsense, was still dominated by the robust sanity of Fielding and Smollett, and was about to be dominated by the equally robust sanity of Scott. Chateaubriand lived in England for some years; in his later years he translated *Paradise Lost,* and *en revanche* much of his work has been translated into English. But for reasons indicated, perhaps not the right ones, he was not widely read in England. To modern Frenchmen his rhetoric is displeasing, but they know that he was a master in a transitional period between the time when French prose lost its head, as many Frenchmen did on the guillotine and elsewhere, and the time when it got its clear head back on strong shoulders.

The shoulders were growing up and the head was many heads with great diversity of power. At the beginning of the century—a few years one way or the other do not count —were born Balzac, Victor Hugo, Alexandre Dumas, George Sand, all novelists, and Sainte-Beuve, the critic and essayist. Balzac, the most fertile and powerful of French novelists, undertook, though he did not realize or declare his purpose until after he had written many stories, to draw all aspects of life, and he called his total work in fiction *The Human Comedy.* He did not live to complete his plan; he died at the age of fifty. The human comedy is beyond the scope of any one man or country or epoch. But no novelist before or since Balzac has a better right to such a universal title. He made a multitude of people whom all readers in any language—most of his books have been translated into all the languages of Europe—recognize as themselves and their friends and enemies, whatever the local or temporal situation. Balzac studied all types, citizens of Paris, peasants, and the little bourgeois of provincial towns. Since most of his life was spent at his desk and he involved himself in business troubles which were enough to take all the energy of an ordinary man, it is a wonder how he found time to know at first hand so many kinds of society. The answer is that he had supremely the essential gift of the novelist, insight. He needed to see but once in order to understand, to absorb scene and character, make them part of himself, so that he could render them with exact detail—sometimes too much detail. His insight was reinforced by his great intellectual honesty and courage. In this he is like Scott whom he so much admired, and like Scott he had to keep his troubled pot boiling and he wrote too much; but he never shirked his responsibility as a writer, he labored titanically, sometimes sixteen hours at a stretch, recasting and perfecting his work, pouring into it the all but inexhaustible vigor which makes most of it, even the too prolix pages, everlastingly alive.

The work of Balzac should have settled practically, almost before it started, the long theoretic controversy, which is still going on rather futilely, between romance and realism. It is an academic question of interest to critics and to novelists who theorize about their art. Is it not answered for the French by the fact that in their own precise language every long fiction, no matter what its substance or treatment, is called a *roman?* And is it not answered by the practice of the greatest French novelist, who saw all or most of life as romantic adventure of soul and circumstance and spared no pains to give the impression of truth to fact? In Balzac literalism and fantastic imagination were not in conflict; the reader may see such a conflict but Balzac was not aware of it. His greatness lies in the range of his sympathies. In *Eugénie Grandet* he draws a simple country girl in narrow surroundings. In other books he portrays the "Splendors and Miseries" of women of another sort. He is the first to introduce into fiction the sordid romance of business and money, utilizing in *César Birotteau* his own disastrous experiences in the commercial world. And in many, indeed most, of his novels, *Cousin Pons, Cousine Bette, Père Goriot,* run the sinister motives of greed and avarice and selfishness in their various forms. Balzac is not a lover of life in any caressing, sentimental way; his view of it is just, often hard, often tender when young girls are concerned. His attitude toward young men is on the whole severe; he drew the "egotist" more than once many years before Meredith began to write. He carries the emotional life far beyond the wedding bells of happy couples; marriage is an episode, people live on, live on to old age—Balzac's old folks, the crotchety, the disagreeable, the pathetic are marvelously well done. Consider too that this observer of men and women has a feeling for scene and place, and though not a poet in style as a rule, he can come near to prose poetry as in *Séraphita,* which is an experiment in Swedenborgian mysticism. He is truly a colossus, or a colosseum, for later novelists have taken stones from his great structure to make buildings on a smaller design.

Balzac's friend and fellow-giant, Victor Hugo, lived through almost the whole of the nineteenth century, and was for fifty years the greatest literary force in France. He was poet, dramatist, novelist, political pamphleteer. The fortunes of politics added to his fame by exiling him from his country for twenty years, and when he returned he was so laureled and glorified that cooler French critics somewhat rebelled against his eminence.

To English readers and to Europe outside France he is best known, certainly most read, in his prose fictions, *Notre-Dame*

VICTOR HUGO

de Paris (commonly called in English the *Hunchback of Notre Dame*) *Toilers of the Sea,* and *Les Misérables.* They are melodramatic, in some scenes feverishly thrilling. Who has not shivered at the fight between Gilliat and the octopus or at the terrific moment when the hunchback forces his

BALZAC

enemy to let go his grip on the gutter of the cathedral and
fall to destruction? But Hugo's melodrama, like Shakespeare's, and indeed all other good melodrama, has thought

JEAN VALJEAN

and passion behind it, the sensational grip by which the
thought takes hold and clings unforgettably. Hugo uses startling situations somewhat as Dickens does, to electrify social

motives that in themselves are dull and dark. Both men of course, and all other writers with dramatic imagination enjoy the striking scene for its own sake. In *Les Misérables* Hugo put together, rather loosely strung on the career of Jean Valjean, five or six novels and the makings of more. There is almost everything in it that a novel can hold; the title is untranslatable into English, for it does not mean "miserable," nor "poor," nor "wretched," nor "unfortunate;" it means all of those and something more; perhaps it was Hugo who gave the word its rich meaning in French. What he means, what he does, is to show all life below the level of ease, of privilege. It would be sociological special pleading, tiresome stuff, if Hugo were not a blazing story-teller. Swinburne in one of his blind rushes of enthusiasm called *Les Misérables* "the greatest epic and dramatic work of fiction ever created or conceived." We do not need to go so far as that but can concur in Stevenson's cooler opinion that Hugo's prose romances "would have made a very great fame for any writer, and yet they are but one façade of the monument that Victor Hugo has erected to his genius." Of the other façades, his poetry and drama, we shall say a word in the next chapter.

Alexandre Dumas has probably entertained more readers than any other writer in a hundred years, not excepting Scott. He is the unrivaled master of the swashbuckling cloak-and-sword romance, with a background of history, some of which is spurious, some of which is true, all of which is flamingly vivid. If Dumas had been less an artist his stories might have fallen to the rank of dime novels; they would have pleased the multitude, perhaps, but they would not have held the permanent place in literature which they do hold and the respect of readers who demand more of a novel than intrigue and adventure. But Dumas was an artist who did more than contrive exciting plots; he created characters who stand up and walk, or swagger, in their own boots, and who speak with living voices. His vivacity never failed him even when he was writing at a rate of speed compared to which the productivity of Scott, Balzac, and Trollope is leisurely and deliberate. He had many collaborators and he was accused of running a fiction-factory; but he was the head and heart and dynamo of it. The surprising thing is that of his innumerable romances (not to speak of plays, histories and memoirs) so many are masterpieces in their kind. At least two, the *Three Musketeers* and the *Count of Monte Cristo,* are so much a part of the boyhood of English readers (and of course of French readers) that we cannot remember a time when we did not know them. We never outgrow Porthos, Athos, and Aramis, the immortal trio, and if eternity admits of comparisons, the still more immortal d'Artagnan. But we do grow up to realize that Dumas was much more than a clever yarn-spinner, that *Olympe de Clèves* and others are novels of all but the first order, solidly conceived and capably wrought. Dumas was hasty, splashy, commercial, theatrical. He (and his circumstances) did not give himself time to think, and he relied too much on his fertility and power to improvise. But under his rapid-fire entertainment is an abundant sense of life and an amazing intelligence.

Dumas found romance in external adventures and far away times. George Sand, the greatest woman among French novelists or the greatest novelist among French women, found romance in herself, in her own affairs of the heart, and in the French country and the peasants whom she loved with a maternal passion. Whatever the scene or plot of her novels, she has one theme, the right, duty, and liberty of love. In developing this theme in many forms she is frankly feminine, and her masculine pseudonym means even less than that of the English woman to whom she is inevitably compared and

GEORGE SAND

whom she very little resembles—George Eliot. All that they have in common is their affection for simple people, their rebellion against the cruelties of the world, and the ability to make their honest thoughts articulate. The finest of George Sand's novels are those which deal with village life, charming idyls, or "eclogues" as she justly called them, *The Little Fadette, François the Waif*, and *The Devil's Pool*.

The great critic of the period, friend or enemy of these romancers and poets, in the long run friend of the best that was and had been in French literature, was Sainte-Beuve. His importance is in large measure confined to France. Criticism is a form of writing which does not go directly very far beyond the interests of literary people; few critics have become internationally important; indeed it may be said that a critic is without honor in any country except his own. Sainte-Beuve had an influence on Matthew Arnold and other English

SAINTE-BEUVE

critics, and probably every literary critic in Europe has taken lessons from him. His great service was his lucid interpretation of French literature to the French, and to the world, but the world does not read criticism. Some of Sainte-Beuve's essays have been translated into English. But he remains a sealed book to those who cannot read French. To those who read French he is not only an open book but an opener of the books of others, of all French literature before him and of his contemporaries whom he often misjudged (Balzac, for instance) but on the whole he saw with the immediate discriminating light of critical intelligence. After Sainte-Beuve no literate Frenchman had any excuse for not understanding the literature of his country, and no foreigner groping for the best in French literature can do better than follow the lead of Sainte-Beuve.

TAINE

The rationalistic and critical side of the French mind—perhaps its most powerful side. though the French have had masters in all forms of literary art—is exemplified in Ernest Renan and H. A. Taine. Renan is best known for his *Life of Jesus,* which is both sceptical and reverent. It became a matter of controversy, as every book on a religious subject is sure to become; Christians did not like it, heretics made capital out of it which Renan did not intend; and Renan himself further complicates the business by disavowing all interest in literature; to himself he is a truth-seeker and historian with no interest in style. But literature takes its revenge by pardoning its enemies and sees in the *Life of Jesus* a book which may or may not be good analytic or "scientific" history, but is undeniably a work of art; it is a clarifying reconstruction of the New Testament with touches of color painted in on the spot, for Renan wrote much of it in Syria in the midst of the scene. He intended to be an historian, a critic, a philosopher, an Orientalist. He was a literary artist. Men deceive themselves and write better than they know. And Literature, the vague, inscrutable goddess, adopts them.

Like Renan, H. A. Taine regarded himself as a scientific historian and logician rather than a man of letters. In the second half of the nineteenth century the scientific spirit took possession of all branches of thought, and the word "scientific," and even the idea or method for which it stands, was somewhat overworked. There was a science of every human activity, even of love-making. The movement was a reaction against the loose thinking of the romantic period, and Taine was a leader of the movement in France. He thought that every man of genius, whether statesman or poet, could be accounted for if we ascertained his race, his time, his social circumstances, and his controlling faculty. Under this formula criticism becomes largely a matter of biography and history. Later there was a revolt against Taine's method by critics who felt that it did not quite account for human genius. And indeed Taine himself was more of a poet than he knew and in his essays his æsthetic enthusiasm often took him outside his avowed principles. To English readers his value is immeasurable, for his great *History of English Literature* can never be wholly superseded by later studies, and it is most illuminating to see our literature from the point of view of a great French mind. The English translation is excellent.

It is usually thought that melancholy is peculiar to the romantic temperament. But in France it was the Romantics, Hugo, George Sand, Dumas, who celebrated the joy of living, and the rationalistic realists who were melancholy and pessimistic. Taine looked upon the human being with almost

gloomy resignation. And the novelists who followed Balzac—
Flaubert, Maupassant, Zola—shared Taine's dark mood, not
because of his influence but because the air was black, partly
on account of the war of 1870.

Gustave Flaubert regarded human beings with a cold contempt and at the same time with penetrating clairvoyant intelligence. His view of life which is satiric and not mellowed
by the humor that makes us laugh has prevented his books
from becoming widely popular even in his own country; but
to readers who are interested in the art of writing Flaubert
is the acme of perfection. He worked for a week on a single
page, striving to find the right word, and the result is not
finical or fussy or artificial, but exact, vigorous, and so natural
that the word seems to have found itself. His most famous
novel is *Madame Bovary,* a portrait of a pitifully weak romantic woman, and her desolate love affairs with commonplace men in a dull provincial town. Such an account of it
seems uninviting; yet it is a very great novel, not only on
account of its perfect style, but by virtue of fidelity to character. The story is wrought of unheroic, even uninteresting
material, but the ordinary becomes extraordinary, and the
progress of it is as inevitable as the tides. This sense of progress and veracity is not lost in translation (there is a satisfactory English version) though it is difficult to reproduce
Flaubert's "right word."

Why *Madam Bovary* should be the best known of Flaubert's
work is not quite explicable. For *L'Education Sentimentale* is
a much greater book, the tragedy of the blasted hopes of youth.
Flaubert's vision is very wide and he simply sweeps aside
distinctions between the past and the present, between fact
and fancy, between romanticism and realism. In *Salammbô*
he goes to the past for color like a romantic novelist, a Scott

or a Dumas, but he keeps the attitude of an objective scientific student. His genius for finding the tragic in the simple, the ironic in the tender, the passionate in the commonplace, the present in the past, is not the genius of paradox and contradiction, but the genius of wisdom which sees life whole. Toward the end of his life the spirit of irony took possession of him and in the unfinished *Bouvard et Pécuchet* he portrays all humanity in the persons of little provincial people as fools. This aristocratic hater of the commonplace finds us all commonplace at last. Flaubert brought reason into romance and taught the realism which was to follow him a lesson which only the masters learned, that the facts of life can be transmuted into exquisite beauty, that truth is not dull, and that elegance of phrase consists in simplicity, exactness, clarity, logic.

A pupil of Flaubert, but an original genius not dependent on any teacher, is Guy de Maupassant, the master of the short story. For Maupassant nothing exists but the story, the people who enact it, and the barest outlines of the place where it happens. No writer was ever less interested in the non-narrative issues of life. Except Dumas. And it is contradictorily just to name the glowing romancer and the hard realist in the same breath; they have in different ways a common gift, the gift of refraining from all comment on their characters. People *are* and *do*. There is no analysis of human nature, no choice between good and evil, no expository "psychology." Of course the resemblance ends there, for Dumas lives in a colored past, and invents exciting situations, whereas Maupassant lives in drab houses and streets, and pretends to invent nothing, which is a romantic fallacy deceiving nobody. But Maupassant within his range of observation has that faculty which Dumas has in another way, of letting life tell itself through action, of keeping his hand off and not seeming to manipulate human affairs. It is a quality found in Boccaccio and *The Arabian Nights,* but too often lacking in most modern fiction. If life is pathetic or funny or brutal or indecent, it is life and not Maupassant who seems to be responsible. Because Maupassant chose to portray some aspects of life which are not conventional subjects for parlor conversation, some of his stories were objected to even in France, and perhaps they should not be read by the young and the weak. But Maupassant's ethical outlook is on the whole sound and severe. On this point we can trust Tolstoy, who said at a time when he had reached his most austerely moral stage: "Next to Victor Hugo, Maupassant is the best writer of our time. I am very fond of him and rank him above all his contemporaries." The best of his stories from *Boule de Suif,* the first tale that showed his genius, are profoundly sympathetic, though often on the surface cold and hard. He looks at people and things solely for the purpose of finding out what sort of story they yield. And whether the story is pleasant or unpleasant, he tells it impartially for its own sake, taking sides neither with good nor with evil, neither with hero nor with villain, pressing no point beyond the immediate effect of his narrative. His language is strong and spare, without a superfluous detail, a useless word. Maupassant is so supreme an artist in the short story that we may forget that he was a novelist of sustained power. *Une Vie* and *Fort Comme la Mort* are as nearly perfect novels as even French literature can show.

Maupassant makes his effect by economy of word and idea. Emile Zola, the most prolific of the naturalists or realists, piles detail upon detail and achieves his result by sheer weight. Compared with him even Balzac is brief and

parsimonious and Maupassant is a mere skeleton. Zola's
novels are great in their massed power; all life is crowded into
them until the reader almost wearies of life and wishes there
were not so much of it. Zola had not the charm and grace of
the best French style, and French criticism treated him with
sharp severity. In all Zola's work there is no masterpiece,
no jewel. But to choose two or three of his innumerable novels,
we may name *Nana, La Débâcle,* and *La Terre,* all of which,
and many more, have been translated into English. He loses
little in translation because his strength is in his substance, not
in any peculiar magic of style. Zola's critics—and his novels
are the undeniable evidence—accuse him of overemphasizing
the sordid, the grim, the bestial. But his conception of life
is not unwholesome, it is simply that of the physician who
describes painful symptoms or of the social reformer who
tells us what is wrong with the world in the hope of making
it better. His first successful book, *L'Assommoir,* (*The Bludgeon*) is a huge tract against alcohol. There is never any
question of the honesty of Zola's purpose, and the nobility
of his character is attested by his courageous fight in the
Dreyfus case which made him after his death a national hero.

The oration at Zola's grave was delivered by Anatole
France, a man as unlike Zola as two Frenchmen can be unlike
each other. Monsieur France took the name of his country
for his literary name (it was really the short form of his
father's name, François), and no man could have a better
right to it. He is original and independent, whimsical on the
safe side of eccentricity, yet his eclectic spirit includes the best
of French tradition. If we had only his books, it seems that
we should be able to learn from them his country, his time,
the French language in its most perfect form. What side of
life has he not touched with his keen, robust, serene scepticism?

Penguin Island is a satirical history of civilization. Jonathan Swift would have laughed at it, and Voltaire would have saluted a superior. The four novels grouped as *Contemporary History* are "realism"—with a wink. And *The Crime of Sylvester Bonnard* is romance—with a tear and a smile. He is in great issues as serious and passionate as his friend Zola,

ANATOLE FRANCE

and he carries easily upon his shrugging shoulders a burden of erudition that would stagger a mere academic. His thought is often revolutionary; his style is pure and simple. He hates sham and hypocrisy, but his hatred is temperate, ironic, philosophic, never hot with indignation. His genius is critical, inquisitive, and his fiction is a vehicle, ingeniously handled, for his thoughts and opinions.

The nineteenth century is one of the richest periods of French prose. Fiction and criticism flourished mightily in quantity and quality. Even without the preëminent masters modern France would have a great prose literature. And it is difficult to say, perhaps unnecessary to say, who is preëminent in a century that is crowded with talent. This difficulty is especially perplexing, though it need not worry us, in the case of fiction which is subject to rapid fluctuations in the taste of the public and in the judgment of critics.

A man of genius whose reputation increases with time is Henri Beyle, Stendhal, as he called himself. His novels, *Le Rouge et Le Noir* and *La Chartreuse de Parme,* are remarkable for their analysis of character. They were published in the first part of the century, but made little impression until after Stendhal's death. Balzac appreciated him, and later French writers have acknowledged his influence and proclaimed his genius. The finest of modern critics, Remy de Gourmont, regards Stendhal as a touchstone; if we do not like him we do not belong to the "happy few," the elect who understand.

A writer whose fiction is the possession of the happy many is Prosper Mérimée. His *Colomba,* a story of Corsica, is a perfect narrative, exciting in substance and written like all of Mérimée's work in a style classically clear and at the same time full of poetic color. His *Carmen* has a double title to immortality, for it is the source of the text of Bizet's perennial opera.

Alphonse Daudet, called with some justice the Dickens of France, was like the English master in his pathos and humor, his hearty sympathy with all kinds of folk, especially those whom life had used unkindly. In this aspect he is as closely akin to Victor Hugo as to Dickens. *Fromont Junior and*

Risler Senior, the novel which first made him famous, has a great-hearted kindliness, but is free from mawkish sentimentality; and this is true of the succeeding books which made him more and more secure in the affections of the public. The charm of his style (and perhaps of the man himself) held the respect of writers whose view of life was much more critical and analytic than his, of Zola, Flaubert, Edmond de Goncourt. He belonged to the school of naturalists; he belonged also to the laughers and farceurs of the race of Rabelais. His *Tartarin of Tarascon* is one of the best jokes in literature.

Daudet's friends, Edmond de Goncourt and his brother Jules, were the leaders of the naturalists, or, better, the visualists; they saw life less as matter for narrative than as matter for pictures, for detailed description. But narrative, which, as Stevenson said, is the typical mood of literature, got the better of their theories, and in several of their novels, *Renée Mauperin,* to name but one, they united the old art of the story with the art, which was more or less new in their hands, of minute analyses or impressions of the inside workings of character. Even more important than the novels is the *Journal* which is not only the expression of the beliefs and personalities of the authors but a brilliantly direct light on French literature of the nineteenth century. Edmond de Goncourt left his fortune for the foundation of an *academie,* which was in its inception a protest against the official French academy, but is now a well recognized institution, whose crown and substantial prize for literary merit is coveted by every young French writer. It has been a strong force on the side of freedom and daring in French literature.

A man deeply influenced by the Goncourts but of an eccentrically violent will and power to go his own way is J. K. Huysmans. He begins as a Zolaesque realist in stories like *En Menage* and ends in religious mysticism, for example, *The Cathedral.* Huysmans has not been fully or, in the few books that have been attempted, adequately translated into English. His highly colored style is difficult to render, and he is distinctly an author's author, a delight to the literary. But he is sure to become better known in the future both in France and in other countries.

An exquisite artist whose charm is felt by all kinds of readers is Pierre Loti, who died in 1923. He was a naval officer, had seen much of the world, and felt the spell of the sea and strange lands. His experiences and impressions he reproduces with subtlety and sincerity in novels and reminiscences. He found in the south seas the *Marriage of Loti;* in Japan, *Madame Chrysanthemum;* on the coast of Breton and in the north seas, *An Iceland Fisherman.* And he informed the external description and event with his sensitive personality.

Loti is an impressionist, to whom the world is color, sensation, experience, wherever it may be, without regard to morals in the sense of goodness or badness. Paul Bourget is an acute, rather solemn student of society, with an increasing tendency toward a conservative and moralistic view of life. He goes to the hearts of his own characters and would strike to ours if his attitude were less snobbish. But he is an artist and the *Disciple,* the *Promised Land,* are novels of first-rate merit. Bourget and his age were a little hard, factual in their analysis and conservative in their views of life. Before the war there were younger men, but not children, who saw life in the light of a new idealism. The chief of these is Romain Rolland, whose *Jean Christophe* is an international novel, having for its hero a German musician, part of whose experiences are in France. Though it is interminably long, it was widely read in France and in the English translation. The spirit of it is world embracing. But the world embrace became a deadly clutch in 1914. Rolland tried to rise above it in a booklet called *Above the Conflict,* for which and other humane writings he was not popular with his militant countrymen. Anatole France maintained the serenity of privileged old age. Henri Barbusse (in *Le Feu*), and other writers made capital out of the war.

In reviewing contemporaneous English and American literature we find it impossible to indicate what is being done, what are the prevailing movements. It is much more difficult to estimate, discriminate, even to know at first hand the workers in a literature to which one was not born, in the midst of which one does not live. We may, however, venture, without prophesying, to suggest that the close of an era is marked by the death of Marcel Proust, whose novel, *A la Recherche du Temps Perdu* (there is an English translation), a minute study of modern society as seen by a sensitive observer, seems like a culmination of half a century of psychological fiction, a summary of what has been and a prelude to the unknown future of the novel.

In one branch of literary art the French are supreme, that is criticism. From Boileau to Remy de Gourmont and to a score of younger living men, French criticism has been creative in the highest sense, excellent in and for itself and also invaluable for its influence on the other forms of literature. The race of Sainte-Beuve, of Renan, Taine, Scherer, Sarcey, still flourishes. After the elder masters came the two academics, Brunetière and Faguet, and the greatest of impressionistic critics, Anatole France, who even in his fiction is always the critic. Two brilliant men who died young were

Marcel Schwob, whose interest in English literature was almost as alert and instructed as his interest in French, and Emile Hennequin, whose all too brief studies of French writers and of foreign writers who became part of French literature, like Poe and Dickens, are the last word in the art of the literary essay. In the department of criticism the whole world of letters bows to France.

French Poets of the Nineteenth Century   421

CHAPTER XXXIX

FRENCH POETRY OF THE NINETEENTH CENTURY

The seer and singer of righteousness and wrong
Who stands now master of all the keys of song.
—*Swinburne* to Victor Hugo.

S I ventured to say apropos the English lyric poets of the seventeenth
century, schools or types of poetry
blend into each other in a way to
baffle whoever seeks sharp lines; we
cannot say where one ends and the
next begins. French poetry of the
nineteenth century (and a few years
before and a few years after) divides
not very clearly into three groups:
the Romantic, the Parnassian, the
Symbolic. The romantics both in
England and in France (the move-
ments in those two countries are curiously alike and yet different) broke away from a cramping convention, both of form
and of substance, went for subject matter to the past, to the
depths of their souls and to the stars, and let the reins go loose
on Pegasus. The Parnassians rebelled against the license, the
personal whining and Byronic egotism of the Romantics and
tried to make poetry objective, impersonal, "impassible," not
hard and cold as marble, but pure, solid, shapely as fine
sculpture. It was a new classicism which regarded even

Shakespeare and Dante as "barbarous." Then there came the symbolists who insisted on the personal, on the necessity of singing oneself, on the impossibility of doing anything else sincerely; their critical spokesman, Remy de Gourmont, says that the only excuse a man has for writing at all is to express his own personality. These three "schools" and several subsidiary off-shoots (it is said that France has a new school of verse every fifteen years), are not at bottom mutually hostile or exclusive, for after all poetry is poetry. Leconte de Lisle, greatest of the Parnassians is in his way just as personal as Verlaine is in his way. The Parnassian preaches and practices beauty of form, of sound. Verlaine's great motto is "music before everything else." The symbolist, expressing his own heart, his mood, conveying to the reader by suggestion his feeling and sensations surely has no quarrel with the early romantics; for what else does Lamartine do in *The Lake,* in *Solitude?* If the Parnassian corresponds in some ways to the realist in fiction, the old question arises just where is the line between romance and realism? But to our poets! We shall not understand them much better by trying to determine on just what bench they sit in school.

The romantic movement in French poetry begins, so far as a definite beginning can be assigned to it, with that remarkable young poet, André Chénier, who died on the scaffold at the age of 32. He derives his inspiration from Greek and Latin, and though the romantics claimed him as a precursor, he is a thoroughgoing classicist. But his classicism is not pedantic, it is a fruitful classicism, not borrowed or consciously studied but a part of his nature. His verse is flexible and lovely and that is why the romantics called him father. Some of his verses would be in place in the Greek Anthology.

Béranger, the great balladist and singer of popular songs, did not belong to the romantic group but stood quite alone, though his vigorous songs were surely not out of key with his romantic contemporaries by whom he was greatly admired. His songs, or ballads, are sparkling, vivacious, neatly turned, simple and sincere in vocabulary, singable if not subtle in rhythm, perfect in their kind if not the greatest poetry. There is no more spirited ballad than the one directed against Napoleon:

There was a king of Yvetot.

The first great poet of the romantic group is Lamartine. His *Meditations,* which he never surpassed, is one of the crucial books of French literature. Such melody had not been heard in French poetry since the seventeenth century. It was spontaneous, fresh, genuine. The melancholy, the gentle sadness which verges on sentimentality, the "twilight-and-memory" mood are perfectly sincere. His range of feeling is limited, and his delicate colors faded almost out of sight in the presence of the gaudy splendor of Hugo and his followers. But there is no doubt that later poets and critics have regarded him with increasing admiration. His best known poem is *The Lake,* from which I take two stanzas in Thorley's translation:

O lake! Now hardly by a year grown older
    And nigh the well-known waves her eyes should greet,
Behold! I sit alone on this same boulder
    Thou knewest for her seat.

Thus didst thou murmur in thy rocky haven,
    Thus didst thou shatter on its stony breast;
Thus fell the wind-flung foam on sands engraven
    Where her dear feet had pressed.

Another of the innovators is Alfred de Vigny, whom English readers know best for his historical novel, *Cinq-Mars.* His first book of verse, *Poèmes Antiques et Modernes,* has the originality which he claims for it, philosophy in dramatic and narrative form. He is of great importance in the progress of French verse, because he did not stop with the poetry of youth; his poems grew more thoughtful and more shapely as he grew older. Most of these new poets were religious, following the lead of Chateaubriand. But de Vigny's religion is rational, still in the eighteenth century. Lamartine's God is the father of the suffering; de Vigny's is the God of thought:

> The true God, the strong God, is the God of ideas.
> Upon our brows where the seed is cast by chance
> Let it spread Knowledge in fertile waves;
> Then, gathering the fruit as it comes from the soul,
> All imbued with the perfume of the holy solitudes,
> Let us throw the work in the sea, the sea of the multitudes;
> —God will take it with his finger and lead it to port.

The prince of poets was Victor Hugo, who held his throne for fifty years. The variety and abundance of his work is past belief, and the disposition of later criticism to reduce his stature is in part a protest against his very bulk. Hugo's plays had a great vogue; he lived to see *Le Roi s'amuse,* which King Louis Philippe had forbidden after its first performance, produced fifty years later amid storms of applause. And in our time, nearly a century after they were written, hardly a week goes by without a performance of *Hernani* or *Ruy Blas* at the Comédie Française. Hugo's plays are melodramas without much truth to character or plausibility of plot. But the story *goes* and the lines are charged with superb rhetoric which sometimes mounts to a very high poetic plane.

The dramas of Hugo, for all their passionate rhetoric, are

beginning to get stale. His prose novels, of which we have spoken, have more enduring vitality (though modern French critics underrate them) ; a prose romance, even when it is written in words of fire and is full of false situations, is closer to life and freer from theatricality than a play of the same melodramatic quality. And I suspect that immortality has set its seal even more securely on the best of Hugo's lyric and narrative poems. He was a great singer, and it is true of him if of any man that his songs poured out of him. Volume after volume of shorter poems appeared between his plays and romances. And in the shorter poems (many of which are long enough!) is the soul of the man. He could turn a lyric measure to praise a baby or curse a king. Many of his poems have been translated into English, for he has been greatly admired by English poets. But most of the translations are of poems that are too long for our limits. The following piece, in a rough version, reveals one aspect of his faith:

> The child was singing; the mother on the bed, exhausted,
> Was dying, her beautiful brow bowed above the shades;
> Death hovered over her in the cloud;
> I heard that death-rattle, and I heard that song.
>
> The child was five years old, and near the window
> Its laughter and play made a charming sound;
> And the mother, beside that poor sweet being
> That sang all day, coughed all night.
>
> The mother went to sleep beneath the stones of the cloister;
> And the child began to sing again.—
> Grief is a fruit; God does not make it grow
> Upon a branch too feeble to bear it.

This illustrates rather sentimentally Hugo's belief in the goodness of God and the triumph of life, a belief which he maintained in the face of many bitter experiences. It distinguishes him from some of his pessimistic contemporaries and is allied with the great sense of pity which informs all his work, even when it is stagey and flamboyant. The whole world, including people who found fault with his art and disagreed with his politics, respected the man.

> Nor doubt nor hope could bend
> Earth's loftiest head, found upright to the end.

A poet less vigorous than Hugo is Alfred de Musset, who had a deep strain of melancholy which might have been morbid and maudlin but for the preserving salt of his humor. His strength is in his critical intelligence which not only controlled his wayward moods but enabled him to see that there was something futile in the contest between classic and romantic drama. He combined the two kinds of plays, and his work for the theater, notably *Les Caprices de Marianne,* is still alive on the French stage, and his excellent comedies, *A Quoi Rêvent Les Jeunes Filles (What Young Girls Dream About)* and *On Ne Badine Pas Avec L'Amour (One Does Not Trifle with Love)* and *Proverbs* are an established part of the repertory of the French theaters. His emotional lyrics which have in them something of the wild, willful, improvised quality of Byron, whom Musset admired but obviously could not imitate if he would, are shaped by an artistic mastery of classic French verse. In his noble *Lettre à Lamartine* he sums up himself and the spirit of his time, its melancholy and hope. The following poem *Sorrow,* in Thorley's neat translation, gives an idea of Musset's melancholy strain:

> Strength and Life have fled afar,
> Friends are not, and Mirth is dead;
> Gone is pride that erstwhile fed
> Faith in my frail star.

Once I hailed a friend in Truth
　　Ere I knew her changing guise;
　　When the scales fell from mine eyes,
Ah, the bitter ruth!

Everlasting is her power,
　　And all men that pass her by
　　Unperceiving, fruitlessly
Live their little hour.

God doth speak and man that hears
　　Needs must answer; all of good
　　Life hath given me is the flood
Eased my heart of tears.

There are three poets of this period who would be more prominent if they were not surrounded by greater men. They are Brizeux, Barbier, and Gerard de Nerval. Brizeux was a Breton and turned to his native province for his material, so that his poetry is of the soil, sincere and human. He also translated the whole of Dante's *Commedia* into terza rima. Barbier, a disciple of Chénier, denounced the evils of the time in vigorous satiric verses. De Nerval was a lyric poet of delicate finish, who kept the elegant form of the preceding century but revelled in romantic color. His translation of *Faust* made Goethe known in France. His prose stories, notably *Les Filles du Feu*, which contains his masterpiece *Sylvie*, are exquisite.

Through the troubled seas of romanticism, Theophile Gautier steered a clear course in a small vessel so admirably managed that its white sail shines clear among the larger craft. His poems, *Emaux et Camées* (*Enamels and Cameos*) have a perfection of form remarkable even in French verse. Gautier's jewel has a French facet and cannot be, as a jewel ought to be, carried across the boundaries of language. A hint of his poetic theory and practice is *Art,* which in the original is a delight to French ears and a gospel to French poets. Following are a few stanzas from the translation by George Santayana:

> All things return to dust
> Save beauties fashioned well.
> > The bust
> Outlasts the citadel.

> Oft doth the plowman's heel,
> Breaking the ancient clod,
> > Reveal
> A Cæsar or a god.

> The gods, too, die, alas!
> But deathless and more strong
> > Than brass
> Remains the sovereign song.

> Chisel and carve and file,
> Till thy vague dream imprint
> > Its smile
> On the unyielding flint.

Gautier's prose is as finely polished as his verse. His famous *Mlle. de Maupin* and the less well-known but equally delightful "bantering" romances, *Les Jeunes-France*, are in flawless style. Gautier is not a profound thinker, not perhaps a great poet, but he is the very pattern of elegance, of taste, of freedom from banality. His ideal as expressed in *Art* and in the phrase which he perhaps invented, "art for art," or as we say, "art for art's sake," is the ideal of the Parnassian group of which he is the eldest member.

In this group the profoundest poet is Leconte de Lisle, who despises romanticism and all the joys of life except art and devotion to objective truth. Like Schopenhauer he is a brave pessimist who finds the only refuge from an impossible world in contemplation, and who is not almost in love with easeful death, but loves it above life. He would have the entire universe including God annihilated. This gloomy soul like Schopenhauer has a sense of beauty so fine that it tortures him:

> Even as the Naiad in the distant woodland
>   Asleep beneath the tide,
>   Fly from the impious hand and eye, and hide
>   Light of the soul, O Beauty!

Leconte de Lisle is a great classical scholar. He not only found inspiration in the ancients for much of his own poetry, but made ultimate translations of Homer, Aeschylus, Sophocles, Horace. All the Parnassians were lovers of antiquity, and that is really a mood of romance. If Leconte de Lisle feels that it is beneath the dignity of a true artist to show his wounds in the market-place, he nevertheless does much the same thing by embodying his heartache in the pains of the whole human race. And in spite of his attitude of impersonality and impassibility, he suffers acutely and says so. No tearful romantic could be more personal, more egoistic, than this (Thorley's translation):

> O splendid blood, come shrive me in thy waves,
>   So may I, while the vulgar rabble shout,
>   Pass to my endless home with spirit clean.

A younger contemporary of Gautier and Musset, who belonged to no school but went his own darkly wonderful way, is Charles Baudelaire. In his *Fleurs du Mal,* some of the ideas are sinister, but the evil is only an element in the soil and the flowers are imperishable. Baudelaire found a kindred spirit in Poe, whose ideas, he said, had existed in his own mind but had never taken form. His admirable translations of Poe made the American writer a part of French literature. It would require a genius equal to Poe's to translate Baudelaire into English. But an English poet, Arthur Symons, has made excellent versions of Baudelaire's *Poems in Prose.*

Like Leconte de Lisle Baudelaire dreams of death and has a marmoreal ideal of beauty:

> I am lovely as a dream of stone.

He stands apart and though sharing some of their ideals does not belong among the Parnassians because he bares his soul openly, emphatically in the first person.

Theodore de Banville is a disciple of Gautier and quite equal to his master in his dexterous handling of meters. His thought is shallow but the little he has to say he says perfectly. He revived and turned gracefully the old French forms, the rondeaux and the villanelle, and with Gautier influenced the lighter versifiers of England.

Sully Prudhomme's Parnassian objectivity takes the form of philosophy and science. His *Justice* and *Bonheur* are versified discourses in ethics and metaphysics. But he is not wholly abstract, for he has a tender sense of the sufferings of people, and though he is miles away from anything like lyric ecstasy he has real poetic feeling and unquestionable command of phrase and form.

The most authentic Parnassian after Leconte de Lisle is Hérédia, whose one volume, *Les Trophées,* is the most remarkable collection of sonnets in French or, I dare say, in any language since Shakespeare. Hérédia's objectivity is historical; he searches the past of mankind for his subjects; his fellow-Parnassian, Coppée called his poems "a legend of the centuries in sonnets." They have been well rendered in English, but it would take Rossetti himself to translate them adequately, the lines are so packed with substance, so polished, luminous and brilliant with imagery.

BAUDELAIRE

A writer of genius who does not fit into any school but is most eccentrically himself is Richepin, a man of erratic life and thought but of great original power. His first volume of verse *Chanson de Gueux (Song of the Scoundrels* or as we might say "tramps" or "hobos")*, was so audacious that Richepin was imprisoned for violating public morals. But he did not stay his hand and France got used to him and recognized his essential honesty, his fearless will to grapple with life. Moreover, his works grew wiser, and though uncompromisingly violent his novels and plays gained in psychological insight. He is an accepted classic of the French theater.

Before the Parnassians had quite run their course they were superseded by the rising school of symbolists. That word, which we touched on at the beginning of the chapter, is hard to define, but perhaps it is no harder to define than poetry itself. We can suggest what symbolism is by an example familiar to us. If the raven in Poe's poem is fate or some dark aspect of his soul, there is a double meaning under the surface of the verses and the poem is symbolic. It is more than mere imagery, in which one thing stands for another; it is the representation of a whole idea by an associated idea. Symbolism is as old as poetry. The French poets made a conscious method of it. A disciple of Baudelaire, Stéphane Mallarmé, carried it to a point beyond obscurity in the ordinary sense of failure to express an idea. He gives the secondary thought and significance of words, suppressing deliberately the primary and leaving the reader no clew to it —except his own imagination. This was something new and strange in a literature distinguished for its clarity, and it puzzled even admiring French poets and critics. But many of the poems of Mallarmé are clear as daylight or lie in the enchanting twilight zone, the misty mid-region, where readers of English poetry are at home. Mallarmé, like Baudelaire, found a fellow artist, if not a master in Poe, and made beautiful translations of the American poet.

The mysterious voice of Mallarmé has reached but an elect few of his countrymen and it is not likely to win the ears of the world outside France. A symbolist of a different kind,

Paul Verlaine, lived to be known as one of the great poets of France and of modern Europe. Verlaine's poems are the spontaneous utterance of his sensations, loves, hates, hopes, despairs. He uses language with little regard to the classic rules of French verse, but in obedience only to his inner sense of melody, which is almost infallible. In his famous *Art Poétique* he gives his principles, which of course are his and not of much help to other poets, though many of the younger poets have been under his sway. The first principle is music above all else, no cleverness, no wit, no rhetoric, but music always.

As Verlaine preached so he practiced. He scattered his verse to the morning wind, as if he sang because he must, songs as natural as the songs of birds. They are the delight of composers, who have set many of them to music, and the despair of those who try to supply English texts. Verlaine was a man of many and violent feelings, yet a great simple child a drunken child of Bohemia, with a strain, toward the end of his life, of religious mysticism. He was often not master of himself but not often less than master of his art. Verlaine began as a Parnassian and became a symbolist, but he shook off all schools and went his own way, creating an idiom of his own, free from rhetoric, simple yet infinitely subtle. He despised the merely literary and never used a word that he did not mean. His strange and haunting minor cadences are like nothing else in poetry. In emotional power, in the directness with which he touches the heart of the reader he is like Heine, like Shelley, and yet of course utterly different from them.

Associated with Verlaine is the boy Rimbaud, a more curious prodigy than the English Chatterton—and a much better poet. Before he was twenty he wrote verses which fascinated Verlaine and they went wandering together. In a drunken fit Verlaine shot his companion, but his aim was bad and the wound did not prove fatal. Verlaine served two years in prison where he was converted from a pagan to a Catholic,

STEPHANE MALLARME

and whence he came forth with the finest volume of religious poetry in French literature. Rimbaud meanwhile turned his back on literature and went tramping round the world. His slender volume contains extraordinary verses in a vocabulary of old and new words, bizarre but effective. Verlaine did

not sum up a period; rather he inaugurated and inspire
the period that was to follow. Whether or not due to hi
influence (the influences that flow into the wells of genius ar
many), the living poets of France, and those but recentl
dead, are, taken together, as splendid as France has eve
had.

Of these contemporaneous poets a few stand out from th
rest, though it may be that a later time will assign to then
different relative values from those that seem to us just and
discriminating. A poet of magnificent power is Verhaeren, a
native of Flanders, German strength in a French mould. Hi
virility, his northern roughness sometimes strains the French
language, which is indeed capable of passion but has inheren
in its nature a certain philosophic restraint. To Verhaeren
life is a tumult, confusion, full of beauty but full too of unhap
piness. However, the final note of Verhaeren is in the epi
logue of one of his volumes; it is called *Toward the Future*
and the concluding note is of the "dreams which the youth
of the world dreams before each new hope."

Another Belgian poet is Maeterlinck, but he is unlike his
less known and more vigorous countryman, in that he is delicate, fanciful, refined and thin, even precious. Maeterlinck
is a *prosateur* rather than a poet. He is known all over the
world for his plays, of which *The Bluebird* is the most
popular, and for his essays on nature and literature. One
suspects that he loves children and dogs and bees and flowers
better than he does men and women, for his adult characters,
especially the women, are flat as wall paper.

The most aristocratic and elegant of living French poets is
de Régnier, master of form, urbane, serene, philosophic, a
poet who lives in a well kept park, not in the wild forests
where Verhaeren roams. De Régnier has a natural kinship

with the classics and perhaps the form which he invented and named "odelette" is a development from Horace. But his thought is very modern, penetrated everywhere with psychological insight. He does not grapple with life, but retreats like his friend Remy de Gourmont, if not into an ivory tower, into a very pleasantly furnished and quiet library. Not that either of these fine cultivated men of letters is bookish. They know too much, know how to use books and convert them to the nourishment of their own spirit.

A poet of classic learning and elegance and also of delightfully humorous roguery is Pierre Louys. His *Chansons de Bilitis,* purporting to be a translation from the Greek, is in tone and substance so like the Greek that some young critics were deceived, and the older critics examined his Hellenism with approving seriousness. Louys is called a decadent, but such lovely decadence as his is quite charming and harmless.

Probably the world of French letters would almost unanimously acknowledge de Régnier as the dean and master of them all, now that de Gourmont and Anatole France are dead. But the elected prince of poets (the method of election is not quite clear) is Paul Fort, a robust prolific poet who has published volume after volume of *Ballades Françaises* which deal with every conceivable aspect of French life and history from Louis XI to the war of 1914. He is vigorous and fecund, superficially slap-dash and rebellious, but underneath all that a very careful workman with a respect for traditional form from which no Frenchman, perhaps no real man of letters, can ever emancipate himself. Fort writes his lines in the form of prose, but when you read them aloud you find, or rather you hear, that most of the lines are perfectly straight verse. What is captivating about the poet is his inexhaustible rush of images, his fertility of invention, his command of emotion from pell-mell devil-may-care to the tender pathos and indignation of some of his war poems. Most war literature is journalistic and tiresome and is fading in interest. It is possible that Paul Fort's verses will live, for he was born and brought up under the shadow of Reims cathedral.

Much more slender, less muscular than Fort is Samain, a faint and wan poet, an invalid in substance but a very firm artist. He is for all his languid sadness what in his poem *Vigil* he wished to be, "a flame, pure, subtle, and quick with light."

A poet somewhat out of the current of French poetry yet eagerly welcomed and encouraged by the editors of the *Mercure de France* is Francis Jammes, who lives in the Pyrenees far from the madding crowd. He writes excellent narratives of local legends; his peasants or mountaineers seem to be real, at any rate the poetic diction is *vox humana*. I do not place him as a climax to modern French poetry. But there is one title of his which seems a fitting close to this small chapter or to any chapter on poetry: *The Triumph of Life.*

CHAPTER XL

THE CLASSICAL PERIOD IN GERMAN LITERATURE

Goethe appears to us as a person of that deep endowment, and gifted vision, of that experience also and sympathy in the ways of men, which qualify him to stand forth, not only as the literary ornament, but in many respects too as the Teacher and exemplar of his age.

—Carlyle.

N our account of literature I hope we have made it clear that the habit of thinking and the art of writing are more or less continuous processes; they have ups and downs, unaccountable flashes of genius and times of depression. No "period" is really a period, for that word seems to imply sharp beginnings and ends. There are very few such sharp moments in the story of literature or, so far as I can make out, in any other part of the story of the human being. Events and ideas flow and blend into each other. So when we say nineteenth century we do not mean that an idea was born promptly on the first day of January in the year eighteen hundred one. A good deal of nineteenth century thought goes back into the eighteenth century.

The German classical period lies about equally on both sides of the year 1800. In this sketch I have purposely refrained from exact dates, which anybody can look up in an encyclopedia; but to keep our general bearings we may remind ourselves that Goethe died in 1832 (the same year that Scott died), his vigorously productive years being of both the eighteenth and the nineteenth centuries. The forerunners are all in the eighteenth century.

To understand Goethe and his contemporaries we shall have to go back some years and trace rapidly what led up to the supreme master and the classic age of German literature.

When the peace of Westphalia ended the Thirty Years' War in 1648 it left all German-speaking lands devastated and with only half the population they had had before the war. The Reformation and the resultant wars made for the complete failure of the Renaissance in Germany and left the folk-song the only inheritance of German literature. Even during the great war literature did not, of course, die utterly. It was the aim of sporadic writers to keep some flame alive amid the decay of civilization. These writers naturally did not aspire after more than correctness, introducing a smooth versification, keeping the language pure. Such was the aim of Martin Opitz, the Waller and Malherbe of his day and country, who introduced the alexandrine, wrote a little treatise on German versification, and in other ways sought to introduce the forms and ideals of the French literature of the *grand siècle*. Perhaps the most original writer of that barren period was the epigrammatist Logau, some of whose little poems are familiar to us in the versions of Longfellow. We need stop neither over the dramatist Gryphius nor over the various little local academies that sought to keep the language correct and interest in literature alive.

Three figures only deserve notice in the period from the Thirty Years' War to the Seven Years' War. The horrors of

the first war were described by Christopher von Grimmels-
hausen in his *Simplicius Simplicissimus,* a novel of the picaresque tradition and thoroughly realistic temper which is very
readable to this day.   A word must be given to Paulus Gerhardt, greatest of German hymn writers after Luther, many
of whose sacred songs in translation by John Wesley and
others are familiar wherever English is spoken.

By 1740 Leipzig was the literary capital of Germany.   It
was a sort of Mecca in which Gottsched was the prophet of
Boileau.   It is necessary to emphasize the predominance of
the barrenest and most superficial Gallicism in order to explain
the critical side of the work of the great classic masters of
German literature.   That work had its faint forerunners in
Switzerland.   The Swiss critics, Bodmer and Breitinger,
broke with France and turned to England.   They founded a
periodical copied from the *Spectator* and, above all, pointed to
the true grandeur of Milton as opposed to the false and icy
eloquence of the French.   The poet Albrecht von Haller, also
a Swiss, imitated Thomson's *Seasons* in his poem on the Alps
and, somewhat later, the elegiac poets, Salis and Matthisson,
imitated Gray in verses some of which are familiar to us in the
renderings of Longfellow.   In Germany itself poetry, in the
meantime, remained imitative of France.

Such was the literary situation when there emerged the
earliest figures of the classic age, Friedrich Gottlieb Klopstock
and Christoph Martin Wieland.   In a sense these two men
represent the two tendencies described above, the Miltonic
and the French.   But both went deeper.   It is true that Klopstock's long hexameter epic, the *Messiah,* is unreadable today.
It remains true, also, that its vigor and nobility of diction
convinced the Germans, whom war and hunger had shut out
from the literature of Europe, that their native speech was a

medium easily equal to the other great literary languages. Klopstock's *Odes,* moreover, have often more than mere dignity and eloquence; they have, at their best, imagination and poignancy and may still be reckoned among the best of the more formal lyrical poetry of the eighteenth century.

Wieland was the opposite in every way of the solemn and "bardic" Klopstock. He was French in temper. But he went, so far as his age permitted, behind the French to the Greeks; he went to the great Italians, to Ariosto and Tasso; also he went to Shakespeare and made some of the earliest German versions of the plays. His flexibility, ease, brightness, fluency, were of inestimable benefit to the readers and writers of his country, and his philosophical romance *Agathon* and his romantic epic *Oberon,* written in the *ottava rima* of Ariosto, are still readable.

One more forerunner before we come to the masters. This forerunner is Johann Gottfried Herder, who was no poet, wrote no memorable work, produced only anthologies and critical fragments, but was one of those germinal minds that feed the literature of a whole period. His studies of Shakespeare, Ossian, of fundamental critical questions, were fruitful. Of supreme importance was his discovery of the sovereign value of the folk-poetry of all lands. His *Voices of the Nations in Songs* broke down the predominance of the artificial classic-renaissance culture and opened the way for that cultivation of balladry, folk poetry and song from which, later, the entire romantic movement and the romantic sciences of comparative philology, mythology and folk-lore were to spring.

Gotthold Ephraim Lessing was playwright, scholar, thinker, critic. Above all, he wrote good prose. He thought himself lacking in creative power and forgot, as has often been for-

otten, that a great style is in itself creation at its highest.
That some of his critical treatises and theological pamphlets
lack actuality of substance today is a fate shared by Lucian and
by Swift. Yet no critic of either painting or poetry dare be
unfamiliar with *Laocoön* nor any critic or historian of the
drama with the *Hamburg Dramaturgy* nor any student of the
history of thought with the *Education of the Human Race* or

LAOCOON

the *Wolfenbüttel Fragments*. To the lover of literature all
these works and indeed other and quite minor ones, are precious
by virtue of the lucidity, the bright wit, the eloquence, the
structural perfection and sober charm. To come in contact
with the spirit of Lessing is a liberal education whatever sub-

ject he treats, for to him may be truly applied the words tha
Johnson wrote for the tombstone of Goldsmith: "There wa
no kind of writing that he did not practice, nor did he toucl
any but to adorn it." Of Lessing, the dramatist, one must speal
with equal respect but with less warmth. He gave the Ger
mans their first classical comedy in *Minna von Barnhelm*
their first poetic drama of a high order in *Nathan the Wise*
Both pieces still hold the stage. But *Minna von Barnhelm*
is not a little faded and even of *Nathan the Wise* it may be
said that its highest virtue is that it illustrates once more th
nobility, tolerance and lucid-mindedness of its author.

It is difficult to write in brief compass of Goethe, the
greatest of German writers and one of the supreme minds ir
all literature. He was the most modern of the supreme
masters, therefore the most complex in spirit, temper, activity.
Dante assumes the medieval view of the world and the universe, Shakespeare the moral order of the renaissance. Goethe
assumes nothing. He is a modern, one who seeks and strives
and lets life itself crystallize into art. He is a lyric poet of the
first order; he is the author of *Faust,* which bears to modern
man, yesterday, today and for a long tomorrow, the relation
that the *Divine Comedy* bore to the men of the fourteenth century. *Faust* expresses us—our age, problems, moral adventure. And the letters, conversations, gnomic poems, sayings in
verse and prose, constitute a wisdom-literature of vast extent
and constant significance in which every difficulty, problem,
stirring of the modern or scientific period is creatively commented on in terms which find an echo in every instructed
mind.

Like Arnold and Emerson and Morley we are all disciples
of Goethe whether we know it or not, and any liberal mind has
but to be brought into contact with the master to realize that

inevitable discipleship. Whoever prefers moral energy to moral formalism, world federation to international rivalries, a cultivation of essential as opposed to mythical values in literature, life, politics, thought, can draw endless inspiration, vigor, light, from the life, the example, the writings—down to chance letters and brief epigrams—of this one man.

Goethe is a great poet, but he is so much more—and it is that infinitely more that makes up for the fact that certain of his formal works, even the novels, *Wilhelm Meister, Elective Affinities,* even some of the plays, are not today the easiest reading in the world.

In his youth Goethe was a student in the Leipzig of Gottsched and Gallicism and wrote the conventional anacreontics of his day. Thence he proceeded to Strassburg, met Herder, who opened to him the treasures of folk-poetry, and became, almost overnight, a lyrical poet of the first order. There followed the "Storm and Stress" period of Shakesperiolatry and medievalism and romantic melancholy which was marked by the novel *The Sorrows of Young Werther* which swept through Europe and gave Goethe an international reputation at twenty-four. The promising young man was invited to the court of Weimar where, with brief intervals, he passed the rest of his long life. To Weimar he took with him the fragmentary draft of the first part of *Faust,* the second part of which he completed there sixty years later. There followed busy and distracted years, the flight to Italy and the classicizing period during which he wrote the dramas *Iphigenie, Torquato Tasso,* the glowing Venetian epigrams, the exquisite idyl *Hermann und Dorothea.* His middle and later years, up to extreme old age were dedicated to statecraft, the cultivation of the theater, physical and biological science, the writing of his autobiography, the completion of *Faust.* But in every period of his life there was the never-ending stream of lyrics which in extent, passion, wisdom, music, are unsurpassed by those of any other poet.

Whatever else he did he never forgot *Faust*. He began the drama in his twenty-third year; he completed it in his eighty-third. Into it are packed the inspiration, the wisdom of his incomparable mind. The story is simple enough. Faust is a scholar who thirsts for life. He knows that salvation is not through theories but through experience. He throws himself, under the guidance of Mephistopheles, the spirit of negation and of evil, into the world of living experience. He tries vulgar gayety, sensual love, power, an identification with classical antiquity. All these experiences leave him unsatisfied. He finds an ultimate satisfaction in the simplest, most practical service to his fellowmen. But this, too, is but a step in his striving; this, too, is not the goal. The road itself is the goal, life is its own end and must justify itself from within; perfection is beyond our reach; we do not know what it is and indeed, to the human mind, it seems akin to stagnation and to death. Thus our highest achievement is a noble striving, a tireless creative living. That it is which saves Faust and defeats Mephistopheles; it is with an affirmation of this truth that the eternal armies welcome Faust.

This brief account of *Faust* does not even touch upon the poetry of the text. The entire drama, it must be remembered, is considerably longer than *Paradise Lost,* and every line has freshness and vitality of music, significance, characterization unequaled by any work of comparable length in the history of the world's literature. *Faust* is as important to us today as it was when the aged Goethe laid down his pen.

It was Goethe who brought Schiller to Weimar and procured for the younger man, who had had a rather bitter fight

GOETHE

GOETHE

with worldly circumstances, a professorship of history at the university of Jena. Schiller, ten years the junior of Goethe, had begun with prose dramas, *The Robbers, Cabals and Love,* in which the new domestic bourgeois tragedy of the eighteenth century culminated. These plays are in prose; they have a fine, high, revolutionary vigor of plot and characterization and laid the foundation of the modern art of tragic dialogue in prose. But they have touches of wildness and excess, like Schiller's early poetry. The maturing man, deeply versed in history and in the Kantian philosophy, turned during the remainder of his short life to the cultivation of the historical and tragic drama in verse and produced in Jena and Weimar that series of plays which constitute the most important body of dramatic literature between Molière and Hebbel: *Don Carlos, The Maid of Orleans, Mary Stuart, William Tell,* and the *Wallenstein* trilogy. In recent years the dramas of Schiller, though they have all continued to hold the stage, have somewhat lost in reputation. The naturalists preferred the early prose plays; severe criticism of Schiller's rhetoric and of his occasional sentimentality, especially in the *Maid of Orleans,* became common. Despite that the finest of the plays, *William Tell* and the whole of *Wallenstein,*—and this is equally true of the philosophic poems—remain vital, dramatic, spirited.

With Schiller's death in 1805 the strictly classical period of German literature may be said to have ended. Goethe survived until 1832. But by that time the Romantic School had done its work, the July revolution was over, Heine had fled to Paris. The new age was almost at its noon.

CHAPTER XLI

GERMAN LITERATURE SINCE GOETHE

And now let us look at the work of German poets and prose writers of recognized ability. With what care and what devotion did they not follow in their labors an enlightened conviction!

—*Goethe.*

MANY literary, intellectual, political motives caused the rise and determined the character of the Romantic School in German literature. Germany lay broken, powerless, at the feet of France. What was more natural than that poets and idealists should turn in their reveries to the medieval idea of German empire? And that brought them to the Gothic and the Catholic—to the architecture of Nürnberg, to the Cathedrals of Cologne and Strassburg, to the Minnesingers of the Middle High German period, to the folksongs and legends of haunted woodlands and streams and valleys. Blended with this motive was a philosophic one. The thinkers who came after Kant refined the hard world of reality away more and more until Fichte proclaimed it to be but the projection of the creative spirit of man. Thus poets had the right to dream and dream only, and act out their dreams and let that suffice.

The Romantic school produced no solid works of art. In

the translations of Shakespeare by Schlegel, Tieck and others, in the philological labors of the Grimms, it permanently enriched the world of knowledge. Its writings are all fragments and are important chiefly on account of the influence exerted by them directly or indirectly on the literature of Europe. Only in the lyric did the Romantics do work of the first order. The *Fragments* of Novalis make a profound book, but they are fragments. The tales of Hoffmann are not first-rate literature. The lyrical poems of Novalis, Brentano, Eichendorff, Hölderlin, Uhland, Rückert are good. And they are known all over the world because they were, like the lyrics of Heine, set to music by Schubert, Schumann, Franz, Brahms.

The romantic lyric had a long life. It continued that life in the melancholy strains of Nicholaus Lenau and still later in the lyrical work of Eduard Mörike, rendered more famous by the musical settings of Hugo Wolf; it reaches its highest point in the few faultless verses of Theodor Storm.

More or less directly from the Romantic school there proceeded three important men: Schopenhauer, and the two dramatists, Prussian and Austrian respectively, Heinrich von Kleist and Franz Grillparzer. Schopenhauer is known as the classic exponent of pessimism. He was convinced that the sum of pain in life so outweighs anything else that he identified the biological and psychical will to live with evil itself and preached quietism and absorption in art as the only course of wisdom. The reason for placing him in this account is that not only his chief work, *The World as Will and Representation,* but all his minor works, especially the two volumes of *Miscellanies,* are excellent prose. On literature, philology, art, music, he is richly suggestive.

Kleist, who committed suicide at an early age, left a handful of plays and novelettes that have steadily grown in reputation.

He was modern.   He abandons the heroic psychology of the
tragic drama that had become stereotyped and leads us into
the obscure inner conflicts that take place in the minds of men.
His *Prince of Homburg,* his admirable comedy, *The Broken
Jug,* a few stories like *Michael Koolhaas* are among the earliest

SCHOPENHAUER

documents in any literature that exhaust unusual and yet highly
representative psychological situations with strangly persuasive if often morbid passion and power. Grillparzer, the
most famous of Austrian dramatists, is far more a poet, less
a psychologist than Kleist.   He is also more strictly a roman-
ticist. His psychology often approaches the modern. Yet

his plays, wherever he chooses the scene of the action, are in essence plays of a human fairy-land. His politics as well as his motivation are poetical and romantic. Asceticism fought in him with high passion, and the traces of that struggle are in the management of every fable he built. He is not modern; he has no sagacity. Yet these lovely and legendary and shimmering dramas—*Sappho, The Golden Fleece, Dreams Too Are Life, Libussa, The Waves of Love and of the Sea*—are charming things.

It has been pointed out that the Romantics were dreamers, conservatives, often Catholics. There came the July revolution; liberty once more asserted itself after the eclipse that followed Waterloo; there arose the group of writers known as "Young Germany," men of more realistic temper, freer ideas. Few of them have left permanent works. To mention the brilliant pamphleteer Ludwig Börne suffices. We can proceed at once to Heine, Jew and German, child of Romanticism and also of the revolution, dreamer and realist, full of yearning and full of passion for human freedom, who sang both the glories of fairy-land and the woe of the same Silesian weavers that Hauptmann made immortal—Heine, storm-center of controversy in Germany to this day, a personality, like Byron's, of European influence, importance and fame.

The works of Heine are perhaps of less importance in themselves than his personality and influence. It would be doing him an ill-service today to speak of him, as Arnold did, as the lyrical inheritor of Goethe's genius. Hundreds of the early verses of Heine are wilted, almost tawdry. Fortunately the body of his poetic work is enormous. There remain the best of the *North Sea* cycle, the most earnest and sincere of the later poems, true in substance, stripped of the roses and raptures of the earlier work. His prose has suffered less justly in reputation. It is colorful, rich, swift, eloquent and witty. He was, as he said of himself, a good fighter in humanity's war of liberation and his prose holds, in a thousand brilliant, eloquent, and impassioned pages the record of that fight.

HEINE

During the middle years of the nineteenth century, while Heine was at the height of his fame, two great men were laboring in obscurity. These were Richard Wagner and Friedrich Hebbel. Wagner, despite the verse of his texts and his theoretical treatises, does not strictly belong to literature. It is otherwise with the dramatist, Friedrich Hebbel, a great writer and a greater thinker and man. Through difficult, barren, lonely years Hebbel thought out the modern drama—the drama that came into being first in his works, then in those of Ibsen and of all who followed. He transferred dramatic conflict from the people who embody rigid moral concepts to those concepts themselves; he brought the universe and the history of civilization to the judgment bar of the dramatic poet; he conceived drama to arise primarily at periods when one set of *mores* is dying and another is arising, when man and his morals die to live. His chief works, *Maria Magdalena, Herodes and Mariamne, Gyges and His Ring, Agnes Bernauer,* all illustrate this theory with a tense and eloquent closeness of dramatic action and reasoning. Years after Hebbel's death appeared his diaries, the record of a strong and honest mind, and perhaps an even more important work than his plays.

Two eminent novelists belong to this period: Theodor Fontane and Gottfried Keller, the most distinguished of Swiss writers. Fontane is the precursor of the realistic, even of the naturalistic novel; he produced minor but authentic masterpieces, such as *Effi Briest* and *Life's Confusions*. Keller is a figure of international importance. His long novel *Green Henry,* which is the story of his own inner development, is not throughout the easiest reading. His novelettes are masterpieces. Keller had an eye for the quaint and the humorous aspects of life and saw the foibles of the Swiss peasantry and town-folk. He was master of prose, and his stories from the past and present of his country belong to what is soundest, most enjoyable in nineteenth century fiction.

In Germany, as in France, the years from 1850 to 1870 saw the cultivation of pure form in verse. The Munich school parallels the Parnassians in many interesting ways. Chiefs of this school were Paul Heyse whose novels and tales, long famous, seem faded and feeble today and whose fame must rest on a selection from his very pure and lucid verse, and Emmanuel Geibel who wrote lovely romantic lyrics in the traditional German fashion and was for some years a national poet by virtue of his grave, polished, sonorous stanzas. The best poet of this kind that wrote German was, however, another Swiss, Konrad Ferdinand Meyer. In him the lucidity and tempered eloquence of the "art poets" was married to high imagination and enchanting music.

NIETZSCHE

We are on the threshold of the modern period and there we meet the strange figure of the poet philosopher, Friedrich Nietzsche. Nietzsche is primarily an artist and a great one. He is a thinker, too, and he more than anyone else taught mankind the central lesson of modern thought that the moral like the physical world is one of change and life, not of change-

lessness and death and that, therefore, man may utterly tran-
scend his present self. These ideas of change and of the superman are germinal; they are the leaven that is leavening the
whole lump of modern life. What makes them and all the
deductions from them so flame-like is Nietzsche's incomparable power of speech. We meet not only in *Thus Spake
Zarathustra,* but in all his other works, in *The Revaluation of
Values,* in *Human All Too Human,* one of the great creative
speakers. His words burn and soar and sing. His books have
a message that beats upon the hearts of men in this epoch; they
have a persuasiveness, a rapture of speech that may be compared to the eloquence and persuasiveness of the gospels. His
books are filled with pregnant sayings each of which opens a
new vista into "man and nature and human life," and he has
this further mark of the sage who is also a poet that these sayings are often part of lyrical structures, of parables, of stories,
that make them live and breathe.

To understand the last revolution in German literature, we
must remember that in 1880 Hebbel, Keller, Meyer, Nietzsche
had not come into their own. The public saw shoddy plays
imitated from the works of Augier and Dumas, the younger;
it read sentimental novels and verse drained from the lees of
romanticism without its original beauty and power. Hence
the young generation of the early eighties rose in revolt,
formed societies, sent programs abroad, enunciated the theory
of "consistent naturalism" and laid the foundations of a vigorous literary movement. The pamphlets and the examples of
Arno Holz soon bore fruit. A true poet arose, Detlev von
Liliencron, and a great dramatist, Gerhart Hauptmann. The
novel lagged a little, but not for long. A new literature was
born.

With Liliencron the lyric, always the glory of German literature, regained concreteness, poignancy, truth. His songs and ballads have in them the savor of earth and wine and bread. And, at the same time, though he deals so concretely and vividly with simple things, he recovered for German poetry a fine stringency of form.

An outburst of lyrical poetry followed the leadership of Liliencron. The next, and perhaps the most eminent poet of all, is Richard Dehmel. To Liliencron's vividness and concreteness Dehmel added a philosophic vision and a power —in this he stands alone among the poets of Europe—of transferring into verse the whole psychical and mechanical complexity of modern life. He can write a folk-song; he can write with the simplicity of a medieval carol. But his eminent achievement, in a hundred single poems and in the cycle, *Two Souls,* is to have created the poetry of the life of modern men and women, a bicycle trip, a telephone conversation, a woman playing the piano in the next-door flat, and the verses in which he tells of these things are clear and elevated.

Almost simultaneously with Liliencron and Dehmel there arose in Vienna another school of poetry which deliberately turned away from the concrete realism of the North and cultivated a transmutation of all the elements of life into the realm of a serene and timeless beauty. Among the many accomplished writers of this group three emerge as most memorable: Stefan George, Hugo von Hofmannsthal, Rainer Maria Rilke. George is an austere and faultless master. There is no flawed stanza in his works nor one that is not imaginatively and philosophically pregnant. Hofmannsthal, by his choice of the dramatic form and by his collaboration with Richard Strauss, has given the work of his group and school international currency. But translations betray him; they cannot give the perfection and the glow, the mystery and

magic of his verses. A little aside from these stands Rainer
Maria Rilke, son of the ancient city of Prague, strict in form
and yet mystic, master of all the young expressionist lyrists
because he recreates the world from within and remolds
reality nearer the desire of his delicate and musical soul.
Around him arose in recent years the new expressionist storm
and stress which has achieved its solidest work not in the novel
or the drama, but in lyrical and philosophic poetry. Among
these younger contemporaries there is at least one whose
name deserves to be recorded; that one is Franz Werfel.

The modern drama that arose after the experiments of Holz
and first gathered about the famous Free Stage Society of
Berlin, consists of a body of work extraordinary in range,
wealth, variety, power. Hermann Sudermann, who has an international reputation, is an interesting but not a great dramatist. The two men of emergent genius are Gerhart Hauptmann and Arthur Schnitzler.

Although Hauptmann is a poet and the only contemporary
dramatist who has successfully written poetic drama in the
grand style—*The Sunken Bell, Henry of Aue*—his naturalistic plays are probably his greatest and most characteristic
achievement. In these plays, in *Lonely Lives, The Weavers,
The Beaver Coat, Drayman Henschel, Michael Kramer, Rose
Bernd*—there is perfect illusion of reality. No speech more
authentic and piercing had ever before been recorded in writing. There is, secondly, a complete reversal of the mythic
notion of human guilt. Tragic guilt, in these dramas, inheres
either in the universe or in the corporate, not the individual
life, of mankind. Hauptmann's protagonists are all sufferers;
they are all more sinned against than sinning. He is the dramatist of compassion, the representative poet of an industrialist
and social-minded age. His highest achievement is in the cre-

ation of character. No living writer has created a world so full of breathing souls, a world in which aftertimes will be able to see the very life of an age and a country.

Schnitzler, the Viennese, is in his way as realistic and authentic as Hauptmann. But he deals with a sophisticated society, a society devoted to art, and given to introspection and a little disillusioned and weary. He has not Hauptmann's vigor. He has elegance, subtlety, suaveness. His best plays—*Light o' Love, The Fairy Tale, The Wide Domain, The Lonely Way*—have a union of veracity and elegiac melancholy and spiritual charm. The same may be said of his stories which are written in a lucid and musical style.

The novel lagged behind both the lyric and the drama in Germany. It was handicapped by the character of German prose which matured late and did not attain modern simplicity, elegance and telling quality until after Nietzsche. Among many interesting and often able writers of fiction something approaching an international reputation has been attained by Gustav Frenssen, chronicler of North German peasant life, and by Clara Viebig, sturdy realist, equally at home among the proletarians of Berlin and the happier children of the Rhine. Such a reputation is bound to come sooner or later to that gifted woman, Ricarda Huch, scholar, poet, novelist of artistic purity and imaginative reach. But above all these stand two masters—masters not only of the novel, but of prose as an art—Thomas Mann and Jacob Wassermann.

Thomas Mann is a very austere writer. One long novel *Buddenbrooks,* two volumes of novelettes and short stories—these, setting aside his essays, constitute almost his whole work. But *Buddenbrooks,* a story of the decline and disintegration of a family of Lübeck patricians, is a book at once massive and perfect, glowing and serene, and the short stories and novelettes, especially *Death in Venice*, are of an incomparable beauty and sobriety. No prose more noble than his has been written in this generation.*

Wassermann, whose chief work, *The World's Illusion,* has made its way with readers of English, is a mystic, a writer of vast creative energy, large passion, long development. He has a touch of the fantastic; he has been compared to both Dickens and Dostoievsky. Through long years of effort he evolved eloquent poetic form and style adequate to the rendering of his impassioned vision of things. Wassermann has something of the prophetic power of his blood. He, like Schnitzler and Hofmannsthal, is a Jew. The contrast between him and Mann, as between Schnitzler and Hauptmann, illustrates the passion and turmoil, the rapture and God-seeking that mark the work of many younger contemporary German poets, playwrights, novelists, whose work belongs to the future rather than to the present.

* Since this paragraph was set in type Mann has published *The Magic Mountain,* his supreme masterpiece—so far. One can only await with glowing assurance what his still vigorous genius may yet produce!

CHAPTER XLII
RUSSIAN LITERATURE OF THE NINETEENTH CENTURY

Among us things have taken such shape that a story—the most frivolous and insignificant form of literature—becomes one of two things: either it is rubbish, or else it is the voice of a leader sounding through the empire.
—Drouzhinin.

TO the western reader who does not know the language, Russian literature means the Russian novel of the nineteenth century and today. This is a limited view, blind to the genius of Russian poetry and other forms of expression. But there is good reason for the limitation. The novel has wide appeal, it crosses more easily than other kinds of writing the frontiers between nations. And the Russian novel is a powerful institution. It is more than a story, as the critic quoted above suggests, it is a voice sounding not only through the empire but through Europe. So it is the very richness of Russian fiction which justifies us in neglecting the rest of Russian literature—even if we knew much about it. Moreover, before the age of the great novelists the Russians were borrowing from western Europe, and before they had much that was new and original to contribute in return,

460

the currents of influence flowed eastward. They took their inspiration from France, Italy, and England, to the neglect of their native sources of song and story.

Though it is the prose fiction that chiefly interests us, the founders of modern Russian literature were two poets, Pushkin and Lermontov, who also wrote prose. Both men belong to the romantic period at the beginning of the nineteenth century and both were strongly influenced by Byron as were half the young writers of Europe.

Pushkin had all the literary gifts; he was a lyric poet, a dramatic poet, and a story-teller. But he is primarily a dramatist of great force and beauty. Russian composers have gone to him repeatedly for their themes. The best known operas founded on his stories and poems are *Eugene Onegin, Boris Godounov, Rusalka* and *Dame Pique.* He had a great and good influence on all Russian literature after him, for he developed or was born with a simple style and got his powerful effects by clarity and directness.

Lermontov, like Pushkin, was Byronic but he also had a touch of Shelley. He was a visionary, interested in the mystical and spiritual qualities of the Russian soul, and this interest prevailed throughout much of the literature that followed and is more dominantly characteristic of Russian fiction than of the fiction of any other country. Lermontov's chief novel is *A Hero of Our Time,* which has been translated into many languages including English. It is laid in the Caucasus and discloses with a kind of romantic chivalry the virtues of the mountaineers against whom the Russian gentleman had to fight. That too is said to be characteristically Russian: not to take sides in fiction, however necessary it may be to take sides in practical life, but always to see the qualities of the other fellow. It gives us a glimpse into the state of literature and society of the time to learn that Pushkin and Lermontov, the two leading men of letters, were both killed in duels.

The first master of fiction to leave romantic convention and go to life for his subjects was Nikolai Gogol. His *Dead Souls,* which is much livelier than the title suggests, depicts in a series of adventures many aspects of Russian society of the smaller sort, and is full of humorous sympathy with plain people and satirical contempt for sham and hypocrisy. It is said that much of the humor is lost in translation; this is probably true, for Gogol is a close observer of small provincial folk. But in the English translation enough of the essential humanity shines through to make us aware of the greatness of the book. Beside his gift for ironic observation Gogol had a talent for the more excitingly dramatic, which is shown in *Taras Bulba,* a tale of the fights between the Cossacks and the Poles. But he is above all the founder of Russian realism, and succeeding Russian novelists acknowledged his primacy, though they went far beyond him. It is the opinion of the venerable Russian scholar and erstwhile revolutionist, Kropotkin, that the later Russian novelists descend in a more direct line from Pushkin than from Gogol. However that may be, it is certain that Gogol was and still is a great power, in his own work, which has never ceased to be read, and in his effort, not a critically conscious effort, to pull the novel away from romanticism and make it identical with life.

The first great advance was made by Ivan Tourgenev. He and Dostoievsky and Tolstoy are a triumvirate who rule Russian fiction. Tourgenev's first important work, *Memories of a Sportsman,* describes the miserable life of the peasants and had some effect in bringing about their emancipation from serfdom. It is an illustration of the fact already noted, and to be seen even more strikingly in Tolstoy, that Russian fiction is not a mere idle tale, but has a practical bearing on life. In *Fathers and Sons*, Tourgenev describes the conflict between the rising new generation and the old, between the young who have scientific and intellectual aspirations and the old-fashioned home-loving aristocracy. He applied to some of the

DOSTOIEVSKY

new doctrines the term "nihilism," and the word was used by the government to stigmatize all liberal ideas, with the result that Tourgenev for a time lost the favor of those with whom he sympathized. A few years earlier he had displeased the government by some remarks on officialdom and had been punished by a brief imprisonment and exile. The life of a

Russian writer was one of excitement and danger. Tourgenev was not, however, primarily a propagandist. He was an artist, a student of character, a lover of beauty, with a sense of form which we think of as French. He was both simple and profound. It has been said that nobody but Tourgenev ever wrote a perfect novel—an exaggeration, but true if it means that most of his novels are nearly perfect. In *On the Eve* and the *Waters of Spring*, he portrayed the pathetic loveliness of young women. He felt what was futile and brutal in Russian people and understood their brooding melancholy, for he shared it himself. His unhappiness is not sickly, but brave and tender. The clearness of his analysis and the intelligibility of his narrative make him perhaps the most transparent interpreter of Russian nature to the rest of the world; certainly he is the most readable. Whether he is truer than his great contemporaries, only Russians can tell us. His novels are built upon a European framework rather than upon the loose plotless Russian model. He lived in Paris much of his active life, and Dostoievsky and Tolstoy both thought him Frenchified, or in danger of becoming so. But he went back often to Russia to get new material. His self-imposed exile made him an idolator of the Russian language, which Russians say he used with final perfection. He wrote with exquisite care and perhaps that was the one thing he learned from the French. Certainly French influence did not hurt the artist, whatever it may have done to the Russian. And the Russian as artist did not suffer, for only an artist in a sort of invocation to his native tongue could have written, in effect: "It is unthinkable that such a language should have been given to any but a great nation."

Tourgenev's novels are finished and restrained. The novels of Feodor Dostoievsky, a man of more intense or less controlled passion, are poured out of him into no mold but the lawless irregular confines of fact. In his youth he was arrested for his revolutionary activities (which were little more than talk), and was sent to Siberia for four years. His bitter experiences are narrated in *Recollections of the House of the Dead*. The iron entered his soul, and he remained all his life a man of sorrows. But with his bitterness, perhaps as a result of it, was a great compassion for all who suffer, for criminals and outcasts, for the *Injured and the Insulted,* as one of his novels is called. His best known work, *Crime and Punishment,* is terrible and touching. A poor student, Raskolnikov, commits an atrocious murder, the motives of which are not the ordinary ones, jealousy, revenge, robbery, but a complexity of morbid egotism and resentment against life. He confesses to his sweetheart, Sonia, a poor girl of the streets, and she persuades him to expiate his crime. He surrenders to the police and is sent to Siberia, where Sonia joins him. Her devotion is his redemption. In the suffering of these two children Dostoievsky, without being a symbolist, saw all Russia and dreamed of a future when love should redeem all Russia and all the world. He did not believe in violence as a cure for oppression; in *The Possessed* he shows the folly and tragedy of revolutionary conspiracies. He thought the peasant was the hope of Russia and endowed him with virtues which Maxim Gorky now tells us were only the literary and political idealizations of the time.

The sadness of life in all Dostoievsky's novels has sometimes been mistaken by western readers for morbidity. It is morbid only in so far forth as the human being has some unwholesome motives. But the novelist is not to blame for that, any more than the newspaper editor is to blame for putting on his front page a murder and a fire and a kidnap

ping, and also a fine piece of human courage, like a flight to
the North Pole or the death of a surgeon who gives his life
in an effort to find a way of saving the lives of some of his
fellowmen. Not that Dostoievsky takes his material from
newspapers. He takes it from universal life. His greatest
novel, *Brothers Karamazov*, handles the problems of good and
evil as they present themselves in the weaknesses and difficulties of quite unimportant people. In all Dostoievsky there
is no "hero." And the heroines were not made for the moving
pictures. They are too pathetic, too tragic and too true. The
only thing lacking in Dostoievsky's genius is a sense of humor.
Tourgenev had it in a rather pale and philosophically sympathetic kind. The greatest of them all, Tolstoy, had only a
solemn wry humor, a smile but never a laugh. Between
Gogol and Chekov there is not much fun in Russian literature.

The Russians are sometimes difficult to understand but not
more so than the rest of us. And one suspects that the Slavic
temperament, miscalled "psychology," is to be found in our
next door neighbor. In this connection it is significant that
Dostoievsky's first story, *Poor Folk,* seems to have a strong
flavor of Dickens, of whose work he actually knew very little.
It is a small round world. Yet that Dostoievsky thought of his
people and their literature as apart from Europe is shown by
his strange comment on Tolstoy's *Anna Karénina,* that it was
the most palpable proof Russia could offer to the western
world of Russia's capacity to contribute something great to
the solution of the problems that oppress humanity. The problems that oppress humanity are not solved, east or west, by
fiction, nor the problems of human character, which fiction
presents and illuminates but does not solve. What comes
through to us from Dostoievsky's Russia is his power to communicate and evoke emotion, to compel interest in diffuse

detail and rather hard fundamental material, as in the *Brothers Karamazov*. He was not known in England or America until after Tourgenev and Tolstoy had at least been heard of. His intense nationalism checked him at the frontiers, but his humanity has finally triumphed, at least among the intelligent, in all countries, and Dostoievsky is now one of the acknowledged great masters of the nineteenth century.

The Russian novelists carried the burden of the world upon their shoulders, and whether that burden strengthened them as artists we cannot say. It is enough that they are strong and that their art is noble and honest. When Tolstoy died in 1910, he was the preëminent man of letters in all the world. He would not have been so universally honored if he had been only a novelist, and his stature as reformer and champion of liberty would not have been so towering if he had not been a novelist. There have been many men of letters who have used their pens—their manhood and their souls—bravely in non-literary conflicts, for example, Milton and Hugo. Some sacrificed their energy or postponed their art at times for the sake of a "cause"; others put aside the pen and took up the sword, like Byron. Tolstoy is probably the only artist of first-rate creative power who tried to deny and suppress his art as something hostile or irrelevant to his higher purposes. Fortunately those purposes did not take complete possession of him until after his creative impulse had expressed itself in his novels and stories. In his youth he was a conventional aristocrat and soldier, conventional in outward circumstances, not by nature. His experiences in the Crimean War gave him the material for *Sebastopol* and other military tales which brought him immediate fame and established him in a literary career. Their quality, their hero, as he himself said, is truth, without a touch of false heroics or sentimental glory. He saw war for what it is, horrible and useless, in which common men show a simple blind courage. He was not then a pacifist or propagandist; indeed, the emperor ordered him removed from the danger zone. Even after his reputation was brilliant and secure he was more interested in people and things than in letters—and that is the source of his strength. He spent his time on his country estate trying to educate the village children and improve the condition of the peasants. In the midst of many activities he wrote his two great novels, *War and Peace* and *Anna Karénina.*

War and Peace is more than a novel, it is an epic of Russian social life and history at the time of the Napoleonic wars. The scope of it is enormous; it contains a score of ordinary novels. The individuals move against an immense background. And they are individuals. Every member of the four families who are the chief actors in the vast drama is a person. Tolstoy has supremely the gift of characterization; he cannot touch a human being without making him alive. And he has descriptive power, the sense of scene, whether it be the panorama of a battlefield or the inside of a house in Moscow. His narrative is crowded and complex because there are so many crossing lines of interest. He follows instinctively a method which he somewhere phrases as a principle, never to force a story to a conclusion but to let it seem to go its own way. His "naturalism" was not a theory but an expression of his nature, of his habit of mind; he looked at things literally and through things imaginatively.

The only fault of *War and Peace* is that there is too much of it, that its very magnitude makes it formless. In *Anna Karénina* the field of vision is not so broad and the power is more concentrated. The story of Anna moves with the inevitability of the greatest tragedies. Her character and her circumstances carry her to her doom as steadily as a river that flows toward a cataract. The sinning woman leaves a husband who is a perfect specimen of repulsive rectitude, for a lover who is brilliant and vain, and finds herself cut off both from the lover who has wearied of her and from the society which she has abandoned. She is punished not by any abstract code of goodness or badness but by the implacable morality of fact. There is no longer a place for her in life, and suicide is the only solution.

As a foil to the feverish passion of Anna and her lover is the quiet story of the domestic life of Levine and Kitty. This part of the book is but loosely related to the main tragedy, but it is important because Levine is Tolstoy himself struggling with the riddle of existence and finding peace in religious mysticism. Tolstoy spent most of the rest of his life developing and expounding his views of ethics, religion, government, art. Tourgenev, who said of him, "In contemporary European literature he has no equal," thought that Tolstoy's apostasy from literature was an unpardonable sin. But to Tolstoy one of the unpardonable sins was to indulge in mere literature—of which he was past master!—and in *What Is Art?* he swept into the rubbish heap almost all our cherished masterpieces, including his own novels. Once when he was seventy years old he returned to the novel and wrote *Resurrection*. His motive, however, was not artistic but practical, to raise money for a persecuted sect of Christians, the Doughobors. Tolstoy abjured money but was willing to make it for somebody else. The book is overloaded with moral purpose, but shows undiminished power of characterization and realization of scene. The artistic spirit in him took advantage of the opportunity and got its revenge. Tolstoy's religious beliefs, arrived at by great travail of soul, are simple enough: the teachings of Jesus—as he interpreted them—freed from ecclesiastical authority and theological sophistry. The Orthodox Church feared his influence and increased it by excommunicating him and censoring his books. His religious ideas led naturally to non-resistance and pacific anarchism. If he had been a poor and obscure man, he would have been clapped into prison or exiled to Siberia. But he was the king of literature, stronger than temporal kings. Had the government laid hands on him there would have been a storm of protest throughout Europe. So the authorities took it out on his humbler followers, to Tolstoy's infinite sorrow. It is as well that he died before 1914.

ANDREYEV

Tolstoy's principal works have been translated into English and are available in cheap editions. The best translations are those by Aylmer Maude, of which several volumes, including the most important works, have already appeared in the World's Classics. Mr. Maude is the author of the *Life of Tolstoy*, in two volumes. The reader will find Tolstoy interesting in every aspect, even when he is riding a hobby over too long a course. His terrific vitality makes his least important pages alive.

TOLSTOY

It seems to be the opinion of Russian critics that the mantle of the great elders, or at least a comfortable corner of it, fell on the shoulders of Chekov. He was a writer of short stories and plays, a country physician for whom literature, at least in the beginning of his relatively short life, was a recreation, a side-play. Tolstoy, growing more and more austere, thought that Chekov had no philosophy, but he loved the man and his stories and plays. Chekov, in a quite artlessly artful way, wrote with a delightful fantastic humor of life as he saw it about him. His manner is perfectly simple. The tale tells itself. It is often not an important tale. Certainly the peddler's pack of notions that the Russian so often carries, Chekov threw into a ditch. For his humor let us read *The Little Darling,* a mild satire on the female of the species, but done with perfect good humor. And of his dramas the finest is *The Cherry Orchard,* a curious play in which a gentle sadly humorous sense is combined with a painful situation. Tragic humor—that is a mood seldom attained in literature. Chekov had it. His short stories are so good in their simplicity and directness that some enthusiastic critics have compared him to Maupassant. That is a mistake. When an actual stream of influence, of real stuff, passes from one country to another it is interesting to follow it and it is even interesting to find resemblances between writers who never heard of each other. But it helps little to refer one man to another man with whom he has no intellectual relation. Chekov has only this in common with Maupassant: he writes good stories.

Maxim Gorky has a curious and important place in recent Russian literature. Aristocrats like Tourgenev and Tolstoy were friends of the peasant, and more than one well-born Russian has gone to Siberia for taking up the cause of the workman. Maxim Gorky (as he calls himself, Gorky being the Russian for "bitter") was born of the peasants and the workers. His hero is himself, whether in his fiction or his avowedly autobiographic books, an individual born in the dark and trying to get into the light. Every book of Gorky's is a struggle. He is not a great artist. He fights too hard and streaks every page with propaganda. All the same you

GORKY

shall go far to find a more touching and disturbing book than *Mother.* For some reason which is not quite explicable he took hold of the imagination of the world outside Russia, and he is probably the best known to the English speaking world of all contemporary Russian writers.

Andreyev, as contrasted with Gorky, is an intellectual sceptic, not fighting with life but trying to understand it and turning on it the light of disillusion and doubt. His

stories, *The Seven That Were Hanged* and *The Red Laugh*, are terrible in their intensity and his plays, *The Life of Man* and *He Who Gets Slapped*, are pessimistic symbolism (to use words which are getting worn out), of a strain almost too sad even for Russia. It is said that the performance of *The Life of Man* in its sinister gloom caused many suicides among the students of Petrograd (or as it is now, Leningrad).

If so, the play is more powerful than it seems to us or there is something weak about the Russian students.

Several other living or but recently dead Russians are part of the literature of the world but how large a part nobody can yet determine. Kuprin, whose rather happy nature places him with Chekov, and whose skill in the short story and the longer novel, *The Duel,* can be known to readers of English in satisfactory translation; Artzybashef, a queer genius, whose *Sanine* seems to me monstrously untrue, but who wrote at least one story of the failure of a good man in an impossibly unchristian world, *The Death of Ivan Lande.* Korolenko should be remembered for at least one book, *The Forest Murmurs*, which is sentimental but is as good an account of the blind as any seeing person has ever written. But we cannot touch the living and promising writers of Russia. In our limited scope we cannot even see more than ten writers altogether in France, England, Germany, America, who may be remembered a century from now. Russia is a perplexing country; the political and economic life for more than a century, and especially since the great war, has baffled all economists west of Moscow, and at the moment when this book is published official governments do not seem to know whether to treat Russians as civilized people or savages. Meanwhile Russian literature and Russian music and Russian dancing and Russian stage-craft have conquered the world.

CHAPTER XLIII

ITALIAN LITERATURE SINCE THE RENAISSANCE

> You by whom our pain is assuaged,
> Live forever, O beloved arts divine,
> A consolation to our unhappy people.
> —*Leopardi*.

TASSO was the last great genius in the golden age of Italian literature. After him and his time all the arts of Italy declined, and did not revive until the nineteenth century when a new renaissance dawned over all Europe. In the intervening centuries, the seventeenth and eighteenth, literature flourished mightily in England and France because they were, for all their troubles, politically and economically powerful. We cannot say exactly what the relation is between the prosperity of a nation and its art, or of an individual and his creation. But it seems that physical health is necessary to produce the creative vigor which in turn produces art. For two hundred years Italy was torn by internal strifes and battered by foreign enemies. The once strong city republics had exhausted each other, and the Italian spirit wilted and withered and tried to live on the glory of the past. Of all the imitators of Petrarch and the other masters of the Renaissance not one produced ten lines of poetry.

But the spirit did not quite die, and there are several important men to touch on before we come to the second rebirth in the nineteenth century. In the twilight of the Renaissance there were two or three men of talent, in whom, however, glowed no spark of the real divine fire. One was Guarini, whose *Pastor Fido* (*Faithful Shepherd*) continued the tradition of the artificial Arcadia, was read in all the courts of Europe, and influenced for two centuries the pretty literature of the powdered, perfumed, silk-stockinged pastoral. A man of keener intellect was Tassoni, who ridiculed the imitators of Petrarch and whose burlesque, *Secchia Rapita* (*Stolen Bucket*) though long out of date still has some fun in it. Tassoni is not for us, but he is important enough to have commanded the editorial labor of the great modern Italian poet, Carducci. But from Tasso to Alfieri, two centuries, there was no genuine poetry in that sunny peninsula which seems drenched in ages of poetry.

The strength of the late Italian Renaissance is in its prose philosophers, Bruno, Campanella, and Galileo. It is a pity that we cannot linger over the works of these magnificent thinkers. But they belong rather to technical philosophy than to general literary art. Yet who shall say where to draw the line between philosophy and literature? Bruno and Campanella wrote verses which are deservedly forgotten; their power is in their prosaic, their logical thought. Bruno, long suppressed by ecclesiastical authority and by the neglect which obscures and half buries much of the finest thought, has within the last fifty years been recognized as one of the giants of philosophy. His main thought is that the whole universe is an animated being—a thought beautifully developed centuries later by the German philosopher, Fechner.

Galileo was an extraordinary genius, man of science and

man of letters. We know him as the founder, with Coper-
nicus, of modern astronomy. Probably not many readers,
even Italians, know him as one of the masters of Italian prose.
It is only within the last forty years that his essays and correspondence have been collected. In Italian only; so far as I
know, there is no English version of the writings of this
amazing man. The story of Italy's contribution to the sciences, physics, medicine, electricity, and the rest, is still to
be written. In the story Galileo is the most eminent figure,
the most illustrious individual in the long straight lineage of
Italian thought from Greek and Roman masters. This inheritance Italy has kept undefiled until very recent times when
her sons began to go to German universities, where they
learned not the power and profundity of German thought but
its sluggish stupidity; an example is the most distinguished
living Italian philosopher and critic Croce, who is so thick
that he is almost unreadable.

Italian dramatic literature merges very early with music,
and the music soon dominates the words. For three centuries
the whole world has sung and hummed and whistled airs from
Italian operas and not one of us in a thousand remembers
who wrote the words. The genius of modern Italy in the
eyes, or rather the ears, of the rest of the world is no poet, no
novelist, not even the statesman soldier Garibaldi, but the
unrivaled *maestro,* Giuseppe Verdi, whom not even the magnificent Wagner overtops. Music is not in the range of our
brief survey. But we must never forget the close relation
between drama, poetry, and song (song meaning music with
all its highest orchestral developments). All the nations of
Europe (and—who knows?—of Asia, Africa, America) have
made songs. The Italians have been the teachers of the
world in the art of music—even the Germans must concede

this. And here is a matter of interesting speculation (we can never find a sure answer) : Is there any antithetical relation between a certain weakness of Italian verse after Dante and the continuous brilliancy of Italian music? And to carry the question to another country, why should England, for all the lovely folk songs, be rather notoriously weak in music and probably the strongest of all modern countries in the art of verse, strongest in variety of substance and form and in the number of poets of genius?

The modern Italians, as we have said, are direct heirs of the classics. But their classicism is not piously servile. The romantic movement which began in the eighteenth century and reached its climax in the first half of the nineteenth century caught and conquered the Italian imagination. Cesarotti translated the *Fingal* of Ossian, a real or spurious translation from the Gaelic by a Scottish poet James Macpherson. Whether the Scotsman's work was a true translation or a fraud makes no difference. In either case he proved his talent, and his romance swept all over Europe. Perhaps it is worth recording that Cesarotti's version was one of Napoleon's favorite books.

A man of eccentric genius whose genuine literary merit has not been recognized until recent times is Casanova. He was not primarily a man of letters, but in his *Memoirs* he discovered an excellent prose style. It may be that the subject-matter is not for the young and innocent; but for older people who know how to read between the lines and *through* the lines Casanova is one of the great self-revealers who happened to know how to say things, like the English diarist Pepys, and was an artist without knowing it. His reputation increases as time goes by; the English critic and philosopher, Havelock Ellis, has written a beautiful and wise essay about him. His *Memoirs* belong to French literature, but he also wrote in Italian.

Italy has always been rich in comic drama, but in the seventeenth and eighteenth centuries the Italian stage became rather stiffly artificial (so did the French stage after Molière and the English stage after Dryden). There was one Italian genius of merry talent who recreated the comedy of character. That was Goldoni, a native of Venice. His characters are Venetian; more broadly, they are Italian; more broadly still,

GOLDONI

they are universally human. He was well known in France. But English translators seem to have neglected him. Perhaps his plays would not "get across" on our stage, for all their rich and really funny humanity. We can, however, read his *Memoirs*, which were translated many years ago with an introduction by the most distinguished American consul to Venice, the novelist, Howells.

The herald of the new era in poetry, the most important man in serious Italian dramatic literature of the eighteenth century was Alfieri, a man of first-rate dramatic power and sincerity of style. His subjects are mostly classic, Greek legends and ancient history. But the style, although somewhat dependent on Machiavelli, is Alfieri's own, fresh and vigorous, and immensely influential in Italian literature. Alfieri's dramas have never crossed the boundary into English literature. But he is important as dramatist, poet, and prose-writer, and his odes on the independence of America should be known to us (he was a fiery lover of liberty and foe of tyrants) ; so far as I can discover they have not been translated into English.

The most brilliant Italian writer of the eighteenth century was Parini, whose *Day* (*Il Giorno*) is a keen satire and by virtue of its fresh use of heroic blank verse won deservedly the title with which L e o p a r d i crowned the older poet: "the Virgil of modern Italy." In spite of his love of the classic past, Parini was independent and original. A less original and more servile man, but of excellent talent, was M o n t i,

LEOPARDI

whose importance is largely due to the fact that he illustrates the relation of literature to practical affairs. He wrote rather sycophantic poems in praise of Napoleon. But his claim to a high place in literature is his translation of the *Iliad*, which is the ultimate and accepted version in Italian.

With Ugo Foscolo we come in time and spirit well into the nineteenth century. His *Jacob Ortis*, published two years before the new century was born, makes him a sort of Italian

UGO FOSCOLO

Goethe, though of much narrower range than the great German. The book reflects the suffering of Italy under the

double weight of Austria and her accomplice, Napoleon.
Foscolo is a most interesting illustration of the literary relation between two countries that one might think almost at
opposite ends of Europe—Italy and England. A great essay
is still to be written on this relation. Many English poets
lived in Italy and died there. At least one superb English
poet, Rossetti, was of pure Italian stock. Foscolo spent many
years in England and was a recognized and respected figure in
English criticism. His verse is of short compass but excellent.
His *Poem of the Tombs* (*Carme sui Sepolcri*) is a sadly beautiful lyric. His immediate connection with English literature
is his translation of Sterne's *Sentimental Journey*.

And so we pass to a supreme Italian genius of the nineteenth
century, Leopardi, a great poet, melancholy, sad, pessimistic,
but a born singer. We can roughly identify him as the Byron
of Italy, less vigorous and prolific than the English poet, and
more delicate and finished. The magic of him has not been,
probably cannot be, transplanted into English. There is an
interesting and instructive book on Leopardi by an English
scholar, G. L. Bickersteth. But the English verse "in the
meters of the original" is a thousand miles away from the
Italian. Translation should be one of two things, strictly
literal, or re-created art in the language of the translator.
I should dare recommend that we all get a reading knowledge
of Italian if only for Dante and Leopardi.

The romantic spirit in fiction is best represented by Manzoni, who, to make another loosely uncritical but suggestive
comparison, is the Walter Scott of Italy. His novel, *The
Betrothed* (*I Promessi Sposi*) is a first-rate story; it went
into every language of Europe and is still enjoyable, though
it is not such a masterpiece as the Italians like to believe it.
But there is in it something charmingly tender and fine, and

the style of it, over which Manzoni spent many years, has done much to keep Italian prose on a sound basis, when there

was a danger of its flying off into windy rhetoric. He was a man of various gifts. His tragedies are now known and admired chiefly because he wrote them. But his first play, *The Count of Carmagnolia*, independent of tradition and novel in form, caught the eye of that wise man who was always alert to fine things, Goethe. Manzoni was a lyric poet of power, of exuberant splendor. His poem on the death of Napoleon (*Il Cinque Maggio*) is known wherever Italian is spoken. It is worth at

MANZONI

least one line in the briefest story of literature, especially if we are trying to discover the unity of the arts, the continuity of human expression, to record that Verdi's splendid *Requiem* is in honor of Manzoni.

An Italian poet of the middle of the century, a poet of great importance, absolutely impossible to translate, is Carducci. He was both poet and critic and edited with acute skill the older Italian poets—an extraordinary case of a professor of literature who was also an artist. His

CARDUCCI

verse is compact, austere, profound; no modern Italian poet
has excelled him in depth of meaning and perfection of form.

In fiction modern Italy has had several men of talent, but
few of first-rate genius. Perhaps the most distinguished is
Verga, the Sicilian, who is known outside Italy chiefly

THE BETROTHAL
(Illus. for *Don Abondio*)

for his story, *Cavalleria Rusticana,* which is the basis of the text of Mascagni's immensely popular opera.   But Verga's work is greater than that romantic little story; it is the social and emotional history of Sicily and southern Italy.

Of modern Italians we can say but a word.   D'Annunzio is

D'ANNUNZIO

poet, dramatist, novelist, aviator, politician; his versatility and energy are past belief; the most vigorous men of the Renaissance did not excel him in power.   His command of language is stupendous; probably no other Italian of any period has been master of such a vast vocabulary.   There may be in him a touch of the charlatan and poseur, but his work not only captured his countrymen but took all Europe by storm; and surely the man who wrote *The Triumph of Death* (*Il Trionfo della Morte*) and *Fire* (*Il Fuoco*) belongs in the company of the immortals. His lyrics are full of eloquence, on the verge of the danger of verbosity and his dramas are intense and vivid, though somewhat rhetorical. His version of the story of Francesca da Rimini, with Duse as the heroine, is a sensation such as the stage has not afforded many times in our generation—or any other.

Preëminent among Italian dramatists and, with the acknowledged supremacy of Hauptmann, the most beautiful imagination now contributing to the theatre is Pirandello. Of his many plays at least two, *Six Characters in Search of an Author* and *As You Desire Me,* have won American audiences, and several novels, including *The Outcast* and *The Late Mattia Pascal,* are available for English readers. A short phrase for his genius is fantasy made perfectly logical, a dream idea or day-fact completely worked out and realized. Pirandello is also a prolific writer of short stories, some of which place him securely, in degree if not in kind, with Chekov and Maupassant.

The younger Italians, such as Papini and Marinetti, have tried daring experiments in new forms and revolutionary thoughts. A brilliant writer of short stories, not revolutionary but classically perfect in structure, is Giuseppe Errico. One thing seems sure: tastes change and schools come and go; Italy, the violent, the romantic, the country of gestures, will remain on the whole true to its ancient parents, the child of the classics.

CHAPTER XLIV
MODERN SPANISH LITERATURE

'Tis the warm south, where Europe spreads her lands
Like fretted leaflets, breathing on the deep:
Broad-breasted Spain, leaning with equal love
On the Mid Sea that moans with memories,
And on the untraveled Ocean's restless tides.
            —*George Eliot.*

AFTER the golden age which faded out in the seventeenth century, Spanish literature, like Italian, became decadent, without authenticity or originality. And as in the case of Italy I will suggest for study or speculation, without giving a dogmatic answer, the question whether the political and economic decline of a nation is accompanied by a decline of its artistic, its intellectual power. During the eighteenth century all Europe was in a terrible condition. The war of the Spanish Succession involved England, France, Austria, Prussia, Spain, Holland at about the same time that Sweden and Russia were fighting in eastern Europe. Later in the century came the French Revolution which also involved most of Europe. No country was serenely devoted to the things of the spirit. Yet English literature and French literature showed continuous vitality in one way or another

and there was about to be new life in non-Prussian parts of
Germany.   In the other countries literature went flat.

France was the supreme intellectual monarchy on the continent and Spain was one of her most servile vassals.   The
great Spain of laughter and tragedy, of charming natural folk-
song and of good yarn-spinning in the picaresque fashion, lost
its nerve and became a commonplace pupil of Paris.   And even
in the first part of the nineteenth century, when Spain was
trying to throw off the yoke of Napoleon, the peninsula remained the intellectual dependent of its political oppressor.
Strangely enough, in spite of this dependence, Spain, literary
Spain, did not catch the great spirit of France.   The romantic
revival, which glows in most of the thought of Europe and
in the great literatures breaks into flame, kindles in Spain nothing more than a smudge.   The most romantic country in Europe does not catch fire.

The reason, or one reason, is that the Spaniard, for all his
gestures, who seems such a fine stage figure, seems so only to
the rest of Europe, to Hugo, to Mérimée, to John Sargent, to
the literary tourist.   The Spaniard takes himself most literally
for granted in his best books and (I hazard this at the risk of
rousing painters and art critics) in his painting.   So that
when about the middle of the nineteenth century Spanish literature picks up and becomes important in the literature of
the world, the new men are novelists and dramatists, much
more "realistic" than "romantic" in their fidelity to the Spanish life which they draw but, of course, universally romantic
in feeling and treatment, or the world would never have heard
of them.

The one Spanish dramatist of modern times who has become
part of the literature of western civilization is Echegaray.
He was a strange genius, a mathematician by profession, who

rather late in life determined to try the drama. His singular genius is not clearly of the race of Calderón but is clearly of that inquisitive nineteenth century restlessness, the genius of Ibsen, of Hauptmann, of Bernard Shaw, of a type of theater which seems to be growing stronger in our time rather than weaker—a good sign for truth on the stage and not exclusive

JOSE ECHEGARAY

of the fun of the drama in which the Spaniards were once preëminent. Echegaray is not a humorist except in a grim and laughterless way. His best plays, *The Son of Don Juan* and *The Great Galeato,* are studies of human character intensely "Spanished" but understandable in any part of this round world. And Echegaray became a distinguished figure in universal literature. It is said that his reputation wanes, but there is no branch of literature where fame and fortune are so shifty as the literature of the stage, none in which glory can be more permanent—Æschylus, Shakespeare, Molière. One would like to live a century to learn what posterity will think of the plays of Echegaray, Ibsen, Hauptmann, Shaw. Today they are tingling with vitality. And tomorrow there will perhaps be other dramatists to supersede them.

The Spanish novel, which never quite died—how could it in the country of Cervantes?—came to life again about the middle of the nineteenth century. And its substance was realistic, for, as we have suggested, romantic Spain was not romantic in literature. One of the truth-tellers was a woman who called herself Fernán Caballero. Her best known novel, *La Gaviota* (*The Sea-Gull*) was widely read outside Spain, and though somewhat faded, still survives because it has the essential things, truth to character and scene. There is something of this truth in the work of Alarcón, who carried on the tradition of the picaresque novel, the rambling formless form in which Spanish fiction is at its best. His novel of country life, *El Sombrero de tres Picos* (*The Cocked Hat*) is honest fun. Alarcón is not a great artist but he belongs to the continuous breed of Spanish story-tellers.

After Alarcón in time and in literary development is Pereda, who writes of peasants and sailors and of the scene which is the foundation of their lives, the hills and the sea. He has been called the founder of modern realism in Spanish literature and probably he deserves this title. It should be remembered, however, that one of the virtues of Spanish fiction for three centuries, the fiction of life not of traditional romance, is its realism, its truth to character; Pereda did not invent a new type of story, he inherited it. It should also be remembered that the modern Spanish novel in scene and in the drawing of character is intensely local; this may be a real merit but it has confined Spanish fiction to Spain and very little of it has come over the mountains and become part of the universal literature of Europe.

Pereda is very serious, an austere religious conservative. His contemporary, Valera, is a gayer nature, a mystical sceptic, a man of the world and gifted with charming urbanity. Valera's chief novel, *Pepita Jiménez,* shows both sides of his genius; it is the story of a mystical priest of saintly aspirations which go to pieces in the presence of fact, a large part of the fact being, of course, a woman. Valera was already known as poet and essayist before at the age of fifty he took his contemporaries by surprise with his first novel. After that he repeated himself—in real Shakespearean fashion—by improving his art in novels and short stories. And he lived till the end of the century when he was regarded as the dean of Spanish letters.

Younger than Pereda and Valera and leading the way for many of the still younger Spaniards is Galdós, who marks the transition to contemporary fiction. But every man of talent is a transition, for no man begins or ends any literary movement, not even Dante or Goethe; it is transmission rather than transition. Galdós went for his subjects to the history of the nineteenth century, and in a series of novels made a sort of epic: *Episodios Nacionales.* The limitation is that the epic quality, even the good romantic novel stuff, does not seem to be in the actual material; it remains provincially Spanish—when all Europe was involved. But there are good stories there, exactly what he called them, *episodes,* and he had the gift of drawing character. Beside his historical tales he wrote a score of novels on many subjects, and he has been compared to Balzac and Dickens, because of the variety of his people and his sense of story and his humor.

It has been brought against Valdés, who belongs to the second half of the last century, that he is too much influenced

BENITO PEREZ GALDOS

by the French. The inter-influence of literatures is good and not an infringement upon national rights. Great writers have been expert thieves. Valdés is by instinct a fine artist and he has a closer relation to the French novel than most Spanish writers, who, as a rule, lack French precision and shapeliness. His *Espuma* (*Froth*) and *La Fe* (*Faith*) are realistic studies of modern life with an excellent strain of irony.

A woman of genius who may fairly be called the George Sand of Spain is Emilia Pardo Bazán. She resembles her French sister in her enthusiasm for the country and country people. In *de Mi Tierra* (*Of My Country*) she writes with a vivid glowing sense of scene—the scene is northwestern Spain—and observant sympathy with characters sometimes not attractive in themselves. In this novel and in others, such as *La Madre Naturaleza* (*Mother Nature*) she takes her place among the so-called naturalists. I do not find that these novels have been translated into English, though it is likely that we have versions of some of them. For there has been a multiplying interest in Spanish fiction among English and American writers and publishers—which means readers.

The novel, or any form of narrative, is the type of literature that acclimates itself most easily under other skies than its own. And it is of course the prose narrative that is most easily rendered. Spanish poetry of the nineteenth century has not made much impression outside Spain but has been rather under the influence of foreigners. Espronceda, a young poet of the first half of the century, was a disciple of Byron, as were many of the young poets of continental Europe. He was naturally attracted to Byron, being a swaggering, adventurous revolutionist, mixed up in all the political and bellicose turmoil of his time. That he was a born poet and that his many activities were only part of a fiery, gallant and impudent nature, the other part of which went ringing and dashing through his poetry, all intimate readers of Spanish verse attest.

A poet who in the middle of the century seems to have

made a great impression in Spain and to have crossed the mountains and perhaps the sea (for a large part of the Spanish world does not live in Spain) is Campoamor. He is, quite simply, a symbolist, as poets have been for many centuries. In a kind of short poem which he repeated many times—he gives it a critical name which does not help us to get the essential stuff, any more than does sonnet or ode or ballad— he sings that there is a relation between the thoughts of people and everlasting ideas. I leave this notion to my readers and to wiser students of Spanish than I: Campoamor was a reader of Horace, Ovid, and Juvenal. I find no translations of the Spanish poet in English, though there are probably fragments scattered through the later English poets. For as I have suggested, the interest in Spanish literature among English-speaking people is increasing.

There is no doubt of this interest when we come to the most modern Spanish fiction. As in the case of the other modern literatures we cannot say very much about our Spanish contemporaries. It seems to me that the living reader should shake the furnace down for himself. Not that any man can take care of the furnaces of the whole world. But all intelligent readers together can take part in the sifting process.

Of the emergent writers among living Spaniards, the man who most faithfully sticks to his trade, his business, his art as novelist, is Pío Baroja, whose *Feria de los Discretos* (*Marketplace of the Discreet*) gives a sense of a city and of many streets and back alleys and of conflicts between people, or escapade and adventure. And Baroja has a feeling for the rather hopeless opposition of the different social classes, for example, in a novel (the title of which in English, *The Quest*, is not the Spanish at all. but the text of which is good enough) he gives the contrast between the night life and the day life, both unhappy, of a modern city.

In general, the younger men are in rebellion against the established social and political order, and it has been said by the best British critic of Spanish literature that the Spanish

BLASCO IBANEZ

artist is always spoiling his art by mixing it with politics. This may be so, and yet in other countries some of the best and bravest of artists have taken their sword or pen in hand against a kind of government they did not like or for one that they did like. Recall Victor Hugo, the Cavalier poets of seventeenth century England, Tolstoy and almost every other Russian! One asks what is the relation of poetry to

politics. However that may be, one of the most interesting
men of modern Spain, not very well known, I think, in Eng
lish translation, is Unamuno, who, essayist, satirist, journalist
poet, achieved the glory of being exiled from his native land
Exile is a form of punishment that is not much practiced by
modern governments in the case of men of letters. For i
adds immediately to their reputations, ideas now shoot al
round the world, a man worth exiling may be assumed to
know how to write back.

Another Spaniard who is in rebellion against the govern
ment is that immensely popular writer, Blasco Ibáñez. I an
told by competent critics that in Spain he is regarded as a
joke. Well, he is a very good joke. *The Four Horsemer
of the Apocalypse,* which made his international reputatior
(or confirmed it, for several of his books before that had beer
translated into English and other languages) contains excel
lently touching and dramatic scenes, cleverly devised to ap
peal to the allied human heart while everybody was suffering
in or from the war. But since we are allowed to joke, w
may quote from an essay on Blasco Ibáñez by the late W. D
Howells: "Ibáñez achieves effects beyond the art of Henr
James, below whom he nevertheless falls so far in subtlet
and beauty."

Mr. Howells, who loved Spain and read many Spanish
books, might have found a subtlety and picturesqueness i
two of the contemporary Spaniards, Valle-Inclán and J. M
Ruiz, who calls himself Azorín. Valle-Inclán is a delicat
artist, author of *The Pleasant Memories of the Marquis o
Bradomín* and a fine trilogy on the Carlist wars. Azorín i
author of *Las Confessiones de un Pequeño Filósofo* (*The Con
fessions of a Little Philosopher*), a book of wit and worth, and

estined (if we may play with destiny) to get into the library
f the world. There is much in contemporaneous Spanish
iterature of promise and of achievement. We can merely
uggest it and then jump into an airplane and travel to a
country which long ago political Spain did not treat kindly

CHAPTER XLV

DUTCH AND FLEMISH LITERATURE

To men of other minds my fancy flies,
Embosom'd in the sea where Holland lies.
Methinks her patient sons before me stand,
Where the broad ocean leans against the land.
                                        —*Goldsmith.*

MOST of the writers touched on in this small chapter lived before the nineteenth century. So that we are violating our chronological plan. But this seems to be the most convenient place to put the chapter, which, oddly enough, is not of much importance.

For Dutch literature is not important. Two learned Dutchmen who have generously given me advice on this subject agree in an almost contemptuous attitude toward the literature of their country, especially the later literature. The most casual visitor to the galleries of Europe (and America) will be struck by the richness of Dutch painting. During the Renaissance Italians were the only competitors of the Dutch and Flemish artists. The Italians were immensely great in all forms of literature. But the Dutch put their whole strength into other arts than letters. It may be that the Dutch language was not highly developed but remained thick and inflexible like the neighboring German languages until modern times.

Two of the greatest of Dutchmen did not write Dutch but Latin, Spinoza and Erasmus. Erasmus, the humanist, the friend of Thomas More, whom we have met in an earlier

SPINOZA

chapter, tended, like all humanists, to set back the clock and check the growth of modern languages. Because to the humanist all virtue resided in Greek and Latin. Erasmus was a man of learning in a real sense: he loved literature, classic literature and the literature of the Church especially, for in that he found what he thought was truth, like most of the men of his time (remember that the year 1500 divides his life of seventy years into two equal parts). Much of the classicism of men of the Renaissance was not pagan, not Greek or Latin, as an old Roman would have understood it, but Christian. The best side of Erasmus is in his letters and *Colloquies*, dia-

ERASMUS

logues on a great variety of subjects. It would not be bad criticism if without saying a word of comparative values we put Plato's *Dialogues*, the *Colloquia* of Erasmus and Landor's *Imaginary Conversations* on the same shelf and looked at them together.

About a century after Erasmus died there was born in Amsterdam one who was neither Christian nor pagan but Jew-

ish, Spinoza. He is one of the founders of modern philosophy, with Bacon, with Descartes, with Bruno. Spinoza belongs, as I suggested, doubtfully in our record, for he is a
strict, difficult, technical philosopher, writing a rather condensed scholastic Latin, which Latinists tell me is sound and
accurate. The thinker is there; the man of letters with a
touch of the artist (Erasmus had it, so did Bacon, so in our
day did Nietzsche, Bertrand Russell, William James, Santayana) is lacking. His method is a kind of philosophic
geometry, propositions laid down and numbered, with proofs,
corollaries, axioms. He went into oblivion for a hundred
years until about the beginning of the nineteenth century philosophers and men of letters rediscovered him, Herder,
Lessing, Novalis, Goethe, and he is now one of the heroes
of philosophic thought. And perhaps he is not altogether
lacking in the literary touch. The title of one part of his
Ethics (in the English translation, of course), *Of Human
Bondage,* was taken as the title of one of the deepest and finest
novels of our time, by W. Somerset Maugham.

In Dutch as in all literatures we must go for the most savory
stuff to the folk tales, the ballads, the popular romances.
Holland contributed at least one, a poetic version of the universally popular *Reynard the Fox,* by Willem the Minstrel.
This is one of the earliest versions of the famous story; it was
translated by Caxton from a prose version, undoubtedly
Dutch, into English. These legends, romances, satires passed
from one country to another. It was only a question, and it
is now in fiction, poetry, criticism, only a question, of the skill
of the adapter, of the importer. In the Middle Ages there
was no sense of literary proprietorship. A writer took an idea
wherever he found it without saying by your leave. *Reinaert*
(*Reynard the Fox*) seems to be the only great story of which

the Dutch version prevailed and it had an immense vogue. The most spirited modern version is Goethe's *Reinecke Fuchs*.

An important medieval mystic whose religious writings have come down to us is a Brussels friar, van Roesbroec, who lived in the fourteenth century. The Belgian poet, Maeterlinck, has written about him in *The Treasure of the Humble* and has translated (into French) one of his works: *La Beauté des Noces Spirituelles*.

An illustration of the international exchange of ideas is the Dutch morality *Elckerlijk* which is without much question the original of the greatest of English moralities, *Everyman*.

Another example of the international exchange of ideas, of especial interest to English readers, is the connection between the first poet of the Renaissance in the Netherlands, van der Noot and Spenser. The relation is obscure, like most Elizabethan literary biography, but the Dutch poet seems to have been instrumental in introducing to the young English poet the work of du Bellay and Petrarch.

The greatest Dutch writer is the poet Vondel who was born late in the sixteenth century and lived through three-quarters of the seventeenth. He wrote tragedies which combine dramatic power with lyrical beauty. On one hand, since he dramatized heroic stories from the Bible, he has been compared to Racine. On the other hand, his masterpiece *Lucifer* allies him to Milton. It is likely that Milton had at least a scholar's knowledge of the great Dutch drama. But it is doubtful if he derived anything from it. *Paradise Lost* and *Paradise Regained* and *Lucifer* have nothing in common except the subject and the elevation of style. The two poets have quite different methods of treatment, *Lucifer* being dramatic and lyric, Milton's poems epic narratives. An excellent account of the poet and of his political and religious background is the biography of Vondel by Professor A. J. Barnouw.

After the age of Vondel Dutch literature declined and most of the work of the eighteenth century is utterly dull. The revival came toward the end of the century and the beginning of the nineteenth. The forerunner of the new era was Bilderdijk, a didactic poet, whose clever verses were immensely popular in Holland, but have not made any impression in other countries. In England he would have been among the secondary rhymesters. He was a very learned man who commanded the respect of so good a judge as Robert Southey. But a notion of his sense of beauty can be deduced from the fact that he thought Shakespeare puerile and detested the new poetry of Germany.

In spite of Bilderdijk's opposition to German romanticism, it made its way into Holland, largely owing to the universal influence of Goethe which no country escaped, and a contemporary influence was English romanticism, chiefly in the novels of Scott. But the new era was not very brilliant and Dutch literature became conventional. The rigidity of the verse forms was broken up by a young poet, Jacques Perk, who died at the age of twenty-one. His posthumous poems showed an original talent and deep feeling and roused the enthusiasm of the younger men who formed a sort of school round his memory.

By far the most eminent figure in contemporary Dutch literature is Louis Couperus, whose verses show him in sympathy with the young school but who is less important as poet than as novelist. His fiction, which has been widely translated, has, so to speak, put Holland back on the literary map of Europe. His best known work in English, excellently translated, is a series of four novels called *The Books of Small Souls.*

Allied to Dutch literature is Flemish which has a peculiar vitality on account of the political situation. When Belgium was separated from Holland in 1839, the Flemish turned against everything Dutch and cultivated French and Flemish. The government tried to suppress Flemish as an official language and that had the effect of stimulating the cultivation of it by writers and scholars. The first fruits of this movement were the novels of Hendrik Conscience. His first story, *In the Wonderful Year,* dealing with the War of Dutch Independence, stirred the patriotism of his countrymen and established the literary dignity of modern Flemish. He wrote many stories of Flemish home life and became a national hero. By his fidelity to life he took his place not only as the leading novelist in Flemish literature but as an important figure in European literature. But this fidelity is highly idealistic and romantic. A novelist of quite different method, the naturalistic, is Sleeckx, who gets his effect by precise accurate observation and accumulation of detail.

It is one of the ironies of history that Flemish writers are at least as much admired in Holland as in Belgium. Intellectually Flanders and the Netherlands are no longer separated. And in Belgium as a whole with its dual culture it is French not Flemish which dominates.

CHAPTER XLVI

SCANDINAVIAN LITERATURE

Skoal! To the Northland! *Skoal!*
—LONGFELLOW.

 SOME years ago an English critic said that Norway with less than three million people counted for more intellectually than the United States with a hundred million people. Such comparisons are rather futile but in this one there is at least a half truth: it is remarkable how many men of genius there have been among the Scandinavians. We have seen how the Icelandic branch of the Norsemen early developed a great literature. The modern Scandinavians have certainly lived up to the traditions of the ancient islanders. Let us look at Denmark first.

The founder of modern Danish literature was Ludwig Holberg. He was born in Norway, but at the time of his birth, the end of the seventeenth century, and until the beginning of the nineteenth century, Norway belonged to Denmark and Norwegians wrote Danish or more often French or German. Holberg was a satirist and humorist of the first rank and in his time was equaled by no other European except Swift and Voltaire. His humorous narrative, *Peder Paars,* is the first

Danish classic and its wit is still relished by Danes. He founded the Danish theater with a long series of comedies. Before him on the Danish stage only French and German plays were given. Holberg taught his people to laugh in their own language. He was more than a humorist. He was one of the most learned men that ever lived and he wrote serious treatises on a great variety of subjects in a firm straightforward style which was the first and final education for Danish writers. His influence is still active after two centuries, and it extended outside Denmark, of course to the other Scandinavian countries and to Germany. He influenced Lessing whose play, *Der Junge Gelehrte,* is a close imitation of Holberg's *Erasmus Montanus,* and since Lessing was the father of the modern German stage, Holberg has at least an indirect influence there. A selection of his plays is published in English translation by the American-Scandinavian Foundation, that admirable institution which has done so much to open to the English-reading world the rich Scandinavian library.

The greatest poet of Denmark is Oehlenschläger who lived from 1779 to 1850. The dates here, almost exactly the dates of Wordsworth's life, are important, for they cover the period of the romantic movement which completely dominated the literature of every country in Europe. Oehlenschläger was the leader of the romantic movement in his country. His inspiration came from Goethe and Schiller. But he was not imitative in style or substance. He went back to the old legends of his ancestors and turned them into romantic tragedies and narratives in a spirit partly antiquarian, partly patriotic, and wholly poetic; his worship of the past and his enthusiasm for old poetry resemble the spirit of Scott. Before he was thirty his countrymen unanimously recognized him as the foremost Danish poet and his fame went to the other Scandinavian countries and to Germany. In Sweden he was crowned "Scandinavian King of Song" by Bishop Tegnér, himself a fine poet. Only Holberg has had so great an influence as Oehlenschläger, and like Holberg he gave his native tongue a new elevation, and he also gave it what it had seldom attained before, tragic dignity.

Thanks partly to the great impetus which Oehlenschläger gave to the romantic movement it continued to be strong through most of the century, and there were several great poets, Grundtvig, Hauch, Winther, Herz. These names are not well known to us, because Denmark is a small country and few foreigners take the trouble to learn Danish. But there is one poet whose name and work are known all over the world—Hans Christian Andersen. What child in any country has not read or listened to some of his *Fairy Tales?* Many of them are traditional folk-tales; others he invented. To all he gave a peculiar flavor, his humor, his tenderness, that artless simplicity which is very exquisite art. Let any reader who happens to have (as every household ought to have) the Fairy Books edited by Andrew Lang, the Red, the Blue, the Yellow and the rest. Read any tale from any source— many of them are well written—and then turn to the same tale, or any other, in Andersen; the reader will find that few of the fairy fables, not even the famous and excellent *Kinder- und Hausmärchen* of the brothers Grimm have quite the charm of Andersen. What the charm is it is hard to say —that is one of the secrets of genius. Andersen wrote much besides the *Fairy Tales,* poems, travels, novels, and fantastic stories in the manner of the German Hoffmann. But he is one of those fortunate authors, like Cervantes, whose greatest work is so great that we forget the other good things he wrote.

A generation later than the romantic poets, but still a romantic as every imaginative poet must be, is Drachmann, who was born in the middle of the nineteenth century and lived

DRACHMANN

into the twentieth. He began his adult life as a marine p a i n t e r, but dropped the brush to take up the pen and paint the sea in words. He is a sort of Danish John Masefield. His heroes a r e sailors and fishermen. He became a patriot of a wholesome sort and by celebrating the lives of the people in vigorous poetic plays he made himself the recognized head of the Danish theater. He made long voyages to study aspects of the sea and the characters of sea-faring folk, thus ever refreshing his substance and keeping it vital and real. But one can know the sea for a life time and not be able to express it. To be a Conrad or a Drachmann is given only to him who has poetic genius which is not outside on great waters but inside the man.

Of the prose writers of the second half of the nineteenth century there are several of great distinction. Jens Jacobsen was the greatest prose artist that Denmark produced. He was an invalid and died young and wrote with painful care. Like Flaubert, he spent hours seeking the right word, the right rhythm. The result is two novels of such beauty as Denmark had not seen before, *Marie Grubbe* and *Niels Lyne,* also a volume of short stories called by the first one, *Mogens.* Although he wrote so little, his influence has been great and his perfection set a standard for all Danish and Norwegian writers who cared for beauty, style, art. And his influence extended beyond Denmark. He was translated into German and at least in part into English.

After the untimely death of Jacobsen the leading novelist for a while was Schandorph, a realist who made close observations of country people and the lower middle classes of the city. His best novel is *Little Folk.* Another novelist who belongs to the naturalistic school is Herman Bang. His best novel, *Near the Road,* is a work of depth and

GEORG BRANDES

power. Mention should be made of Edvard Brandes, whose reputation has perhaps suffered a slight eclipse from the fact that he is the younger brother of the great critic Georg Brandes. But Edvard is a critic of great ability, a playwright,

and author of two novels of distinction. A little later came
the great novelist who is in time and spirit our contemporary,
Pontoppidan, of whom probably most English and American
readers never heard until he received the Nobel prize in 1917.
Here again is an illustration of the restrictions imposed on a
great literature which is the creation of a small country. Pontoppidan is a novelist of such power and sympathy as we find
among the great Russians. His finest novel, *Lykke-Per,*
though it deals with simple people and has not a touch of
heroics, is epic in its proportions.

Presiding over these poets and novelists, steering them
straight and welcoming their best is Georg Brandes, the most
learned and catholic critic in Europe for more than half a
century. The range of his knowledge is enormous; he seems
to have read everything ever written in Europe. He has written many studies of individuals, Shakespeare, Ibsen, Anatole
France. His monumental work, his philosophy of criticism,
is *Main Currents in Nineteenth Century Literature.* It is
now complete in English in six volumes. It is the best possible introduction to the literature of the last hundred and
fifty years. Readers of Danish say that his style is charming
and lucid. I can well believe that, for the English translation is clear and fluent. His countrymen, even when they
disagree with him, hold him in highest respect, and he is
probably the best known critic in Europe, all countries included. I cannot do better than quote from him a paragraph
which sums up the characteristics of Danish literature and
German. It is pertinent to remember that Brandes looks at
the Danes from a somewhat detached point of view, for he
is not a Scandinavian but a Jew. He says in *The Romantic
School in Germany,* which is the second volume of *Main
Currents:*

"To the Danish authors, as a body, may be attributed the merit of avoiding the fantastic, tasteless extravagances of which the Germans are frequently guilty. The Danes stop in time; they avoid paradox or do not carry it to its logical conclusion; they have the steadiness due to naturally well-balanced minds and naturally phlegmatic dispositions; they are hardly ever indecent, audacious, blasphemous, revolutionary, wildly fantastic, utterly sentimental, utterly unreal, or utterly sensual; they seldom run amuck, they never tilt at the clouds, and they never fall into a well. This is what makes them so popular with their own countrymen. Unerring taste and elegance such as . . . characterizes Oehlenschläger's and Hartmann's best works, will always be prized by Danes as the expression of noble and self-controlled art. . . . Think of Hoffmann, and his pupil, Hans Andersen, and observe how sane, how sober and subdued Andersen appears compared with his first master."

Norwegian literature is inseparable from Danish. After the political separation at the beginning of the nineteenth century there was a movement to establish an independent Norwegian literature. Many of the great men in Danish literature were Norwegians, and some over patriotic Norwegians are trying to get them back, which is as futile as trying to determine whether Henry James and John Sargent were Americans.

Modern Norwegian literature may be divided into three periods, The Forerunners, The Age of Ibsen, The New Movement.

The forerunners were two poets, Wergeland and Welhaven. Wergeland may be called the creator of Norwegian literature though no man does anything alone. He was a wildly energetic and enthusiastic poet, an eloquent revolutionist, a sort of northern Rousseau. But he never mastered style. Obscurity and willfulness impeded his teachings and his thought. Some of his lyrics are very beautiful. He died young after having done a prodigious amount of work. Welhaven was a conservative, a champion and exponent of clearness. He attacked the extravagance of Wergeland in a vigorous pamphlet. His contention for moderation, for lucidity, had an excellent influence on Norwegian thought and style, and his authority is still great. For he is more than a critic, he is a poet, and his poems on old Norse themes are established classics in Norwegian literature.

The age of Ibsen includes Björnson, Jonas Lie, and Kjelland. Lie and Kjelland are novelists of first-rate ability. Of the two Lie is the more powerful. He was the foremost novelist of his generation and his first great book, *The Pilot and His Wife,* made him undisputed leader of Norwegian fiction. His novels were widely popular at home and won a considerable reputation abroad. Several of them have been translated into English: *One of Life's Slaves, The Commodore's Daughter, Niobe.* His strength lies not in any high astounding scenes but in his quiet observation of ordinary people.

Ibsen is the supreme dramatist of the last hundred and fifty years and no writer of plays in any country can dispute his eminence. In the dramatic literature of the world he is with Æschylus, with Shakespeare, with Corneille—this is not to institute comparisons but to indicate greatness. His dramas are of two kinds, lyrico-romantic and realistic. The poetic dramas are on the whole early and the prose dramas late. Among the poetic dramas are *Brand* and *Peer Gynt,* which raised Norwegian literature to the level of the best in Europe. *Peer Gynt* is a fantastic satire not only on the Norwegian

IBSEN

IBSEN

nation but upon universal human nature. It is a classic that belongs to the world, and its greatness has been confirmed by the gorgeous music of Grieg. The first of Ibsen's realistic prose plays to attract much attention is *A Doll's House,* in which a woman asserts her right to herself in revolt against the old idea that the wife is servant of the man. It was discussed all over Europe, and though "feminism" is now an old story and most of its problem literature has faded, Ibsen's play is still vital. His next provocative play is *Ghosts* which deals with the inheritance of disease. That play is rather out of date because it is unsound biology. It was furiously attacked and Ibsen as furiously returned the attack in a play called *An Enemy of the People.* Ibsen is sometimes treated as if he were a problem seeker and propagandist trying to reform society. He was as far from any such intention as he was from founding a medical school or starting a new religion. He was first of all a dramatist looking for dramatic effects and he cared for society only as it furnished him material. This is evident in *Rosmerholm,* where the problem is simply dramatic, the contest between a weak man and a strong woman, and it is evident in *Hedda Gabler,* a striking play if the title part is played by such an actress as Nazimova; here is no social problem but an individual situation. In his later plays he becomes poetic again, not with the poetry of his youth but with a wise and thoughtful symbolism. This is best seen in *The Master Builder* and in a strange play which closed his career, *When We Dead Awaken.* We have all the plays in English translated by William Archer. Those who enjoy pungent and very sound criticism will wish to read a small book by another dramatist, G. Bernard Shaw, called *The Quintessence of Ibsenism.*

Ibsen concentrated all his thought on poetry, drama and

the theater.   His contemporary, Björnson, a man of lesser genius, scattered his power not only over every form of literature but over the vexed field of politics.   He is at his best

BJORNSON

in the novel and never surpassed his early tales of peasant life, *Arne* and *A Happy Boy*.   These made him famous in many countries.   Like Ibsen, he had a practical knowledge of the stage and was manager of the Christiania Theater. His plays have action and speed and where the author is not in too much haste they have many fine poetic passages. His heroic dramas based on Icelandic legends, *Sigurd the Bastard* and *Sigurd the Crusader* place him among the great poets of the century. His comedies are amusing. He had much

KNUT HAMSUN

more humor than Ibsen or at any rate humor of a more genial sort. In his twofold capacity as poet and political reformer, in his fiery zeal for republicanism, which resulted in his being accused of treason, he reminds us not a little of Hugo.

Ibsen and Björnson and Lie lived long and continued to be the leading literary figures after they were dead in the flesh.

But the younger men were already arriving. Garborg, the son of peasant parents, wrote stories in the peasant dialect. He did not get a hearing until he wrote in the ordinary language a remarkable novel called *Tired Men*. A romantic novelist of delicacy and distinction is Thomas Krag, whose best known story is *Ada Wilde*. Popular in his own country and recently well received in English translation is Bojer, who combines the romantic with the satiric. But the towering figure in recent Norwegian fiction is Hamsun. He has written forty novels, many of which are masterpieces, notably *Hunger* and *The Growth of the Soil*. He writes of the hard side of life—"sordid" is not the word for it—and he writes bitterly, but his bitterness is cleansing, antiseptic. More important, he writes with a rugged beauty, some of which comes through in translation.

Swedish literature has a long history. It did not begin at any definite time as did Danish and Norwegian. But this much definition is possible: in the seventeenth century when Gustavus Adolphus brought the country to its highest military and political development, literature, which had been flat during the sixteenth century, began to flourish. There is at least one great writer in the century, Stjernhjelm, "the Father of Swedish poetry." He found the language rough and made it smooth and adapted it to many forms of verse. Another poet, Rosenhane, brought the Renaissance into Sweden in a cycle of sonnets based on French models. During the eighteenth century Sweden was intellectual vassal to France and England both in prose and in verse, and we find no great name in literature. But there is one great name which it is not impertinent to mention, though it lies outside our province, that of Linnæus, the first genius in botany. As in other countries the ideal of literature in Sweden during the eighteenth century was academic, formalistic, but with no genius approaching the academics of France and England. And as in every country so in Sweden there was a revolt against the academics early in the nineteenth century and the romantics finally won the day. In the Swedish romantic movement there was one great poet, Tegnér. In 1835, Longfellow, who was studying in Sweden, wrote: "Sweden has one great poet and only one. That is Tegnér." Longfellow's translations from Tegnér are very interesting, poetic, and metrically dexterous. Like most of the romantics Tegnér found his

richest material in the past, in ancestral legend. His chief work is *Frithiof's Saga*, which carried his name all over Europe and secured for him a place for which he was totally unfit, that of bishop.

In this period, the first part of the nineteenth century, there were many lyric poets and prose writers of real distinction. The prose writer and poet most widely known is F r e d e r i k a B r e m e r. Her novels, *Sketches of Everyday Life, The H Family,*

ESAIAS TEGNER

Neighbors, The President's Daughter, caught the heart of her own people and through a good translation by Mary

Howitt went all over the English speaking world. They are sentimental, but the sentimentality is not mawkish. She is as honest as George Sand, but much less interesting. She was a vigorous propagandist for the emancipation of women, but fortunately that worthy zealotry did not spoil her stories.

Miss Bremer was a Finn. The foremost Swedish poet of the middle of the century, Runeberg, was also a Finn, in place of birth if not in blood. He wrote mostly of Finnish subjects and lived in Finland most of his life. He achieved great popularity. An obscure schoolmaster in a small college in Finland, he was the recognized poet laureate of Sweden, second only to Tegnér in modern Swedish poetry and first after Tegnér's death. We have some selections from his lyric verse in English.

STRINDBERG

During the middle of the century Swedish prose was lifeless and conventional. As compared with Norway and Denmark Sweden was backward. Toward the end of the century there came a kind of renaissance due to the influence of French realism, Norwegian drama in the person of Ibsen, and Danish criticism in the person of

Brandes. The most striking figure in the new literature is Strindberg, an eccentric genius of immense power. Ibsen, so the story goes, looking at a portrait of Strindberg, said: "There is one who shall be greater than I." Ibsen and Strindberg in their outlook on life are quite unlike. In Ibsen's finest plays the woman has an independent mind and strives for emancipation even if she does not realize it. Strindberg, on the other hand, is a woman-hater, violently hostile to the feminist movement. In his best novel, *The Red Room*, which depicts the lives of poor struggling artists and authors, it is always the women who cause the ruin of the men. His short stories called *Married* are so deliberately aimed at woman and marriage that they lose their effect as art. Strindberg's work is very uneven, at its lowest coarse and crude, at its best rising to the highest poetic beauty. One virtue prevails through it all, its unflinching honesty, the will to see things as they are and to record them without fear.

In singular contrast with Strindberg is Selma Lagerlöf, the most eminent woman among

SELMA LAGERLOF

Swedish writers. She has a tender sympathetic imagination. The book which made her famous and which she never surpassed is *The Saga of Gösta Berling*. A delightful book for children—and for grown people—is *The Wonderful Journey of Nils* which would have pleased Hans Christian Andersen; it narrates the adventures of a small boy who flies through Sweden on the back of a wild goose. Selma Lagerlöf has become a world figure; her books have been translated into many languages, most of them into English. She is greatly admired and honored at home and is the only woman ever elected to the Swedish Academy. Another distinguished woman is Ellen Key, a philosopher and critic rather than an artist, but very important in the literature of modern Sweden. Her *Love and Marriage* and *The Century of Childhood* are valuable contributions to the problems of sex and of education.

The most influential writer in Sweden is Verner von Heidenstam, an idealist in direct opposition to Strindberg. He is a lyric poet of the first order, an excellent critic and in his prose romances, *Endymion* and *Hans Alienus,* he gives the lie to realism. It is fitting to leave the Scandinavian countries on a note of romance and idealism.

CHAPTER XLVII

AMERICAN FICTION

A tale which holdeth children from play and old men from the chimney corner.

—*Philip Sidney.*

E have seen how at the end of the eighteenth century and the beginning of the nineteenth there was a glorious outburst of romanticism both in poetry and in prose. The master of romantic fiction in English literature was Walter Scott, and he was soon followed by the people's elected king of laughter and tears, Charles Dickens. The leaders of the romantics in France were Victor Hugo and Alexandre Dumas. In Germany Goethe, the greatest poet and critic of his time, had given intellectual dignity to the German sentimental novel. Soon after his death in 1832 Goethe was being vigorously introduced to English readers by Thomas Carlyle. In Italy Alessandro Manzoni took his place among the world's tellers with his novel, *The Betrothed.*

Meanwhile what was happening in the young republic across the Atlantic? America had become politically independent and was living a vigorous life of its own. But intel-

lectually it was, and still is, part of Europe, not only of England, whose language Americans spoke and wrote, but of the
continent of Europe from which many of our people came.
American contributions to the art of literature were romantic
because all Europe was writing romance. And, strange as it
may seem, our lusty young country did not express itself in
wild and woolly tales of startling novelty. Except James
Fenimore Cooper, the American writers of fiction who
charmed our great-grandfathers are notable for their delicacy
and highly cultivated manner.

Washington Irving, welcomed by Thackeray as the "first
ambassador whom the New World of Letters sent to the Old,"
was a shy and dignified gentleman with a roguish twinkle in
his eye. He began his literary career with a sparkling bit of
humor, a burlesque *History of New York,* the pretended
author of which was a descendant of the old Dutch settlers,
Diedrich Knickerbocker. The name, Knickerbocker, has
stuck to New York City, and the old man in the cocked hat
is still the figure that modern cartoonists draw to represent
the largest American municipality. In his last peaceful years,
when Irving was recognized at home and abroad as the dean
of American letters, he was amused to note that there were
already Knickerbocker insurance companies and Knickerbocker bread and ice!

Another figure that Irving made immortal is also Dutch,
Rip Van Winkle. The story of good-for-nothing Rip, whom
the goblins got and who slept for twenty years, has become one
of the legends that everybody knows. It is based on a German
tale, but Irving localized it in the Kaatskill Mountains of
New York State and made it native American fiction. Those
goblins are the ghosts of Hendrik Hudson and his crew,

and when it thunders on the banks of the river that bears his name we know that they are playing nine-pins in the clouds.

A fantastic and humorous game of nine-pins, with Irving as smiling spectator, is a pleasant picture of the beginning of American fiction. Before him Americans had tried to write stories, but they are not of much value and are almost forgotten. Before him, too, there had been something like what we think of as American humor in the writings of Benjamin Franklin, but Franklin was a philosopher and essayist, not a professional story-teller. Just what American humor is and how it differs from the comic sense of people who do not live in the United States is a question that nobody has answered in a satisfactory way. When Irving was at the height of his literary power and after a long residence in Europe returned to the United States, he made a tour of the western part of his native country. He could not know, as he passed through Missouri, that a boy was born, or about to be born, who was later to be known as Mark Twain. Is there any relation between Irving and Mark Twain except that they were both born on the same continent and wrote the same language? It is an amusing question to think about, but not one to be settled.

Irving, the citizen of New York and the biographer of the father of his country, after whom he was named, took pride in his nationality. But he was cosmopolitan in spirit, free from narrow provincialism. He spent many years in England, and some of his best stories, those in "Bracebridge Hall," are laid in English scenes and might have been written by an Englishman. He also lived in Spain. The fruits of his residence there were *The Conquest of Granada* and *The Alhambra*, sketches of Moors and Spaniards, full of color and adventure. One reward that Irving received for this work was the appointment to the post of Minister to Spain.

As man and as artist, Irving was refined, sensitive, gracious, everywhere admired and beloved. In contrast with this gentle serene humorist and historian was his most famous contemporary in American literature, James Fenimore Cooper.

Cooper was a vigorous, ill-tempered man, rough and pompous in his personal bearing and in his literary style. He quarreled with his neighbors, took himself with top-lofty seriousness, and had not a spark of humor. Yet this stormy, awkward man, who could not write two pages without doing violence to the English language, has held for a century the imaginations of all readers of romance in all countries. He is known in Europe, even in Asia. And is there an American schoolboy who has not read *The Spy* and *The Last of the Mohicans?*

It is the story that counts. And Cooper was a story-teller. He had the gift of invention and he had first-hand knowledge of life on land and at sea which gave him the stuff for thrilling tales of adventure. Central New York State, where he was born, is now a region of thriving cities; it was in his day almost a wilderness; his red Indians and white pioneers, woodsmen, hunters, and trappers lived near the town that his father founded. He actually knew them or made them up from material which lay within the range of his observation. He had been to sea and had learned American sailors and ships so thoroughly that he is the acknowledged authority on the American merchant marine of a century ago.

Civilization has pushed the wilderness hundreds of miles north and west of the territory through which Natty Bumppo, Leatherstocking, hunted with his long rifle. The Indians have disappeared, and their few peaceful descendants are on reservations. Ships of the type that Cooper knew are as obsolete as a stage coach. But Cooper's forests still flourish in literature, not many miles from Irving's Sleepy Hollow. It is no wonder that European boys who visit America expect to find red Indians a short distance from New York City, just as an American boy visiting Scotland hopes to catch a glimpse of Rob Roy.

Forests vanish and the wilderness recedes. The eternal sea remains unchangeable, though it has many moods and the ships that sail it have grown from wooden barks to Mauretanias. Cooper must have caught the everlasting qualities of the great waters, for every writer of sea tales in English has saluted him as captain of the whole fleet. The finest tribute has been paid to him by Joseph Conrad, who is the greatest living * writer of romances of the sea. Cooper, says Conrad, "loved the sea and looked at it with consummate understanding . . . the colors of sunset, the peace of starlight, the aspects of calm and storm, the great loneliness of the waters, the stillness of watchful coasts, and the alert readiness which marks men who live face to face with the promise and the menace of the sea."

Cooper and Irving found romance in the external adventures of life, in what happens to people from the outside. Two younger romancers, Nathaniel Hawthorne and Edgar Allan Poe, were more concerned with what happens to people from the inside, their mental and spiritual adventures. They were both melancholy men without the genial fun of Irving or the athletic power of Cooper.

Hawthorne came honestly by his deep interest in the souls of men. For he was descended from the New England Puritans, and though he was not a Puritan himself, he brooded, like his ancestors, over problems of conscience. But he brooded as an artist, studying conflicts of character in order

* He died, alas, since this paragraph was written.

to make stories of them, whereas the old New Englanders were not artists at all; they were solemn prosy folks who had not much sense of beauty, who, indeed, seemed to believe that anything beautiful must be sinful. Hawthorne turned them inside out and made them entertaining in spite of themselves.

His father and grandfather were sea captains in Salem, Massachusetts, which was once a bustling port. He might have gone to sea and written nautical romances. Instead of sailing a literary ship, he remained on land and, as his friend Ralph Waldo Emerson said about him, he rode a dark horse, and rode it well. For some time after he graduated from Bowdoin College he lived in seclusion writing short stories and carefully polishing his style. It is an excellent style and some of the stories are little masterpieces. But for a long time the American public did not give his work a very cordial welcome. Only a few literary men, including Edgar Allan Poe, appreciated his merits. Hawthorne called himself the obscurest man of letters in America.

However, he finally won popular approval with *The Scarlet Letter,* his first long narrative, which was published in 1850, when he was forty-six years old. The success of this now world-famous romance surprised both the author and the publisher. Hawthorne thought that it could not appeal to the broadest class of sympathies because it "lacks sunshine." The publisher issued five thousand copies and then had the type distributed; in a few days the edition was sold and the book had to be set up again to meet the continued demand. This illustrates a great and important fact in the story of literature that when a work of genius first appears some readers may see its value at once, but nobody, author, critic, or publisher can guess how other people are going to judge it. Time alone is

THE SCARLET LETTER

the only safe and sane judge, and Time plays queer tricks with books, as with everything else.

If *The Scarlet Letter* lacks sunshine, it is full of purple clouds and shadows and mysterious moonshine. The pathos of the story of Hester Prynne moved Hawthorne profoundly, and some of his readers were so affected that they wrote to him as to a father confessor asking for help in their sorrow and temptation. We do not take the moral burden of the story quite so hard as that. For us Hester has become one of the lovely unhappy heroines of romance, like the unfaithful nun in Scott's *Marmion,* like King Arthur's Guinevere, like Helen of Troy. Hawthorne was the first maker of tragic myth in American literature and he remains the most important one.

In his second long story, *The House of the Seven Gables,* Hawthorne plays upon a theme which has always been a favorite with writers and readers of mystery tales. It is a haunted house, occupied by perturbed spirits in the flesh and by the ghosts of the past; and there are musty documents hidden behind secret panels. It is the sort of stuff that has been used so many, many times that it has lost some of its thrill. But Hawthorne put the stamp of his genius on commonplace material. His haunted house stands after many weaker ones have fallen.

Hawthorne was not so much interested in the houses that people inhabit and that ghosts haunt as he was in the souls that inhabit the people and the ideas that haunt the souls. And upon the country that surrounds the house he looked only with the eye of a painter in words. He thought that America was not an inspiring country for a writer of romance, because, he said, "there is no shadow, no antiquity, no mystery, no picturesque and gloomy wrong." Yet he seems to have been somewhat mistaken, as men of genius often are, and to have disproved his belief by his own creations. If he did not find picturesque and gloomy wrong ready made, he invented it which is, perhaps, only additional proof of his originality. When he went outside New England, to Italy, "a sort of poetic or fairy precinct," for plot and scene, he did not do his best work. *The Marble Faun,* fine as it is, is not so enchanting as the stories that he laid in a real or imaginary New England.

High up on the side of a mountain in New Hampshire is a group of rocks that form the gigantic profile of a man. It is one of the natural wonders of the world and is a familiar sight to tourists. Hawthorne made The Old Man of the Mountain peculiarly and characteristically his own. He imagined what its effect would be on a sensitive boy who should grow up under its shadow, and so in his tale *The Great Stone Face* he conceived it as a symbol, an inspiration. He translated the stone into a poetic sermon. Before Hawthorne wrote, New England may not have been a "fairy precinct," but after he wrote, Romance adopted it as one of her permanent abodes.

Cooper and Irving and Hawthorne lived to see their work widely accepted and to enjoy as much practical prosperity as an author can ask for. They never lacked a coat or a meal or a comfortable bed. Their younger contemporary, Edgar Allan Poe, who died before them, struggled all his short life with poverty, and it was not until after his death that the world recognized him as the greatest American man of letters. No other American has had such a powerful influence upon the literature of Europe. In 1909, the hundredth anniversary of Poe's birth, every competent writer from New York to Moscow would have acknowledged his debt or the debt of his country to the genius of Poe.

Poe was more than a romancer. He was poet and critic as well as the creator of a new and original kind of short story.

But it is fair to treat him as a romancer if for no other reason than that the story of his life is itself a romance and Poe is a sort of real-fictitious hero, a subject for novels and plays. The theme of the story appeals to a feeling in us, which may or may not be peculiarly American, our admiration for a man who makes his way against hard circumstances. We like the self-made man, in business and politics. Of course no man is self-made, but if we accept the term in its usual meaning we may justly call Poe a self-made author. He was born with talent, no doubt, but he fought to keep his talent pure and make it prevail amid discouragements and difficulties.

When Poe was twenty-four years old he won a prize of a hundred dollars, offered by a Baltimore paper, for a short story called *Ms. Found in a Bottle*. The story is remarkable for two things. It revealed at once Poe's command of his style and method. And it is probably the only story he ever wrote for which he was well paid. For Poe made his meager living not by his finest fiction and certainly not by his poetry, but by laborious journalism and routine editing. He was a careful and scrupulous craftsman, and he could not do hasty work merely for the sake of the money which he so sorely needed. The history of literature records many cases of poverty and hardship and sacrifice of material welfare to high ideals of art. But there is no example more honorable to the literary profession than that of Poe. He was a proud man, arrogantly sure of his ability, happy in the knowledge that his best work was stamped with immortality. It would be untrue to his spirit to whine about his poverty or to accuse the world in which he lived of neglecting a man of genius. But there is one little scene, or fact, which dramatizes his life. For a few months he had been a cadet at The United States

POE

POE

Military Academy. Sixteen years later, when his wife was
dying, the only covering for her bed was his army cloak.

Poe's stories deal with mysterious situations and with the
still more mysterious effects that situations have upon the
mind. His absorbing interest was in what it is now the fashion
to call psychological. He created the detective story long
before Sherlock Holmes and Arsène Lupin were born. To
him a detective story was not at all a question of whether a
criminal was caught and punished; it was wholly a question
of how the logical part of the mind acts in the presence of a
fact. Not only did he invent detective stories, the best of their
kind, *The Purloined Letter* and *The Murders in the Rue
Morgue,* but he took an actual case, the mystery of which
remained unsolved at the time when he wrote, and turned it
into a piece of fiction, *Marie Roget,* the plot of which later
proved to be an almost exact parallel of the real events. Poe
was very vain of his own power of ratiocination, as he called
it, and he believed and proved that any puzzle, mechanical or
intellectual, which one mind can contrive another mind can
disentangle.

We seldom find in literature a poet and dreamer like Poe
whose intellect is so highly developed in its capacity for pure
reason. Not that there is any hostility between reason and
poetry. Quite the contrary. We know that Dante and Shakespeare and Goethe were capable in all departments of thought.
But it rarely happens that all kinds of ability are given to
one human brain. As time goes on we realize more and more
surely that Poe, cut off in his brilliant prime before he had
reached the full height of his power, was one of the few
supreme intellects.

Poe's skillfully reasoned mystery tales are perhaps only
clever tricks, though in three-quarters of a century no other

writer has been clever enough to surpass him. His most beautiful prose is found not in his ingenious yarns but in pieces
which have an immediate effect on the emotions and sensations, like poetry or music. Such pieces as *Legeia* and
Shadow are perfect. If Poe was not the originator of that
sort of prose-poem—every original creation can be traced to
something earlier—he is the still unrivaled master of its
enchanting magic.

The poet Swinburne, who was himself a magician, called
Poe "the complete man of genius," "who always worked out
his ideas thoroughly, and made something solid, rounded, and
durable of them." Poe was complete in two senses. He perfected his ideas, bringing each to its final form. And he had
great versatility. His short stories are sufficient to give him
distinction. But even without them he would be remembered
as critic and poet.

Some of Poe's criticisms have lost a little of their interest
because the books that called them forth were of slight importance and, but for his comments, would be forgotten. Yet
even in a passing newspaper review he often expressed some
thought of permanent value in literature. His literary essays
taken together have more light and learning than those of any
other American of his day. They constitute for the general
reader and for the professional student the best account of
American literary thought before 1850. And let it be remembered to his everlasting honor that he maintained for himself
and for others standards of fine work amid surroundings that
were far from favorable. He carried his banner almost alone,
and there were few of his contemporaries who had the courage and the strength and the right kind of humility to follow him. It is the excellence of his criticism quite as much
as the wizardry of his stories or the loveliness of his verse

that makes it a matter of never-ending wonder to European critics that Poe lived and wrote in America. He is an example of the strange truth that a great intellect can be born in any environment, and nobody can explain how or why it happens. It is one of the romantic mysteries of life which Poe himself could not have reasoned out to a satisfactory conclusion.

Among the writers of the first half of the century is one of great importance in her time and still memorable, Mrs. Stowe. *Uncle Tom's Cabin* made an impression beyond any dream or intention she had while she was writing it. Lincoln with more gallantry than historical accuracy called her "the little lady who caused this great war." Tolstoy, who was always looking for moral issues in fiction, admitted it to the very limited list of books which he called true art. It seems to me art of a secondary order, for it is special pleading, propaganda, not serene enough to lift it above the burning issue which inspired it. But except for some old-fashioned moralizing, it is not badly written, the story moves, the genuine passions triumph over the obvious sentimentalities.

In the generation which came to maturity after the Civil War are three writers of first importance and several of real though lesser merit. The three are Mark Twain, Howells, and Henry James.

Mark Twain is the most original of all our writers and the most deeply and broadly American. Howells called him the Lincoln of our literature. No other writer is comparable to him in the extent of his knowledge, his digested, meditated knowledge, his understanding of so many phases of American life. He was born in Missouri, which is middle-western and half southern, he lived for some time in California and for many years in New York and Connecticut. He travelled all over the world and knew all sorts and conditions of men. A notion recently current among younger critics that his wings were clipped, that the respectability of American life kept his genius from expressing itself fully is simply nonsense. No writer was ever better fitted to interpret the country in which he lived, and no country ever had a writer better equipped to interpret it. He said all that he had to say, he knew how to say it, and circumstances fostered his genius.

He began as a newspaper man in Nevada and California and achieved a local reputation as a humorist. His newspaper sent him as correspondent on an excursion to Europe and the Holy Land and his letters constitute his first important book, *Innocents Abroad*. This is not a funny book. It has much fun in it and a good deal of the fooling is somewhat cheap. But most of it is honest, independent, serious observation and report of actual experience. The sober passages are in excellent prose, and he discovered in some passages a sense of beauty which developed as he grew older, wiser, more reflective. There never was a better reporter of travel; his keen eyes saw through everything and he had a born genius for realizing and communicating a scene. This special talent is exemplified in later books, *A Tramp Abroad* and *Following the Equator*.

In fiction his masterpiece is *Huckleberry Finn*. It is solitary in his work, for *Tom Sawyer* does not compare with it, though Mark Twain, who had no critical sense, seemed to prefer the lesser book to the greater. *Huckleberry Finn* is solitary in American literature; there is nothing like it in extent of scene and variety of narrative interest. It is not solitary in the literature of the world if we think only of magnitude, for there was at least one great humorous novel of wandering and adventure called *Don Quixote*. *Huckleberry Finn* is more than the story of a boy, and it is not a book for boys, though young readers enjoy it, as they enjoy *Gulliver's Travels* without knowing what it means. Through the innocent eyes of

MARK TWAIN

Huck we see an entire civilization (or lack of civilization), we get an almost epic view of the geographical center of the country at the center of its history. In Mark Twain's lighter fiction there is a good deal of fun, some shrewd observation of character, but a disappointing unevenness of workmanship, and signs of impatient haste. The value of *Pudd'n-head Wilson* is almost wholly in the "Calendar" which Mark Twain continued as chapter headings in other books, aphorisms as keen and brilliant as have ever been uttered. In *Joan of Arc,* which is fiction of a sort, there is much beauty and a sustained dignity. But best of all (next to *Huckleberry Finn*) are two satirical stories, *The Man That Corrupted Hadleyburg* and a curious parable published after his death, *The Mysterious Stranger.* Mark Twain had a deep strain of Swiftian bitterness, tempered, like Swift's, with pity, and often when he is laughing loudest he is most savage. *A Connecticut Yankee in King Arthur's Court* is superficially a somewhat amusing farce with a touch of parody. At bottom it is a study of democracy and a violent attack on human stupidity. It is there that Mark Twain expresses the wish that the whole human race might be hanged.

With his marvellous command of language, his bitter indignation, and his deadly skill in ridiculing what he hated he was a great pamphleteer and readers who overlook his occasional essays of protest miss one of his most manly and admirable aspects.

It may be that much of the fun of Mark Twain will grow stale; some of it is ephemeral, foredoomed to oblivion except as his other work keeps it alive. But the serious Mark Twain is a classic as sure of immortality as any prose writer of the century. When he speaks his mind directly without the intervention of any conventional literary form as in *Life on the Mississippi,* he is a master of style. He is the prose laureate of our democracy—as he would say, what there is of it.

Associated with Mark Twain on one side, the California side, is Bret Harte. He exploited the pioneer life of the western coast for the entertainment of readers on the eastern coast. And he did it very well. His gamblers and miners are sentimentalized and he seems to have taken lessons from the weakest parts of the genius of Dickens. But he wrote good prose, he knew the art of the short story, and he was skillful in touching romantic emotions. He was very prolific and most of his work is already forgotten, but such stories as *The Outcasts of Poker Flat* are still fresh. One work of his I trust will not be forgotten, for it is excellent humor and first-rate indirect literary criticism. That is the two series of *Condensed Novels.*

The official dean of American letters during the last half of his long life, the friend and tactful schoolmaster of the unruly Mark Twain and the patron of promising talent in the younger generation, is William Dean Howells. He is an amiable personality, an artist to his finger tips, from his first work to his last a master of style. To find a bad sentence in Howells would be as surprising as to find one in Flaubert or Anatole France. But Howells is timid. He lacks power; reticence of the "reticent realism" which he preached and practised is not the fine restraint of art by which intelligence subdues passion. It is a vacant reticence because Howells has nothing in him to be reticent about. Of his many novels— he was an industrious as well as a most scrupulous craftsman— three or four come near to being works of genius. *A Modern Instance,* in which commonplace little people are shipwrecked because they are little was something entirely new in American fiction. *The Rise of Silas Lapham* was perhaps the first novel to have for hero an ordinary business man. A later novel, *The Kentons,* is one of his best and seems to me not to be as heartily appreciated as it ought to be even by consistent admirers of Howells. He thought that he was under the influence of Tolstoy, but there is no more trace of Tolstoy in his work than there is of Fielding in Hawthorne.   Howells was a tremendous reader and he wrote well about books. Whether you agree with him or not you are in the company of a thoroughgoing man of letters.

The supreme American novelist is hardly American at all except by birth.   That is Henry James, who spent most of his mature life in Europe and whose outlook is European, cosmopolitan.   He is one of the prose masters of the century, a superb artist with only one serious limitation: he is an incurable snob, not a mean one, for his nature is most generous and sympathetic, but an intellectual "shut-in," with no knowledge of life except what can be learned in a hotel drawing room and an art museum, and, of course, a well appointed library.   That limitation granted, he is a profound student of human character, that is, to use the scientific word, a psychologist.   He is said to be the inventor of the international novel because many of his characters are Americans in Europe, but a real international novelist would play the game both ways and show the European in America.   However, the European in America is usually a workman and the American in Europe is usually an idler, and that is the class that James knows.   His work is divided into two periods.   To the first belong the excellent story *Roderick Hudson,* the title-hero of which is a weak-willed American sculptor; *Daisy Miller,* a genuinely pathetic tale of an innocent American girl who does not understand the sophisticated morality and immorality of the old world; *The Portrait of a Lady,* a rather poignant study of American cheek, freshness and vulgarity (vulgarity is a favorite word with James; he uses it so often as almost to make it vulgar), and also of spiritual tragedy finely conceived; *The American,* a true tragedy, the hero of which is a real man, unsophisticated but intelligent, caught in a situation which is too much for him.

In his second period James grew more and more subtle and complex to the great delight of his limited circle of sincere admirers and to the disgust of those who have not learned his method. This method is a complete objectification of character. The persons of the story move about in what may be quite ordinary circumstances or unusual and trying situations. First one, then another trait or characteristic flashes out from the circumstances. If the reader follows the novel all the way through, he will find that the novelist has built up for him a complete human character.

HENRY JAMES

Two novels which illustrate this method are *The Wings of the Dove* and *The Golden Bowl*. James takes his time in his novels and traces the development of some motive through many pages. But he is also a master of the short story. A volume containing eight or ten of his best briefer works of fiction would be quite without rival in the literature of our time. He is also a penetrating critic of French and English literature. If he had not turned to fiction he would be among the foremost writers of literary essays.

The story of a country is told not only by a few writers of genius but by many lesser narrators whose work all put together constitutes its social history. America is necessarily divided into intellectual provinces. How is one man to know the Vermont farmer and the Georgia negro? A few of these secondary story-tellers hold what should be a permanent place in the social record as it is preserved in the art of fiction. T. B. Aldrich, a poet of considerable distinction, wrote some charming short stories, of which *Margery Daw* is the best known. There is not much in that whimsical bit of American life. But there is excellent humorous art. The same is true of the tales of Frank Stockton, whose most famous tale is *The Lady or the Tiger?* The life of the south found expression in the fiction of several writers of real ability. Cable discovered romantic material in the old creole life of New Orleans. The negro is immortalized in Harris's *Uncle Remus.* An important phase of the Middle West is preserved in Edward Eggleston's *Hoosier Schoolmaster,* the first American novel in which a local dialect is carefully studied (for it was published several years before *Huckleberry Finn*). The people and the landscape of New England are drawn for all time in the delicate stories of Mary Wilkins-Freeman and Sarah Orne Jewett. I do not know in the work of any other American writer a better story of humble people than Mrs. Wilkins-Freeman's *Revolt of Mother.*

Of writers who died but yesterday the most memorable is Stephen Crane, whose short life ended with the nineteenth century, the most talented American writer of his generation. His *Red Badge of Courage,* a story of the Civil War, may be somewhat dimmed by the more terrible war that has intervened but the art of the story cannot fade. Another man of talent who died young is Frank Norris, an honest realist, who showed a growing power to handle large themes. His great subject was the epic of wheat. Of living novelists, the finest artist is Edith Wharton. Her scene is New York or the country places where well-to-do New York people spend the summer. She is an aristocrat, highly intelligent, a trifle snobbish, but fundamentally sympathetic. In *Ethan Frome* and *Summer,* she deals with the tragedy of the New England country with a grasp as firm as that of Mrs. Wilkins-Freeman at her best. Many of our story writers seem to be under the spell of O. Henry, a man of real talent and excellent humor, a born story-teller, ingenious and inventive, but deficient in point of style, too journalistic. To suggest the defects of this very clever man, the reader has but to turn back to the O. Henry of an earlier generation, H. C. Bunner, and see how good fooling can be conveyed in a vehicle perfectly finished and civilized. Human substance combined with literary art are the elements of fiction which is to live beyond its day. I find signs of growth in the human substance of American fiction and abundant examples of competent technique. Of the younger writers (yet old enough to be established) those who have the finest sense of words are Willa Cather (*O Pioneers!; My Antonia; The Song of the Lark*) and James Branch Cabell (*Beyond Life; Jurgen; The Rivet in Grandfather's Neck; The Cream of the Jest; Figures of Earth*). Joseph Hergesheimer also has a feeling for beauty, notably in *Linda Condon.* Theodore Dreiser, crude, ungainly, lives in at least three of his books (*Sister Carrie; Jennie Gerhardt; An American Tragedy*) by his immense power, his sympathy with human beings, his integrity and courage. Sinclair Lewis made "Babbitt" almost a common noun in the language and he all but renamed the Main Street of any ordinary western town "Lewis Avenue."

CHAPTER XLVIII

AMERICAN ESSAYS AND HISTORY

America is beginning to assert herself to the senses and to the imagination of her children.

—*Emerson.*

DURING the nineteenth century the intellectual center of America was Boston and the neighboring towns, Cambridge and Concord. New England did not have exclusive control of American thought. There was an active literary life in New York and Philadelphia. Irving and Cooper were sons of New York state; and Poe, the straying genius from no-man's-land, lived during his few most productive and relatively prosperous years in New York, from which stronghold he made sharp attacks upon the New England supremacy. But that supremacy was a fact as definite, in its drab way, as the supremacy of Florence in Italy. Boston used to be called, in humorless praise or derision, the Athens of America.

It is certain that the thought that radiated over America and has not yet lost its mild glow came from a small group of thinkers in a small provincial civilization. There is a disposition in our time to underrate that civilization, and indeed it had many weaknesses. Its poetry was feeble, lacking both originality of substance and command of form. The only true artists in prose were Hawthorne and Holmes. The limitations of the few memorable individuals are obvious and have been card-catalogued and accounted for. Yet the group of New England writers, taken together, did express and create a genuine culture which extended beyond New England and became national so far as nationality was possible in a country of widely disparate, even hostile sectionalisms.

The leading thinker of the time was Emerson, son of a long line of Puritan preachers, a liberal revolter against the austerities of his forefathers and the refined distillation of their virtues. The virtues that he taught and exemplified are simple: self-reliance; optimism, but not ignorance of the rougher facts of life; serenity; geniality; faith in man and in the God who dwells in the heart of man, not the God of the formal religions.

Emerson's essays and addresses are sermons; he was a preacher all his life, though he resigned from the Unitarian ministry and was not for most of his life an adherent of any creed or sect. In tone and substance his sermons are far above dull pulpit-pounding; their eloquence is natural and sincere, and the wisdom is enlivened by poetic illustration, analogy, shrewd epigrammatic phrasing, and humor. Hundreds of Emerson's sentences are quotable for their sagacity, pith, compact finality of expression.

One reason for the pungent richness of his thought is that he knew how to select and assimilate from other writers the idea exactly suited to his purpose. "Next to the originator of a good sentence," he says, "is the first quoter of it." That expresses an important part of his talent. Yet he was not imitative or derivative in a secondary sense; he thoroughly Emersonized everything he touched. The charm of voice and personality which captivated his contemporaries is lost to us, but there is a vocal persuasiveness in his printed words. Open to any page of the *Essays,* or the *Conduct of Life* or *Representative Men,* or *Society and Solitude* and you will hear a man talking. The ideas are grouped under broadly

EMERSON

abstract titles, such as *Nature, Politics, Compensation,* but the ideas themselves are direct, specific, clear.

Emerson had no interest in systems and logical arguments, and it has been said that his essays have so little constructive unity that they can be read backwards. They are strings of pearls, which can be counted from either end of the string. But the pearls are genuine. Or, to change the figure swiftly, as Emerson often did, the underlying personality of the man gives unity to detached thoughts. There have been more profound and orderly philosophers; there have been essayists whose literary art was finer; his poetry, though it contains a few excellent lines, has clipped wings and does not fly among the immortals. Yet Emerson's greatness is undeniable. It is himself. He illustrates his own saying that "the best of beauty is a finer charm than skill in surfaces, in outlines, or rules of art can ever teach, namely a radiation from the work of art, of human character." And he suggests himself, though he was too modestly humorous to intend the personal application which we make of it, when he says in one of his most oracular utterances: "Beware when the great God lets loose a thinker on this planet."

God seems to have let loose several thinkers in that small corner of the planet which is New England. One was Emerson's friend and neighbor, Thoreau, who had little influence on his generation but whose genius is more and more widely recognized as new readers find him out. His chief book, *Walden,* is the record of his life for two years in the woods near Concord, an experiment in solitude and self-reliance. He proved that he could live independent of society and that he and nature were sufficient unto themselves. The charm of the book is Thoreau's hearty enjoyment of the life that he chose to lead and was free to lead. "Every morning was a cheerful invitation to make my life of equal simplicity, and I may say innocence, with Nature herself." The Nature that he worshiped was indeed simple and innocent, and his observations of the moods of his goddess are direct, primi-

tive, original, without too much display of the technical knowledge of the professional "naturalist."

Thoreau is a moralist rather than a naturalist. Though he
takes a grave delight in the external world, he is chiefly interested in the internal world, his soul and conscience, and
he writes, as he lived, to please and perfect himself. He is
not a misanthropic hermit, but a gentle and highly civilized
man, his mind stored full of the essence of books, of which
he discourses in the intervals between paddling a canoe and
hoeing beans. In one sense he is the least literary of writers,
making his notes in a casual, informal way and depending
not at all materially or spiritually upon the reception which
his readers accorded him. In another sense he is a literary
man with a delicate feeling for style, and master of a style
pure as was ever written and individual though not in the
least cranky or eccentric. The passage on style in *A Week
on the Concord and Merrimack Rivers* is the best short essay
on the subject that I have ever seen not excepting the beautiful essay by Walter Pater. The increasing conservatism
of New England has tended to suppress or diminish the
revolutionary side of Thoreau's thought and to put the
emphasis on his life out-of-doors. He was, however, a political rebel and his essay *On the Necessity of Civil Diso-
bedience,* the leading idea of which is that when government
is organized oppression it is the duty of honest men to op-
pose it, is one of the classics of radical revolutionary thought.
Once when Thoreau tried to carry out a kind of passive resistance and refused to pay taxes, which he believed government used for criminal purposes, he was put in jail. But
he stayed only a day, for a friend paid the taxes, and so ended
the rebellion. When Thoreau died, Emerson thought that
the world had still to discover what a great man he was.

There is something artificial and untrue to the human spirit in dividing men of letters into essayists, poets, novelists, when so many of the most brilliant writers have made their mark in more than one of these divisions of literature. In a few words let us remind ourselves that Poe, whom we consider more in detail as poet and story-teller, was a first-rate essayist; and I will not dispute with any reader of Poe who regards some of his essays and "miscellanies" as the most shining moments of his extraordinary genius.

Poe's brief and twisted life was slightly warmed by the sunlight of journalistic notoriety and partial recognition of his really fine achievement. Emerson went his serene way as a sort of unofficial parson. Thoreau lived mostly by and for himself, making lead pencils for a living, in his essays touching now and again on public affairs but taking no practical part in them. There were two of the New England essayists who enjoyed, whatever the enjoyment may have been, a more radiant career in the world, Lowell and Holmes.

Holmes was a physician, professor of anatomy in the Harvard Medical School, a Boston aristocrat with a house on Beacon Street. He knew how to turn a light verse with wit and ease. But the gods did not intend him to be a poet. They made him an essayist and a very good one. *The Autocrat of the Breakfast Table* with its delightful rambling manner and its multitudinous variety of subjects is as fresh as when it appeared in the *Atlantic Monthly* more than sixty years ago and entitles Dr. Holmes to a secure place in the company of Montaigne and Lamb. He was gifted, as his friend Lowell neatly said of him, with "Fame's great antiseptic, Style."

And Lowell himself had the gift of prose, much more

authentic to my ear than his slender talent in verse. Lowell
was a well-bred man of the world, professor of literature
at Harvard but never academic, minister from the United
States to Great Britain, a considerable figure in his time.
The range of his interests was extraordinary. There is nothing better than his essay on Chaucer. And at a time when
people were in doubt about that strange man from Illinois
and the conservative politicians were giving advice which
later proved superfluous, Lowell understood Lincoln, "sized
him up" with final wisdom. I will say a word presently
about the only part of his verse which seems to me still vital.
For the moment take a look at that supremely humorous
and very Yankee essay, *On a Certain Condescension in
Foreigners.*

America has been very rich in men who were makers of
history or writers of history and knew how to express themselves. Among the makers of history who had the gift of
oral or written speech are Franklin, Jefferson, Webster, Lincoln. My selection, to which other readers will immediately
add, is determined—if we can separate one department of
human thought from another—by purely literary standards,
not by the judgments of political history.

Franklin's *Autobiography* and his occasional papers and
letters are not perhaps of high importance in the history of
literature, but they portray in a smug way an honest and
humorous character and they have a peculiar literary interest
because Franklin, a practical man who today would be an
"efficiency expert," wishing to perfect his style, studied Addison's *Spectator* and so, without losing his own vigorous personality, learned how to write.

Jefferson's state papers and correspondence are of more

than merely historical interest. He may have been perversely wrong or eminently right in his political theories and practices. That does not concern us here. He had in his nature a touch of the artist, and the Declaration of Independence, which he composed, is a model of clear and eloquent phrasing.

Daniel Webster is still worth remembering as a figure in public life. For us he survives by virtue of his literary style, a spoken style in its first form, for he was a professional orator

THOMAS JEFFERSON

of a school which has now gone out of fashion. There is nobody capable of carrying it on—the most eloquent congressman nowadays is rather ridiculous when he tries it. Many of the issues of Webster's time are dead; only students of history will wish to dig them up. But two or three of his speeches are still alive, for example the Bunker Hill oration, which should be part of the education of every American boy. The style, for all its rhetorical flourishes, is solid and pure. By the testimony of his contemporaries Webster was an impressive speaker with an effective voice and dignified bearing. Carlyle, who was not too friendly to political orators —or to Americans—speaks of Webster's "crag-like brow." He did not always win his case, for sometimes his case was inherently weak, but he won a sure place among the world's orators who are also men of letters.

Lincoln very early in his career developed an admirable literary style. He arrived at it by hard study and not, as the Lincoln story of popular legend tells us, by a divine gift miraculously bestowed upon an ignorant man. He was finely sensitive, highly intellectual, deliberate, cautious, meditative, uncommonly gifted with that rare thing miscalled common sense, to which was added a slight mixture of superstition and prophetic vision. That roughly explains, not the states- man who belongs to history, but the style of the man who belongs to literature. Read again the Gettysburg Address and see it for what it is, a short prose-poem, a work of art. In a few words he expresses the essential emotion of that moment, and he does it without flourish, without screaming in a quiet, calm style, with rhythms carefully designed for the effect which he intends to produce.

Most of Lincoln's writing is in grave earnest, for he had laborious problems to solve. But he had a fair measure of humor which was salt to his style and was, moreover, a practi cal defense against office-seekers and bores. To protect him self he made them laugh. When he called his cabinet to gether, not to ask their advice but to tell them what he had made up his mind to do about the Emancipation Proclama

LINCOLN

tion, he first read them some pages from Artemus Ward. But he was by nature and by circumstance, after the war began, a sad man, miles away from the smart politician who tries to get votes by telling his audience a funny story. One of the lessons to be learned from any study of the art of expression is that a man who has a definite aim and personality, though

he be a politician whose policy we disapprove, will learn how
to use words. Cæsar, Cromwell, Napoleon, Bismarck, and
Lincoln (remember I group them only from the literary point
of view) were masters of style, the kind of style adapted to their

work and so adapted that
it is still living. Without
a hint of that over-per-
cented Americanism
which seems to me very
bad for criticism, for art,
for life, I will drop a suggestion for my readers to
consider: that of all statesmen in the world—recall
Pitt, Disraeli, Gladstone,
whom you will in France
—Lincoln had the finest
and strongest literary
touch.

The professional his-
torians in America have
done excellent work. I
mean those historians
who are in the holy

PARKMAN

temple of literature rather than those who are doing extremely
good work in documentary history. Washington Irving in
his studies of American and Spanish history was more than
the gentle humorist who created Rip and Father Knicker
bocker. He yielded with magnificent courtesy to Prescott
a young man, hampered by partial blindness, who had begun
to study and write the history of Mexico. That book made
Prescott's reputation. He went on to a study of *The Con*

quest of Peru and then to a history of *Philip the Second.* I understand from later historians that much of his work, as history, has been superseded, but that he did not go wrong in his facts, as far as they were procurable. His books are readable—I give the testimony of a literary man, not of an historian.

Mark Twain said in laying out a list of books that he valued: "A thousand volumes of Parkman, if he wrote that many." Parkman was interested in the northwest of America and in the strife between Englishmen and Frenchmen before our republic began. There may be more learned histories than *La Salle* and *Montcalm and Wolfe,* and a strictly scientific historian would score Parkman rather heavily as a romantic. But the subjects that he handled were essentially romantic, and his books are, if not accurate to the last statement, fascinating to the last sentence.

CHAPTER XLIX

AMERICAN POETRY

I hear America singing, the varied carols I hear.
                                                —*Whitman.*

F all forms of literature, of all specimens of the forms written on the
northwest side of the Atlantic Ocean
American poetry has least of the
stuff, the color, the peculiar vitality
of the continent on which it was
made. Except Whitman, whom
many readers do not find representative of the American spirit, except
also a few poems in local or racial
dialects and some poems that deal
with scenes and subjects that belong
especially to this country, most
American poetry might have been written by the minor poets
of England.

The derivative, dependent and secondary quality of American verse is not necessarily a proof of servility on the part of
American poets but is rather one of the proofs of the overwhelming power of English poetry. We may in our prose
think American, but we have to sing English. Our poets too
often do not feel the country, or the part of the country, in
which they live, as a Frenchman or a German or an Englishman feels his country. There is no question here of patriotism; the Muse scorns patriotism except when she can make

music of it. And after all it is less important that a poet should be American than that he should be a poet.

The first American poet with a sense of verse and honestly emotional substance was Philip Freneau, who lived in the time of the American Revolution. He is remembered for a few short poems in the romantic vein which would be better remembered if there had not been a great century of lyric poetry after him. *The Wild Honeysuckle* and *The Indian Burying-Ground* have a faint poetic flavor.

A poet who enjoyed a great reputation in his day was Bryant. He wrote with the precocity of Chatterton a poem on death, *Thanatopsis,* which is an echo, probably, of the graveyard poets of England, but is his own and well done. Chatterton died young. Bryant, who began by celebrating death, lived to be a venerable, even imposing figure in New York journalism as editor of *The Evening Post.* He continued all his life to write good verse, as mature in technical skill and as juvenile in thought as his first poems. His best work consists of nature poems of a mild loveliness like the lines *To a Waterfowl.*

Not far from Bryant's desk in a neighboring office there worked for a few years the strangest poet in American literature, one of the strangest in all literature, Poe. His poems are contained in a very thin volume (for undoubtedly the labor of journalism took too much of his vitality) but they are all notable for excellence of form, and the best of them, perhaps ten or twelve including *Israfel* and *To Helen* have the mystery, the indefinable magic which is given only to the true poet. Within his limited range Poe is a genuinely inspired poet; his voice is golden and he is minor only in the sense that Coleridge is minor, as are many other authentic poets who sing true but never with the final power of Dante and Shake-

speare. We have said on another page that "minor" is a
unsatisfactory word, even though astronomers use it for stars
it suggests, as applied to poets, some sort of military ranking
from field marshal down to petty officers. The poets resis
all attempts to grade them. There must be something
wonderful in a poet, an English poet, who scales the walled
garden of the most exquisite French poets. Poe did that
Baudelaire and Mallarmé translated him beautifully. And
who that has an ear for English verse can miss the haunting
charm of such lines as these which conclude *Israfel* (Israfe
is the angel whose heart-strings are a lute):

> Yes, Heaven is thine; but this
> Is a world of sweets and sours;
> Our flowers are merely—flowers,
> And the shadow of thy perfect bliss
> Is the sunshine of ours.

> If I could dwell
> Where Israfel
> Hath dwelt, and he where I,
> He might not sing so wildly well
> A mortal melody,
> While a wilder note than this might swell
> From my lyre within the sky.

Poe's instinct and ambition were those of a poet. But w
often find that the poet writes good prose, and when Po
descended to the lesser harmonies he showed his genius, i
his fiction and in his criticism. We have said a word abou
his prose in other chapters and merely remind ourselves agai
that if his lyrics were destroyed the prose writer would remair

The laureate of America was Longfellow. He sat fc
years on the democratic throne, with modest dignity, for h
was the most modest and gentle of men. He wrote man

American legends, like *Hiawatha,* and *Miles Standish, The Wreck of the Hesperus, Paul Revere's Ride*, and he wrote many more (and much richer) translations and adaptations from European literatures. Besides, he made many songs and lyrics which have neither space nor time, for example, the famous *Psalm of Life* which is commonplace matter not raised to the pitch of a true lyric by any miracle of phrase or melody. His *Village Blacksmith* is the kind of thing for the "Poets' Corner" of a country newspaper, but it is technically good, for Longfellow was an artist who understood the management of verse. The masterpiece of this most popular American poet was his translation of Dante's *Commedia.* And the most nearly original things that he wrote in the grand manner were the sonnets that he prefixed to the canticles of

LONGFELLOW

the Italian poet. The explanation seems to be that the New England professor-poets were conscious of their literary inferiority and went to Europe for inspiration. Somehow *The Skeleton in Armor* fails and so does *The Hanging of the Crane.* But *The Belfry of Bruges* is good balladry.

The professor poet who succeeded Longfellow as teacher

at Harvard and maker of bookish verse was Lowell. He also
was conscious of his American inferiority, and took his de-
fensive revenge, not in his verse but in his essay *On A Certain
Condescension in Foreigners.* His verses in classic English
have little savor, and his *Commemoration Ode*, distinguished
by the occasion, which was the dedication of a building at
Harvard University in honor of the students killed in the Civil
War, is mere rhetoric. He accused himself in his loosely
versified *A Fable for Critics* of

> Striving Parnassus to climb
> With a whole bale of *isms* tied together in rhyme

But he happened to be his very best when he let his *isms* have
free play in the *Biglow Papers,* satirical verses in a literary
imitation of New England Yankee dialect. They have
sparkle, humor, and sting, and cut deep into the follies of
American politics. No other satiric verse in America has
kept fresh so long, for satire is a perishable plant which
dies with the contemporary events in which it is rooted, and
American satirists have been writers of prose rather than
versifiers.

Lowell's friend across the Charles River, Dr. Holmes, was
also at his best—so far as his verse is concerned—when he
wrote in a pseudo Yankee dialect, in *The One Hoss Shay*.
The greatest admirer of Dr. Holmes, one who sees at least
the genius of style in *The Autocrat,* cannot take his serious
verses very seriously. But he was clever, witty and genial
in occasional verses in celebration of class reunions and other
such pleasant affairs.

The sage of Concord, Emerson, was primarily a writer of
prose, some of which is eloquent and imaginative. He also

WHITMAN

RUDOLO S.

WHITMAN

wrote verse as so many writers do who are not God-made poets. Emerson said of his friend Thoreau that his myrtle and thyme were not quite converted into honey. That is a good account of Emerson's verse. Yet once or twice Emerson struck a real poetic note, a very jolly and open-air note in *The Honey Bee,* the deeper philosophic note in *Brahma.* The rest of his verse seems to have less of his flashing imagery than his prose.

A friend of these gentlemen of Cambridge, Concord and Boston was a gentle Quaker with more fire in his heart than ever burned visibly or audibly in theirs. That poet was Whittier. Never did so unpoetic a poet try the difficult art since perhaps the English poet Crabbe. Like Crabbe, Whittier had a vivid sense of the life and the scene in which he lived. His religious poetry is flat, as religious poetry is wont to be. His balladry is often simply bad literature, but sometimes it has the folk-accent, as in *Skipper Ireson's Ride.* His approach to a masterpiece is *Snow Bound* which has the chill and seclusion of the old New England winter. The scenes are true and roughly well phrased. Whittier burned to be a poet, had the impulse to expression, but as he said of himself in an ingenuous poem, he suffered from "the harshness of an untaught ear."

While the older men were growing old and established, (and Poe in his comparative youth was dead) a great poet almost as old as the acknowledged veterans was being gradually discovered and appreciated. Walt Whitman was called the "Good Gray Poet" because in the second half of his life he was indeed gray. But his *Leaves of Grass* was the youngest, most audacious and challenging book of verse published in this country. It is a curious mixture of crudity and beauty. The magnificent lines and sequences of lines are powerful. The worst lines are as bad as any poet ever wrote, but even they are redeemed by a kind of consonance and coherence with the whole book. For *Leaves of Grass* is a whole book, the poetic life of a man for many years. Whitman celebrates democracy. He celebrates himself as an interesting person—and he was. In his middle period he cele-

LONGFELLOW'S HOUSE

brates Abraham Lincoln in noble verse. There was a kind of foreordained relation between Lincoln and Whitman. Howells called Mark Twain the Lincoln of our literature, and he made the right association; for Lincoln would not have understood Whitman as a poet; Lincoln's sense of verse was far below his own instinctive or cultivated sense of the poetry of prose. But Whitman is Lincoln's laureate in a way that has been increasingly felt as time puts a halo round Lincoln's head and reveals the aureole beauty of the wreath that Whitman placed upon that tortured brow. *When Lilacs Last in the Door-Yard Bloomed* is undoubtedly the high mark of American poetry. And there are moments in all Whitman's moods of distinguished beauty. He wrote much rubbish. So did Wordsworth and other poets. At his best Whitman is the authentic poet of the sea and the sun, of the million men who tread the earth. Whitman fancied that he had made a new form of verse and had shaken off the conventional bonds of rhyme and meter. It is not the originality or eccentricity of his form that makes him great. His splendor is in essential rhythms which are as old as English poetry. And his originality is simply that he was a great poet and a new and original poet—at his best. It is the best of a poet that remains.

After Whitman most American verse is an anticlimax. But any good anthology will contain some of the curiously compact and half-expressed verses—yet fully expressed in their mode—of Emily Dickinson; delicate elfin verses by Louise Guiney, who though she did not cease to be American remained Irish and therefore a poet; the "homely" verses of James W. Riley; the poems of Thomas Bailey Aldrich, with their thin excellence; and a poet much greater potentially than his ill health and a hundred difficulties permitted the Muse to realize in him, Sidney Lanier: you shall go far even in the "major" poets for anything more sweepingly gorgeous than Lanier's *Marshes of Glynn* and *Sunrise*. Sometimes American poets are weak, inexpressive, hoarse. But the harp of Israfel is not yet unstrung. And if America is not a nation of singers, there is now and again a pure and lovely note.

CHAPTER L

CONTEMPORARY WORLD LITERATURE

AMERICAN LITERATURE

THE twentieth century saw a poetic renaissance in America that was indeed remarkable. There was no market for poetry in a world torn by a strife and disillusionment. Critics of the titanic stature of Emerson had long since disappeared and there was no one to lend a helping hand to the unknown artist. In the face of a continually growing materialism which had no ear for poetic beauty, many poets and novelists ran away to more sympathetic environments—to France, Italy, England, even the Far East.

Most remained and often their poetry was a protest against the conditions they had to struggle with. The miracle was that in the face of discouragement a *truly native, distinctive American poetry appeared.*

Edgar Lee Masters aimed his satire at the narrow-minded, small town mentality of many of the middle Western communities of America. *Spoon River Anthology,* written in unrhymed verse forms, consists of 19 stories with 244 characters and covers almost every occupation in its biting commentary on the town of Spoon River. Like Zola, Masters was a naturalist who left out nothing in life that helped to describe his characters.

Vachel Lindsay, like Masters, helped to relax the face of American poetry from its dependence on English tradition. Anything but a formal poet, he wrote stage directions for his primitive, chanted poems such as *General Booth Enters into Heaven* and *The Congo*. Lindsay had a terrible time trying to publish most of his work. Usually, he mimeographed a few hundred copies and peddled them on street corners for two or three cents each. A fervent believer in democracy, he wrote for the average working-man reader in simple, powerful language that has made his poems among the most popular in the English language.

Another poet who had a hard struggle against poverty and for recognition was Edward Arlington Robinson. He refused to write the florid, fancy diction typical of the late nineteenth century. His poems have a straight-to-the-point quality that combines both beauty and a philosophical pessimism. See *The Man Against the Sky* and *Minever Cheevy*.

Following in Robinson's footsteps was the plain speech, New England logic, and homespun optimism of Robert Frost. He writes poetry in simple, understandable language that relies on a subtle wit and keen observation for effect rather than on any literary techniques. Frost is not a philosopher. He takes life as it comes and sees the good as well as the bad in people. He is perhaps the best lyric poet of our generation. The best characterization of his poetry is his own remark: "A poem begins with a lump in the throat; a homesickness or a lovesickness. It is a reaching-out toward expression; an effort to find fulfillment."

One of the most famous or infamous poets of recent years is Ezra Pound. He was born in Paley, Idaho and studied at the University of Pennsylvania, where he was an Instructor for a few years. Repelled by the materialism of American

life, Pound sailed to Italy where he published his first book of
poems. In Europe, he was the recognized leader of the Imagist school in poetry. An astounding but pedantic scholar,
familiar with Greek, Latin, Chinese, Oriental philosophy, and
the building costs in Florence in the early Renaissance, his
poetry is full of the most difficult illusions that often make
it sound like gibberish to the uninitiated reader.

Pound is probably most significant as the founder and guide
of much of modern poetic development. Leader of the Imagist
Movement, he influenced Amy Lowell, T. S. Eliot, (who
dedicated his *Wasteland* to Pound), William Carlos Williams,
and H. D. (Hilda Doolittle). From his changing head-
quarters in Europe, he sent a constant flow of the best in the
new poetry back to the little poetry magazines of Harriet
Monroe, Marianne Moore, and others. Some of the authors
he helped to publish were Robert Frost, Richard Aldington,
James Joyce, Rabindranath Tagore, T. S. Eliot, D. H. Lawrence, and William Butler Yeats.

After the second World War, Pound was indicted for treason, having broadcast anti-American propaganda for Mus-
solini. Later, he was declared insane by the courts and confined
to a mental institution, where he wrote his controversial *Pisan
Cantos.*

Unlike Pound, T. S. Eliot is probably a better poet than he
is a critic. Thomas Stearns Eliot was born in St. Louis, Missouri. After studying in Europe, he decided to remain in England and become a British subject. Like Pound, Eliot made
a cult out of learning and deliberately filled his poetry with
the most difficult intellectual references. He believes that
mature poetry must shock the reader out of his lethargy into
consciousness by harsh language, planned obscurity, and complete phrases borrowed unchanged from the Latin, Sanskrit,

Greek, Spanish, and from the works of literally dozens of other authors. "Immature poets imitate, mature poets steal", he has remarked. *The Love Song of J. Alfred Prufrock* leads off with quotations from Dante's *Inferno*. *Gerontian* uses lines from the *Education of Henry Adams* and from a poem of Robert Browning's. But like the "metaphysical" poets with whom he is often compared, his poetry has a deep emotional and often a truly melodic appeal. Eliot's best known work is *The Wasteland*, a study of the sterility of modern industrial society.

Carl Sandburg is the very opposite of Pound and Eliot. He inherited the mantle of Walt Whitman. Educated on the Illinois prairie, he barnstormed across the country much as Whitman did, working as a barber, dishwasher, coal-heaver, and soldier. The language of Sandburg's poetry is the language of the people, the people he has known and worked with all his life. Happily, he is able to combine his honest realism with a sensitive lyric imagination. One of his finest poems is *Prayers of Steel*.

A poet who has often been compared to John Keats is the tragic Hart Crane. With his whole career ahead of him, he committed suicide by jumping off the deck of a ship in the Gulf of Mexico. Like Whitman before him, Crane tried to depict the mythical epic of American civilization—the Brooklyn Bridge, Pocahontas, the subway train, cutty sark—in his long unfinished poem, *The Bridge*. Crane's sensuous words and images, his effects of tonal music, are matched only in the work of the best symbolist poets.

The twentieth century renaissance in American poetry was only a part of the latent flowering of American literature. The American novelist almost overnight has become famous throughout the world and his books are translated into many languages. Some of this popularity is doubtless due to the leadership the United States has assumed in world affairs, but more important is the raw physical courage with which the American novelist has faced the problems of modern civilization.

Sherwood Anderson struggled with the complexities of the revolutionary theories of Sigmund Freud as he attempted to analyze American village life in *Winesburg, Ohio*. Psychology and sex were to be the answers to frustration and discontent. *Dark Laughter* and *Beyond Desire* continued Anderson's effort to break down the wall of sex ignorance and prejudice in American life.

In the forefront of the critics of the American scene was Sinclair Lewis. His *Main Street* was the satire to end all satires on American small town life. In *Babbitt*, he went on to lampoon the smugness and Philistinism of the American business man. So true to life was his characterization that the terms Babbitt and Babbittry have become a part of the everyday language of the people.

Of all American writers, perhaps the best known abroad is Jack London. His books are a strange mixture of supermen who recognize no authority but their own, militant radicals, and just plain adventurers. Many of his short stories and incidents from his novels are based on his own experiences as a merchant mariner and gold-hunter in Alaska.

Another Socialist writer whose work achieved an international reputation is Upton Sinclair. Sinclair was strongly influenced by Émile Zola and the French naturalists. In *The Jungle,* he tells the story of the Chicago stockyards. To obtain the material for his book he went to live with the poor immigrants who were brought over in wholesale lots to work for miserable wages in the slaughter houses. He piles up masses of first-hand detail to achieve an overpowering effect. The publication of *The Jungle* had repercussions on the floor of Congress and led to the passage of the Pure Food and Drug Act in the United States.

Out of the great depression of the 1930's came two memorable American novels of social protest, *U. S. A.* and *The Grapes of Wrath.*

U. S. A. by John Dos Passos is a black picture of the future of the United States. It expressed the disillusionment of a young intellectual with the chicanery and politics that marked the peace conference after the first World War and the pessimism of an artist confronted with the Jazz age and the blind worship of money. No less amazing than Dos Passos' ability to embrace the historical events of so dynamic a period, was his original and effective literary technique. Every device that by now has become familiar in the motion picture is used. There is no main narrative that holds the book together. Characters come and go, and then reappear. The continuity is maintained by means of three devices; the newsreel, the camera eye, and factual biographical sketches. The newsreel is a collection of headlines spelling out the current events of the time; the camera eye is a psychological analysis of the story-teller's reactions; and the factual biographical sketches are of the lives of some of America's contemporary leading figures.

The Grapes of Wrath by John Steinbeck is an American "epic" novel. It is the story of the Joad family—the "Oakies" —driven off their land by drought and the depression, making the long trek to California, the land of "milk and honey". There they found the same poverty and despair they had fled from in Oklahoma. The pitiful story of the Joads struck at the conscience of the country. The losing struggle of Ma Joad to keep her family together and the smouldering hunger of Pa

Joad for just a small piece of earth to farm echoed the cry of the army of farmers who had lost their land to the dust storm and the tractor.

Two other significant novels of Steinbeck's are *Of Mice and Men* and *In Dubious Battle*.

Much of Dos Passos' material and style in *U. S. A.* came from his experiences as an ambulance driver in the first World War and his association with Gertrude Stein in Paris. Another member of this so-called "lost generation" was Ernest Hemingway. Hemingway brought to the novel the short sentence, the clipped conversation, the violent action, and morbid preoccupation with death that have become the standard trademark of the American murder mystery. His best works include *A Farewell to Arms, To Have and Have Not,* and *For Whom the Bell Tolls,* a story of the Spanish Civil War.

Thomas Wolfe had the potential for becoming the finest novelist of all the younger crop of writers until his premature death at the age of 38. Relying heavily on autobiographical material—so much so that his home town of Asheville, North Carolina threatened to run him out of town if he ever came back—he recreated the life of a boy growing to manhood in a small American community. His richly sensuous style, overflowing with emotion, seems closer to poetry than to prose. Many critics have compared his descriptive prose passages to the poetry of Whitman.

Of the regional novelists, William Faulkner has best captured the spirit of the South. His characters, however, are brutally distorted and a moody introspection on the place of the individual in modern society makes his books difficult reading.

On the stage, the end of the first World War saw New York become the drama center of the world. The plays of George

Bernard Shaw and Ibsen were presented in American theatres and helped to prepare audiences for the revolutionary work of Eugene O'Neill, Sidney Howard, Lawrence Stallings, Maxwell Anderson, Clifford Odets, Lillian Hellman, Tennessee Williams, and Arthur Miller.

O'Neill got his start with the Provincetown Players, an amateur group in Provincetown, Mass. O'Neill's first one-act plays were based on his experiences as a sailor in the Caribbean Sea and demonstrated his keen ear and sense of the theatre. Like Aeschylus, the Greek tragedian, O'Neill is concerned with the relationship between man and his God. While his techniques are revolutionary, his themes stem from classical tradition. *The Emperor Jones,* utilizing the psychological value of the continuous beat of tom-toms, shows that every man belongs to some God. In *The Great God Brown,* the use of masks by the characters helps bring out man's psychological duality—his appearance on the surface and what he is really like inside. Other great plays by O'Neill are *Desire Under the Elms,* debunking the puritans of New England, and *Mourning Becomes Electra,* a modern interpretation of the Greek myth of Orestes as found in the Agamemnon trilogy of Aeschylus. (See page 105.)

ENGLISH LITERATURE

Great Britain after the first World War found almost all of its writers suffering from a common feeling of despair. Modern civilization seemed sterile, empty, enslaving man to an inexorable machine that destroyed every shred of individualism. Accepting the researches of Freud into the subconscious mind with its corollary that reason is imperfect and cannot be relied on, authors felt compelled to search for new values that could compete with the airplane, the automobile, and the assembly line. Novelist D. H. Lawrence, leaning heavily on Freud, thought that an all-embracing theocratic love—including a purified sex—would solve mankind's problems. Poets Auden and Spender turned to radicalism, and T. S. Eliot fell back on tradition and authority.

The great tradition of English poetry suffered from this searching "between two worlds, one dead, the other powerless to be born". From the trenches in France, muddy and reeking of poison gas, came poetry not so much beautiful as bitter, brooding, and harshly realistic. These were the poems of Wilfred Owen, killed in combat scarcely a year after his first volume was published. Owen felt himself to be a part of a lost generation, a generation of men without arms and legs, unable to breathe, with nothing to believe in or live for.

T. S. Eliot, who is discussed more in detail elsewhere in this chapter, was the most important poetic spokesman for this "lost generation". In *The Wasteland* he catches the prevailing moods of materialism, vacillation, sordidness, and despair and made it the symbol for the intellectuals of the twenties and thirties.

Some few poets were aware of the dead end that such thinking led to. Wynstan Hugh Auden, critic as well as poet, satirized the decadence of these British intellectuals in the poetic plays he wrote in collaboration with Christopher Isherwood. *The Ascent of F6* is a political allegory showing the plight of the intellectual torn between left and right and finally disloyal to both. Auden had little to offer besides satire. He could see the diseases of the old order, but beyond that his vision faded badly. In his personal life he vacillated like the hero of F6, embracing first religion and then Communism which he later renounced.

Another poet who believed that pessimism had no place in literature was Stephen Spender. Strongly stirred by the social and political movements of his day, Spender became active in left-wing movements. *Vienna* and an allegorical drama *Trial of a Judge* reflect the radical views which he too later repudiated.

In the novel, this same stifling disillusionment had its effect on the writing of D. H. Lawrence, Aldous Huxley and Virginia Woolf. Here, however, only Aldous Huxley succumbed to the easy way out of skepticism and weak satire.

D. H. Lawrence, the high priest of sex in contemporary English literature, offered a rustic theocracy as a remedy for modern confusion. He had no use for democracy and his book *The Plumed Serpent* in which Don Ramón, an ideal dictator, imposes a fascist organization on Mexico, was taken as a text by native British fascists in the thirties.

In *Lady Chatterley's Lover* (banned in Britain and the United States), Lawrence's description of the passionate love affair between an English noblewoman and a game-keeper on her husband's estate is aimed at showing the infinite possibilities of physical and spiritual love in his new society. Lawrence, a very Puritanical man, with the strictest moral code, meant to do anything *but* shock the reader with his seeming crudity. Lawrence had tuberculosis, with which he battled all his life; and his effort to harmonize the physical with the spiritual in his philosophy was a reflection of all his suffering.

The most significant woman writer of her generation was indisputably Virginia Woolf. Like Joyce, she was a devotee of the stream-of-consciousness in her writing, and her work is marked by probings of psychological motives, reactions, and implications. The smallest action, the most insignificant remark can serve her as the source of an entire story.

The abstract conception of time fascinated Virginia Woolf and her novels were preoccupied with it. In *The Waves,* the lives of six characters are observed as they react to the sea, which itself is a symbol of abstract Time. *To the Lighthouse* and *Orlando* are also studies in time. Much of this preoccupation is philosophical dabbling with the theories of Henri Bergson, the French philosopher of creative evolution. The rest is Virginia Woolf's total obsession with the nuance of the inner life. Many readers, attracted by her keen, delicate prose, have turned away from her, unwilling to struggle with the psychological minutiae and repelled by her complete refusal to admit the slightest reality into her work.

Aldous Huxley is the grandson of Thomas Henry Huxley, the ardent defender and popularizer of Charles Darwin and the theory of evolution. He was in his twenties when the first World War ended, and the shock of the betrayal of his youthful idealism in the peace that followed made him a confirmed skeptic. He had lost his faith and he blamed it in large measure on the faith-shattering teachings of his grandfather Thomas Huxley.

To him, nineteenth century science had left a curse on the English mind. Lyell, Darwin, Tyndall, Huxley, Marx, Freud had destroyed every decent motive and substituted for them a world full of animals bent only on satisfying their material needs. His two satirical novels *Point Counter-Point* and *A Brave New World* have characters whose actions are motivated by animal impulses that lead inevitably to violence, lust, and perversion.

IRISH LITERATURE

Irish contributions to the main stream of English literature have always been of the first order. Satirists like Jonathan Swift and Oscar Wilde, novelists like George Moore, are but representatives of dozens of Celtic writers who have contributed to English literature. However, the period known as the Irish Literary Renaissance which began at the end of the nineteenth century has been so remarkably fertile that no study of world literature can deny it a special place.

The director and leader of the movement was William Butler Yeats, poet, prose writer, and dramatist. Yeats modeled his poetry—called by some critics the finest since Shakespeare—on the Pre-raphaelites and the French symbolists. His poetry divides itself into two periods. The early work is full of music, gay and sprightly, based in large part on folk lore and mythology. Such poems as *The Stolen Child* and *The Lake Isle of Innisfree* are typically charming. His later poetry takes on a sharper tone, is more direct and powerful. See *Leda and the Swan* and *Sailing to Byzantium.*

Yeats in company with Lady Gregory, George Russell (AE), Edwin Martyn, and George Moore established the Irish Literary Theatre which later became the world famous Abbey Theatre of Dublin.

One of the first plays produced in the new theatre was Yeats' *The Countess Kathleen,* the story of an Irish Lady Godiva who sold her soul to the devil to obtain food for the people. Plays by AE, Lady Gregory, and others in the circle were put on with varying degrees of success. It was not until Yeats discovered a young Irishman, John Millington Synge, starving in a garret in Paris that a truly great playwright was introduced. Yeats and Lady Gregory encouraged Synge to use the inexhaustible wealth of folk mythology as material for his plays. Such plays would appeal to everyone and help to stimulate Irish nationalism. To obtain material for these, Synge went to live on the Aran Islands. *Riders to the Sea* was the happy result. It is the story of a peasant family who wrest their meagre living from the sea. Maurya, the mother, has lost her husband to the implacable ocean and one by one is losing her sons. The play was stark, harsh reality and though written in prose was lyrically poetic. It is one of the finest one-act plays in any language.

After Synge, there were again a succession of mediocre playwrights—Lord Dunsany, Lennox-Robertson, Paul Carroll—until Sean O'Casey came along.

O'Casey was the product of the Civil War in Ireland that matched brother against brother instead of uniting them against the common enemy, Great Britain. Born in bitter poverty in the Dublin slums, the son of a bricklayer, it is not strange that O'Casey's plays have common people as heroes, the people one can see any day on a walk through Dublin's tenement-lined streets. *Juno and the Paycock* and *The Plough and the Stars* are his best plays.

Across the channel in France, another Dubliner, James Joyce, was writing literary history. No man has ever had more fervent supporters or rabid detractors. Unlike his compatriots, Joyce had no interest in Irish nationalism, even attacking the Irish theatre, and became a voluntary exile on the continent.

His masterpiece, *Ulysses,* is a study of the events in the lives of three people during a twenty-four hour period. These people are Leopold Bloom, an advertising solicitor of Dublin; his wife, Molly; and Stephen Dedalus, a young artist searching for a spiritual father. He finds such a man in Leopold

Bloom. The book picks up Bloom as he rises in the morning and follows him through the day as he wanders about the city. Every daydream and sub-conscious reflection is recorded by Joyce in an amazing stream-of-consciousness technique. Late at night, Bloom returns home to an unfaithful Molly whose frank mental soliloquy at the close of the book was mainly responsible for its early banning in Great Britain, Ireland, and the United States.

In *Finnegan's Wake,* Joyce continues his experiments with spelling, syntax, and vocabulary. One word to Joyce may suggest a set of words not only in English but in Italian, Latin, Hebrew, etc. Most of *Ulysses* is difficult but at least intelligible; *Finnegan's Wake* is incomprehensible.

Joyce's influence on later writers was immense. His stream-of-consciousness technique that portrayed the thought-processes of his characters has been widely adopted. His distortion of language and uninhibited frankness became a cult with his followers and today is a recognizable trade mark.

The third of the triumvirate of great Irish dramatists is George Bernard Shaw, Fabian Socialist, unabashed egotist, and biting satirist. Shaw has become a legend, thanks to his pungent tongue and acid wit. His plays cover a wide range, are whimsical, witty, and caustic. In *Widowers' Houses,* he attacks the landlords of slum property. In *The Philanderer, Mrs. Warren's Profession,* and *The Woman Who Did,* he follows Ibsen in portraying women as complete equals with men. Other plays by Shaw are *Candida, Man and Superman,* and *Pygmalion.*

FRENCH LITERATURE

The dominant figure in French literary life since the first World War has been Andre Gide. His penetrating novels of psychological insight and his literary criticism delineated the aesthetic standard of a generation. Gide began his career as a symbolist under the influence of Stephen Mallarmé, Paul Valéry, and Maurice Maeterlinck. He has written many volumes of prose and poetry of which three are universally recognized as masterpieces: *The Immoralist, Strait Is the Gate,* and *The Counterfeiters.*

The *Immoralist* is the story of a cruel but bewildered superman, Michel, who breaks with conventional morality in his search for self-realization only to come to a tragic end. In his most ambitious work, *The Counterfeiters,* Gide has written four novels in one, each interlocking with the others. The four themes are youth revolting against the older generation, the slow decay of the family, the creation of a work of art, and the "counterfeit" of life. Fundamental in his work is Gide's moral philosophy—the fullest realization of the individual at any cost.

Friend of Gide, follower of Mallarmé, the leading French poet in modern times is Paul Valéry. His poetry and few essays are marked by intense sensitivity and impressionism. See *The Serpent* and *The Graveyard by the Sea.*

The Nobel Prize for Literature in 1937 went to Roger Martin du Gard, author of the ten volume series, *The Thibaults,* the last will and testament of a middle-class family disintegrating under the social conditions of our day.

From an assistant surgeon-major, Georges Duhamel, who performed over 2300 operations at the front in the first World War, came another series of novels that attempted to analyze the changing society of France through the fortunes of another middle-class French family, *The Fortunes of the Pasquiers.*

But slowly, out of the destruction and chaos of two world wars fought largely on the soil of France, traditional French literature began to change. One after another, her best writers leaped into the battle of politics.

Louis Aragon, a veteran of both wars, was first a surrealist poet attacking all forms of respectability. He later became a Communist and editor of *L'Humanité*. He played a leading role in the French underground struggle against the Nazis.

A vigorous anti-fascist in the beginning of his literary career, André Malraux turned in the other direction after the end of World War II and joined forces with the extreme right wing party led by General De Gaulle. Malraux's best work, *Man's Fate,* a story of the Chinese Civil War, is a novel of action that is both authentic and powerful.

The third force in French literature is the Church. Francois Mauriac is a liberal Catholic writer whose work is permeated with a strong religious flavor. Paul Claudel is another mystic Catholic poet.

GERMAN LITERATURE

German literature has always been strongly influenced by foreign sources. From Goethe and Heine to Thomas Mann, German writers have acknowledged their debt to world literature. Much of this influence has been a direct result of the large number of translations published in Germany every year. After the first World War many publishers had the major part of their lists composed of translations from the American, English, French, and Scandinavian languages.

This eclectic gleaning encouraged a many-faceted development in poetry, drama, and the novel. There were poets Richard Beer-Hoffman, Rainer Maria Rilke, Stefan George, and Bertold Brecht; novelists Thomas and Heinrich Mann, Hermann Kesten, Leonhard Frank, Anna Seghers, Erich Maria Remarque, and Arnold Zweig; the historical fictioneers

Lion Feuchtwanger and Stefan Zweig; and playwrights Ernst Toller and Bertold Brecht.

The first German novel to achieve an international success after the chaos succeeding the first World War was Remarque's *All Quiet on the Western Front*. It was an antimilitarist novel that made sense to a war-torn world. Millions of copies and dozens of editions were sold in nearly every language. It was a humble story told simply with no adornment in the best realist tradition of the French naturalists. A flag-waving school teacher drums up a war hysteria in his classes and a few schoolboys enlist in the army to fight for the "glorious fatherland." Their illusion-shattering awakening to the bestiality of war in front-line combat sparked pacifist movements all over Europe.

Not so popular as Remarque's but an equally outspoken antiwar book was Arnold Zweig's *The Case of Sergeant Grischa*.

Yet Remarque and Zweig were not leaders but offshoots of German literature between two wars. The great majority of writers drawing their inspiration from the cosmopolitan atmosphere of German letters turned to Humanism, to the philosophical speculation on the nature of man and the meaning of existence. The leader of this new Humanism was Thomas Mann.

When the Nazis seized power in 1933, among the first books they burned were *The Magic Mountain* and *Joseph and His Brothers*. The *Kultur Gauleiters* realized that Mann's books, filled with a passionate democracy and rooted in mankind's cultural heritage, were violently opposed to everything they stood for. Forced into exile, Mann fought to save Germany as best he could with his pen and from the lecture platform.

The Magic Mountain is widely acknowledged as Mann's masterpiece. It is the story of a young man, Hans Castorp, confined to a tubercular sanitorium in the mountains of Switzerland. The many levels of meaning that Mann manages to convey as Hans speculates on the place of the individual in society provides a veritable storehouse of ideas that one can return to again and again.

Some of his other books are *Buddenbrooks, The Beloved Returns, Joseph and His Brothers,* and *Dr. Faustus.*

Writing in the same humanistic tradition are two other Manns; Heinrich, the elder brother, and Klaus, the second son of Thomas Mann. Heinrich Mann's best known works are *The Subject, Diana, The Royal Woman,* and *The Hill of Lies.* Before fleeing from the Nazis, Heinrich had been elected President of the literary division of the Prussian Academy. The cream of Germany's writers were members— Gerhart Hauptmann, Jacob Wassermann, Franz Werfel, Leonhard Frank, and others.

In the drama, two authors attained a major stature. Ernst Toller wrote his plays in prison while serving a five year term for revolutionary activity against Prussian troops after the end of World War I. His plays reflect his intense belief in social justice and are almost all concerned with the peoples' struggle for freedom. Some of the best of these are *Masses and Man, The Machine Wreckers,* and *Hoppla! Such Is Life!* His life ended on a tragic note when he committed suicide in a New York hotel room.

Bertold Brecht is both poet and playwright. A fluent writer, he is equally at home in the theatre, radio, and the novel. With Lion Feuchtwanger, he adapted one of Marlowe's historical tragedies, and his radio play *The Trial of Lucullus* was popularly received.

Other dramatists are Carl Sternheim, Georg Kaiser, and Fritz von Unruh.

CZECHOSLOVAKIAN LITERATURE

Czechoslovakia has been an independent nation for only a short span of years. To expect a native literature steeped in Czech tradition to spring up overnight was the last thing anyone thought would happen. But it did! Led by Thomas Masaryk, one of the leading forces in Czech literary criticism (as well as in politics), a literature of social consciousness appeared and attracted world attention.

A Prague bank clerk, Jaroslav Hasek, made literary critics sit up and take notice with his Chaplin-like comic hero, *Schweik, the Good Soldier.* A master of Czech vernacular, he utilized his own experiences as a soldier in the first World War to mercilessly satirize the Austro-Hungarian army, its inefficiency, graft, and corruption. Schweik is an incredibly simple-hearted and gullible rear rank private from the streets of Prague who refuses to take his officers, the army, or the war seriously. He makes the whole institution of militarism appear ridiculous.

Another novelist and dramatist who wrote with humor, but in a serious vein, was Karel Capek. Like his contemporary, the more stylish Franz Kafka, he is absorbed with the themes of human inferiority and the significance of death. Works such as *The Manufacture of the Absolute* and *War with the Newts* have heroes and heroines who, while continuing as humans mentally, take on the shapes of birds or insects.

The most famous modern Czech writer, Franz Kafka, wrote in German but has been translated into dozens of languages throughout the world. Kafka is an intensely individual writer who falls back on his sensations for much of his material. The result is a feeling of frustration and bewilderment in all his work that makes his books very hard reading. *Metamorphosis*

is a symbolic novel of a young salesman who goes to sleep one
night to wake up the next morning transformed or metamor-
phosed into a cockroach. Kafka died of consumption at an
early age and directed that his unfinished novels be burned.
Max Brod, his executor, ignored the will and published *The
Trial* and *Amerika*.

ITALIAN LITERATURE

Only two modern Italian men of letters have succeeded in
gaining a considerable world reputation—Ignazio Silone and
Alberto Moravia. Silone's *Fontamara* and *Bread and Wine,*
both violent attacks on the Fascist state, helped begin a new
school of realism among Italian writers. Written in the classical tradition of the Italian Renaissance, they are a chronicle of
the misery of a generation of Fascism.

Moravia, also a realist, is more introspective than Silone,
more concerned with his characters' inner lives than the external reality around them. His most successful novel, *The
Woman of Rome,* the revealing story of a courtesan in the
postwar capital, has been highly acclaimed in literary
circles.

Other Italian writers who are gaining in reputation are
Giuseppi Marotta, Elsa Morante, Corrado Alvaro, Italo
Svevo, Elio Vittorini, Vasco Pratolini, Cesare Pavese, and
Carlo Levi. Of these, Pratolini with his *A Tale of Poor
Lovers* has shown the most promise. Like Zola's *Nana,* this
is a novel that makes no compromise with reality. All the
sordidness of life on a dead-end street of a Florence tenement
—the murders, lust, and poverty—are here. Yet *A Tale of
Poor Lovers* retains a quality of humanity that gives it a depth
and understanding that Zola was never able to attain.

SPANISH LITERATURE

Outside of Vicente Blasco Ibáñez, there are few Spanish writers who are familiar to the English-reading public. Under the Republic, Spain had entered on a short-lived literary renaissance. The poetry of Guillén, the social novels of Ramón Sender, Arconada, and Arderíus, the plays and poetry of García Lorca, the critical studies of Ortega y Gasset, were summarily expunged by the censors of the Franco regime and the authors either murdered or driven into exile.

Frederico García Lorca was the leading poet and playwright before his death at the hands of a firing squad. His books, including *Blood Wedding* and *Five Plays,* were burned and today are banned in Spain.

One of the best known modern Spanish novelists is Ramón J. Sender whose novel *Seven Red Sundays* was well received in Europe and America. *Seven Red Sundays* is the story of a Spanish demonstration that police brutality goaded into a general strike. Six of the seven red Sundays are the days of the strike, the seventh is the day of rest, the victory to come in the near future. The development of the strike into an unsuccessful revolutionary uprising is told by a journalist who has thrown in his lot with the revolutionists.

Sender was a lawyer active in politics. In Madrid, he was on the staff of *El Sol,* the leading Spanish liberal newspaper. He fought the dictatorship of Primo de Rivera and was forced to flee from Spain after the fall of the Spanish Republic.

The intellectual leader of modern Spain is a quiet university professor of philosophy, José Ortega y Gasset. He has been extremely influential in shaping ideas through the newspaper *El Sol* which he founded, and the magazines *Faro* and *Europa.* Two of his books have achieved a great popularity, *The Revolt of the Masses* and *The Modern Theme.* He is now a professor of philosophy at the University, Lima, Peru.

RUSSIAN LITERATURE

Russian literature since the revolution has been marked by its uncompromising realism and strict avoidance of the symbolism and impressionism that influenced so many writers in Western Europe. The magnificent flowering of the nineteenth century Russian novelists and dramatists has been the inspiration for many of the post-revolution authors. Novelists Mikhail Sholokhov and Alexander Fadeyev take their inspiration from Tolstoy. Ilya Ehrenburg and Leonid Leonov are rooted in Dostoyevsky. The satire of Zostchenko reminds the reader of Gogol.

Alexei Tolstoy is a descendent of Leo Tolstoy and Ivan Turgenev. During the revolution he fought against the Bolsheviks but in 1921 he returned to the Soviet Union to become a Soviet citizen. His novel, *The Road to Calvary,* has been translated into several languages. He is the winner of three Stalin prizes.

The Soviet writer whose name is most familiar to the rest of the world is the journalist and author, Ilya Ehrenburg. During World War II his flaming articles against the Nazi invaders won him a huge national popularity. He won the Stalin prize for his novel *The Fall of Paris.*

Considered the finest poet in the Soviet era is Vladimir Mayakovsky. His satiric plays, especially *The Bed Bug,* are as biting and grandiose as those of Aristophanes. His poetry is very expressive and makes use of a colloquial free verse style.

One of the literary masterpieces that will probably be remembered and read a long time from now is Mikhail Sholokhov's *The Silent Don*. The hero, Gregor, is a Cossack like the author himself. Sholokhov portrays the passionate nationalism of the Cossacks and also, their distorted hatred of minority peoples that led them to become the devoted body guards and executioners for the Czars.

BRIEF COMMENTS ON CONTEMPORARY WRITERS

Every reader will have his favorites and there will always be differences of opinion. Some of these authors and their work will be long-remembered, others less so and some perhaps not at all. Yet to even risk their omission is unthinkable. Space limitation prohibits more than mention of a number of the contemporary writers who have established themselves in our hearts and our literature. Among these (and they by no means are meant to be all-inclusive) are Joy Adamson, for her fascinating *Born Free*—Rachel Carson, for *The Sea Around Us*—Winston Churchill, for his now famous memoirs of the war years—James Gould Cozzens, author of *By Love Possessed,* and other books—Allen Drury, Pulitzer-prize winner, for *Advise and Consent*—Ernest K. Gann, for *Fate Is the Hunter*—Graham Greene, for a *Burnt-Out Case,* and other novels—John Hersey, for *The Child Buyer*—Paul Horgan, Pulitzer-prize winner, for *The Great River*—James A. Michener, for his exceptional novel, *Hawaii*—John O'Hara, for a number of popular titles, *From the Terrace, Rage to Live* and *10 North Frederick*—Ayn Rand, for *Atlas Shrugged*— Arthur M. Schlesinger, Jr., a powerful writer, for *The Politics of Upheaval*—William L. Shirer, for *The Rise & Fall of The Third Reich,* which literally created a sensation— C. P. Snow, a novelist and writer on science and government, for *The Affair* (1953-1954), and *Strangers and Brothers*— Irving Stone, for *The Agony and The Ecstasy*—Robert Penn

Warren, author of *All the King's Men* (1940)—and for specialized writing, the name of Leon Uris, for *Exodus,* should be listed.

The extensive development of paperback books has made a tremendous impression and increased the number of book readers quite substantially. The pocket-size editions have always been accepted in Europe and at this writing some 12,000 titles are available in this format, in the United States. These include popular novels, westerns, detective stories, mysteries, fiction, classics, avant garde and experimental novels, biography, history, economics, philosophy, science, religion and fine arts. They are being improved gradually and larger-sized paperbacks added. Each day nearly one million books are sold in the U.S. alone. Problems of distribution and the ability to locate volumes are still to be satisfactorily solved, but hopes for these solutions are high. With the increase in school attendance and the availability of these lower-priced editions, good books are available to everyone.

CONTEMPORARY FOREIGN WRITERS, TRANSLATIONS, ETC.

In French literature, *Memoires d'une Jeune Fille Rangée,* by Simone de Beauvoir, one of the outstanding figures of literary existentialism and author of *Memoires,* 1954 *Prix Goncourt winner*—a story of the childhood and youth of a "well-brought-up girl"—Albert Camus, winner of the Nobel Prize in 1957, for his new book, *Resistance, Rebellion, and Death* —in which he records his testament of faith in human freedom. Francoise Sagan must be included for her *Bonjour Tristesse,* and *Aimez-Vous Brahms.*

From India, we have R. K. Narayan, a born storyteller, and his, *The Man-Eater of Malgudi*—a delightful story of the little world of an imaginary town in South India—and probably the best novelist that India has produced, comparable to distinguished contemporary writers anywhere.

From Japan, following the great popularity of Ryunosuke Akutagawa's *Rashomon,* collection of thrilling stories written in an intriguing style, providing several versions of an incident as seen through different eyes, have come—*Japanese Inn* by Oliver Statler, a story of the Minaguchi-ya, a typical better-class Japanese Inn—the story of the Eastern Sea Road that connects Kyoto and Tokyo, covering a period from the 16th Century to the present, in which readers learn of Japan's history—and *The Key,* by Junichiro Tanizaki, a novel about a married couple (a best seller in Japan) each of whom keeps a diary. More is to be expected from this progressive nation.

From Jugoslavia, we have Dobrica Cosic's trilogy, *Deobe* (Divisions)—his earlier book—*Far in the Sun,* translated into English and published in 1951—a bold approach in war literature with excellent characteristics and insight—a turning point in Jugoslavian writing. Another popular Jugoslavian writer is Ivo Andric, for his short-story collection *Lica* (characters).

In Russian literature, the greatest difficulties are those of translation and political interference by the U.S.S.R. Apart from scientific literature, the three most outstanding writers, Vladimir Nabokov, for *Lolita*—a powerfully written best seller—Boris Pasternak, for his *Doctor Zhivago,* which created international controversy and became a political involvement—and Sholokhov, for his new Don novel—*Harvest on the Don*—one of Russia's greatest living writers again presents his beloved Cossacks—people torn from their ancient ways and forced into a new way of thinking—are deserving of special consideration.

There are of course, distinguished writings from other countries, but they are already covered in the previous pages.

BIBLIOGRAPHICAL NOTE

Since this is a book about books, there is a sort of bibliography, implicit or explicit, in the text. In this short note I shall list a few books which I have found useful or which are the accepted standard authorities. Obviously, we cannot approximate completeness in the case of any national literature, or period or author of first-rate importance. An adequate bibliography of Shakespeare or Dante, for example, would more than fill a book of this size, and so for our purposes would be out of proportion. Nor can we go very far into the complicated questions of editions and texts, except to indicate in some instances the most easily accessible text for the ordinary reader. And it is for the ordinary reader, the lover of books, that this list is selected. The professional student of literature will know where to turn for sources of information.

Some standard encyclopedia is indispensable not only for the scholar but for the amateur. *Encyclopædia Britannica* contains articles on the several national literatures, on the various types of literature, such as novel, drama, pastoral, etc., and, of course, on each of the great writers. Most of these articles are written by critics of recognized authority, some by distinguished men of letters, and though other scholars and experts may object to this and that detail, the general reader will find the essential facts and much enlightening criticism. Each article has a bibliography which will guide the reader as far into the subject as he cares to go. With one or two exceptions, I mention only books in English.

BIBLIOGRAPHY

CHAPTER I

For the art and history of printing, Robert Hoe: *A Short History of the Printing Press;* T. L. de Vinne: *The Invention of Printing.* The articles in *Encyc. Brit.* on *Book, Parchment, Paper, Papyrus, Inscriptions, Palæography,* and *Writing* are interesting and lead to further study of a fascinating subject. See also the chapter on Books and Writing in James T. Shotwell: *Introduction to the History of History,* also in the same volume the chapters on Egyptian Annals and Babylonian, Assyrian and Persian Records. This book and the articles cited in *Encyc. Brit.* contain much that is pertinent to Chapter II.

Chapter II

For the origin of myths,—J. G. Frazer: *The Golden Bough.* For the distinction between poetry and prose, the articles in *Encyc. Brit.: Poetry, Prose,* though these articles deal rather with later artistic developments than with origins. For Rosetta Stone and hieroglyphics, article in *Encyc. Brit.: Egypt.* For alphabet, see article under that caption in *Encyc. Brit.* Also Isaac Taylor: *The Alphabet, an Account of the Origin and Development of Letters.*

Chapter III

China,—J. Legge: *The Chinese Classics;* H. A. Giles: *A History of Chinese Literature;* Arthur Waley: *The Temple* (translations of Chinese poetry) ; Brian Brown: *The Wisdom of the Chinese;* Shigeyoshi Obata: *The poems of Li Po.* Japan,—W. G. Aston: *A History of Japanese Literature;* Lafcadio Hearn: *Japanese Lyrics; Kotto, a Japanese Miscellany; Japanese Fairy Tales.* India,—Max Müller: *History of Ancient Sanskrit Literature; The Vedic Hymns; The Upanishads;* A. Weber: *History of Indian Literature;* Vincent A. Smith: *The Oxford History of India;* Edwin Arnold: *Indian Poetry; Light of Asia;* A. W. Ryder: *Kalidasa, Translations of Shakuntala and Other Works;* Rabindranath Tagore: *The Songs of Kabir; Getanjale;* Brian Brown: *Wisdom of the Hindus.* See also a collection of translations called *The Sacred Books of the East.* Arabic,—Clement Huart: *A History of Arabic Literature;* W. A. Clouston: *Arabian Poetry for English Readers;* E. H. Palmer: *The Koran* (English translation). There is another translation by J. M. Rodwell. Richard Burton: Tr. *Arabian Nights.* Burton is complete. There are many selections and expurgated versions for popular reading, for example, the edition by Andrew Lang. Persia,—E. G. Browne: *Literary History of Persia;* Edwin Arnold: *Gulistàn of Saadi* (English translation). FitzGerald's translation of the *Rubáiyát* of Omar Khayyám needs no further mention. There is an abridgment of the poet Firdusi in English by J. Atkinson, and a verse translation by A. G. and E. Warner.

Chapter IV

The literature of the Bible is an appallingly huge library. We can give but a few titles of books dealing with the literary history of the Bible; with theological explanation and exegesis we have little to do, though we cannot quite escape it. W. Robertson Smith: *Old Testament and the Jewish Church; The Prophets of Israel;* C. A. Briggs: *General Introduction to the Study* of *Holy Scripture;* A. Harnack: *What Is Christianity?;* Ernest Renan: *Origins of Christianity* (including the *Life of Jesus*); *History of Israel;* Matthew Arnold: *God and the Bible; Literature and Dogma; St. Paul and Protestantism;* J. E. Carpenter: *The Bible in the 19th Century;* A. S. Cook: *Biblical Quotations in Old English Poets;* B. F. Westcott: *History of the English Bible;* J. A. Bewer: *The Literature of the Old Testament in Its Historical Development;* G. Milligan: *The English Bible, a Sketch of Its History;* other histories are by F. Moulton and T. H. Pattison. The fullest compendium of all aspects of Bible scholarship is Hastings: *Dictionary of the Bible.* A readable book is J. H. Gardiner: *The Bible as English Literature.* Another is H. W. Van Loon: *The Story of the Bible.* See also Shailer Mathews: *A History of New Testament Times in Palestine.* The Talmud,— M. L. Rodkinson: *History of the Talmud;* articles in *Encyc. Brit.* and Hastings' *Dict. of the Bible.*

CHAPTER V

James T. Shotwell: *An Introduction to the History of History,* Section III; Botsford and Sihler: *Hellenic Civilization;* J. P. Mahaffy: *History of Classical Greek Literature;* Gilbert Murray: *History of Ancient Greek Lit.;* George Grote: *History of Greece;* J. B. Bury: *The Ancient Greek Historians.* Since this chapter is our first on Greek literature, we may mention here the *Loeb Classical Library,* which contains more than a hundred and fifty volumes of Greek and Latin authors, original text and English translation. I have heard classical scholars quarrel with some of the volumes, but those that I have seen seem to be well done. Also the old Bohn's Classical Library is not outworn intellectually, but the type is defective and seems never to have been renewed. Jowett, as we noted in our brief paragraph, made the final translation of Thucydides. The great translation of Herodotus is by George Rawlinson. A convenient, clear and readable handbook is *A History of Ancient Greek Literature* by H. N. Fowler. The best English version of Plutarch is A. H. Clough's revision of Dryden's translation.

CHAPTER VI

The general histories and handbooks of Greek literature noted above. The principal English translations of Homer are discussed in the text. See also R. C. Jebb: *Introduction to Homer;* Gilbert Murray: *Rise of the Greek Epic;* Andrew Lang: *Homer and His Age.* For Hesiod and the Homeric Hymns,—tr. by H. G. E. White in the Loeb Class. Lib. See also, on both Homer and Hesiod, Shotwell, work cited. For Hesiod,—A. W. Mair, in the Oxford Library of Translations.

Chapter VII

General works on Greek lit. cited. Sappho, see H. W. Smyth: *Greek Melic Poets.* On Greek poetry,—J. A. Symonds: *Studies of the Greek Poets;* R. C. Jebb: *Growth and Influence of Classical Greek Poetry.* For Alcæus, Anachreon, Sappho,—H. W. Smyth: *Greek Melic Poets.* For Theocritus and the Pastoral, Andrew Lang's trans. of Theocritus, Bion, and Moschus. For Bacchylideas,—R. C. Jebb: Text, translation, and especially the introduction. For the Anthology,—W. R. Paton's text and translation in the Loeb Class. Lib.; Graham R. Tomson: *Selections from the Greek Anthology;* F. A. Wright: *The Girdle of Aphrodite* (in the Broadway translations).

Chapter VIII

General works on Greek lit. cited. R. G. Moulton: *The Ancient Classical Drama.* For Greek theory of the drama, Aristotle's *Poetics* in the translation of S. H. Butcher (especially fine supplementary analysis); J. W. Donaldson: *Theatre of the Greeks;* A. E. Haigh: *The Tragic Drama of the Greeks; The Attic Theatre;* Ph. E. Legrand: *The New Greek Comedy* (Eng. trans., Loeb). Æschylus,—translations by E. H. Plumptre, Lewis Campbell. See also Browning's translation of the *Agamemnon* and Mrs. Browning's translation of *Prometheus Bound.* Sophocles,—the great translation is by Jebb. Others by E. H. Plumptre, L. Campbell. Euripides,—Gilbert Murray's translation, already an English classic; A. S. Way: complete translation in verse. See also in Browning's *Balaustion* the "transcript" of the *Alcestis,* and in *Aristophanes' Apology* another "transcript," from the *Herakles.* Aristophanes,—Translations: B. B. Rogers, W. J. Hickie (in Bohn Lib.) J. H. Frere (in Everyman's Lib. and Morley's Universal Lib.). Menander,—F. G. Allinson: text and trans. in Loeb Clas. Lib. Here especially Legrand's *New Greek Comedy.*

Chapter IX

General handbooks and histories of philosophy. W. Windelband: *History of Ancient Philosophy* (Eng. trans. H. E. Cushman); E. Zeller: *Hist. of Greek Phil.;* T. Gompertz: *Greek Thinkers* (Eng. trans. L. Magnus). Empedocles,—W. E. Leonard: an excellent verse trans.; Socrates-Plato,—G. Grote: *Plato and the Other Companions of Sokrates;* B. Jowett: the supreme translation of Plato into English; whoever intelligently reads that with the admirable introductions will know all that it is essential to know about Plato. The commentaries and literary essays are innumerable. English readers should know Walter Pater's *Plato and Platonism*. Aristotle,—there is an Oxford translation by various scholars under the editorship of J. A. Smith and W. D. Ross. The principal works are in Bohn's Class. Lib. A standard essay on A. is that by Grote. For the Stoics and Epicureans the authoritative work is E. Zeller: *Phil. of Epicureans, Stoics, and Sceptics* (Eng. trans. J. Reichel); see also H. Sidgwick's *History of Ethics*. On Greek oratory,—R. C. Jebb: *Attic Orators from Antiphon to Isæos*. Demosthenes,—C. R. Kennedy (trans. in Bohn's Class. Lib. S. H. Butcher): *Introduction to the Study of Demosthenes*. Lucian,—trans. by A. M. Harmon, in Loeb Class. Lib. W. H. and F. G. Fowler: a complete translation in modern racy English; the essay on L. in R. C. Jebb: *Essays and Addresses*. Longus,—trans. by J. M. Edmonds in Loeb Class. Lib.; trans. by W. D. Lowe. Origen belongs to church history rather than to Greek literature, but a good account of him will be found in any history of Greek phil., *e. g.*, Zeller, Ueberweg, Windelband.

CHAPTER X

Shotwell: work cited, section IV on Roman History; for this chapter and all on the three following chapters, J. W. Mackail: *Latin Literature* (as good a short handbook about any literature as has ever been written). Wight Duff: *Literary History of Rome;* W. S. Teuffel: *History of Roman Lit.* (Eng. trans. by Warr). Any good general history of Rome, *e. g.*, Mommsen, in English translation; Dean Merivale: *History of the Romans Under the Empire;* Gibbon: *Decline and Fall of the Rom. Empire.* One or two more modern historians, *e. g.*, the Italian, G. Ferrero: *Greatness and Decline of Rome,* said to be unsound, but interesting and vivid. The picturesque *History,* by the French scholar, V. Duruy, has been translated into English. Cæsar,—*Civil War,* Eng. trans. A. G. Peskett in Loeb Class. Lib.; *Gallic War,* Eng. trans. H. J. Edwards in Loeb Class. Lib.; Ferrero: work cited; T. R. Holmes: *Ancient Britain and the Invasion of J. Cæsar; Cæsar's Conquest of Gaul.* Sallust is available in the Loeb Class. Lib., Eng. trans. by J. C. Rolfe. Livy,—in the Loeb Class. Lib. by B. O. Foster; in Everyman's Lib., trans by W. M. Roberts. Tacitus,—trans. by A. J. Church and W. J. Brodribb; in Everyman's Lib. by A. Murphy; in Loeb Class. Lib. by W. Peterson and M. Hutton.

CHAPTER XI

Several translations of Virgil are briefly commented on in the text. There are essays on Virgil by J. R. Green: *Stray Studies;* F. W. H. Myers: Com-

paretti: *Virgil in the Middle Ages* (Eng. trans. by E. F. M. Benecke).
A great book on Virgil is Sainte-Beuve's *Etude.* For this chapter and the
next see W. Y. Sellar: *Roman Poets of the Augustan Age.*

<h2 style="text-align:center">CHAPTER XII</h2>

For the influence of Plautus and Terence on later drama, for example,
Ralph Royster Doyster, Shakespeare's *Comedy of Errors,* Jonson's *The Case
Is Altered,* Dryden's *Anphitryon,* we must go to criticisms of the English
dramatists. There should be (perhaps there is) a complete study of the
influence of Latin drama on modern drama. In the Loeb Class. Lib. the
Plautus is by Paul Nixon, the Terence by John Sargeaunt. In the same
series the Seneca is trans. by F. J. Miller. For Lucretius,—trans. by W. E.
Leonard; essay by G. Santayana in *Three Philosophical Poets.* Catullus
has been trans. into Eng. verse by J. Cranstoun and by T. Martin.
The version in the Loeb Class. Lib. is by F. W. Cornish. Horace has
tempted more translators than any other Latin poet. Among English translations in verse may be mentioned those by Theodore Martin, John Conington,
W. E. Gladstone. Eugene Field's paraphrases and imitations (they are
hardly translations) are amusing. The English poets of the seventeenth and
eighteenth centuries knew Horace and the other Latin lyrists by heart and
made excellent versions. See Ben Jonson's trans. of the *Ars Poetica.* Pope's
rendering of a few of the odes and his imitations of Horace are brilliant.
For Propertius,—The few admirable translations by the poet Gray; verse
trans. by J. Cranstoun. The trans. in the Loeb Clas. Lib. is by H. E.
Butler. Tibullus,—trans. by R. Whiffin, by C. A. Elton, by J. Cranstoun
(complete). Ovid,—many times imitated, quoted and parahrased throughout the Middle Ages, exerted a greater influence on modern poetry than any
other Latin poet, not excepting Virgil or Horace. See the essay on the
influence of Ovid on Shakespeare in T. S. Baynes' *Shakespeare Studies.*
Dryden's translations are as good as translation can be from the point of
view of English verse and are probably true to the original, for Dryden was
a thorough scholar. See especially the preface to the trans. of the Epistles
of Ovid, a fine essay on the art of translation. For Lucan,—the best trans.
is by E. Ridley. Marlowe made a vigorous rendering of the first book.
For Statius,—the only available translation seems to be D. A. Slater's version
of the *Silvæ.* For Martial,—the trans. of the *Epigrams* by W. C. Ker in
the Loeb. Class. Lib. For Juvenal,—the complete trans. by G. Ramsay in
Loeb. Class. Lib.; Dr. Johnson's well-known imitations and Dryden's trans.
of five of the Satires. The *Pervigilium Veneris* from the Latin Anthology

Bibliography 571

is trans. by J. W. Mackail in the Loeb Class. Lib. There is also a version by the eighteenth century poet, Thomas Parnell.

CHAPTER XIII

The literature relating to Cicero is very extensive. A good short biography is that by J. L. Strachan-Davidson in "Heroes of the Nations." A good account of Cicero's philosophy is J. S. Reid's introduction to the *Academica.* Most if not all of the considerable body of Cicero's work that survives has been translated into English. The Letters, the *De Officiis* and the *De Finibus* are in the Loeb Class. Lib. There are nine volumes in the "Handy Literal Translations" (in general literal translations, though they do not exemplify the *art* of translation and so are not fine literature, are a great help to the student and to the general reader. The use of "trots" is discouraged by most school teachers, but a wise use of them is helpful, not harmful). The great satire of Petronius, The *Satyræ* or *Satyricon* is in the Loeb Class. Lib., trans. by M. Heseltine. Apuleius is completely translated in the Bohn Class. Lib. The sixteenth century trans. of *The Golden Ass,* by W. Adlington, revised by S. Gaselee, is published in Loeb Class. Lib. The episode of Cupid and Psyche is in William Morris's *Earthly Paradise* and has been translated into verse by the poet laureate Robert Bridges. Quintilian's *Training of an Orator* is in the Loeb Class. Lib., trans. by H. E. Butler. Almost all of Augustine is in English in the *Select Library of the Nicene and post-Nicene Fathers of the Christian Church.* Since Augustine is one of the great figures in the history of the church, there have been innumerable commentaries on him in all European languages. An interesting sketch is Joseph McCabe's *St. Augustine and His Age.* For both Augustine and Jerome, see F. W. Farrar: *Lives of the Fathers.* Selections from Jerome in English (trans. by W. H. Freemantle) will be found in the *Select Library of the Nicene and post-Nicene Fathers of the Church.* Since Thomas Aquinas is the chief philosopher of the Roman Catholic Church, there is a vast library relating to him. Any good handbook of philosophy must give an account of him. Two books in English are R. B. Vaughan: *St. Thomas of Aquin, His Life and Labours,* and H. C. O'Neill: *New Things and Old in St. Thomas Aquinas.*

CHAPTER XIV

For the Middle Ages,—any good short history, such as E. Emerton: *Introduction to the Study of the Middle Ages,* and *Medieval Europe;* J. H. Robinson: *History of Western Europe,* especially the chapter on the Culture of the Middle Ages. Much of the literature of a thousand years is not quite intelligible without at least a superficial knowledge of the historical and social background. See the article on the Middle Ages in *Encyc. Brit.* For romance, W. P. Ker: *Epic and Romance;* also by the same author, *The Dark Ages;* the important article on Romance by Saintsbury in *Encyc. Brit.;* and his book: *The Flourishing of Romance and the Rise of Allegory.* For Celtic Romance, E. Anwyl: *Prolegomena to Welsh Poetry;* The *Mabinigion* in Alfred Nutt's edition; T. Stephens: *Literature of the Kymry;* Magnus Maclean: *Literature of the Celts;* P. W. Joyce: *Old Celtic Romances.* A. Nutt: *Ossian and the Ossianic Literature.* For the Arthurian Cycle and the associated story of the Holy Grail,—E. Rhys: *Studies in the Arthurian Legend;* A. Nutt: *Studies on the Legend of the Holy Grail;* T. Bulfinch: *Age of Chivalry;* Sebastian Evans: *High History of the Holy Grail;* Jessie L. Weston: *The Legend of Sir Gawain; The Legend of Sir Perceval; Popular Studies in Romance and Folk-Lore,* nos. i and iv. For Anglo-Saxon,—in addition to the translations noted in the text, see J. Duncan Spaeth: *Old English Poetry;* Saintsbury: *Short History of Eng. Lit.* (first book) ; Stopford A. Brooke: *History of Early Eng. Lit.* These three books treat also Cædmon and Cynewulf. For Middle English,—any of the standard histories, e. g., Saintsbury; more especially, I. Gollancz; *Pearl, an Eng. Poem of the Fourteenth Cent., edited, with a Modern Rendering;* the same author's article in *Cambridge Hist. of Eng. Lit.*

As we here approach English literature for the first time, I will make two or three observations which apply to all the following chapters relating to English literature. We have many handbooks and histories dealing with all English literature or with special sections or periods. Some are dull, uninspired and uninspiring. Others are works of creative scholarship. The reader cannot go far wrong who follows Professor Saintsbury, in his *Short History of Eng. Lit.,* the books that deal with the several types and periods of literature and his two monumental studies, *History of Criticism* and *History of English Prosody.* He has written so much that sometimes his sentences are hasty and loosely put together. But his judgment is sound, his learning is vast and fruitful, not in the least pedantic, and his pages are aglow with enthusiasm for the best things in literature. *The Cambridge History of English Literature* in several volumes, written like an encyclopedia by many scholars, is indispensable for the student. Necessarily the work is uneven ; some of the chapters are commonplace, others are very fine examples of criticism. The supplementary volumes on American literature are inferior ; the editors in several cases selected as contributors men whose only qualification was that they had the degree of Doctor of Philosophy. Most of the volumes in the *English Men of Letters* are sound biography and clear criticism. Useful histories are Henry Morley's *First Sketch of English Literature,* and his great work in eleven volumes, *English Writers.* Another excellent guide is W. J. Courthope's *History of English Poetry.* Almost as good as the *Cambridge History,* though not so nearly complete, is the *Illustrated Record of English Literature,* edited by Richard Garnett and Edmund Gosse. Another encyclopedic work of great value is the *Dictionary of National Biography.* Very important are the *History of English Literature,* by B. E. K. Ten Brink, and J. J. Jusserand's *Literary History of the English People.* The *History of English Literature,* by the great French critic, Taine, is a classic; the English translation is good. A convenient book to have at hand is F. Ryland's *Chronological Outlines of English Literature.* Stopford Brooke's brief *English Literature* is excellent.

CHAPTER XV

For this chapter and all following chapters on French literature, the standard reference book is Gustave Lanson's *Histoire de la Littérature Française.* If there is not an English translation, there is sure to be one before long, for the English-reading world cannot afford to be without it. A shorter *Histoire,* very compact and meaty, is that by Petit de Julleville. The best book on the subject in English is Saintsbury's *Short History of French Literature.* Readers who are near one of the university or larger public libraries can consult the monumental *Histoire Littéraire de la France.* On Provençal literature and the troubadours I find very little in English. In *Encyc. Brit.* the only English book mentioned is Francis Hueffer: *The Troubadours.* There are abundant references in French, German, Italian, Spanish. On the *Chansons de Geste* and *Charlemagne* the great authority is Gaston Paris: *La Littérature Française au Moyen Age* (not, I think, in English). For Chretien de Troyes,—*Legend of Sir Lancelot* and *Legend of Sir Percival* in Grimm Library; T. Bulfinch: *Legends of Charlemagne.* For Froissart,—the excellent essay in W. P. Ker: *Essays on Medieval Literature.* For Spanish Romance and the Cid,—J. Fitzmaurice-Kelly: *History of Spanish Literature.*

CHAPTER XVI

For this and later chapters on German literature,—W. Scherer: *History of German Literature* (trans. by Mrs. F. C. Conybeare); Kuno Franke: *German Literature as Determined by Social Forces;* J. G. Robertson: *History of German Literature;* Max Müller: *The German Classics from the Fourth to the Nineteenth Century;* J. S. Nollen: *Chronology and Practical Bibliography of Modern German Literature* (applies less to this chapter than to later ones). For the Minnesingers, C. F. Nicholson: *Old German Love Songs.* For Walter von der Vogelweide,—*Selected Poems of W. v. d. V.,* trans. by W. A. Phillips; see also the trans. by the poet T. L. Beddoes. For Wolfram and the Parzival (Perceval) story, see the trans. by J. L. Weston; by the same author: *Legends of the Wagner Drama* (also for the *Nibelungenlied*). For Gottfried von Strassburg,—J. L. Weston: trans. of *Tristan.* For *Nibelungenlied,*—English translations by A. G. Foster-Barham, by Margaret Armour, by Alice Horton; G. B. Shaw: *The Perfect Wagnerite;* any good book on Wagner, for example, H. E. Krehbiel: *Studies in the Wagnerian Drama.* For Icelandic literature,—F. Jonsson: *Old Norse and Old Icelandic Literature* (trans. by R. B. Anderson); W. Horn: *History of the Literature of the Scandinavian North.*

CHAPTER XVII

There is an enormous literature about Dante. On the six hundredth anniversary of Dante's death Paget Toynbee compiled a bibliography called *Britain's Tribute to Dante in Literature and Art.* This book, which does not include American contributions, runs to nearly two hundred pages, about ten entries to a page. I can give but a brief list of biographies, critical studies and translations. Biographies by Paget Toynbee, by C. H. Grandgent, by C. A. Dinsmore. Essays and introductions: R. W. Church: *Essay on Dante;* M. Rossetti: *Shadow of Dante;* J. A. Symonds: *A Study of Dante;* E. Moore: *Studies in Dante;* W. W. Vernon: *Readings in Dante;* E. G. Gardner: *Dante* (in the "Temple Primers"); introductions and notes to the various translations. Translations of the *Commedia,*—by H. F. Cary, one of the earliest and best, in blank verse; H. W. Longfellow, in blank verse, very good; C. E. Norton, in prose, admirably clear and simple; in the "Temple Classics" with the Italian on the left-hand page and a close prose trans. on the right hand, the *Inferno* by J. A. Carlye, the *Purgatory* by T. Okey, *The Paradise* by P. H. Wicksteed; H. F. Tozer in prose; *The New Life* by C. E. Norton and by D. G. Rossetti; *The Monarchy* by F. C. Church and P. H. Wicksteed.

CHAPTER XVIII

R. Garnett: *History of Italian Literature;* J. A. Symonds: *Renaissance in Italy.* For Petrarch,—M. F. Jerrold: *Francesco Petrarca, Poet and Human-*

ist; H. Reeve: *Petrarch.* For Boccaccio,—the best biography is by E. Hutton. For Machiavelli,—the standard biography is by P. Villari: *The History of Niccolo Machiavelli and His Times* (Eng. trans. by L. Villari); John Morley: The Romanes Lecture, Oxford, 1891; Essay by L. A. Burd, in *Cambridge Modern History.* For Ariosto,—E. Gardner: *Ariosto: the Prince of Court Poets.* For Bruno,—any good history of philosophy, for example, Falckenberg, or H. H. Höffding or J. M. Robertson: *Short History of Free Thought;* the biography by J. L. McIntyre; I. Frith: *Life of Giordano Bruno;* C. E. Plumptre: *Life and Works of Giordano Bruno.* For Galileo, see Falckenberg or any other good history of modern philosophy; J. J. Fahie: *Galileo: His Life and Work.*

CHAPTER XIX

Histories of French literature cited. Also A. Tilley: *Literature of the French Renaissance;* G. Saintsbury: *The Earlier Renaissance.* For Rabelais,—W. Besant in "Foreign Classics for English Readers." For Montaigne,—Saintsbury's introduction to the edition of Florio's translation in the "Tudor Translations"; biographies by E. Dowden and by M. E. Lowndes; J. Feis: *Shakespeare and Montaigne;* Emerson's essay in *Representative Men.* For Calvin,—W. Walker: *John Calvin the Organizer of Reformed Protestantism.* For Descartes,—any good history of modern philosophy, Falckenberg or R. Adamson: *The Development of Modern Philosophy;* or L. Lévy-Bruhl: *History of Modern Philosophy in France.* For Pascal,—Life by Tulloch in "Foreign Classics for English Readers." For Bossuet,—Life by Mrs. S. Lear. For Fénelon,—E. K. Sanders: *Fénelon, His Friends and Enemies;* Viscount St. Cyres: *François de Fénelon.* For Madame de Sévigné and Madame La Fayette,—Sainte-Beuve's essays in *Celebrated Women* (Eng. trans. by H. W. Preston); see also A. T. Ritchie on Mme. de Sévigné and J. Aldis: *Mme. de Sévigné: The Queen of Letter-writers.* For Diderot,—The biography by John Morley. For Voltaire,—the life by S. G. Tallentyre; J. S. Lounsbury's *Shakespeare and Voltaire;* essays by John Morley and Carlyle; J. C. Collins: *Voltaire in England* and *Voltaire and Rousseau.* For Rousseau,—biographies by John Morley and by Mrs. F. Macdonald.

CHAPTER XX

For this chapter, as for the preceding, consult A. Tilley: *Literature of the French Renaissance;* G. Saintsbury: *The Early Renaissance.* There seems to be no good life of Villon in English; Stevenson's essay in *Familiar*

Studies of Men and Books is excellent, as is also the essay on Charles D'Orleans. For Du Bellay, Ronsard, etc., see G. Wyndham: *Ronsard and La Pléiade.* For Malherbe,—G. Saintsbury: *History of Criticism.* Corneille and Racine have been translated and adapted in English, but I find little good biographical or critical matter outside French. For Molière,—Brander Matthews: *Molière.* What seems to be the only available work in English on Beaumarchais is the translation by H. S. Edwards of *Beaumarchais and His Times,* by L. de Loménie.

CHAPTER XXI

For this period,—C. H. Herford: *Studies in the Literary Relations of England and Germany in the Sixteenth Century.* For Luther,—Lindsay: *Luther and the German Reformation;* any standard history of Germany or such a special study of Luther's period as W. Robertson's *History of the Emperor Charles V.* I find little in English about Hans Sachs and the Meistersinger; for information about them, if the very rich German sources are closed to us, we must rely on the standard histories and handbooks.

CHAPTER XXII

For Spanish Literature,—the *History* by J. Fitzmaurice-Kelly; and that monument of American scholarship, G. Ticknor's *History of Spanish Literature.* For Cervantes,—J. Fitzmaurice-Kelley: *Cervantes in England.* For Lope de Vega,—H. A. Rennert: *The Life of Lope de Vega.* There is a volume of Select Plays of Calderon edited by N. MacColl. For Camoens, —R. Burton: *Camoens: His Life and His Lusiads;* also Burton's translations of the *Lusiads* and the *Lyrics;* another translation is by J. J. Aubertin.

CHAPTER XXIII

Beside the general histories there are several manuals that deal with special aspects of this period; one of genuine value is J. M. Berdan: *Early Tudor Poetry,* which discusses not only the poets but More and the Humanists. From this point on in our glance at English literature we can make advantageous use of various anthologies and collections, *e.g.*: Ward's *English Poets* and Craik's *English Prose,* the first volumes of which contain selections from this period; the ever indispensable *Golden Treasury of Songs and Lyrics; The Oxford Book of English Verse.* For Chaucer,—A. W. Ward: *Chaucer* in "English Men of Letters"; R. E. G. Kirk: *Life-Records of*

Chaucer; T. R. Lounsbury: *Studies in Chaucer.* For Gower,—W. P. Ker: *Essays on Medieval Literature.* For Langland,—H. Morley: *English Writers.* For Ballads,—Introduction by G. L. Kittredge to the one-volume edition of Child's *English and Scottish Popular Ballads; Oxford Book of Ballads,* with introduction by A. T. Quiller-Couch; a modern edition of Percy's *Reliques of Ancient Poetry,* notably that by H. B. Wheatley. For More,—F. Seebohm: *Oxford Reformers;* biographies by T. H. Bridgett, by W. H. Hutton, by A. Cayley, by J. Hoddesdon; R. Southey: *Sir Thomas More, or Colloquies on the Progress and Prospects of Society.* For Caxton, —the standard biography is William Blades: *Life and Typography of William Caxton.* For Mallory,—G. L. Kittredge: *Who Was Thomas Mallory?* For Cranmer and Latimer,—any good history of England, J. A. Froude or J. R. Green's *Short History.*

CHAPTER XXIV

Saintsbury: *History of Elizabethan Literature;* F. E. Schelling: *Elizabethan Lyrics.* For Sidney,—biographies by H. R. Fox-Bourne and by J. A. Symonds (in "English Men of Letters"). For Spenser,—introductions to the various editions of the poems, notably that by J. W. Hales in the Globe Edition; R. W. Church: the biography in "English Men of Letters"; F. I. Carpenter: *Guide to the Study of Spenser.* For Raleigh,—biography by M. A. S. Hume in "Builders of Greater Britain"; R. Southey: *Lives of English Admirals;* the Life by E. Edwards, the standard authority; E. W. Gosse: *Raleigh* in "English Worthies"; H. de Selincourt: *Great Raleigh.* For Bacon,—the standard life is by J. Spedding; life by R. W. Church in "English Men of Letters"; W. H. Dixon: *Personal History of Lord Bacon* and *Story of Lord Bacon's Life;* any good history of modern philosophy.

CHAPTER XXV

G. Saintsbury, as above; J. M. Manly: *Specimens of Pre-Shakespearean Drama;* article on *Drama* in *Encyc. Brit.;* B. E. K. Ten Brink: *History of English Literature;* J. J. Jusserand: *The Theatre in England from the Conquest to the Immediate Predecessors of Shakespeare;* F. S. Boas: *S. and His Predecessors; Shakespeare's Predecessors in the English Drama;* J. P. Collier: *History of English Dramatic Poetry and Annals of the Stage to the Restoration;* A. W. Ward: *History of English Dramatic Literature to the Age of Queen Anne;* F. E. Schelling: *A History of English Drama;* F. G. Fleay: *A Chronicle History of the London Stage,* 1550-1642, and *Biograph-*

ical Chronicle of the English Drama. For Marlowe,—J. A. Symonds: Introduction to the plays in the "Mermaid Series"; A. C. Swinburne: *Study of Shakespeare;* W. Hazlitt: *Dramatic Literature of the Age of Elizabeth.*

CHAPTER XXVI

The Shakespeare literature is endless and no man can have read it all. See the general histories of Literature and of the drama already noted. W. Hazlitt: *Characters of S.'s Plays;* S. T. Coleridge: *Notes and Lectures upon S.;* E. Dowden: *S., a Critical Study of His Mind and Art;* F. K. Elze: *Essays on S.* (Eng. trans.) ; F. G. Fleay: *S. Manual;* J. W. Hales: *Notes and Essays on S.;* R. G. Moulton: *S. As Dramatic Artist;* R. G. White: *Studies in S.* and *Memoirs of the Life of W. S.;* F. J. Furnivall: *Modern Shakespearean Criticism;* J. M. Robertson: *Montaigne and S.;* B. Wendell: *W. S., a Study in Elizabethan Literature;* G. Brandes: *Shakespeare* (Eng. trans.) ; A. H. Thorndike: *The Influence of Beaumont and Fletcher on S.;* A. C. Bradley: *Shakespearean Tragedy;* J. C. Collins: *Studies in S.;* W. Raleigh: biography of S. in "English Men of Letters"; F. E. Schelling: *English Literature during the Lifetime of S.;* J. O. Halliwell-Phillips: *The Life of W. S.;* T. De Quincey: *S., a Biography;* Victor Hugo: *W. S.* (Eng. trans.) ; F. G. Fleay: *Chronicle History of the Life and Work of W. S.;* Sidney Lee: *Life of W. S.;* Goldwin Smith: *S. the Man;* W. J. Rolfe: *Life of W. S.;* Frank Harris: *The Man S. and His Tragic Life Story;* W. L. Rushton: *S. and the Arte of English Poesie.*

CHAPTER XXVII

General works on Elizabethan literature and drama already noted under foregoing chapters. Introductions to the several volumes in the "Mermaid Series." C. Lamb: *Specimens of the English Dramatic Poets.* For Chapman,—Matthew Arnold: *On Translating Homer;* A. C. Swinburne: *George Chapman, an Essay.* For Jonson,—J. Dryden: *Essay on Dramatic Poesie;* A. C. Swinburne: *Study of Ben Jonson;* F. E. Schelling: *Ben Jonson and the Classical School.*

CHAPTER XXVIII

General works on English poetry already noted. E. Gosse: *From Shakespeare to Pope;* F. E. Schelling: *Seventeenth Century Lyrics;* E. H. Garrett: *Elizabethan Songs* (Introduction by A. Lang) ; For Donne,—Izaak Walton:

Life of Dr. Donne; E. Gosse: *Life and Letters of John Donne.* For Herrick,—F. W. Moorman: *Robert Herrick.* For Herbert,—Izaak Walton: *Life of George Herbert.* For Marvell,—the life by A. Birrell in "English Men of Letters." For Cowley, Denham, Waller,—Dr. Johnson: *Lives of the Poets.*

Chapter XXIX

Dr. Johnson: Essay on Milton in *Lives of the Poets;* D. Masson: *Life of John Milton; narrated in Connexion with the Political, Ecclesiastical, and Literary History of His Time;* Mark Pattison: *Milton* ("English Men of Letters") ; R. Garnett: *Life of John Milton* in "Great Writers" series; T. B. Macaulay: Essay on Milton in *Edinburgh Review* (in *Miscellaneous Essays*) ; S. T. Coleridge: *Seven Lectures on Shakespeare and Milton;* A. Birrell: Essay on *Milton* in *Obiter Dicta;* A. T. Quiller-Couch: *Studies in Literature* (second series).

Chapter XXX

For Thomas Browne,—introduction to the edition of *Religio Medici, etc.,* by W. A. Greenhill ; W. Pater: Essay in *Appreciations.* For Fuller,—J. E. Bailey: *The Life of Thomas Fuller, with Notices of his Books, his Kinsmen and his Friends.* For Taylor,—E. W. Gosse: *Jeremy Taylor* ("English Men of Letters") ; S. T. Coleridge; *Literary Remains.* For Walton,— biography prefixed to the *Angler* by H. Nicholas; S. Martin: *Izaak Walton and His Friends.* For Hobbes,—any good history of modern philosophy; G. C. Robertson: *Hobbes* in "Blackwood's Phil. Classics": Leslie Stephen: *Hobbes* ("English Men of Letters").

Chapter XXXI

For Dryden,—Dr. Johnson: Essay in *Lives of the Poets;* G. Saintsbury: *Dryden* ("English Men of Letters"). For Locke,—any good history of modern philosophy; H. R. Fox-Bourne: *Life of Locke;* T. H. Fowler: *Locke* ("English Men of Letters"). For Congreve,—introduction by A. C. Ewald to *Best Plays of William Congreve* in "Mermaid" series; Thackeray: *English Humorists;* E. Gosse: *Life of William Congreve* in "Great Writers." For Bunyan,—J. Brown: *John Bunyan: His Life, Times and Work;* R. Southey: *Life* of Bunyan in his edition of *Pilgrim's Progress;* biographies by W. H. White, by J. A. Froude ("English Men of Letters"), by E.

Venables; T. B. Macaulay: *John Bunyan* (in *Miscellaneous Essays*); For Pepys,—H. B. Wheatley: *Samuel Pepys and the World He Lived In;* E. H. Moorhouse: *Samuel Pepys, Administrator, Observer, Gossip;* P. Lubbock: *Samuel Pepys.*

<h2 style="text-align:center">CHAPTER XXXII</h2>

For this chapter and the next,—E. W. Gosse: *History of English Lit-*
erature in the Eighteenth Century; A. Dobson: *Eighteenth Century Vignettes.*
For Swift,—Leslie Stephen: *Swift* ("English Men of Letters"); essay by
Dr. Johnson in *Lives of the Poets* (prejudiced); essay by Thackeray in
English Humorists (very unfair); W. R. Wilde: *Closing Years of Dean*
Swift's Life; W. E. H. Lecky: *Leaders of Public Opinion in Ireland.* For
Addison,—W. J. Courthope: *Addison* ("English Men of Letters"); Dr.
Johnson: essay in *Lives of the Poets* (very good); Thackeray: essay in
English Humorists (praises Steele at expense of Addison); T. B. Macaulay:
The Life and Writings of Addison. For Steele,—Austin Dobson in "English
Worthies"; G. A. Aitken: *Life of Steele* and introduction to the edition of
Steele's plays in the "Mermaid" series. For Berkeley,—any good history of
modern philosophy; A. C. Fraser: *Life* in his edition of Berkeley; A. J.
Balfour; biographical introduction to the edition of Berkeley by G. Sampson;
L. Stephen: *English Thought in the Eighteenth Century;* J. McCosh: *Locke's*
Theory of Knowledge (for both Locke and Berkeley); J. S. Mill: in vols.
ii and iv of *Dissertations;* T. H. Huxley: in *Critiques and Addresses.* For
Defoe,—W. Wilson: *Life of Defoe,* in three vols., the standard work; W.
Minto: *Defoe* ("English Men of Letters"); T. Wright: *Life of Defoe;*
H. Morley: *Earlier Life and Chief Earlier Works of Defoe;* C. Lamb:
three short notes in his literary essays; John Forster: *Historical and Bio-*
graphical Essays; G. Saintsbury: Introduction to Defoe's *Minor Novels.*
For Richardson,—Austin Dobson: *Richardson* ("English Men of Letters").
For Fielding,—G. M. Godden: *Life of Fielding;* A. Dobson: *Fielding*
("English Men of Letters"); Thackeray: *English Humorists.* For Smol-
lett,—W. Scott: Memoir to Bellantyne's edition of Smollett's novels; D.
Hannay: *Life of Smollett;* D. Masson: *British Novelists;* Thackeray: *Eng-*
lish Humorists. For Sterne,—W. L. Cross: *Life and Times of Laurence*
Sterne; Walter Sichel: *Sterne: A Study;* Thackeray: *English Humorists.*
For Johnson,—J. Boswell: *Life of Johnson* (most famous of all literary
biographies in English) in A. Birrell's edition; T. B. Macaulay: Essay on
Johnson in *Encyc. Brit.*) (in *Miscellaneous Essays*); F. Grant: *Johnson*
("English Writers"); L. Stephen: *Johnson* ("English Men of Letters");
T. Carlye: *Boswell's Life of Johnson.* For Goldsmith,—J. Boswell: *Life*

of *Johnson;* J. Forster: *Life and Times of Oliver Goldsmith;* W. Irving: *Life of Oliver Goldsmith;* W. Black: *Goldsmith* ("English Men of Letters") ; A. Dobson: *Life of Goldsmith;* T. B. Macaulay: *Oliver Goldsmith* (in *Miscellaneous Essays*). For Burke,—J. Prior: *Memoirs of the Life and Character of Edmund Burke, with Specimens of His Poetry and Letters;* T. MacKnight: *Life of Burke;* J. Morley: *Burke* ("English Men of Letters"). For Gibbon,—J. B. Holroyd (Lord Sheffield): *Gibbon's Miscellaneous Works, with Memoirs of his Life and Writings, Composed by himself; Illustrated from his Letters, with Occasional Notes and Narratives;* J. C. Morison: *Gibbon* ("English Men of Letters") ; S. Walpole: Essay on Gibbon in *Essays and Biographies.* For Hume,—any good history of modern philosophy; more especially, L. Stephen: *English Thought in the Eighteenth Century;* J. Orr: *David Hume* and *His Influence on Philosophy and Theology;* T. H. Huxley: *Hume* ("English Men of Letters") ; J. H. Burton: *Life and Correspondence of David Hume.*

Chapter XXXIII

For Pope,—L. Stephen: *Pope* ("English Men of Letters") ; W. J. Courthope: biography in Courthope and Elwin's edition of the *Works;* G. Paston: *Mr. Pope: His Life and Times;* Thackeray: *Prior, Gay and Pope* in *English Humorists;* W. Hazlitt: *Dryden and Pope,* Lecture IV of *English Poets.* For Gay,—Dr. Johnson: Essay in *Lives of the Poets;* Thackeray: essay cited; J. Underhill: introductory Memoir to edition of *Poetical Works* of Gay in "Muses' Library." For Gray,—E. Gosse: *Gray* ("English Men of Letters") ; Matthew Arnold: *Gray* in *Essays;* W. Hazlitt: *English Poets,* Lecture VI on *Swift, Young, Gray, Collins,* etc. For Collins: M. Thomas: *Life;* Dr. Johnson: Essay in *Lives of the Poets.* For Cowper,—R. Southey: *Life and Letters of Cowper;* Goldwin Smith: *Cowper* ("English Men of Letters") ; W. Benham: Introduction to the *Poetical Works* in the Globe Edition; W. Hazlitt: Lecture V in *English Poets* (this also discusses Thomson). For Thomson,—G. C. Macaulay: *Thomson* ("English Men of Letters") ; Dr. Johnson: Essay in *Lives of the Poets.* For Burns,—J. G. Lockhart: *Life of Burns;* J. C. Shairp: *Burns* ("English Men of Letters") ; W. E. Henley: Essay in the "Centenary Burns," *Robert Burns, Life, Genius, Achievement;* T. Carlyle: *Burns;* R. L. Stevenson: *Familiar Studies of Men and Books;* Lord Rosebery: *Robert Burns: Two Addresses in Edinburgh;* W. Hazlitt: Lecture VII of *English Poets;* Alexander Smith: *Biographical Memoir* in Globe Edition; W. A. Neilson: *Burns, How to Know Him.* For Blake,—A. Gilchrist: *Life of Blake;* A. C. Swinburne: *William Blake,*

a Critical Essay; E. J. Ellis and W. B. Yeats: Introduction to their edition
of the *Works of William Blake;* A. G. B. Russell: *Letters of William Blake,
together with a Life by Frederick Tatham;* B. de Selincourt: *William Blake.*
For Crabbe,—G. Crabbe (Jr.): *Life of the Rev. George Crabbe, LL.B., by
his Son;* R. Huchon (Eng. trans. by F. Clarke): *George Crabbe and his
Times: a Critical and Biographical Study;* T. H. Kebbel: *George Crabbe*
in "Great Writers"; Canon Ainger: *Crabbe* ("English Men of Letters").

Chapter XXXIV

For this period in general,—G. Saintsbury: *History of Nineteenth Century
Literature;* G. Brandes: *Main Currents in Nineteenth Century Literature:*
vol. iv, *Naturalism in England.* For Wordsworth,—W. Knight: *Life of
Wordsworth;* F. W. H. Myers: *Wordsworth* ("English Men of Letters");
Walter Raleigh: *Wordsworth;* Leslie Stephen: *Wordsworth's Ethics* in
Hours in a Library; Walter Pater: *Appreciations;* M. Arnold: Introduction
to *Selections;* W. Hazlitt: *On Wordsworth's "Excursion"* and the paragraphs
about Wordsworth in *Living Poets.* For Coleridge,—J. D. Campbell: *Life;*
Coleridge's own *Biographia Literaria,* with the notes and supplementary
biography by his daughter Sara; H. D. Traill: *Coleridge* ("English Men of
Letters"); W. Pater: *Appreciations.* For Scott,—J. G. Lockhart: *Memoirs
of the Life of Sir Walter Scott;* R. H. Hutton: *Scott* ("English Men of
Letters"); G. Saintsbury: *Scott* in "Famous Scots" series; A. Lang: *Scott*
in "Literary Lives"; W. Hazlitt: *Spirit of the Age;* W. Bagehot: *The
Waverley Novels* in *Literary Studies;* A. Lang: *Letters to Dead Authors;*
L. Stephen: *Hours in a Library.* For Byron,—T. Moore: *Letters and Jour-
nals of Lord Byron with Notices of His Life;* Leigh Hunt: *Correspondence
of Byron and some of his Contemporaries;* J. C. Jeaffreson: *The Real Lord
Byron;* W. Hazlitt: *Spirit of the Age;* E. J. Trelawney: *Records of Shelley,
Byron and the Author;* M. Arnold: Introduction to *Selections;* J. C. Collins:
Studies in Poetry and Criticism; J. Nichol: *Byron* ("English Men of Let-
ters"). For Shelley,—E. J. Trelawney: *Records;* E. Dowden: *Life of
Shelley;* R. Garnett: *Relics of Shelley;* J. A. Symonds: *Shelley* ("English
Men of Letters"); H. N. Brailsford: *Shelley, Godwin, and Their Circle;*
Francis Thompson: *Shelley.* For Keats,—R. M. Milnes (Lord Houghton):
Life, Letters, and Literary Remains of John Keats; S. Colvin: *Keats* ("Eng-
lish Men of Letters") and the larger work, *John Keats, His Life and Poetry;*
M. Arnold: in *Essays.* For Landor,—J. Forster: *Works and Life of Walter
Savage Landor;* S. Colvin: *Landor* ("English Men of Letters"); the glowing
article in *Encyc. Brit.* is by Swinburne.

CHAPTER XXXV

For Scott,—see preceding chapter. For Jane Austen,—J. E. Austen
Leigh (her nephew) : *Life;* H. C. Beeching: *Jane Austen* ("English Men
of Letters") ; G. E. Mitton: *Jane Austen and her Times;* Goldwin Smith:
Jane Austen; Her Contemporaries and Herself. For Dickens,—J. Forster:
Life of Charles Dickens; G. Gissing: abridgement of Forster's *Life* and
Charles Dickens, a Critical Study; A. W. Ward: *Dickens* ("English Men
of Letters") ; F. G. Kitton: *Charles Dickens, His Life, Writings, and Per-
sonality;* G. K. Chesterton: *Charles Dickens;* G. Santayana: *Dickens* in
Soliloquies in England; A. Lang: *Letters to Dead Authors.* For Thackeray,
—A. Trollope: *Thackeray* ("English Men of Letters") ; Merivale and
Marzials: *Life of Thackeray;* A. T. Ritchie (his daughter): biographical
introductions to the several volumes in the complete edition (1897-1900) ;
Charles Whibley: *Thackeray.* For the Brontës,—E. Gaskell: *Life of Char-
lotte Brontë;* A. C. Swinburne: *A Note on Charlotte Brontë;* C. K. Shorter:
Charlotte Brontë and her Circle; A. Birrell: *Life of Charlotte Brontë;*
A. Symons: Essay in *Dramatis Personæ.* For George Eliot,—J. W. Cross:
Life of George Eliot; L. Stephen: *George Eliot* ("English Men of Letters") ;
Oscar Browning: *George Eliot* in "Great Writers." For Reade,—C. L.
Reade and Compton Reade: *Charles Reade, a Memoir;* A. C. Swinburne:
essay in *Miscellanies.* For Trollope,—his *Autobiography;* L. Stephen:
Studies of a Biographer; J. Bryce: *Studies in Contemporary Biography;*
Henry James: *Partial Portraits.* For Meredith,—R. Le Gallienne: *George
Meredith: Some Characteristics;* M. Sturge Henderson: *George Meredith:
Novelist, Poet, Reformer.* For Hardy,—L. P. Johnson: *The Art of Thomas
Hardy;* H. Lea: *Thomas Hardy's Wessex;* J. W. Beach: *The Technique
of Thomas Hardy.* For Stevenson,—G. Balfour: *Life of Robert Louis
Stevenson;* Walter Raleigh: *R. L. Stevenson;* I. Strong and L. Osbourne:
Memories of Vailima; F. Watt: *R. L. S.* For Gissing,—M. Yates: *George
Gissing.* For Joseph Conrad there are many enthusiastic essays, for example,
A. Symons: *Dramatis Personæ;* J. Macy: *The Critical Game.* For contem-
porary English literature,—H. Williams: *Modern English Writers;* A
Chevalley: *The Modern English Novel* (trans: from the French by B. R
Redman).

CHAPTER XXXVI

For Lamb,—His *Letters* with the life by T. N. Talfourd; B. Cornwall:
Charles Lamb: a Memoir; W. C. Hazlitt: *Mary and Charles Lamb;* E. V.
Lucas: *The Life of Charles Lamb.* For Hunt,—His *Autobiography;* C.

Monkhouse: *Leigh Hunt* in "Great Writers." For Hazlitt,—A. Birrell; *Hazlitt* ("English Men of Letters"); W. C. Hazlitt (his grandson): *Memoirs of William Hazlitt;* Leslie Stephen: *Hours in a Library.* For De Quincey,—D. Masson: *De Quincey* ("English Men of Letters"); A. H. Japp: *Thomas De Quincey: His Life and Writings;* H. S. Salt: *De Quincey;* L. Stephen: *Hours in a Library.* For Southey,—E. Dowden: *Southey* ("English Men of Letters"); J. Dennis: *Robert Southey, the Story of His Life Written in His Letters.* For Macaulay,—G. O. Trevelyan: *Life and Letters of Lord Macaulay;* J. C. Morison: *Macaulay* ("English Men of Letters"); W. Bagehot: *Literary Studies;* L. Stephen: *Hours in a Library;* John Morley: *Critical Miscellanies.* For Carlyle,—his *Reminiscences,* edited by C. E. Norton; J. A. Froude: *Life of Carlyle;* J. Nichol: *Carlyle* ("English Men of Letters"); D. Masson: *Carlyle Personally and in His Writings;* B. Perry: *Carlyle.* For Ruskin,—W. G. Collingwood: *Life of Ruskin;* F. Harrison: *Ruskin* ("English Men of Letters"); J. A. Hobson: *John Ruskin, Social Reformer;* C. Waldstein: *The Work of John Ruskin.* For Arnold,— H. Paul: *Matthew Arnold* ("English Men of Letters"); G. Saintsbury: *Matthew Arnold* in "Modern English Writers"; G. W. E. Russell: *Matthew Arnold* in "Literary Lives"; S. P. Sherman: *Arnold;* J. M. Robertson: *Modern Humanists.* For Mill,—his *Autobiography;* H. Elliott: *Letters of John Stuart Mill;* F. Harrison: *Tennyson, Ruskin, Mill;* W. L. Courtney: *Life of John Stuart Mill;* John Morley: *Miscellanies;* L. Stephen: *The English Utilitarians.* For Newman,—his *Apologia pro Vita Sua;* R. W. Church: *The Oxford Movement.* For Darwin,—F. Darwin (his son): *Life and Letters of Charles Darwin, including an Autobiographical Chapter;* A. R. Wallace: *Darwinism.* The vast literature of biology since Darwin's death is thick with references to him and criticisms of his theories. But most of this literature lies outside our view, which must on the whole remain literary. For Spencer,—any good history of modern philosophy; his *Autobiography;* W. H. Hudson: *Introduction to the Philosophy of Herbert Spencer.* For Huxley,—Leonard Huxley (his son): *Life and Letters of Thomas Henry Huxley;* P. C. Mitchell: *Thomas Henry Huxley, a Sketch of His Life and Work.* For Pater,—T. Wright: *Life of Walter Pater;* A. C. Benson: *Pater* ("English Men of Letters"); F. Greenslet: *Walter Pater* ("Contemporary Men of Letters").

CHAPTER XXXVII

For the poetry of this period two books to have at hand and know by heart are *The Oxford Book of Victorian Verse* chosen by A. Quiller-Couch, and F. T. Palgrave's *Golden Treasury of Songs and Lyrics,* second series; less well selected but valuable is E. C. Stedman's *Victorian Anthology.* For Tennyson,—Hallam Tennyson (his son): *Alfred, Lord Tennyson: A Memoir;* A. C. Benson: *The Life of Lord Tennyson;* A. Lang: *Alfred Tennyson.* For Browning,—Mrs. S. Orr: *Life and Letters of Browning* and *Handbook to the Works of Browning; Letters of Robert Browning and Elizabeth Barrett Browning;* E. Gosse: *Robert Browning: Personalia;* A. Symons: *An Introduction to the Study of Browning;* G. K. Chesterton: *Browning* ("English Men of Letters"); W. Sharp: *Life of Robert Browning.* For Mrs. Browning,—the various biographies of Browning; S. R. Townsend Mayer: *Letters of Elizabeth Barrett Browning Addressed to R. H. Horne with Comments on Contemporaries;* A. T. Ritchie: *Records of Tennyson, Ruskin and the Brownings;* J. H. Ingram: *Elizabeth Barrett Browning* (in "Eminent Women" series); F. G. Kenyon: *Letters of Elizabeth Barrett Browning.* For FitzGerald,—T. Wright: *Life of Edward FitzGerald;* A. C. Benson: *FitzGerald* ("English Men of Letters"). For Arnold,—see preceding chapter. For Rossetti,—W. M. Rossetti (his brother): *Dante Gabriel Rossetti as Designer and Writer,* and *Ruskin, Rossetti, Pre-Raphaelitism,* and *Some Reminiscences;* Lady Burne-Jones: *Memorials of Edward Burne-Jones.* A. Symons: *Dramatis Personæ;* F. G. Stephens: *D. G. Rossetti;* W. Sharp: *Dante Gabriel Rossetti: A Record and a Study;* T. H. Caine: *Recollections of Dante Gabriel Rossetti;* W. Pater: *Appreciations.* For Christina Rossetti,—the various memoirs about her brother; W. M. Rossetti: Memoir in *Poetical Works* and *Family Letters of Christina Rossetti;* E. Gosse: *Critical Kit-Kats.* For Morris,— J. W. Mackail: *Life and Letters of William Morris;* May Morris (his daughter): introductions to the several volumes of the *Collected Works.* For Swinburne.—E. Gosse: *Life of Swinburne* (the official biography, critically sound but mincing in manner). For Meredith and Hardy,—see under chap. xxv. For James Thomson,—H. S. Salt: *Life of James Thomson.* For Francis Thompson,—Everard Meynell: *Life of Francis Thompson;* A. Symons: *Dramatis Personæ.*

Chapter XXXVIII

Histories and handbooks on French literature already noted, Saintsbury, Lanson, de Julleville, etc. To these should be added the English translation of F. Brunetière's *Manual of the History of French Literature* and G. Brandes: *Main Currents in Nineteenth Century Literature,* vol. iii, *The Reaction in France* and vol. iv, *The Romantic School in France.* The French are the best critics of themselves—and of others—and whoever reads French will of course go to the originals. For Chateaubriand the standard work in English is the translation by A. Teixeira de Mattos of the *Memoirs of Chateaubriand.* For Balzac,—lives or studies in English by K. Wormely, by F. Wedmore, by F. Sandars; W. J. Helm: *Aspects of Balzac;* H. James: *The Lesson of Balzac.* For Hugo,—F. T. Marzials: *Life of Hugo;* A. C. Swinburne: *Study of Hugo.* For Dumas,—A. F. Davidson: *Alexandre Dumas Père, His Life and Works;* P. Fitzgerald: *Life of Dumas;* A. Lang: *Letters to Dead Authors;* Brander Matthews: *French Dramatists;* R. L. Stevenson: *Memories and Portraits.* For George Sand,—R. Doumic (Eng. trans. by A. Hallard): *George Sand: Some Aspects of Her Life and Writings;* Matthew Arnold: *Mixed Essays;* F. W. H. Meyers: *Essays Ancient and Modern; The George Sand—Gustave Flaubert Letters* (trans. by A. L. McKenzie, with introduction by S. P. Sherman). For Sainte-Beuve,—the classic essay in English is that by Matthew Arnold in *Encyc. Brit.* (and in his *Essays*). For Renan,—E. Grant Duff: *Ernest Renan in Memoriam;* Brauer: *Philosophy of Ernest Renan.* For Taine,—*H. Taine, His Life and Correspondence* (Eng. trans. by Mrs. R. L. Devonshire). For Flaubert,— The correspondence with George Sand noted above; H. James: *French Poets and Novelists.* For Maupassant,—If there is an official life of Maupassant, it seems not to have been translated into English. For short critical studies see introduction by H. James to a selection of stories, *The Odd Number,* and A. Symons: *Studies in Prose and Verse;* Joseph Conrad: *Notes on Life and Letters.* For Zola,—E. A. Vizetelly: *Emile Zola, Novelist and Reformer;* R. H. Sherard: *Emile Zola: A Biographical and Critical Study.* There are several good studies of Anatole France in French but not much that is authoritative in English. See Joseph Conrad: *Notes on Life and Letters;* J. J. Brousson: *Anatole France Himself* (Eng. trans. by J. Pollock). Magazine reviews are abundant, for Anatole France has a large audience of English readers. For Stendhal,—A. A. Paton: *Henry Beyle, a Critical and Biographical Study.* For Mérimée,—introductions to translations of *Colomba* and *Carmen,* and especially Saintsbury's introduction to the *Chronicle of Charles IX.* For Daudet,—There seems to be no complete life of Daudet in English; for critical essays see a brief but penetrating paper in Joseph Conrad's *Notes on Life and Letters;* A. Symons: *Studies in Prose and Verse;* and the introductions to the translations of the novels and stories of which there are many in English. For E. and J. de Goncourt,—M. A. Belloc-Lowndes and M. L. Shedlock: *Edmond and Jules de Goncourt, with Letters and Leaves from their Journals.* For Huysmans,—A. Symons: *Studies in Two Literatures* and *The Symbolist Movement in Literature.* For Loti,—his most characteristic works are half autobiographical confessions.

CHAPTER XXXIX

General books of reference, histories and criticism mentioned above. *Oxford Book of French Verse;* Wilfrid Thorley: *Fleurs-de-Lys: A Book of French Poetry Freely Translated into English Verse;* Ludwig Lewisohn: *The Poets of Modern France.* Amy Lowell: *Six French Poets.* The studies of modern French poets in English are not extensive, though there are some fine essays. For Mallarmé and others,—E. Gosse: *French Profiles;* A. Symons: *The Symbolist Movement in Literature.* For Verlaine,—the *Life of Verlaine* by Lepelletier (Eng. trans. by E. M. Lang) ; A. Symons: *Studies in Prose and Verse;* V. Thompson: *French Portraits.* For Maeterlinck and Verhaeren,—A. Symons: *Dramatis Personæ.*

CHAPTER XL

General History of German literature already noted. G. Brandes: *Main Currents of the Nineteenth Century,* vol. ii, *The Romantic Movement in Germany;* J. F. Coar: *Studies in German Literature in the Nineteenth Century.* For Lessing,—J. Sime: *Lessing, his Life and Works;* H. Zimmern: *Lessing's Life and Works;* T. W. Rolleston: *Lessing* (in "Great Writers") ; there are translations of *Laocoön* and of the *Dramatic Works* in Bohn's Library. For Goethe,—the literature about Goethe is endless; he penetrated every corner of European thought and has had many translators, biographers and critics in many languages. Following are a few English titles: L. D. Schmitz: Eng. trans. of the *Goethe-Schiller Correspondence;* A. D. Coleridge: Eng. trans. of the *Goethe-Zelter Correspondence;* Eng. trans. of the *Goethe-Carlyle Correspondence;* E. Bell: Eng. trans. of *Early and Miscellaneous Letters;* Goethe's *Autobiography,* Eng. trans. by J. Oxenford; G. H. Lewes: *Life and Works of Goethe;* H. H. Boyesen: *Goethe and Schiller;* J. Sime: *Life of Goethe;* A. Bielschowsky (Eng. trans. by W. A. Cooper): *Goethe, His Life and Works;* T. Carlyle: *Essays on Goethe;* J. R. Seeley: *Goethe Reviewed after Sixty Years;* E. Dowden: *New Studies in Literature;* *Goethe's Literary Essays:* a selection in English, arranged by J. E. Spingarn. For Schiller,—T. Carlyle: *Life of Friedrich Schiller;* E. Palleske: *Schiller's Life and Works* (Eng. trans.) ; G. Thomas: *Life and Works of Schiller;* J. G. Robertson: *Schiller after a Century;* Coleridge's translation of *Wallenstein* was one of the earliest introductions of the German poet to English readers.

CHAPTER XLI

General works on German literature cited. G. Brandes: *Main Currents in Nineteenth Century Literature,* vol. vi., *Young Germany.* For Novalis,

—Carlyle's essay. For Schopenhauer,—any history of modern philosophy; H. Zimmern: *Schopenhauer and his Philosophy*. For Kleist and other dramatists up to and including Hauptmann,—G. Witkowski: *German Drama of the Nineteenth Century*. For Heine,—W. Stigand: *Life, Works and Opinions of Heinrich Heine;* W. Sharp: *Life of Heine;* George Eliot: *German Wit: Heinrich Heine;* M. Arnold: Essay. For Nietzsche,—M. A. Mügge: *F. Nietzsche, his Life and Work;* Havelock Ellis: *F. Nietzsche,* in *Affirmations; Selected Letters of Friedrich Nietzsche,* ed. by O. Levy (Eng. trans. by A. M. Ludovici) ; *The Nietzsche-Wagner Correspondence,* ed. by E. Foerster-Nietzsche (Eng. trans. by C. V. Kerr) ; W. M. Salter: *Nietzsche, the Thinker.*

CHAPTER XLII

M. J. Olgin: *Guide to Russian Literature;* L. Wiener: *Anthology of Russian Literature;* P. Kropotkin: *Ideals and Realities of Russian Literature;* A. Brückner (Eng. trans. by E. H. Minns): *History of Russian Literature;* K. Waliszewski: *History of Russian Literature.* For Tolstoy,—the standard biography in English is by Aylmer Maude.

CHAPTER XLIII

R. Garnett: *History of Italian Literature.* For Goldoni,—*Memoirs* (Eng. trans. by J. Black with introduction by W. D. Howells). For Leopardi,—*Dialogues* (Eng. trans. by James Thomson, the poet of the *City of Dreadful Night* and a kindred spirit of Leopardi) ; G. L. Bickersteth: *The Poems of Leopardi, ed. with Introduction and Notes and a Verse-Translation in the Meters of the Original.*

CHAPTER XLIV

J. Fitzmaurice Kelly: *History of Spanish Literature;* A. F. G. Bell: *Contemporary Spanish Literature.*

CHAPTER XLV

There seems to be very little in English about Dutch literature, except Erasmus, Spinoza, and Vondel. For Erasmus,—F. Seebohm: *Oxford Reformers;* R. B. Drummond: *Life of Erasmus;* F. M. Nichols: *Letters of Erasmus* (Eng. trans.). For Spinoza,—any good history of modern philosophy: F. Polock: *Spinoza, his Life and Philosophy;* J. Martineau: *Study of*

Spinoza; J. Caird: *Spinoza.* We have noted in the text the life of *Vondel* by A. J. Barnouw.

CHAPTER XLVI

H. H. Boyesen: *Essays on Scandinavian Literature;* E. Gosse: *Studies in the Literature of Northern Europe;* F. W. Horn; *History of the Literature of the Scandinavian North* (Eng. trans.). For Ibsen,—the introductions to the several volumes of W. Archer's edition; Henrick Jaeger: *Henrick Ibsen* (Eng. trans.) G. B. Shaw: *The Quintessence of Ibsenism.* For Björnson,— G. Brandes: *Critical Studies.* For F. Bremer,—C. Bremer (Eng. trans. by F. Milow): *Life, Letters and Posthumous Works of F. Bremer; America of the Fifties: Letters of F. Bremer* (trans. M. Howitt, revised A. B. Benson, in the publications of the American-Scandinavian Foundation).

CHAPTER XLVII

General references for this chapter (and some apply also to following chapters),—E. C. Stedman and E. M. Hutchinson: *Library of American Literature;* W. P. Trent and J. Erskine: *Great American Writers;* W. B. Cairns: *History of American Literature;* B. Wendell: *A Literary History of America;* W. P. Trent: *History of American Literature;* J. Macy; *The Spirit of American Literature;* J. L. Haney: *The Story of Our Literature;* B. Perry: *The American Spirit in Literature;* G. E. Woodberry: *America in Literature;* S. L. Whitcomb: *Chronological Outlines of American Literature;* G. R. Carpenter: *American Prose;* C. Van Doren: *A Short History of American Literature* and *The American Novel* and *Contemporary American Novelists;* F. L. Pattee: *History of American Literature and History of American Literature Since 1870.* For Irving,—P. M. Irving: *Life and Letters of Washington Irving;* C. D. Warner: *Washington Irving* ("American Men of Letters"); G. S. Hellman: *Washington Irving, Esquire.* For Cooper,—T. R. Lounsbury: *James Fenimore Cooper* ("American Men of Letters"); M. Morris: introduction to Macmillan's uniform edition; Mark Twain: *Fenimore Cooper's Literary Offenses;* Joseph Conrad: *Tales of the Sea* in *Notes on Life and Letters.* For Poe,—G. E. Woodberry: *Life of Edgar Allan Poe* (the standard biography); J. A. Harrison: *Life and Letters of Edgar Allan Poe;* J. Macy: *Edgar Allan Poe,* in "Beacon Biographies." For Hawthorne,—Julian Hawthorne (his son): *Nathaniel Hawthorne and his Wife* and *Hawthorne and his Circle;* Henry James: *Hawthorne* ("English Men of Letters"); M. D. Conway: *Life of Nathaniel Hawthorne* in "Great Writers"; H. Bridge: *Personal Recollections of Nathaniel Haw-*

thorne; R. Hawthorne Lathrop: *Memories of Hawthorne;* G. E. Woodberry: *Life of Hawthorne.* For H. B. Stowe,—C. E. Stowe (her son): *Life of Harriet Beecher Stowe;* A. Fields: *Life and Letters of Harriet Beecher Stowe.* For Mark Twain,—A. B. Paine: *Mark Twain: a Biography* (the official biography); Mark Twain's *Autobiography;* Van W. Brooks: *The Ordeal of Mark Twain;* A. Henderson: *Mark Twain;* W. D. Howells: *My Mark Twain.* For Bret Harte,—T. E. Pemberton: *Life of Bret Harte;* H. W. Boynton: *Bret Harte* in "Contemporary Men of Letters." For Howells,—his autobiographical sketches, *A Boy's Town* and *In the Days of My Youth;* J. M. Robertson: *Essays towards a Critical Method;* H. C. Vedder: *American Writers.* For H. James,—his autobiographical books, *A Small Boy and Others; Notes of a Son and Brother; The Middle Years;* J. W. Beach: *The Method of Henry James;* Joseph Conrad: *Notes on Life and Letters;* E. L. Cary: *The Novels of Henry James.* For Stephen Crane,—the study by Thomas Beer with an introduction by Joseph Conrad.

Chapter XLVIII

For Emerson,—J. E. Cabot: *Memoir of Ralph Waldo Emerson* (the authorized biography); O. W. Holmes: *Emerson* ("American Men of Letters"); *Correspondence of Thomas Carlyle and Ralph Waldo Emerson,* ed. by C. E. Norton; G. W. Cooke: *Ralph Waldo Emerson: his Life, Writings and Philosophy;* Alexander Ireland: *Ralph Waldo Emerson: his Life, Genius and Writings;* A. Bronson Alcott: *Ralph Waldo Emerson, Philosopher and Seer;* M. D. Conway: *Emerson at Home and Abroad;* F. B. Sanborn: *Genius and Character of Emerson;* E. W. Emerson: *Emerson in Concord;* R. Garnett: *Life of Ralph Waldo Emerson;* G. E. Woodberry: *Ralph Waldo Emerson;* M. Arnold: *Discourses in America;* J. Morley: *Critical Miscellanies;* H. James: *Partial Portraits;* J. R. Lowell: *My Study Windows;* A. Birrell: *Obiter Dicta;* S. McC. Crothers: *R. W. Emerson: How to Know Him;* E. L. Cary: *Ralph Waldo Emerson: Poet and Thinker.* For Thoreau,— W. E. Channing: *Thoreau: the Poet Naturalist;* F. B. Sanborn: *Henry David Thoreau* ("American Men of Letters"); H. S. Salt: *Life of Henry David Thoreau;* J. R. Lowell: *My Study Windows;* R. L. Stevenson: *Familiar Studies of Men and Books.* For Poe,—see preceding chapter. For Holmes,—J. T. Morse: *Life and Letters of Oliver Wendell Holmes;* S. McC. Crothers: *Oliver Wendell Holmes and His Fellow-Boarders;* L. Stephen: introductory essay to "Golden Treasury" edition of *Autocrat;* G. W. Curtis: *Literary and Social Essays.* For Lowell,—H. E. Scudder: *Life of James Russell Lowell;* E. E. Hale: *James Russell Lowell and His*

Friends; Letters of James Russell Lowell, ed. by C. E. Norton; F. Greenslet: *Life of Lowell.* For Franklin,—his *Autobiography;* J. Parton: *Life and Times of Benjamin Franklin;* J. T. Morse: *Benjamin Franklin* ("American Statesmen" series) ; J. B. McMaster: *Benjamin Franklin as a Man of Letters* ("American Men of Letters") ; P. L. Ford: *The Many-Sided Franklin;* E. E. Hale and E. E. Hale, Jr.: *Franklin in France;* S. G. Fisher: *The True Benjamin Franklin;* E. Robins: *Benjamin Franklin* ("American Men of Energy" series). For Jefferson,—J. T. Morse: *Jefferson* ("American Statesmen" series) ; W. P. Trent; *Southern Statesmen of the Old Régime.* For Webster,—E. Everett: Memoir in the *Works of Daniel Webster;* G. T. Curtis: *Life of Daniel Webster;* H. C. Lodge: *Daniel Webster;* J. B. McMaster: *Daniel Webster;* E. P. Wheeler: *Daniel Webster, the Expounder of the Constitution;* S. W. McCall: *Daniel Webster;* Norman Hapgood: *Daniel Webster.* For Lincoln,—J. G. Nicolay and J. Hay: *Abraham Lincoln: A History* (the standard biography) ; J. T. Morse: *Abraham Lincoln* ("American Statesmen" series) ; Carl Schurz: *Essay on Lincoln;* J. H. Choate: *Address on Lincoln;* Noah Brooks: *Life of Lincoln* (these last three contained in the Constitutional edition of *The Writings of Abraham Lincoln*) ; R. W. Gilder: *Lincoln's Genius for Expression;* J. R. Lowell: *My Study Windows.* For Prescott,—G. Ticknor: *Life of William Hickling Prescott;* H. T. Peck: *Life of Prescott.* For Parkman,—G. H. Farnham: *Life of Parkman.*

Chapter XLIX

General works on American literature. For American poetry,—E. C. Stedman: *Poets of America* and *American Anthology;* C. H. Page: *Chief American Poets;* T. R. Lounsbury: *Yale Book of American Verse;* J. Rittenhouse: *Little Book of Modern Verse;* L. Untermeyer: *Modern American Poetry;* A. Lowell: *Tendencies in Modern American Poetry.* For Bryant,— P. Godwin: *Biography of William Cullen Bryant with Extracts from his Private Correspondence;* J. G. Wilson: *Bryant and His Friends;* J. Bigelow: *William Cullen Bryant* ("American Men of Letters") ; W. A. Bradley: *Bryant* ("English Men of Letters"). For Longfellow,—Samuel Longfellow: *Life of Henry Wadsworth Longfellow with Extracts from his Journals and Correspondence;* T. W. Higginson: *Longfellow* ("American Men of Letters") ; W. S. Kennedy: *Life of Henry Wadsworth Longfellow;* W. D. Howells: *My Literary Friends and Acquaintance.* For Lowell, Holmes and Emerson,—see preceding chapter. For Whittier,—S. T. Pickard: *Life and Letters of John Greenleaf Whittier;* G. R. Carpenter:

John Greenleaf Whittier ("American Men of Letters"); B. Perry: *Whittier;* W. S. Kennedy: *John Greenleaf Whittier;* T. W. Higginson: *Whittier* ("English Men of Letters"). For Whitman,—J. Burroughs: *Walt Whitman: a Study;* H. Traubel, R. M. Bucke, T. B. Harned: *In re Walt Whitman;* H. Traubel: *With Walt Whitman in Camden;* B. Perry: *Walt Whitman: His Life and Work;* R. M. Bucke: *Walt Whitman;* J. A. Symonds: *Walt Whitman;* W. S. Kennedy: *Reminiscences of Walt Whitman with Extracts from His Letters;* H. B. Binns: *Life of Walt Whitman;* B. de Selincourt: *Walt Whitman: A Critical Study;* R. L. Stevenson: *Familiar Studies of Men and Books;* E. Dowden: *Studies in Literature.* For Sidney Lanier,—E. Mims: *Sidney Lanier;* W. H. Ward: Memorial prefixed to *Poems; Letters of Sidney Lanier.*

INDEX

INDEX

Index

Supplemental Index to Publisher's Appendix